STUDIES ON THE SECOND PART
OF THE BOOK OF ISAIAH

SUPPLEMENTS

TO

VETUS TESTAMENTUM

EDITED BY

THE BOARD OF THE QUARTERLY

G. W. ANDERSON - P. A. H. DE BOER - G. R. CASTELLINO
HENRY CAZELLES - E. HAMMERSHAIMB - H. G. MAY
W. ZIMMERLI

VOLUME XIV

LEIDEN
E. J. BRILL
1977

STUDIES ON THE SECOND PART
OF THE BOOK OF ISAIAH

THE SO-CALLED "SERVANT OF THE LORD"
AND "SUFFERING SERVANT"
IN SECOND ISAIAH

BY

HARRY M. ORLINSKY

ISAIAH 40-66

A STUDY OF THE TEACHING OF THE
SECOND ISAIAH AND ITS CONSEQUENCES

BY

NORMAN H. SNAITH

REPRINT WITH ADDITIONS AND CORRECTIONS

LEIDEN
E. J. BRILL
1977

First published in 1967

ISBN 90 04 05437 5

THE SO-CALLED "SERVANT OF THE LORD" AND "SUFFERING SERVANT" IN SECOND ISAIAH

BY

HARRY M. ORLINSKY

TABLE OF CONTENTS

INTRODUCTORY STATEMENT

"The Servant of the Lord" (עבד יהוה) has long been a technical term used universally by biblical scholars to designate the "Servant" mentioned or implied in four major sections in Second Isaiah: 42.1 ff.; 49.1 ff.; 50.4 ff.; and 52.13-53.12.

There are a number of biblical concepts that are of prime importance to the modern student of the Bible but which, it would seem to me, were actually non-existent, or were only of the slightest significance, in biblical times, when the inhabitants of the land of Israel were in the process of creating what later became Sacred Scripture. Among these, apparently only *allegedly* biblical concepts are the existence of a "soul" (the traditional, but incorrect translation of Hebrew *néfesh*), the "virginal" character of the *'almáh* in Isaiah 7.14, the prophets' hostile attitude toward sacrifice in the worship of the Lord, the international outlook of the biblical writers (including, or especially, the prophets)—and the "Servant of the Lord" in Second Isaiah, above all, the "Servant" in 52.13-53.12, as the "Suffering Servant" par excellence, who, innocent of sin, suffered vicariously in order that others, guilty of sin and hence deserving of punishment, might thereby be atoned for and spared the punishment.

For history is full of the commentary, and supercommentary, of eisegesis grafted upon the original exegesis which differed from it altogether; but it is one of the primary tasks of the historian to remove the layers and crust of subsequent explanation and distortion, to reveal the authentic statement set forth by the original author.

This is not a task easily accomplished, and there is little reason to believe that the immediate future will see real advance in this direction. Already three decades ago HENRY J. CADBURY delivered a courageously forthright and pertinent Presidential Address to the Society of Biblical Literature on "Motives of Biblical Scholarship" (*Journal of Biblical Literature*, 56 [1937], 1-16). In his searching analysis of modern Bible study, CADBURY noted especially (pp. 10-12) three "besetting sins of our present procedure: 1. One is an Athenian-like craving for something new . . . 2. Another bias of our procedure is the over-ready attempt to modernize Bible times. This tendency. . .arises partly from taking our own mentality as a norm and partly from a desire to interpret the past for its present values. . .The modernizing is in many cases. . .due to an even less pardonable defect, the overzealous desire to utilize our study for practical ends. . . 3. A third defect. . .arises not from a modernizing but from a conservative tendency. When new conceptions force us from old positions we substitute for the old positions imitations or subterfuges which are no better supported than their predecessors but which we hope are less vulnerable. . .The history of Biblical scholarship is marred by the too fond clinging to the debris of exploded theories. We are afraid to follow the logic of our own discoveries and insist that we are retaining the old values under a new name. . ."

In my chapter on "Old Testament Studies" (pp. 51-109) for the volume on *Religion* in the series *The Princeton Studies: Humanistic Scholarship in America* (Prentice-Hall, 1956), I wrote (in § 7, Biblical Theology), ". . .It is one thing for a scholar to devote his talents to the detailed study of the Old Testament in its historical development during the second and first millennia B.C., or else to specialize in the study of our own twentieth century society; it is something else again, however, for the same scholar to attempt scientific conquest of these two distinct areas of research. Such scholars, as put recently by someone, 'tend often to mix together scholarship and apologetics'. . .Clearly, until the student of biblical theology learns to deal with his data as critically as the student of ancient Greek, or Roman, or Assyrian or Egyptian religion does, he can hardly expect his studies to achieve, validity in scholarly circles. . ." (pp. 77-79); cf. p. vii of (General Editor) RICHARD SCHLATTER's "Foreword".

Ever young in spirit, Prof. CADBURY has returned to this central theme in a recent article on "Gospel Study and Our Image of Early Christianity" (*Journal of Biblical Literature*, 83 [1964], 139-145), where he deplores the fact "that much in our current image of early Christians is reflected from our own traditions and interests, more than from the early Christian documents themselves," and closes with the exhortation "to challenge where challenge is needed the image of early Christianity that is sometimes read *into* as well as *out of* [italics ours] the gospels." Our present essay will have much to say about "*eis*egesis" as distinct from "*ex*egesis". In this connection, ERWIN R. GOODENOUGH's essay on "The Bible as Product of the Ancient World" and MORTON S. ENSLIN's essay on "Biblical Criticism and its Effect on Modern Civilization"—respectively chapters I (pp. 1-19) and IV (30-44) in *Five Essays on the Bible* (American Council of Learned Societies, New York, 1960)—are pertinent reading.

The present study is part of a major work on some biblical concepts in their historical development, tentatively titled The Hebrew Covenant. A much shorter and less technical version of this study, under the title of *The So-Called "Suffering Servant" in Isaiah* 53 constituted the Goldenson Lecture of 1964 (49 pp.), delivered April 22, 1964, on the Cincinnati campus of Hebrew Union College-Jewish Institute of Religion and published under the terms of the Samuel H. Goldenson Lectureship established by Temple Emanu-El of New York City.

NOTE TO SECOND PRINTING

This second printing differs from the first in that several errors have been corrected and a few minor changes made (pp. 9, 11, 34, 35, 39, 47, 49, 55, 62, 69, 79, 82, 91, 108, 114, 125, and 128a).

It was tempting both to acknowledge and to make use of the helpful reviews of the first printing and to reply to the criticisms that I regard as less than cogent; also, to add bibliographical data of value that have appeared since 1966-67. However, this would have necessitated many more changes than a mere reprinting allows. And so I am grateful that a reprint of this study has been found worthwhile, and I content myself with referring the reader to those studies of mine that have appeared recently and that have bearing on this study: "Nationalism-Universalism and Internationalism in Ancient Israel" (H. G. May *Festschrift*, 1970), "Nationalism-Universalism in the Book of Jeremiah" (M. S. Enslin *Festschrift*, 1972) and "Whither Biblical Research?" (Society of Biblical Literature Presidential Address, *JBL*, 90 [1971], 1-14—now respectively Chapters 5 (pp. 78-116), 6 (117-143), and 11 (200-217) in my *Essays in Biblical Culture and Bible Translation* (KTAV, 1974).

CHAPTER ONE

THE BIBLICAL TERM "SERVANT"
IN RELATION TO THE LORD

The dominant term in the Bible for Israel in relation to God is *'ebed*. This is not surprising in view of the fact that slavery was one of the integral elements in the agricultural and commercial activities of biblical Israel, as it was of Ancient Near Eastern society generally.[1]

With Israel alone did God enter into a covenant, exactly as it was with God alone that Israel made a pact. Accordingly, it is virtually only the Israelites as a people, or individual Israelites, who are designated in the Bible as the *'ebed* of the Lord, as God's loyal follower. Specifically, the individual "servants" (*'abadim*) of God are the patriarchs, Moses (God's individual *'ebed* par excellence; see below), Caleb (who alone, with Joshua, gave a favorable report on the possibility of conquering Canaan, with full confidence in God; Num. 14.24), Joshua (God's chosen successor to Moses and conqueror of Canaan), David (founder of Israel's Royal Dynasty and God's favorite king), Hezekiah (II Chron. 32.16), Eliakim (Isa. 22.20), and Zerubbabel (Hag. 2.23)—all three monarchs, it will be noted, of the dynasty of David; none from the Northern Kingdom—the seers Ahijah (I Ki. 14.18; 15.29) and Elijah, such prophets as Isaiah (Isa. 20.3), Jonah ben Amittai (II Ki. 14.25), and Second Isaiah (see Chapter IV below), and, finally, that great worthy, Job (in the prologue and epilogue of the Book); and note the use of the term "My servants the prophets" (*'abadai ha-nebi'im*) on several occasions (II Kings; Jeremiah; Ezekiel; Zechariah).

Only one non-Israelite in the entire Bible is described as God's *'ebed*, namely, "King Nebuchadr/nezzar of Babylon, My servant" (*N. melek-babel 'abdi*; Jer. 25.9; 27.6; 43.10). In all three, closely related passages, the Babylonian monarch is depicted by Jeremiah

---

[1] Cf., e.g., George Ernest Wright, "The Terminology of Old Testament Religion and its Significance," *Journal of Near Eastern Studies*, 1 (1942), 404-411, where the basic master-servant motif is discussed. Isaac Mendelsohn has written the best survey of "Slavery in the Old Testament," in *Interpreter's Dictionary of the Bible*, IV (1962), 383a-391a, following on his earlier, more general work on *Slavery in the Ancient Near East* (New York, 1949); the data offered in Part II, chapter 3 ("Slaves") of Roland de Vaux's *Ancient Israel, its Life and Institutions* (New York, 1961), are not analytically treated.

merely as God's rod of punishment against Judah and the other nations of the East, a tool in the hands of God; and in the end, Nebuchadnezzar's scions and country will suffer drastic destruction at the
hand of God for having done what they did (25.12-14; and cf.
27. 21-22).[1]) [See "ADDITIONAL NOTE" on p. 11 below].

It is clear, then, that any loyal Israelite adherent of God could be
designated as His ʿebed.[2]) And if, apart from the people Israel, it is
overwhelmingly Abraham, Jacob, Moses, and David among the
individuals who are so designated—to judge from the statistics
readily comprehended by consulting the various forms of ʿebed in
SOLOMON MANDELKERN's *Veteris Testamenti Concordantiae*—it is ob-
viously because Abraham is the first Hebrew, Jacob is the immediate
ancestor of the twelve tribes, Moses is the lawgiver and founder of
the Israelite people, and David is the founder of Israel's Golden Era
and of the long Judean dynasty.

However, before coming to any further conclusions about ʿebed
in relation to God, something should be said about the precise expression עֶבֶד יהוה—as distinct from עַבְדִּי "My servant" and the like.

Scholars tend to talk about the expression ʿebed *Adonai* as though it
were found frequently in Second Isaiah. It is all the more interesting,
therefore, and significant, that this expression occurs in Second
Isaiah only a single time, in 42.19, and it is there the people Israel,
not an individual person, that is referred to:

מִי עִוֵּר כִּי אִם־עַבְדִּי וְחֵרֵשׁ כְּמַלְאָכִי אֶשְׁלָח
מִי עִוֵּר כִּמְשֻׁלָּם וְעִוֵּר כְּעֶבֶד יהוה:

---

[1]) Cyrus of Persia—if original in the text—is described in Second Isaiah
(44.28; 45.1) as "My shepherd...His anointed" (רֹעִי...מְשִׁיחוֹ) rather than as
"My/His servant" (עַבְדִּי/עַבְדוֹ). This may be due to his role vis-à-vis (a) Israel and
(b) the other nations: (a) unlike Nebuchadnezzar, who was picked to destroy
Israel, Cyrus was chosen by God to restore His people Israel (he is God's "shepherd" for His flock); and (b) unlike Nebuchadnezzar's dynasty, which was destined
soon to be destroyed, Cyrus' regime was going to be preserved for some time
(hence God's "anointed").

[2]) Considerable data are compiled in WALTHER ZIMMERLI-JOACHIM JEREMIAS,
The Servant of the Lord (= *Studies in Biblical Theology*, No. 20, 1957; this is the
English version of their article "Παῖς Θεοῦ" in *Theologisches Wörterbuch zum Neuen
Testament*, ed. GERHARD KITTEL-GERHARD FRIEDRICH, 1954, 653-713). However,
there is but meager analysis in ZIMMERLI's chapter (I, pp. 9-34) on "The עֶבֶד יהוה
in the Old Testament," coupled with far too much of our own Twentieth Century
notions of "encounter with God" and "tension" (thus I Ki. 11.34 is said to exhibit
"a tense duality," p. 20); all the more is it a pleasure, therefore, to quote this fine

This happens to be also the only instance in the entire Bible where *'ebed Adonai* doesn't refer to an individual person.[1])

Elsewhere in the Hebrew Bible, *'ebed Adonai* is found a total of 21 times, distributed and identified as follows:

(1) In 17 instances it refers to Moses: Deut. 34.5 (מֹשֶׁה עֶבֶד־יהוה); Josh. 1.1, 13, 15; 8.31, 33; 11.12; 12.6 (*bis*); 13.8; 14.7; 18.7; 22.4, 5; II Ki. 18.12; II Chron. 1.3; 24.6.[2])

(2) In 2 instances it refers to Joshua son of Nun: Josh. 24.29 and Jud. 2.8 (יְהוֹשֻׁעַ בֶּן־נוּן עֶבֶד יהוה).

(3) In 2 instances it refers to David, both times in superscriptions in Psalms: 18.1 (the superscription is lacking in // II Sam. 22.1) and 36.1 (לַמְנַצֵּחַ לְעֶבֶד־יהוה לְדָוִד).

(4) In addition, there are 4 instances of the expression עֶבֶד הָאֱלֹהִים "servant of God," all of them referring to Moses: I Chron. 6.34 and II Chron. 24.9 (מֹשֶׁה עֶבֶד הָאֱלֹהִים); Dan. 9.11 (‥‥אֲשֶׁר כְּתוּבָה בְּתוֹרַת ‥‥לָלֶכֶת בְּתוֹרַת הָאֱלֹהִים אֲשֶׁר נִתְּנָה); Neh. 10.30 (מֹשֶׁה עֶבֶד־הָאֱלֹהִים‥‥ ‥‥בְּיַד מֹשֶׁה עֶבֶד־הָאֱלֹהִים‥‥).

From these data it is clear that the expression *'ebed Adonai/Ha-Elohim* was employed in biblical times as something of a technical term for Moses;[3]) that is to say, if a biblical Jew were asked: Who is

---

statement (p. 15), "...The individual can become the servant of Yahweh only in so far as he is a member of Israel; for the will of God is directed toward Israel..."

[1]) In his very fine analysis of "ὁ παῖς" (Note on "The Titles of Jesus in Acts," pp. 354-375 of Vol. V of *Beginnings of Christianity*; ὁ παῖς occupies pp. 364-370), CADBURY had warned (p. 369) "against the too easy assumption of dependence [of the term παῖς for Jesus] on Second Isaiah's 'Ebed Yahweh," and in the course of his note (2) on this statement he commented, "It is probably misleading to refer to the figures in Isaiah as '*the* servant.' There is always in Hebrew and Greek a possessive, usually 'my.' It is also not quite true to the underlying text to speak of 'the Servant of the Lord' or 'Ebed Yahweh. Even if the early Christian passages were regarded as dependent they attest παῖς Κυρίου only at Barnabas vi. 1. Only late and probably in the sense of υἱός do we get παῖς Θεοῦ .." CADBURY's strictures against HARNACK, TORREY, and others, receive considerable support from a straightforward analysis of Old Testament terminology and usage.

[2]) I have not included such a passage as Jonah 1.9, where the Septuagint reads δοῦλος Κυρίου "a servant of the Lord" (=עֶבֶד יהוה) for preserved (וַיֹּאמֶר אֲלֵי עִבְרִי(אָנֹכִי) הֵם) "(And he[Jonah] said to them, 'I am) a Hebrew." The letter *yodh* was sometimes employed as an abbreviation of the Tetragrammaton.

[3]) It need scarcely be added that our conclusions offer no more support for SELLIN's curious identification of Moses as the central personage in Isa. 53 than they do, say, for Abraham, or Jacob, or David as that personage.

"*the 'ebed Adonai* (or, *Ha-Elohim*)"? he would think of Moses immediately. He would, of course, know of David as "*an 'ebed Adonai*,"
and of Abraham, and Jacob, and Joshua, etc.; but Moses alone would
be "*the 'ebed Adonai/Ha-Elohim*" par excellence—and this, because he
was Israel's lawgiver. Several passages come to mind at once, e.g.,
Dan. 9.11 (where Daniel addresses God): וְכָל־יִשְׂרָאֵל עָבְרוּ אֶת־תּוֹרָתֶךָ)
וְסוֹר לְבִלְתִּי שְׁמוֹעַ בְּקֹלֶךָ וַתִּתַּךְ עָלֵינוּ הָאָלָה וְהַשְּׁבוּעָה אֲשֶׁר כְּתוּבָה בְּתוֹרַת
(··וּבָאִים בְּאָלָה וּבִשְׁבוּעָה לָלֶכֶת); and Neh. 10.30: מֹשֶׁה עֶבֶד־הָאֱלֹהִים··
··בְּתוֹרַת הָאֱלֹהִים אֲשֶׁר נִתְּנָה בְּיַד מֹשֶׁה עֶבֶד־הָאֱלֹהִים. Throughout the
Bible, "the *torah* of Moses" (תּוֹרַת מֹשֶׁה) is virtually synonymous with
the expression "the *torah* of the Lord/God"; Mal. 3.22 put it plainly
enough, in the mouth of the Lord Himself: זִכְרוּ תּוֹרַת מֹשֶׁה עַבְדִּי
"Remember the *torah* of My servant Moses." And that is why the
Gemara (Babylonian Talmud, Shabbat 89a center) could assert:
אמר לו הקב״ה למשה, הואיל ומיעטתה עצמך, תיקרא על שמך, שנאמר זכרו
תורת משה עבדי וגומר, "So the Holy One Blessed be He said to Moses,
'Since you have acted modestly, it [the Torah] shall be identified with
your name, as it is stated [Mal. 3.22]: Remember the *Torah* of My
servant Moses,' etc. "

In this connection it is worth noting that in post-biblical times,
Moses came to be called מֹשֶׁה רַבֵּינוּ "Moses our Teacher/Master" (in
his *Legends of the Jews*, Vol. V, p. 403, LOUIS GINZBERG has discussed
this expression along with the inverted order, רַבֵּינוּ מֹשֶׁה, as well as
such terms as רַבֵּינוּ הַקָּדוֹשׁ for Judah Ha-Nasi, redactor of the Mishnah,
and רַבֵּינוּ רַב for Abba Arika). I wonder whether the biblical term
'ebed Adonai for Moses gave way in time to *Rabbenu* because "Servant
of the Lord" had come in Christian circles to designate Jesus; but the
matter requires very careful study.

We are now in a postion to arrive at some conclusions about the
expression "servant of the Lord" in the Bible and in Second Isaiah.
With the apparent exception of Moses, no single person in the Bible
ever came to be recognized in biblical times as "the *'ebed* of the Lord".
Put differently, if a person who knows only the Hebrew Bible were
asked, "Who is the *'ebed Adonai*"? he would answer, "Moses is the
'ebed Adonai/Ha-Elohim, though God had many an *'ebed*, such as
David and Joshua and Abraham and Jacob." And if questioned
further, "How about the *'ebed* in Isaiah 40 ff."? he would not under-

stand the pertinence of the question, since Second Isaiah's ʿebed had
no significance for him. As we shall see below, this significance first
came into being later in the period of the New Testament, about six
hundred years after Isaiah 53 was composed, and then read back into
the Hebrew Bible—a clear case of eisegesis.

ADDITIONAL NOTE

WERNER E. LEMKE, "Nebuchadrezzar, My Servant" (*Catholic Biblical Quarterly*, 28 [1966], 45-50), has made a good case for regarding
ʿabdi in all three passages in Jeremiah as secondary. The analysis is
worth close study.

A much-overlooked study that makes some excellent points and
that merits careful analysis throughout is WILLIAM H. COBB's
"The Servant of Jahveh," *JBL*, 14 (1895), 95-113.

[In the light of recent study of the received Hebrew text of Jeremiah
vis-à-vis the Septuagint and the Dead Sea Scroll material, all three
passages involved (25.9; 27.6; and 43.10)—lacking as they are in
the Septuagint—may now be safely regarded as secondary. As to
when and why they were added to the Hebrew text from which our
received text derives, that is a problem yet to be solved.]

CHAPTER TWO

THE SO-CALLED "SERVANT OF THE LORD"
SECTIONS IN SECOND ISAIAH

Since the appearance in 1892 of BERNHARD DUHM's commentary, *Das Buch Jesaia* (Göttingen, pp. XVIII, 284 ff., 365 ff.), following on his earlier *Die Theologie der Propheten* (Bonn, 1875), 287 ff., scholars have generally recognized four major sections in Second Isaiah as constituting "Servant Songs": 42.1 ff.; 49.1 ff.; 50.4 ff.; 52.13-53.12. It was DUHM's contention that these four sections—along with some other sections in the preserved text of Second Isaiah—were composed by someone other than Second Isaiah, perhaps even constituting originally an independent book, and that they were then incorporated into the text of Second Isaiah proper whenever unused space in the scroll permitted insertion.[1]

A considerable number of competent scholars since DUHM have argued in favor of comprehending the "Servant" sections within their

---

[1] It was, again, DUHM (*Jesaia*, pp. XVIII-XIX, 390 ff.) who proposed to divide the last 27 chapters (40-66) of the book of Isaiah between two distinct authors: 40-55 being allotted to Second (Deutero-) Isaiah, and 56-66 to Third (Trito-) Isaiah. This division, with all kinds of variations, has been accepted by most scholars; cf. the surveys and bibliographies, e.g., in OTTO EISSFELDT, *Einleitung in das A.T.*[2] (Tübingen, 1956), 399 ff., 413 ff. (3rd ed., 1964: 444 ff., 459 ff.); CHRISTOPHER R. NORTH, *The Suffering Servant in Deutero-Isaiah: An Historical and Critical Study* (Oxford, 1948), chap. IX (2nd ed., 1956); MENAHEM HARAN, *Between Ri'shonôt (Former Prophecies) and Ḥadashôt (New Prophecies): A Literary-Historical Study in the Group of Prophecies Isaiah XL-XLVIII* (in Hebrew; Jerusalem, 1963-5723), chap. III, 73 ff.
I myself am not convinced that there was a Third Isaiah readily distinguishable from Second Isaiah as the latter is from First Isaiah. Of course "the *literary* unity of Is. 40-66 is undoubtedly imperfect, especially in later chapters: naturally the whole will not have been delivered by the prophet continuously, but some alteration, and advance, in the historical situation may be presupposed for its later parts. Thus. . ." (SAMUEL R. DRIVER, *An Introduction to the Literature of the O.T.*, rev. ed. (New York, 1913), 244 ff.; see in general, 211 f. (on Isa. 13.1-14.23), 225 f. (on chaps. 34-35), and 230 ff. (on chaps. 40-66). I regard the bulk of chaps. 40-66 as the product of a single author. However, in dealing with the several problems of "The Servant of the Lord" I shall limit myself to chapters 40-55 when referring to Second Isaiah.

preserved position in the Hebrew text. That is to say, they may disagree on the precise verses which each section constitutes; [1]) or on the
date of compostion; or on the identification of the ʿebed in each of the
sections; [2]) or on the actual number of such sections; [3]) and the like.
They may even disagree on whether Second Isaiah himself or an
editor was responsible for the preserved setting of the "Servant"
sections. But in one major respect they are in substantial agreement:
while the four "Servant" sections belong essentially to Second Isaiah
himself, they may be treated as a distinct group apart from all the
other passages and sections in Second Isaiah in which the term "servant" is employed. NORMAN H. SNAITH, "The Servant of the Lord in
Deutero-Isaiah" (in *Studies in Old Testament Prophecy presented to
Professor Theodore H. Robinson*, ed. H. H. ROWLEY [Edinburgh, 1950],
187-200) put it this way (p. 187): "Some few scholars have argued
against their segregation from the main body of the prophecy. . .The
great majority, however, have followed DUHM, to such an extent that
the existence of the four Servant Songs has come to be regarded as
one of the firm results of modern O.T. study. . ." [4])

Yet it seems to me that a basic, even fatal error in methodology is
committed at the very outset in separating the four so-called "Servant
of the Lord" sections from the other "Servant of the Lord" passages
and sections in Second Isaiah and treating them as a distinct unit,
simply because the term ʿebed (or the idea of an ʿebed) is present. There
is *a priori* no more reason for isolating either certain ʿebed or any ʿebed
passages in Second Isaiah than for lifting out of their preserved
Hebrew context passages that deal with the gentile nations, or with

---

[1]) Cf. the brief, convenient survey in HAROLD H. ROWLEY, *The Servant of the
Lord and other Essays on the Old Testament* (London, 1952), p. 6, n. 1.

[2]) Convenient surveys may be found in NORTH, Part I. "Historical" (pp. 6-116),
and ROWLEY, Chapter I, "The Servant of the Lord in the light of Three Decades
of Criticism" (pp. 1-57). See further, Chapter IV below.

[3]) See, e.g., NORTH, "Are Any Other Passages to be Reckoned as 'Songs'?,"
pp. 127-138.

[4]) The literature on the subject in general is immense. A cross-section of the
scholarly treatment of our problem, together with bibliographical references, may
be found—in addition to the above-cited works by EISSFELDT, NORTH, ROWLEY,
and SNAITH—in such works as EDUARD KÖNIG, *Das Buch Jesaja* (Gütersloh,
1926; cf. his "Deuterojesajanisches," *Neue Kirchliche Zeitschrift*, 9 [1898], 895-935,
937-997); CHARLES C. TORREY, *The Second Isaiah* (New York, 1928); EDWARD
J. KISSANE, *The Book of Isaiah*, 2 vols. (Dublin, 1943); JOHANNES LINDBLOM,
The Servant Songs in Deutero-Isaiah (= *Lunds Universitets Årsskrift N.F. Avd. 1.
Bd. 47. Nr. 5*; Lund, 1951).

foreign kings, or with Israel in exile and the like. Even if the ʿebed in some sections refers to an individual, whoever he may be, why should these sections be treated in splendid isolation? And if the ʿebed in these same sections is identified—as it is by most scholars—with the people Israel, then the entire analysis becomes absurdity itself, for it is patently absurd to set apart "Israel as the Servant of the Lord" in these four sections from "Israel as the Servant of the Lord" in the other eight or so sections in Second Isaiah (41.8, 9; 42.19 ff.; 43.10; 44.1, 2; 44.21; 45.4; 48.20; 49.7. On 52.13 see chapter III below).

In this connection, NORTH's chapter (IX, pp. 156-191) on the "Authorship of the Songs" is most pertinent. After discussing (§ 1) "Their Formal Relation to their Contexts" and concluding (p. 160) that ". . .we can no longer argue, either on the basis of a formal connexion of the Songs with their contexts, or on the lack of such formal connexion, that the Songs are, or are not, from Deutero-Isaiah," NORTH continues,"For want of any surer criterion we are forced to a consideration of the vocabulary, style, metrical forms, and the ideas of the Songs in relation to those of the main prophecy. If this should seem like reducing the whole question to one of statistics, there appears to be no alternative."

His detailed analysis (§ 2, pp. 160-169) of the "Language of the Songs," leads NORTH to conclude that "It is impossible on the grounds of vocabulary to deny (to 42.1-4) authorship by Deutero-Isaiah" (p. 162); ". . .Once more, the parallels with Deutero-Isaiah are so close that it is impossible, on grounds of vocabulary alone, to deny (to 49.1-6) identity of authorship. . ." (163 f.); ". . .there are sufficient correspondences with DI to make it hazardous. . .to deny (to 50.4-9) his authorship. They extend over chaps. xlix-lv as well as xl-xlviii" (p. 165); and "It is not permissible, on grounds of vocabulary, to assert that the passage (52.13-53.12) is by Deutero-Isaiah; but neither is it permissible to deny it" (p. 169).

The identical picture emerges from the, less decisive, analysis of the "Style and Metre of the Songs" (§ 3): "As to the metrical form of the Songs, he would be a bold man who should deny [the Songs] to Deutero-Isaiah on the score that they are different from his. . ." (p. 178). And, finally, his more detailed analysis of the "Theological Standpoint of the Songs" (§ 4, 178-186) led NORTH to assert (p. 186), ". . .The conclusion, therefore, to which I feel compelled is that the Songs are by Deutero-Isaiah. . ."

The over-all analysis and conclusions by NORTH, which took into consideration earlier studies by outstanding scholars, can be appreciated fully only by one who has attempted the same thing with other biblical Books: First Isaiah, Jeremiah, Micah, Zechariah, Hosea, etc. Of course one may, with justification, distinguish between major divisions in authorship of Micah, Zechariah, etc.; and one may, justifiably, isolate an individual chapter or section within each of these major divisions as originating with a different author altogether. Nervertheless, were one desirous, because of a special reason, of isolating most any individual section in any of these Books, none of context, vocabulary, style, meter, theology, etc., would probably prevent him from doing so. Take, e.g., the recent attempt of KARL ELLIGER (*Deuterojesaja in seinem Verhältnis zu Tritojesaja*; 1933) to demonstrate Third Isaiah as the author of 52.13-53.12. "ELLIGER's proof," NORTH noted (pp. 82 f.), "of the Trito-Isaianic authorship of the last Song consists of a comparison, in the minutest statistical detail, of the language and ideas of the passage with those of Deutero- and Trito-Isaiah respectively... But the unity of Isa. lvi-lxvi—a condition precedent to our being able to speak of an individual prophet to be called Trito-Isaiah—is not the general view of scholars, despite ELLIGER's pleadings. The personality of 'Trito-Isaiah' is even more elusive than that of his master. We never get to grips with him. Our only means of knowing him—on ELLIGER's own showing—is as the editor of Deutero-Isaiah, and then through his own editor. How, then, can ELLIGER know him so well as to say that his exilic style, in chaps. xl-lv, is more dependent upon that of Deutero-Isaiah than his post-exilic style in chaps. lvi-lxvi?...On his principle we might reasonably argue that all 'Deuteronomic' writings are from one pen. Further, as between writers so similar in style as Deutero- and 'Trito-' Isaiah, it is antecendently improbable that we can ever be so sure as ELLIGER is which chapter, or which half-verse, comes from the one and which from the other."

And when NORTH gets to analyzing in detail (pp. 169-177) the specific words and phrases that ELLIGER chose as the basis for his view, one realizes in even fuller perspective how baseless ELLIGER's argumentation really is. I do not see how anyone can dispute seriously NORTH's conclusion (p. 177) that "All things considered, the verdict must be that ELLIGER's theory that the last Song is the work of 'Trito-Isaiah' is unproven...He marshals his proofs with relentless thoroughness, and with a complete lack of any sense of humour; and when we come to examine them closely they simply fall to pieces."

And so, once again, it becomes clear that there is nothing within Second Isaiah, or the Old Testament in general, that would have led anyone in the biblical period even to think in terms of "Servant Sections" in Second Isaiah; and indeed, none ever did. It is only the nature and needs of Christianity after the death of Jesus—as we shall see below—that brought this sectional division into being.

CHAPTER THREE

THE SO-CALLED "SUFFERING SERVANT" AND "VICARIOUS SUFFERER" IN ISAIAH 52-53

Not only is the "Servant of the Lord" as a technical term (except perhaps for Moses) foreign to the Hebrew Bible, and not only is there no justification for isolating the "Servant" passages from their preserved contexts, but it will now be seen, further, that the concepts "Suffering Servant" and the servant as "Vicarious Sufferer" are likewise post-biblical in origin—actually the product of Christianity in the period subsequent to the death of Jesus.

A

Do Isaiah 52.13-15 and 53.1-12

Really Constitute a Single Unit
with but one Servant Involved?

Scholarship has generally taken it for granted—since the term *ʿebed* occurs in 52.13, though not in chapter 53 until verse 11—that the last three verses in chapter 52 and all of 53 constitute a single composition; [1]) in this, scholars have followed old Christian tradition. Yet there are several cogent reasons for questioning this, quite gratuitous assumption.

---

[1]) Martin Schian, *Die Ebed-Jahwe-Lieder in Jesaias 40-66*, etc. (Halle, 1895), pp. 34 f., 47, 59 f., isolated the two verses 52.13 and 53.1 as a later addition to 53.2-12, in his opinion the original song; after him Ludwig Laue (*Die Ebed-Jahwe-Lieder im II. Teil des Jesaja exegetisch-kritisch und biblisch-theologisch untersucht* [Wittenberg, 1898]; see also pp. 343 ff. in his "Nochmals die Ebed-Jahwe-Lieder im Deuterojesaja" [*Theologische Studien und Kritiken*, 77 (1904), 319-379]) argued that 52.13-15 was a later addition to chap. 53. In the twentieth century, Willy Staerk (*Die Ebed Jahwe Lieder in Jesaja 40 ff. Ein Beitrag zur Deuterojesaja-Kritik* [*Beiträge zur Wissenschaft vom Alten Testament*, XIV, 1913], 116 ff.), Johann Fischer (*Isaias 40-55 und die Perikopen vom Gottesknecht. Eine kritisch-exegetische Studie* [*Alttestamentliche Abhandlungen*, VI, 4/5, 1916], 115 ff.), Hedwig Janow (*Das hebräische Leichenlied im Rahmen der Völkerdichtung* [*Beiheft zur Zeitschrift für die alttestamentliche Wissenschaft*, 36, 1923], p. 256), John Monteith ("A New View of Isaiah liii," *Expository Times*, 36 [1924-25], 498-502), James D. Smart ("A New Approach to the ʿEbed-Yahweh Problem," *Expository Times*, 45 [1933-34], 168-172), N. H. Snaith (p. 199), and J. Lindblom (*The Servant Songs in Deutero-Isaiah* [*Lunds Universitets Årsskrift*, N.F., Avd. 1, Bd. 47, No. 5, 1951], pp. 37 ff.), appear to stand alone in questioning this tacitly accepted view.

(1) The very first clause in 52.13, הִנֵּה יַשְׂכִּיל עַבְדִּי, "Behold, My servant will prosper," [1]) indicates through the pun יִשְׂרָאֵל-יַשְׂכִּיל that it is the people Israel that is the servant here, with God, of course, the speaker. Like his fellow prophets, and the biblical writers generally, our prophet was given to punning. For the pun on "Israel" here, compare 44.2b where *Yeshurun* represents Israel ("Fear not, My servant Jacob, / Jeshurun whom I have chosen" [2])) and 42.19b where *Meshullam* is so intended ("Who is blind like Meshullam, / Blind like the servant of the Lord?" [3]))[4].) One is reminded at once of the same use of the term *Yeshurun* three times in the Pentateuch (Deut. 32.15; 33.5, 26) [5]) and of the term *Yesharim* once (Num. 23.10) [6]).

---

[1]) There can be little doubt of the meaning "prosper, succeed," or the like, in the light of immediately following יָרוּם וְנִשָּׂא וְגָבַהּ מְאֹד.

[2]) Verses 1-2 read:

(1) וְעַתָּה שְׁמַע יַעֲקֹב עַבְדִּי וְיִשְׂרָאֵל בָּחַרְתִּי בוֹ:

(2) כֹּה־אָמַר יהוה עֹשֶׂךָ וְיֹצֶרְךָ מִבֶּטֶן יַעְזְרֶךָ

אַל־תִּירָא עַבְדִּי יַעֲקֹב וִישֻׁרוּן בָּחַרְתִּי בוֹ:

[3]) Verses 18-19 read:

(18) הַחֵרְשִׁים שְׁמָעוּ וְהַעִוְרִים הַבִּיטוּ לִרְאוֹת:

(19) מִי עִוֵּר כִּי אִם־עַבְדִּי וְחֵרֵשׁ כְּמַלְאָכִי אֶשְׁלָח

מִי עִוֵּר כִּמְשֻׁלָּם וְעִוֵּר כְּעֶבֶד יהוה:

The "deaf" and "blind" in Second Isaiah are the Judeans in exile, who are exhorted to heed Second Isaiah's message.

[4]) TORREY, *The Second Isaiah*, p. 331, has some pertinent remarks on *meshullam*, as on *yeshurun* (p. 344) and *yaskil* (p. 415), and on the prophet's "constant use of paronomasia" (pp. 193 f.); or cf., e.g., SHELDON H. BLANK, *Prophetic Faith in Isaiah* (New York, 1958), p. 79 and nn. 7, 9 (on p. 216). KARL BUDDE ("The So-called 'Ebed-Jahwe Songs' and the Meaning of the Term 'Servant of Yahweh' in Isaiah Chaps. 40-55," *American Journal of Theology*, 3 [1899], 533 f. [= 34 f. in *Die sogenannten Ebed-Jahwe-Lieder*, etc. (Giessen, 1900)]), followed, e.g., by KARL MARTI (*Das Buch Jesaja erklärt* [Tübingen, 1900], ad loc.) and MONTEITH (499 f.), missed the point completely in emending יַשְׂכִּיל to יִשְׂרָאֵל. On *meshullam* see Excursus I in CURT LINDHAGEN, *The Servant Motif in the Old Testament: A Preliminary Study to the 'Ebed-Yahweh Problem' in Deutero-Isaiah* (Uppsala, 1950), pp. 216-219.

[5]) Respectively וַיִּשְׁמַן יְשֻׁרוּן וַיִּבְעָט "So Jeshurun grew fat and kicked (. . .He forsook the God who made him / And spurned the Rock of his support)"; וַיְהִי בִישֻׁרוּן מֶלֶךְ "Then He became king in Jeshurun"; and אֵין כָּאֵל יְשֻׁרוּן "O Jeshurun, there is none like God, (Riding through the heavens to help you, / Through the skies in His majesty)." The translation of the passages in the Pentateuch is taken from the New Jewish (Publication Society) Version of the *Torah* (Philadelphia, 1962).

[6]) The verse reads מִי מָנָה עֲפַר יַעֲקֹב וּמִסְפָּר אֶת־רֹבַע יִשְׂרָאֵל

תָּמֹת נַפְשִׁי מוֹת יְשָׁרִים וּתְהִי אַחֲרִיתִי כָּמֹהוּ:

"Who can count the dust of Jacob, / Number the dust-cloud of Israel? May I die the death of the upright, / May my fate be like theirs!" Note that (singular!)

(2) Independently, and at the same time bearing out the equation "*yaskil* = Israel," the expressions "(powerful) nations" (גּוֹיִם [רַבִּים]) and "kings" (מְלָכִים) in v. 15, as also the description of the woebegone servant in v. 14, point to the people Israel rather than to an individual person as the servant: Israel will be exceedingly exalted and honored,[1]) after shocking the mighty with its wretched condition,[2]) by the same powerful nations and kings who would never have believed possible what they will themselves see and hear.[3]) It may be noted here, in passing, that Second Isaiah employs such terms as "nations" (גוים) and "kings" (מלכים) in contrast not to the prophet himself but to the people Israel, or to Cyrus, God's conquering hero in behalf of Israel.

Second Isaiah has much to say about the degraded condition of Israel in exile; indeed the *raison d'être* of his career revolved precisely about Israel's inferior standing and God's decision and ability to restore Israel to her original home and status. Compare, e.g., the prophet's opening words in chap. 40, where Israel's very presence in Babylonia is described as "her term of service, of penal servitude" (צְבָאָה) and her punishment as far more severe than her sin warranted, so that the entire situation justified fully the exulting clarion cry of consolation and liberation (vv. 1, 9):

(1) Comfort, oh comfort My people,
    Says your God.

. . . .

(9) Ascend a lofty mountain,
    O Zion, herald of joy;
    Raise your voice with power,

כָּמֹהוּ correctly refers back to the "Israel" in *yesharim*, which is parallel to Jacob and Israel. On the rendering "the upright" for *yesharim* in the new JPS version of the *Torah* there is an explanatory note that reads: "*Heb* Yesharim, *a play on* Yeshurun (*Jeshurun*; *Deut. 32.15*), *a name for Israel.*"

1) הִנֵּה יַשְׂכִּיל עַבְדִּי יָרוּם וְנִשָּׂא וְגָבַהּ מְאֹד:

2) כַּאֲשֶׁר שָׁמְמוּ עָלֶיךָ רַבִּים כֵּן־מִשְׁחַת מֵאִישׁ מַרְאֵהוּ וְתֹאֲרוֹ מִבְּנֵי אָדָם. Scholars agree that parts of this verse, as of v. 15 following, are of uncertain meaning; nor is the text altogether certain. Our own interpretation is based upon the generally accepted understanding of the traditional Hebrew text.

3) 52.15   כֵּן יַזֶּה גּוֹיִם רַבִּים עָלָיו יִקְפְּצוּ מְלָכִים פִּיהֶם

כִּי אֲשֶׁר לֹא־סֻפַּר לָהֶם רָאוּ וַאֲשֶׁר לֹא־שָׁמְעוּ הִתְבּוֹנָנוּ:

> O Jerusalem, herald of joy—
> Raise it and have no fear,
> Announce to the cities of Judah:
> Behold your God! [1])

In 41.10-12 Israel is told:

> (10) Fear not, for I am with you,
>   Be not frightened, for I am your God;
>   I strengthen you and I help you,
>   I uphold you with My victorious right hand.
> (11) Shamed and chagrined shall be
>   All who contend with you;
>   They who strive with you
>   Shall become as nought and shall perish. . .
> (12) Less than nothing shall be
>   The men who battle against you. [2])

In 42.22 God's servant Israel is described as follows:

> It is a people plundered and despoiled,
> All of them trapped in holes
> And imprisoned in dungeons.
> They are given over to plunder, with none to rescue,
> To despoilment, with none to say, "Restore!" [3])

And so on.

(3) The situation is quite different in chapter 53. Nothing is said there of nations and kings. The treatment is entirely individualistic.

---

[1]) 40.1, 9

(1) נַחֲמוּ נַחֲמוּ עַמִּי יֹאמַר אֱלֹהֵיכֶם:

(9) עַל הַר־גָּבֹהַּ עֲלִי־לָךְ מְבַשֶּׂרֶת צִיּוֹן
הָרִימִי בַכֹּחַ קוֹלֵךְ מְבַשֶּׂרֶת יְרוּשָׁלִָם הָרִימִי אַל־תִּירָאִי
אִמְרִי לְעָרֵי יְהוּדָה הִנֵּה אֱלֹהֵיכֶם:

[2]) 41.10-12

(10) אַל־תִּירָא כִּי עִמְּךָ־אָנִי אַל־תִּשְׁתָּע כִּי־אֲנִי אֱלֹהֶיךָ
אִמַּצְתִּיךָ אַף־עֲזַרְתִּיךָ אַף־תְּמַכְתִּיךָ בִּימִין צִדְקִי:

(11) הֵן יֵבֹשׁוּ וְיִכָּלְמוּ כֹּל הַנֶּחֱרִים בָּךְ
יִהְיוּ כְאַיִן וְיֹאבְדוּ אַנְשֵׁי רִיבֶךָ:

(12) תְּבַקְשֵׁם וְלֹא תִמְצָאֵם אַנְשֵׁי מַצֻּתֶךָ
יִהְיוּ כְאַיִן וּכְאֶפֶס אַנְשֵׁי מִלְחַמְתֶּךָ:

[3]) 42.22

וְהוּא עַם־בָּזוּז וְשָׁסוּי הָפֵחַ בַּחוּרִים כֻּלָּם
וּבְבָתֵּי כְלָאִים הָחְבָּאוּ
הָיוּ לָבַז וְאֵין מַצִּיל מְשִׁסָּה וְאֵין־אֹמֵר הָשַׁב:

Unlike the people Israel, which did not keep silent in the face of destruction and exile, which was not cut off from the land of the living, and which deserved the divine punishment of destruction and exile because of transgression of the covenant, the servant in 53 is one who apparently did not complain, who ostensibly did not survive, and who experienced suffering through no guilt of his own.

As a matter of fact, there is much in chapter 53 that is hyperbolic rather than factual-descriptive (cf., e.g., NORTH, pp. 148 ff.); so that, in effect, the personage involved did not really keep silent nor was he already dead (see further below). But there is no way of getting around the straightforward statement (v. 9), עַל לֹא־חָמָס עָשָׂה וְלֹא מִרְמָה בְּפִיו "Although he had done nothing lawless / And there was no deceit in his mouth," in contrast to which the servant had previously been considered punished for his own sins rather than in consequence of the sins of others (vv. 4-6; see beginning of next section). SMART (p. 169, § 3) put it bluntly, "Would any prophet of Israel worthy of the name make the statement that Israel 'had done no violence, nor was any deceit in his mouth'? TORREY (p. 421) tries to water this down to mean only that Israel 'was far better than those for whom he suffered'; but the plain meaning remains. The writer of Is 40-66 was under no such delusions about his people. He reminds them of sins of the past, and assails them for sins of the present. . ." And cf. ROWLEY, p. 51.

It is worth noting that even TORREY, who regards 52.13-53.12 as a single major unit, with Israel being the servant throughout—vicariously atoning for the Gentiles (409 f.)—has to distinguish 52.13-15 ("the formal statement," with God as the speaker) from 53.1-9 ("the main body. . . conceived in somewhat dramatic form," with the Gentiles as the speaker) and 10-12 (God again as the speaker). LINDBLOM, who maintains (p. 37) "that it is rather astonishing that most commentators have so lightly passed over the problem of the unity of the passage LII.13-LIII.12", regards 52.13-53.1 as a unit (in which God addresses Israel in exile), with 53.2-12 constituting "a prophetic revelation in the form of a vision. . .The suffering man is. . .a fictitious person, who. . . is conjured up in the prophet's imagination, and. . . is the subject of a divine revelation" (p. 46).

(4) A closer examination of the last three verses in chapter 52 in relation to what precedes will reveal that they constitute a suitable ending for all of chapter 52. The entire chapter—actually the theme begins already in chapter 51 preceding— is a proclamation and exhortation to Zion-Jerusalem to prepare for the triumphant return of

the exiles, a triumph even greater than the Exodus from Egypt:

> But you shall not depart in haste,
> You shall not leave in flight;
> For the Lord is marching before you,
> The God of Israel is your rear guard.[1]

It is with this dramatic proclamation that our section is to be associated: God's degraded servant, His people Israel, will astonish everyone by the great restoration that he will achieve.

(5) As for the few verbal similarities between 52.13-15 and 53.1-12 (even allowing for the relatively few verses involved), e.g., תֹּאַר and מַרְאֶה (each in vv. 14 and 2), and רַבִּים (in vv. 14-15 and 11-12), and the use of „the root שמע as the link-word" [2] (viz., the verb שָׁמְעוּ in 15 and the noun שְׁמֻעָתֵנוּ in 1)—they help to indicate why 53.1 ff. was placed after 52.13-15, and may even help to prove that the author of the one section was responsible also for the second; they do not, however, prove that the two sections constitute a single unit.[3]

(6) It has been noted that—as against the (rather late) chapter division—Jewish tradition begins a section with 52.13 (to the end of 53).[4] However, neither the one division nor the other—when the two traditions fail to agree—is automatically to be followed; each instance has to be decided on its own merits. Interestingly, the complete Isaiah

---

[1] 52.12

כִּי לֹא בְחִפָּזוֹן תֵּצֵאוּ וּבִמְנוּסָה לֹא תֵלֵכוּן
כִּי־הֹלֵךְ לִפְנֵיכֶם יהוה וּמְאַסִּפְכֶם אֱלֹהֵי יִשְׂרָאֵל:

[2] SNAITH, p. 199 bottom. It may be noted that the form שְׁמוּעָה is found only here in all of chapters 40-66 of Isaiah.

[3] This is one of the main aspects of LEON J. LIEBREICH's detailed study of "The Compilation of the Book of Isaiah," *Jewish Quarterly Review*, 46 (1955-56), 259-277; 47 (1956-57), 114-138 (especially 135 f., where נִשָּׂא "be elevated" in 52.13, but נָשָׂא "bore" in 53.4, 12 are cited). And cf. the careful analysis of the "Language of the Songs" by NORTH, pp. 161-177, 189-191.

[4] Cf., e.g., CHRISTIAN D. GINSBURG, *Introduction to the Massoretico-Critical Edition of the Hebrew Bible* (London, 1897; reissued in 1966 by KTAV Publishing House, New York, with an introductory essay on "The Masoretic Text: A Critical Evaluation" by the present writer), Part I, Chap. II, "The Sectional Divisions of the Text (the Open and Closed Sections)," pp. 9-24. Thus EISSFELDT, 150 f. (3rd ed., 171 f.), e.g., after discussing some instances in which "Hier ist also die Kapitelteilung besser," continues with "Umgekehrt verdient die Paraschenteilung Gefolgschaft, die Kapitelteilung dagegen nicht, etwas bei dem letzten der 'Ebed-Jahwelieder Jes 52 13-53 12 und bei dem von uns schon als eine Einheit, nämlich also Volksklaglied erkannten Stück Jes 63 7-64 11..."

Scroll treats both 52.13 and 53.1 as the beginning of sections; [1])
Isaiah Scroll II, however, which coincides far more frequently than
Scroll I with the masoretic division (as with the preserved Hebrew
text),[2]) has a space-division at 52.13 only (none at 53.1).

Looking back, one may well wonder whether 52.13-15 would ever
have been attached to chapter 53 following, instead of with verses 1-12
preceding, had it not been for the fact that verse 13 began with "My
servant" (הֵן יַשְׂכִּיל עַבְדִּי). All in all, then, there is insufficient reason
for treating 52.13-15 and 53.1-12 as a single unit; and our analysis of
the concepts "Suffering Servant" and "Vicarious Sufferer" will be
based on chapter 53 alone.

B

IS THE SUBJECT OF ISAIAH 53
AN INDIVIDUAL PERSON OR THE PEOPLE ISRAEL?

A fundamental, and moot, problem in chapter 53 that requires
solution is whether the personage involved is an individual or the
people Israel. Let it be stated here, at the outset, that it cannot be the
people Israel that is involved.

It is a fact that the central figure in this chapter experienced suffering
and punishment for no transgression or guilt of his own; the latter
half of v. 9 asserts this clearly enough:

> Although he had done nothing lawless
> And there was no deceit in his mouth.[3])

This alone at once excludes the people Israel from further consideration.

The devastation of Judah, the destruction of the Temple, and the

---

[1]) HANS BARDTKE has discussed "Die Parascheneinteilung des Jesajarolle I
von Qumrān" (in *Festschrift Franz Dornseiff*, ed. H. KUSCH [Leipzig, 1953],
pp. 33-75). He has noted (pp. 67 f.) that "Fünf offene Paraschen lassen sich von
52,7 bis 53,12 feststellen. Diese sind: 52,7-12, 52,13-15, 53,1-8, 9-10a, 10b-12; die
erste Parasche wird im MT durch BHK[(2)] bestätigt und Pesch, die zweite ist
vorhanden in Petrop., S, B, A. Von 53,1 an hat MT keine Untergliederung mehr,
auch nicht Pesch und B..."

[2]) *The Dead Sea Scrolls of the Hebrew University*, ed. ELEAZAR L. SUKENIK (-NAH-
MAN AVIGAD; Jerusalem, 1955), Plate X; cf. SAMUEL LOEWINGER, "The Variants
of DSI II," *Vetus Testamentum*, 4 (1954), 155-163.

[3]) 53.9b   עַל לֹא־חָמָס עָשָׂה וְלֹא מִרְמָה בְּפִיו:

exile of so many of her finest citizens to Babylonia was the greatest national tragedy yet experienced by Israel. To account for this unprecedented catastrophe to God's chosen, covenanted people, Second Isaiah asserted—and this is the very core of his message—that God was the only Deity in the universe, omnipotent and just. As a just God, He punished Israel for transgressing the covenant, and in His omnipotence He used the army of Babylonia as the means of bringing this justified punishment upon His people. Now, however, the penalty having been paid by Israel in the fullest measure, God will restore His people to their homeland, to "Jerusalem, holy city" (52.1).[1])

Those who hold—and they constitute a vast, perhaps the majority of biblical scholars—that Israel is the subject of Isa. 53 and that innocently and meekly it went into exile to make, or rather to constitute, expiation for the gentile nations, must explain away or pass over in silence the numerous passages in Second Isaiah that assert clearly, or assume, that it is Israel's own sins that led to her captivity. I have in mind such passages as 40.2, where Jerusalem is told

> That she has completed her term,
> That her iniquity is expiated,
> For she has received at the hand of the Lord
> Double for all her sins.[2])

---

[1]) On the concept ירושלים עיר הקודש, see now HARAN, pp. 96-101.

[2]) 40.2

דַּבְּרוּ עַל־לֵב יְרוּשָׁלַם וְקִרְאוּ אֵלֶיהָ

כִּי מָלְאָה צְבָאָהּ כִּי נִרְצָה עֲוֹנָהּ

כִּי לָקְחָה מִיַּד יהוה כִּפְלַיִם בְּכָל־חַטֹּאתֶיהָ:

It is curious that the expression "double, twofold" (כִּפְלַיִם) has sometimes been understood literally. Thus STANLEY A. COOK, "The Prophets of Israel" (*Cambridge Ancient History*, vol. III, 1925), p. 492, surmised that "if Israel had received double for her sins (Isa. 40.2), might not the surplus have a saving efficacy for others?" In this he was followed, e.g., by EISSFELDT, "The Ebed-Jahwe in Isaiah xl.-lv. in the Light of the Israelite Conceptions of the Community and the Individual, the Ideal and the Real" (*Expository Times*, 44 [1932-33], 261-268), pp. 265 ff., who would have it that Jerusalem, having "received from the hand of Jahwe double punishment for all her sins. . .the possibility is at least suggested that the surplus punishment may be credited to others. . ." In immediate reply, SMART has put it this way (p. 168), "EISSFELDT uses the old explanation that the double punishment mentioned in 40[2] was half for the sins of the world. But surely the evident meaning of 40[2] is that since the nation has been punished twice over for all her sins the new day of forgiveness and blessing must be at hand. The purpose is to emphasize that the time of punishment has been completely fulfilled." PIETER A. H. DE BOER, *Second-Isaiah's Message* (= *Oudtestamentische Studiën*, Vol. XI, Leiden, 1956), p. 115, would have it that ". . .Second-Isaiah's message is that their (viz., part of the people's) suffering, beyond their deserved punishment,

Or 42.22-25:

(22) It is a people plundered and despoiled,
     All of them trapped in holes
     And imprisoned in dungeons.
     They are given over to plunder, with none to rescue,
     To despoilment, with none to say, "Restore!"
(23) Is there anyone among you to give ear to this,
     To attend and give heed from now on:
(24) Who was it gave over Jacob to despoilment,
     Israel to plunderers,
     If not the Lord Himself, against whom we sinned!
     They would not follow His ways
     And would not heed His Teaching;
(25) So He poured out wrath upon them,
     His anger and fierce war,
     And it blazed upon them all about, but they heeded not,
     It burned among them, but they gave it no thought.[1]

Or 43.24-25:

(21) You did not buy Me fragrant reed with money
     Nor sate Me with the fat of your sacrifices.

---

was accepted by YHWH as an atonement for those (Jews) who remained without punishment. . ." We shall see below that the non-Israelite nations did not "sin"— they had no covenant with God to transgress!—nor were they atoned for. Our term "double" is employed rhetorically, not mathematically; cf., e.g., TORREY, p. 305.

[1] 42.22-25

(22) וְהוּא עַם־בָּזוּז וְשָׁסוּי הָפֵחַ בַּחוּרִים כֻּלָּם
וּבְבָתֵּי כְלָאִים הָחְבָּאוּ
הָיוּ לָבַז וְאֵין מַצִּיל מְשִׁסָּה וְאֵין־אֹמֶר הָשַׁב:
(23) מִי בָכֶם יַאֲזִין זֹאת יַקְשֵׁב וְיִשְׁמַע לְאָחוֹר:
(24) מִי־נָתַן לִמְשִׁסָּה [Q =] ; למשוסה [א] יַעֲקֹב וְיִשְׂרָאֵל לְבֹזְזִים
הֲלוֹא יהוה זוּ חָטָאנוּ לוֹ
וְלֹא־אָבוּ בִדְרָכָיו הָלוֹךְ וְלֹא שָׁמְעוּ בְּתוֹרָתוֹ:
(25) וַיִּשְׁפֹּךְ עָלָיו חֵמָה אַפּוֹ וֶעֱזוּז מִלְחָמָה
וַתְּלַהֲטֵהוּ מִסָּבִיב וְלֹא יָדָע וַתִּבְעַר־בּוֹ וְלֹא־יָשִׂים עַל־לֵב:

On חֵמָה אַפּוֹ in v. 25, as against the common emendation חֲמַת אַפּוֹ (cf. IQISa חמת אפוא), see H. M. ORLINSKY, "Studies in the St. Mark's Isaiah Scroll, III: Masoretic חֵמָה in Isaiah XLII, 25" (*Journal of Jewish Studies*, 2 [1951], 151-154).

Nay, you burdened Me with your sins,
Wearied Me with your iniquities.
(25) It is I, I, who—for My sake—
Wipe your transgressions away
And remember your sins no more.[1]

Or 44.21-22:

(21) Remember these things, O Jacob,
O Israel, for you are My servant. . .
(22) I wipe away your sins like a cloud,
And your transgressions like mist;
Come back to Me, for I redeem you.[2]

Or 48.1-8:

(1) Hear this, O house of Jacob,
You who are called by Israel's name. . .
Who swear by the name of the Lord
And invoke the God of Israel—
But not in truth or justice. . .
(4) I know that you are stubborn:
Your neck is an iron sinew
And your forehead copper. . .
(5) I knew that you would deal treacherously,
"A rebel from birth" you were called.[3]

---

[1] 43.24-25   (24) לֹא־קָנִיתָ לִּי בַכֶּסֶף קָנֶה וְחֵלֶב זְבָחֶיךָ לֹא הִרְוִיתָנִי
אַךְ הֶעֱבַדְתַּנִי בְּחַטֹּאותֶיךָ הוֹגַעְתַּנִי בַּעֲוֹנֹתֶיךָ:
(25) אָנֹכִי אָנֹכִי הוּא מֹחֶה פְשָׁעֶיךָ לְמַעֲנִי וְחַטֹּאתֶיךָ לֹא אֶזְכֹּר:

[2] 44.21-22   (21) זְכָר־אֵלֶּה יַעֲקֹב וְיִשְׂרָאֵל כִּי עַבְדִּי־אָתָּה
יְצַרְתִּיךָ עֶבֶד־לִי אַתָּה יִשְׂרָאֵל לֹא תִנָּשֵׁנִי:
(22) מָחִיתִי כָעָב פְּשָׁעֶיךָ וְכֶעָנָן חַטֹּאותֶיךָ
שׁוּבָה אֵלַי כִּי גְאַלְתִּיךָ:

[3] 48.1-8   (1) שִׁמְעוּ־זֹאת בֵּית־יַעֲקֹב
הַנִּקְרָאִים בְּשֵׁם יִשְׂרָאֵל וּמִמֵּי יְהוּדָה יָצָאוּ
הַנִּשְׁבָּעִים בְּשֵׁם יהוה וּבֵאלֹהֵי יִשְׂרָאֵל יַזְכִּירוּ
לֹא בֶאֱמֶת וְלֹא בִצְדָקָה: (2) כִּי־מֵעִיר הַקֹּדֶשׁ נִקְרָאוּ
וְעַל־אֱלֹהֵי יִשְׂרָאֵל נִסְמָכוּ יהוה צְבָאות שְׁמוֹ:
(3) הָרִאשֹׁנות מֵאָז הִגַּדְתִּי וּמִפִּי יָצְאוּ וְאַשְׁמִיעֵם
פִּתְאֹם עָשִׂיתִי וַתָּבֹאנָה: (4) מִדַּעְתִּי כִּי קָשֶׁה אָתָּה
וְגִיד בַּרְזֶל עָרְפֶּךָ וּמִצְחֲךָ נְחוּשָׁה:

In 48.18 God tells Israel:

> If only you had obeyed My commandments,
> Your welfare would have been like a stream
> And your triumph like the waves of the sea. . .[1]

Or, finally, 50.1, where the Lord says:

> It is for your sins that you were sold,
> For your crimes that your mother was dismissed.[2]

It is unheard of in the Bible that Israel, God's "treasured people" (עַם סְגֻלָּה), His partner in the covenant, should suffer innocently for the sins and in behalf of any non-Israelite people.[3] But leaving aside for the moment the problem of Israel as a *vicarius*, as a substitute for gentile nations, let us deal with the matter of alleged sin on the part of these nations: precisely what sins are the gentile nations supposed to have committed to warrant punishment from God, punishment that Israel will allegedly suffer in their stead?

Biblically, gentile nations committed two kinds of crimes which justified God's intervention: (a) transgression against the so-called Noahide laws, what might be called crimes against natural law or humanity; (b) crimes against God Himself or against Israel, God's covenanted partner whom He promised to protect and prosper. Thus

---

(5) וָאַגִּיד לְךָ מֵאָז בְּטֶרֶם תָּבוֹא הִשְׁמַעְתִּיךָ
פֶּן־תֹּאמַר עָצְבִּי עָשָׂם וּפִסְלִי וְנִסְכִּי צִוָּם:

(6) שָׁמַעְתָּ חֲזֵה כֻּלָּהּ וְאַתֶּם הֲלוֹא תַגִּידוּ
הִשְׁמַעְתִּיךָ חֲדָשׁוֹת מֵעַתָּה וּנְצֻרוֹת וְלֹא יְדַעְתָּם:

(7) עַתָּה נִבְרְאוּ וְלֹא מֵאָז וְלִפְנֵי־יוֹם וְלֹא שְׁמַעְתָּם
פֶּן־תֹּאמַר הִנֵּה יְדַעְתִּין:

(8) גַּם לֹא־שָׁמַעְתָּ גַּם לֹא יָדַעְתָּ גַּם מֵאָז לֹא־פִּתְּחָה אָזְנֶךָ
כִּי יָדַעְתִּי בָּגוֹד תִּבְגּוֹד וּפֹשֵׁעַ מִבֶּטֶן קֹרָא לָךְ:

[1] 48.18   לוּא הִקְשַׁבְתָּ לְמִצְוֹתָי
וַיְהִי כַנָּהָר שְׁלוֹמֶךָ וְצִדְקָתְךָ כְּגַלֵּי הַיָּם:

[2] 50.1   כֹּה אָמַר יהוה
אֵי זֶה סֵפֶר כְּרִיתוּת אִמְּכֶם אֲשֶׁר שִׁלַּחְתִּיהָ
אוֹ מִי מִנּוֹשַׁי אֲשֶׁר־מָכַרְתִּי אֶתְכֶם לוֹ
הֵן בַּעֲוֹנֹתֵיכֶם נִמְכַּרְתֶּם וּבְפִשְׁעֵיכֶם שֻׁלְּחָה אִמְּכֶם:

---

[3] SMART (pp. 168 f.), while seeing with everyone else vicariousness in chap. 53, nevertheless recognizes the fact that "The idea of Israel as a suffering Servant, meekly redeeming the nations, is quite foreign to the thought of the prophet, and has been largely instrumental in obscuring his real thought. . ."

28 H. M. ORLINSKY

Amos (1.3-2.3) arraigned Israel's neighboring nations, the inhabitants of Damascus, Gaza, Tyre, Edom, Ammon, and Moab for crimes against humanity; Judah and Israel, however, alone in the world, are arraigned for transgression of the covenant (2.4 עַל־מָאֳסָם אֶת־תּוֹרַת יהוה "because they rejected the instruction of the Lord"). Isaiah —First Isaiah, in 37.23 ff.—condemned Sennacherib king of Assyria for having blasphemed the Lord by proclaiming his own power, rather than God's, the source and cause of his victories (and cf. 10.6 ff.). Jeremiah (chap. 27) promised destruction for those nations who, contrary to God's decision, will not submit to "Nebuchadnezzar king of Babylonia, My servant." Or cf., e.g., Isa. 14.12-16; Jer. 50-51 *passim*.

In Second Isaiah, however, the situation is quite different. If the nations will be smitten by God, if the gentile peoples are repeatedly denounced by the prophet, if Babylonia herself will be utterly destroyed—and all this is exactly what the prophet asserts—that was not because they had sinned but simply because they were the means by which God would show Israel and the whole world His uniqueness and omnipotence, and His abiding love for His people Israel. Passage after passage makes it crystal clear that the gentile nations were to be subjected to ignominy and defeat not because of any sins charged to them but only because God was to show His might in behalf of Israel. One recalls at once the identical fate of Egypt and its Pharaoh in the days of Moses and the Exodus, when God hardened and stiffened Pharaoh's heart so that He could perform His miracles in the land and "so that the Egyptians may know that I am the Lord" (Ex. 7.3-5).

Thus, in 40.9-11 our prophet proclaims joyfully that God will raise His mighty arm against the gentiles—hardly to spread His covenant and commandments among them—in order to gather in His lambs, exiled Israel:

> . . .(10) Behold the Lord God comes in might,
> His arm winning triumph for Him. . .
> (11) Like a shepherd He pastures His flock:
> He gathers the lambs in His arms
> And carries them in His bosom;
> Gently He drives the mother sheep.[1])

---

[1]) 40.9-11

(9) עַל הַר־גָּבֹהַ עֲלִי־לָךְ מְבַשֶּׂרֶת צִיּוֹן הָרִימִי בַכֹּחַ קוֹלֵךְ מְבַשֶּׂרֶת יְרוּשָׁלֵַם הָרִימִי אַל־תִּירָאִי

In verses 15-31 the nations are belittled and mocked, their idols ridiculed, and the leaders threatened with extinction, simply because they are not covenanted partners of God, whereas the Judean exiles who have faith in the Lord will be restored:

(15) The nations—they are a drop in a bucket,
Reckoned as dust on a balance;
The countries—He lifts them like motes. . .

(17) All nations are as nought before Him,
Accounted by Him as less than nothing. . .

(23) He brings potentates to nought,
Makes rulers of the earth as nothing. . .

(27) Why do you say, O Jacob,
Why declare, O Israel:
"My way is hid from the Lord,
My cause is ignored by my God"?. . .

(31) They who trust in the Lord shall renew their strength
As eagles grow new plumes:
They shall run and never weary,
They shall march and not grow faint.[1])

אִמְרִי לְעָרֵי יְהוּדָה הִנֵּה אֱלֹהֵיכֶם:

(10) הִנֵּה אֲדֹנָי יֱהֹוִה בְּחָזָק יָבוֹא וּזְרֹעוֹ מֹשְׁלָה לוֹ
הִנֵּה שְׂכָרוֹ אִתּוֹ וּפְעֻלָּתוֹ לְפָנָיו:

(11) כְּרֹעֶה עֶדְרוֹ יִרְעֶה בִּזְרֹעוֹ יְקַבֵּץ טְלָאִים
וּבְחֵיקוֹ יִשָּׂא עָלוֹת יְנַהֵל:

(15) הֵן גּוֹיִם כְּמַר מִדְּלִי וּכְשַׁחַק מֹאזְנַיִם נֶחְשָׁבוּ
הֵן אִיִּים כַּדַּק יִטּוֹל: (16) וּלְבָנוֹן אֵין דֵּי בָּעֵר
וְחַיָּתוֹ אֵין דֵּי עוֹלָה:

(17) כָּל־הַגּוֹיִם כְּאַיִן נֶגְדּוֹ מֵאֶפֶס וָתֹהוּ נֶחְשְׁבוּ־לוֹ:

(18) וְאֶל־מִי תְּדַמְּיוּן אֵל וּמַה־דְּמוּת תַּעַרְכוּ־לוֹ:

(19) הַפֶּסֶל נָסַךְ חָרָשׁ וְצֹרֵף בַּזָּהָב יְרַקְּעֶנּוּ
וּרְתֻקוֹת כֶּסֶף צוֹרֵף: (20) הַמְסֻכָּן תְּרוּמָה עֵץ לֹא־יִרְקַב יִבְחָר
חָרָשׁ חָכָם יְבַקֶּשׁ־לוֹ לְהָכִין פֶּסֶל לֹא יִמּוֹט:

(21) הֲלוֹא תֵדְעוּ הֲלוֹא תִשְׁמָעוּ הֲלוֹא הֻגַּד מֵרֹאשׁ לָכֶם
הֲלוֹא הֲבִינֹתֶם מוֹסְדוֹת הָאָרֶץ:

(22) הַיֹּשֵׁב עַל־חוּג הָאָרֶץ וְיֹשְׁבֶיהָ כַּחֲגָבִים
הַנּוֹטֶה כַדֹּק שָׁמַיִם וַיִּמְתָּחֵם כָּאֹהֶל לָשָׁבֶת:

(23) הַנּוֹתֵן רוֹזְנִים לְאָיִן שֹׁפְטֵי אֶרֶץ כַּתֹּהוּ עָשָׂה:

(24) אַף בַּל־נִטָּעוּ אַף בַּל־זֹרָעוּ אַף בַּל־שֹׁרֵשׁ בָּאָרֶץ גִּזְעָם
וְגַם־נָשַׁף בָּהֶם וַיִּבָשׁוּ וּסְעָרָה כַּקַּשׁ תִּשָּׂאֵם:

Everyone knows that the traditional Hebrew text of chapter 41 is
not altogether clear and that several individual words are hardly
original; yet the context as a whole is clear: the gentile "nations" and
"kings" will be subdued (vv. 2-3), the "coastlands" and the "ends of
the earth" will tremble in fear (v. 5), and all of Israel's enemies will
be destroyed—in short, in the entire world the Lord is on the side
only of His covenanted people Israel. Here is how the prophet
himself put it (vv. 8-16):

(8) But you, O Israel, My servant,
    Jacob, whom I have chosen,
    Seed of Abraham My friend—
(9) You whom I led from the ends of the earth
    And called from its far corners,
    To whom I said: You are My servant;
    I chose you, I have not rejected you—
(10) Fear not, for I am with you,
    Be not frightened, for I am your God;
    I strengthen you and I help you,
    I uphold you with My victorious hand.
(11) Shamed and chagrined shall be
    All who contend with you;
    They who strive with you
    Shall become as nought and shall perish.
(12) You may seek, but shall not find
    Those in conflict with you;

(25) וְאֶל־מִי תְדַמְּיוּנִי וְאֶשְׁוֶה יֹאמַר קָדוֹשׁ׃

(26) שְׂאוּ־מָרוֹם עֵינֵיכֶם וּרְאוּ מִי־בָרָא אֵלֶּה
    הַמּוֹצִיא בְמִסְפָּר צְבָאָם לְכֻלָּם בְּשֵׁם יִקְרָא
    מֵרֹב אוֹנִים וְאַמִּיץ כֹּחַ אִישׁ לֹא נֶעְדָּר׃

(27) לָמָּה תֹאמַר יַעֲקֹב וּתְדַבֵּר יִשְׂרָאֵל
    נִסְתְּרָה דַרְכִּי מֵיהוה וּמֵאֱלֹהַי מִשְׁפָּטִי יַעֲבוֹר׃

(28) הֲלוֹא יָדַעְתָּ אִם־לֹא שָׁמַעְתָּ
    אֱלֹהֵי עוֹלָם יהוה בּוֹרֵא קְצוֹת הָאָרֶץ
    לֹא יִיעַף וְלֹא יִיגָע אֵין חֵקֶר לִתְבוּנָתוֹ׃

(29) נֹתֵן לַיָּעֵף כֹּחַ וּלְאֵין אוֹנִים עָצְמָה יַרְבֶּה׃

(30) וְיִעֲפוּ נְעָרִים וְיִגָעוּ וּבַחוּרִים כָּשׁוֹל יִכָּשֵׁלוּ׃

(31) וְקוֹוֵי יהוה יַחֲלִיפוּ כֹחַ יַעֲלוּ אֵבֶר כַּנְּשָׁרִים
    יָרוּצוּ וְלֹא יִיגָעוּ יֵלְכוּ וְלֹא יִיעָפוּ׃

Less than nothing shall be
The men who battle against you.

(13) For I the Lord am your God,
I hold you by the hand,
I say to you: Have no fear;
I will be your help.

(14) Fear not, O worm Jacob,
O men of Israel:
I will help you—declares the Lord—
I your Redeemer, the Holy One of Israel.

(15) I will make of you a threshing-sledge,
Sharp, new, with many spikes.
You shall thresh the mountains to dust,
And make the hills like chaff.

(16) You shall winnow them
And the wind shall carry them off,
The whirlwind shall scatter them.
But you shall rejoice in the Lord,
And glory in the Holy One of Israel.[1]

Yet throughout this inspired statement, not a word about the nature of the sin committed by the gentile nations whom God will cause to

---

[1] 41.8-16.

(8) וְאַתָּה יִשְׂרָאֵל עַבְדִּי יַעֲקֹב אֲשֶׁר בְּחַרְתִּיךָ
זֶרַע אַבְרָהָם אֹהֲבִי:

(9) אֲשֶׁר הֶחֱזַקְתִּיךָ מִקְצוֹת הָאָרֶץ וּמֵאֲצִילֶיהָ קְרָאתִיךָ
וָאֹמַר לְךָ עַבְדִּי־אַתָּה בְּחַרְתִּיךָ וְלֹא מְאַסְתִּיךָ:

(10) אַל־תִּירָא כִּי עִמְּךָ־אָנִי אַל־תִּשְׁתָּע כִּי־אֲנִי אֱלֹהֶיךָ
אִמַּצְתִּיךָ אַף־עֲזַרְתִּיךָ אַף־תְּמַכְתִּיךָ בִּימִין צִדְקִי:

(11) הֵן יֵבֹשׁוּ וְיִכָּלְמוּ כֹּל הַנֶּחֱרִים בָּךְ
יִהְיוּ כְאַיִן וְיֹאבְדוּ אַנְשֵׁי רִיבֶךָ:

(12) תְּבַקְשֵׁם וְלֹא תִמְצָאֵם אַנְשֵׁי מַצֻּתֶךָ
יִהְיוּ כְאַיִן וּכְאֶפֶס אַנְשֵׁי מִלְחַמְתֶּךָ:

(13) כִּי אֲנִי יהוה אֱלֹהֶיךָ מַחֲזִיק יְמִינֶךָ
הָאֹמֵר לְךָ אַל־תִּירָא אֲנִי עֲזַרְתִּיךָ:

(14) אַל־תִּירְאִי תּוֹלַעַת יַעֲקֹב מְתֵי יִשְׂרָאֵל
אֲנִי עֲזַרְתִּיךְ נְאֻם־יהוה וְגֹאֲלֵךְ יִשְׂרָאֵל:

(15) הִנֵּה שַׂמְתִּיךְ לְמוֹרַג חָרוּץ חָדָשׁ בַּעַל פִּיפִיּוֹת
תָּדוּשׁ הָרִים וְתָדֹק וּגְבָעוֹת כַּמֹּץ תָּשִׂים:

(16) תִּזְרֵם וְרוּחַ תִּשָּׂאֵם וּסְעָרָה תָּפִיץ אוֹתָם
וְאַתָּה תָּגִיל בַּיהוה בִּקְדוֹשׁ יִשְׂרָאֵל תִּתְהַלָּל:

perish and become as nought. And the same is true, e.g., in 42.23-24, where God Himself is stated to have handed over "Jacob for spoil, Israel to plunderers"; clearly all that the gentile nations did was to serve as tools of God's punishment of sinful Israel.

It should be observed here that the expressions "nations," "peoples," "ends of the earth," "seacoasts" (or "isles"), "far corners" (respectively גּוֹיִם; לְאָמִּים; אִיִּים; קְצוֹת הָאָרֶץ; אֲצִילִים), and the like, do not, as a matter of fact, refer to any particular nations at all. Our prophet has but one specific nation in mind as Israel's foe, and that is Babylonia. Whom else would he have in mind at this point in history: Egypt? Or Phoenicia? Or Edom? Or Philistia? Or Assyria? When he used the terms "nations; peoples; ends of the earth," etc., his audience recognized in them at once poetic language for "the whole world; the universe; everyone," exactly as First Isaiah, among others, meant to be understood when he began with

> Hear, O heavens,
> Give ear, O earth.

By the same token, when the prophet refers to "kings," "rulers," "chieftains," "potentates," "rulers of the earth" (respectively מֹשְׁלִים; מְלָכִים; שֹׁפְטֵי אָרֶץ; רוֹזְנִים; שָׂרִים), and the like, he has no particular chieftain or potentate or king in mind; his Israelite audience understood these expressions to refer to the non-Israelite world of rulers and governments and nations. Even in 41.11-12, e.g., when the prophet inveighs against

> All who contend with you,
> They who strive with you. . .
> Those in conflict with you. . .
> The men in battle aginst you [1]

it is not necessary to look for anyone in particular—not even the Babylonian conquerors, three and four decades after the Judean exiles had been living comfortably among them; indeed, the anta-

---

[1] For the Hebrew text, see p.31, n.1 preceding. And whether it is Cyrus or Abraham or anyone else who is the central figure in this chapter, note that the chapter begins with: "Stand silent before Me, O coastlands, / And let nations renew their strength" (הַחֲרִישׁוּ אֵלַי אִיִּים וּלְאָמִּים יַחֲלִיפוּ כֹחַ), where the לְאָמִּים··· אִיִּים in v. 1, as the אִיִּים···קְצוֹת הָאָרֶץ in v. 5, are, again, simply the non-Israelite world, from whose midst God will liberate His servant Israel.

gonists in these two verses are described previously as from "the ends
of the earth and from its far corners" (v. 9; and cf. vv. 1 and 5).
Again, when the prophet proclaims (42.10-12):

> (10) Sing to the Lord a new song,
> His praise from the ends of the earth—
> You sailors of the sea and its creatures,
> You coastlands and their inhabitants!
>
> (11) Let the desert and its towns cry aloud,
> The villages where Kedar dwells;
> Let Sela's inhabitants shout,
> Call out from the peaks of the mountains.
>
> (12) Let them do honor to the Lord,
> And tell His glory throughout the lands.[1]

he is not referring to the denizens of the sea, or to the inhabitants of
Kedar, or of Sela, or of the desert, and the like; he is resorting to
rhetoric pure and simple.[2]

Even nations not involved in Israel's exile, Egypt, Cush, and the
Sabeans, our prophet asserts, will come under Israel's authority, for
it is only Israel who has God on her side; cf. 43.3-6 and 45.14-17:

> (3) For I, the Lord, am your God,
> The Holy One of Israel delivers you:
> I give Egypt as your ransom,
> Cush and Seba in return for you.
>
> (4) Because you are precious in My sight
> You are honored, and I love you;
> I will give mankind in your stead
> And peoples in exchange for your life.
>
> (5) Fear not, for I am with you:
> I will bring your seed from the east
> And I will gather you from the west;

---

[1] 42.10-12

(10) שִׁירוּ לַיהוה שִׁיר חָדָשׁ תְּהִלָּתוֹ מִקְצֵה הָאָרֶץ
יוֹרְדֵי הַיָּם וּמְלֹאוֹ אִיִּים וְיֹשְׁבֵיהֶם:

(11) יִשְׂאוּ מִדְבָּר וְעָרָיו חֲצֵרִים תֵּשֵׁב קֵדָר
יָרֹנּוּ יֹשְׁבֵי סֶלַע מֵרֹאשׁ הָרִים יִצְוָחוּ:

(12) יָשִׂימוּ לַיהוה כָּבוֹד תְּהִלָּתוֹ בָּאִיִּים יַגִּידוּ:

[2] Even in the terminology revolving about "The Council of Yahweh in
Second Isaiah," discussed by FRANK M. CROSS, Jr. (*Journal of Near Eastern Studies*,
12 [1953], 274-277), one must be careful not to take literally what is simply "ancient literary pattern. . .used as. . .artistic device. . ."

(6) I will say to the north, "Give up!"
And to the south, "Hold not back!"
Bring My sons from afar,
And My daughters from the ends of the earth.[1]

(14) Thus said the Lord:

The wealth of Egypt
And the substance of Cush and the Sabeans. . .
Shall pass over to you and be yours;
They shall follow you,
They shall come over in chains;
They shall bow low to you
And make supplication to you:
God is with you alone,
There is no other, no god besides Him. . .

(16) All of them are shamed and chagrined. . .

(17) But Israel is rescued by the Lord
In everlasting triumph. . .[2]

---

[1] 43.3-6

(3) כִּי אֲנִי יהוה אֱלֹהֶיךָ קְדוֹשׁ יִשְׂרָאֵל מוֹשִׁיעֶךָ
נָתַתִּי כָפְרְךָ מִצְרַיִם כּוּשׁ וּסְבָא תַּחְתֶּיךָ:

(4) מֵאֲשֶׁר יָקַרְתָּ בְעֵינַי נִכְבַּדְתָּ וַאֲנִי אֲהַבְתִּיךָ
וְאֶתֵּן אָדָם תַּחְתֶּיךָ וּלְאֻמִּים תַּחַת נַפְשֶׁךָ:

(5) אַל־תִּירָא כִּי אִתְּךָ־אָנִי
מִמִּזְרָח אָבִיא זַרְעֶךָ וּמִמַּעֲרָב אֲקַבְּצֶךָּ:

(6) אֹמַר לַצָּפוֹן תֵּנִי וּלְתֵימָן אַל־תִּכְלָאִי
הָבִיאִי בָנַי מֵרָחוֹק וּבְנוֹתַי מִקְצֵה הָאָרֶץ:

Here, too, we probably have rhetoric rather than—as many scholars believe (cf., e.g., HARAN, p. 59)—specific geopolitics. Thus TORREY has noted at 43.3 (p. 334), " 'I give Egypt as thy ransom. . .nations in thy stead.' The well-known figure of speech, meaning simply, 'Ye are dearer to me than the other peoples. . .' " And DE BOER, e.g., has noted (p. 42, at 40.28 and 41.1; cf. pp. 89 f.), "*coastlands*. This expression possesses the same meaning as the ends of the earth, i.e. the whole earth. . ." This is, clearly, in keeping with the expressions "east. . .west. . .north. . . south. . .from afar. . .ends of the earth."

Although my own interpretation of the problem at large would not suffer, I cannot agree with E. J. HAMLIN, who would limit "The Meaning of 'Mountains and Hills' in Isa. 41: 14-16" (*Journal of Near Eastern Studies*, 13 [1954], 185-90) specifically to Babylonia and her heathenism; the use of הָרִים and גְּבָעוֹת in both Isaiahs and elsewhere in the Bible, as well as our own immediate context, scarcely justifies this kind of specific restriction.

[2] 45.14-17

(14) כֹּה אָמַר יהוה
יְגִיעַ מִצְרַיִם וּסְחַר־כּוּשׁ וּסְבָאִים אַנְשֵׁי מִדָּה

In chapter 47, for the first and only time in all of Second Isaiah, a reason is given for the downfall of a gentile nation, Babylonia; it is the same as that given in chapter 37 (and in the parallel section in II Ki. 19) for the downfall of Sennacherib and Assyria, namely, that Babylonia ignored the central role of God in making her merely the rod of His punishment of Israel, and, instead, regarded herself as the all-powerful one; in addition, it is charged, she maltreated Israel ruthlessly, beyond the call of duty; for these reasons she will be punished (vv. 5-15):

(5) Sit in silence, and go into darkness,
    O daughter of the Chaldeans;
    For you shall no more be called
    The mistress of kingdoms.

(6) I was angry with My people,
    So I profaned My heritage;
    I gave them into your hand,
    But you showed them no mercy;
    On the aged you laid heavy yoke.

(7) You said, "I shall be mistress for ever. . .

(8) . . . I am, and there is none but me;
    I shall not sit as a widow
    Or know the loss of children.". . .

(11) But calamity shall come upon you. . .
     Disaster shall fall upon you. . .
     And ruin shall come upon you suddenly,
     Of which you know nothing. . .[1])

עָלַיִךְ יַעֲבֹרוּ וְלָךְ יִהְיוּ אַחֲרַיִךְ יֵלֵכוּ בַּזִּקִים יַעֲבֹרוּ
וְאֵלַיִךְ יִשְׁתַּחֲווּ אֵלַיִךְ יִתְפַּלָּלוּ
אַךְ בָּךְ אֵל וְאֵין עוֹד אֶפֶס אֱלֹהִים:

(15) אָכֵן אַתָּה אֵל מִסְתַּתֵּר אֱלֹהֵי יִשְׂרָאֵל מוֹשִׁיעַ:

(16) בּוֹשׁוּ וְגַם־נִכְלְמוּ כֻּלָּם יַחְדָּו הָלְכוּ בַכְּלִמָּה חָרָשֵׁי צִירִים:

(17) יִשְׂרָאֵל נוֹשַׁע בַּיהוה תְּשׁוּעַת עוֹלָמִים
לֹא־תֵבֹשׁוּ וְלֹא־תִכָּלְמוּ עַד־עוֹלְמֵי עַד:

[1]) 47.5-15

(5) שְׁבִי דוּמָם וּבֹאִי בַחֹשֶׁךְ בַּת־כַּשְׂדִּים
כִּי לֹא תוֹסִיפִי יִקְרְאוּ־לָךְ גְּבֶרֶת מַמְלָכוֹת:

(6) קָצַפְתִּי עַל־עַמִּי חִלַּלְתִּי נַחֲלָתִי
וָאֶתְּנֵם בְּיָדֵךְ לֹא־שַׂמְתְּ לָהֶם רַחֲמִים
עַל־זָקֵן הִכְבַּדְתְּ עֻלֵּךְ מְאֹד:

There is hardly need to cite additional passages in this vein to justify
the assertion that, on Second Isaiah's view, Israel suffered destruction
at home and captivity in Babylonia abroad only because she had
transgressed her covenant with God; Babylonia, on the other hand,
having no covenant with God and being under no legal obligation to
Him, committed no such transgression. It was but the rod of God's
anger and punishment against sinful Israel, and the helpless witness
and victim of God's might and of God's restoration of His beloved
and chosen Israel to her homeland.

There is, of course, so much more to be said about Second Isaiah's
attitude toward Babylonia and the gentile world in general. But one
additional aspect must be brought out clearly, namely, that nothing
could have been farther from the prophet's mind than that Israel
was in existence for the welfare of the nations, or that other nations
could achieve equality with Israel in God's scheme of things. This

---

(7) וַתֹּאמְרִי לְעוֹלָם אֶהְיֶה גְּבָרֶת עַד
לֹא־שַׂמְתְּ אֵלֶּה עַל־לִבֵּךְ לֹא זָכַרְתְּ אַחֲרִיתָהּ:

(8) וְעַתָּה שִׁמְעִי־זֹאת עֲדִינָה הַיּוֹשֶׁבֶת לָבֶטַח
הָאֹמְרָה בִּלְבָבָהּ אֲנִי וְאַפְסִי עוֹד
לֹא אֵשֵׁב אַלְמָנָה וְלֹא אֵדַע שְׁכוֹל:

(9) וְתָבֹאנָה לָּךְ שְׁתֵּי־אֵלֶּה רֶגַע בְּיוֹם אֶחָד
שְׁכוֹל וְאַלְמֹן כְּתֻמָּם בָּאוּ עָלַיִךְ
בְּרֹב כְּשָׁפַיִךְ בְּעָצְמַת חֲבָרַיִךְ מְאֹד:

(10) וַתִּבְטְחִי בְרָעָתֵךְ אָמַרְתְּ אֵין רֹאָנִי
חָכְמָתֵךְ וְדַעְתֵּךְ הִיא שׁוֹבְבָתֶךְ
וַתֹּאמְרִי בְלִבֵּךְ אֲנִי וְאַפְסִי עוֹד:

(11) וּבָא עָלַיִךְ רָעָה לֹא תֵדְעִי שַׁחְרָהּ
וְתִפֹּל עָלַיִךְ הֹוָה לֹא תוּכְלִי כַּפְּרָהּ
וְתָבֹא עָלַיִךְ פִּתְאֹם שׁוֹאָה לֹא תֵדָעִי:

(12) עִמְדִי־נָא בַחֲבָרַיִךְ וּבְרֹב כְּשָׁפַיִךְ
בַּאֲשֶׁר יָגַעַתְּ מִנְּעוּרָיִךְ אוּלַי תּוּכְלִי הוֹעִיל אוּלַי תַּעֲרוֹצִי:

(13) נִלְאֵית בְּרֹב עֲצָתָיִךְ יַעַמְדוּ־נָא וְיוֹשִׁיעֻךְ
הברו =K] ;הברי [Q=   שָׁמַיִם הַחֹזִים בַּכּוֹכָבִים
מוֹדִיעִם לֶחֳדָשִׁים מֵאֲשֶׁר יָבֹאוּ עָלָיִךְ:

(14) הִנֵּה הָיוּ כְקַשׁ אֵשׁ שְׂרָפָתַם
לֹא־יַצִּילוּ אֶת־נַפְשָׁם מִיַּד לֶהָבָה
אֵין־גַּחֶלֶת לַחְמָם אוּר לָשֶׁבֶת נֶגְדּוֹ:

(15) כֵּן הָיוּ־לָךְ אֲשֶׁר יָגָעַתְּ סֹחֲרַיִךְ מִנְּעוּרָיִךְ
אִישׁ לְעֶבְרוֹ תָּעוּ אֵין מוֹשִׁיעֵךְ:

may be a very noble and worthy concept, one that would do credit even to the nations of our own twentieth century; but it is unfair and historically unjustifiable to read this concept back into Israelite thinking two and a half millennia ago.

An excellent case in point is provided by Isa. 56.7, where scholars generally have found the last clause to be the very essence of internationalism: "...for My House shall be called a House of prayer for all peoples" (כִּי בֵיתִי בֵּית־תְּפִלָּה יִקָּרֵא לְכָל־הָעַמִּים ...). But this interpretation can be gotten out of the text only by wilfully ignoring or perverting the context, i.e., by eisegesis. For the context (vv. 3-7) asserts unequivocally that it is only the eunuchs and the aliens (סָרִי־ סִים...וּבְנֵי הַנֵּכָר) "who observe My sabbaths and choose what I delight in and hold fast to My covenant...who attach themselves to the Lord to serve Him and to love the name of the Lord, to be His servants—all who observe the sabbath and de not profane it and who hold fast to My covenant—these I will bring to My holy mountain and cause them to rejoice in My House of prayer; their burnt offerings and their sacrifices shall be acceptable upon My altar, for My House shall be called a House of prayer for all peoples." [1]) In other words, only those foreigners who have already converted to God's Torah and accepted the covenant are welcome in His House! (As to whether this section is original or the product of a later hand—that is a separate problem and does not concern us here.)

---

[1]) 56.3-8

(3) וְאַל־יֹאמַר בֶּן־הַנֵּכָר הַנִּלְוָה אֶל־יְהוָה לֵאמֹר
הַבְדֵּל יַבְדִּילַנִי יהוה מֵעַל עַמּוֹ

(4) כִּי־כֹה אָמַר יהוה
וְאַל־יֹאמַר הַסָּרִיס הֵן אֲנִי עֵץ יָבֵשׁ:
לַסָּרִיסִים אֲשֶׁר יִשְׁמְרוּ אֶת־שַׁבְּתוֹתַי
וּבָחֲרוּ בַּאֲשֶׁר חָפָצְתִּי וּמַחֲזִיקִים בִּבְרִיתִי:

(5) וְנָתַתִּי לָהֶם בְּבֵיתִי וּבְחוֹמֹתַי יָד וָשֵׁם
טוֹב מִבָּנִים וּמִבָּנוֹת שֵׁם עוֹלָם אֶתֶּן־לוֹ אֲשֶׁר לֹא יִכָּרֵת:

(6) וּבְנֵי הַנֵּכָר הַנִּלְוִים עַל־יְהוָה לְשָׁרְתוֹ וּלְאַהֲבָה אֶת־שֵׁם יהוה
לִהְיוֹת לוֹ לַעֲבָדִים כָּל־שֹׁמֵר שַׁבָּת מֵחַלְּלוֹ וּמַחֲזִיקִים בִּבְרִיתִי:

(7) וַהֲבִיאוֹתִים אֶל־הַר קָדְשִׁי וְשִׂמַּחְתִּים בְּבֵית תְּפִלָּתִי
עוֹלֹתֵיהֶם וְזִבְחֵיהֶם לְרָצוֹן עַל־מִזְבְּחִי
כִּי בֵיתִי בֵּית־תְּפִלָּה יִקָּרֵא לְכָל־הָעַמִּים:

(8) נְאֻם אֲדֹנָי יהוה מְקַבֵּץ נִדְחֵי יִשְׂרָאֵל
עוֹד אֲקַבֵּץ עָלָיו לְנִקְבָּצָיו:

Or compare, e.g., Isaiah 14.1-2, where the alien may become attached to triumphant and restored Israel, whereas, on the other hand, the gentile peoples who had oppressed them will become their slaves. This statement, clearly, is not internationalism at all, except that it is arbitrarily made so by ignoring the true force of verse 1, the great victory of Israel and the consequent desire of some aliens to join her:

The Lord will pardon (or have compassion on) Jacob and will again choose Israel, and He will set them in their own land; and aliens will join them, attaching themselves to the house of Israel.

and by suppressing altogether verse 2:

The people will take them and bring them to their place; and the house of Israel will possess them in the Lord's land as male and female slaves, making captives of their captors and ruling over their oppressors.[1]

The same thought is expressed elsewhere in the Bible. Thus Zechariah 2.14-16 asserts plainly that only the gentiles who join Israel in her restored homeland can become part of God's people and that it is only in Zion that God will dwell:

"Shout for joy, Fair Zion! For lo, I come, and I will dwell in your midst," declares the Lord. In that day, many nations will attach themselves to the Lord and become His (lit. My) people, and He (lit. "I") will dwell among you; then you will know that the Lord of Hosts sent me to you. And the Lord will take Judah to Himself as His portion upon the holy land, and He will choose Jerusalem once more.[2]

---

[1] Most scholars emend עַמִּים to עַמָּם ("they will take them [viz., the גֵּר of verse 1] with them"); our argument is not affected thereby. The Hebrew text of verses 1-2 reads:

כִּי יְרַחֵם יהוה אֶת־יַעֲקֹב וּבָחַר עוֹד בְּיִשְׂרָאֵל וְהִנִּיחָם עַל־אַדְמָתָם וְנִלְוָה הַגֵּר עֲלֵיהֶם וְנִסְפְּחוּ עַל־בֵּית יַעֲקֹב: וּלְקָחוּם עַמִּים וֶהֱבִיאוּם אֶל־מְקוֹמָם וְהִתְנַחֲלוּם בֵּית־יִשְׂרָאֵל עַל אַדְמַת יהוה לַעֲבָדִים וְלִשְׁפָחוֹת וְהָיוּ שֹׁבִים לְשֹׁבֵיהֶם וְרָדוּ בְּנֹגְשֵׂיהֶם:

MOSHE WEINFELD recently dealt with the passages discussed here (and in n. 2 following), in his article on "Universalism and Particularism in the Period of Exile and Restoration" (in Hebrew; *Tarbiẓ*, 33 [1964/5724], 228-242, especially 231 ff.). In missing the points made here, he was following uncritically his mentor, YEHEZKEL KAUFMANN; see the several references to the latter's תולדות האמונה הי־שראלית, especially (in notes 38, 59, and 60) to vol. 8 (Tel-Aviv, 5716/1956).

[2] Zech. 2.14-16

רָנִּי וְשִׂמְחִי בַּת־צִיּוֹן כִּי הִנְנִי־בָא וְשָׁכַנְתִּי בְתוֹכֵךְ נְאֻם־יהוה: וְנִלְווּ גוֹיִם רַבִּים אֶל־יהוה בַּיּוֹם הַהוּא וְהָיוּ לִי לְעָם וְשָׁכַנְתִּי בְתוֹכֵךְ וְיָדַעַתְּ כִּי־יהוה צְבָאוֹת שְׁלָחַנִי אֵלָיִךְ: וְנָחַל יהוה אֶת־יְהוּדָה חֶלְקוֹ עַל אַדְמַת הַקֹּדֶשׁ וּבָחַר עוֹד בִּירוּשָׁלָםִ:

Or compare in this connection such passages as Isa. 49.22-23 and
66.18-24, written by quite different authors:

(22) Thus said the Lord God:

> I wil raise My hand to nations
> And lift up My ensign to peoples;
> And they shall bring your sons in their bosoms,
> And carry your daughters on their shoulders.

(23) Kings shall be your attendants,
> Their queens shall serve you as nurses;
> They shall bow to you, face to the ground,
> And lick the dust of your feet.
> And you shall know that I am the Lord—
> Those who trust in Me shall not be shamed.[1]

and

(18) . . . to gather all the nations and tongues; they shall come and
behold My glory. (19) I will set a sign among them, and send from
them survivors to the nations: to Tarshish, Pul, and Lud—that draw
the bow—to Tubal, Javan, and the distant coasts, that have never
heard My fame or beheld My glory. They shall declare My glory
among these nations. (20) And out of all the nations they shall bring
all your brothers on horses, in chariots and drays, on mules and
dromedaries, to Jerusalem, My holy mountain, said the Lord, as an
offering to the Lord—just as the Israelites bring an offering in a pure
vessel to the House of the Lord. (21) And from them likewise I will
take some to be levitical priests, said the Lord.

(22) For as the new heaven and the new earth
> Which I will make
> Shall endure by My will
>   —declares the Lord—
> So shall your seed and your name endure.

---

[1] 49.22-23

(22) כֹּה־אָמַר אֲדֹנָי יהוה
הִנֵּה אֶשָּׂא אֶל־גּוֹיִם יָדִי וְאֶל־עַמִּים אָרִים נִסִּי
וְהֵבִיאוּ בָנַיִךְ בְּחֹצֶן וּבְנֹתַיִךְ עַל־כָּתֵף תִּנָּשֶׂאנָה:
(23) וְהָיוּ מְלָכִים אֹמְנַיִךְ וְשָׂרוֹתֵיהֶם מֵינִיקֹתַיִךְ
אַפַּיִם אֶרֶץ יִשְׁתַּחֲווּ לָךְ וַעֲפַר רַגְלַיִךְ יְלַחֵכוּ
וְיָדַעַתְּ כִּי־אֲנִי יהוה אֲשֶׁר לֹא־יֵבֹשׁוּ קֹוָי:

(23) And new moon after new moon,
    And Sabbath after Sabbath,
    All flesh shall come to worship Me
    —said the Lord.
(24) They shall go out and gaze
    On the corpses of the men who rebelled against Me:
    Their worms shall not die,
    Nor their fire be quenched;
    They shall be a horror
    To all flesh.[1])

Even in the extremely difficult latter part of Isaiah 19, verses 18-25, which is doubtless eclectic and derives from more than one historical background (cf., e.g., GEORGE B. GRAY, *ICC on Isaiah*, 1912, pp. 332 ff.), it tends to be overlooked that Egypt will first be crushed (vv. 1-17, 22, 23) before it recognizes the authority of Israel's God, and that in forming a triumvirate with Egypt and Assyria, Israel will constitute a blessing in the world, i.e., it is through Israel that they will be blessed. However, this composite section can hardly, as it stands, serve as the basis for any theory—except for those who would proceed *per ignotum ad ignotius*.

The Israelite composers of the Bible recognized God as the only God in the universe. He was the Creator, the sole Creator, of the whole world; He, and He alone, brought all peoples into being and determined their careers; everyone and everything—even though they

---

[1]) 66.18-24 (the first part of v. 18 is corrupt):

18 וְאָנֹכִי מַעֲשֵׂיהֶם וּמַחְשְׁבֹתֵיהֶם בָּאָה לְקַבֵּץ אֶת־כָּל־הַגּוֹיִם וְהַלְּשׁוֹנוֹת וּבָאוּ וְרָאוּ אֶת־כְּבוֹדִי: (19) וְשַׂמְתִּי בָהֶם אוֹת וְשִׁלַּחְתִּי מֵהֶם פְּלֵיטִים אֶל־הַגּוֹיִם תַּרְשִׁישׁ פּוּל וְלוּד מֹשְׁכֵי קֶשֶׁת תֻּבַל וְיָוָן הָאִיִּים הָרְחֹקִים אֲשֶׁר לֹא־שָׁמְעוּ אֶת־שִׁמְעִי וְלֹא־רָאוּ אֶת־כְּבוֹדִי וְהִגִּידוּ אֶת־כְּבוֹדִי בַּגּוֹיִם: (20) וְהֵבִיאוּ אֶת־כָּל־אֲחֵיכֶם מִכָּל־הַגּוֹיִם מִנְחָה לַיהוה בַּסּוּסִים וּבָרֶכֶב וּבַצַּבִּים וּבַפְּרָדִים וּבַכִּרְכָּרוֹת עַל הַר קָדְשִׁי יְרוּשָׁלַם אָמַר יהוה כַּאֲשֶׁר יָבִיאוּ בְנֵי יִשְׂרָאֵל אֶת־הַמִּנְחָה בִּכְלִי טָהוֹר בֵּית יהוה: (21) וְגַם־מֵהֶם אֶקַּח לַכֹּהֲנִים לַלְוִיִּם אָמַר יהוה:

(22) כִּי כַאֲשֶׁר הַשָּׁמַיִם הַחֲדָשִׁים וְהָאָרֶץ הַחֲדָשָׁה אֲשֶׁר אֲנִי עֹשֶׂה עֹמְדִים לְפָנַי נְאֻם־יהוה כֵּן יַעֲמֹד זַרְעֲכֶם וְשִׁמְכֶם:

(23) וְהָיָה מִדֵּי־חֹדֶשׁ בְּחָדְשׁוֹ וּמִדֵּי שַׁבָּת בְּשַׁבַּתּוֹ יָבוֹא כָל־בָּשָׂר לְהִשְׁתַּחֲוֹת לְפָנַי אָמַר יהוה:

(24) וְיָצְאוּ וְרָאוּ בְּפִגְרֵי הָאֲנָשִׁים הַפֹּשְׁעִים בִּי כִּי תוֹלַעְתָּם לֹא תָמוּת וְאִשָּׁם לֹא תִכְבֶּה וְהָיוּ דֵרָאוֹן לְכָל־בָּשָׂר:

were not cognizant of it—were beholden to Him. At the same time, however, not one of all these peoples, apart from Israel, was God's covenanted people. So that while God was—to the biblical writers—a universal God, He was not an international God, but a national God, the God of no nation in the universe but Israel. An excellent statement of this is expressed in Amos 9.7, where the prophet declares:

> You are like the Cushites to Me,
> O Israelites
> —declares the Lord.
> I brought up Israel from the land of Egypt,
> And the Philistines from Caphtor,
> And the Arameans from Kir.[1])

Since Israel's God is the only deity in the world, who else but He is responsible for all events involving nature and man? Ethiopia, Philistia, Aram—all lands and peoples everywhere are His to act upon as He sees fit. (Note how Amos expresses the identical concept in 1.3-2.3, discussed briefly above.) But this does not make God the God of the Ethiopians, or of the Philistines, or of the Arameans! He is the God of Israel exclusively, by legal and binding contract, by the covenant. Israel's God is a universal God, not an international God.[2])

---

[1])   הֲלוֹא כִבְנֵי כֻשִׁיִּים אַתֶּם לִי בְּנֵי יִשְׂרָאֵל נְאֻם־יהוה
הֲלוֹא אֶת־יִשְׂרָאֵל הֶעֱלֵיתִי מֵאֶרֶץ מִצְרַיִם
וּפְלִשְׁתִּיִּים מִכַּפְתּוֹר וַאֲרָם מִקִּיר:

Cf. my discussion, "Who is the Ideal Jew: the Biblical View," in *Judaism*, 13 (1964), 19-28, where I deal with this passage (and others) in Amos, with Lev. 19.18; Malachi 2.10; Ps. 24; etc.

[2]) For a different approach to the problem, *in re* Second Isaiah, see S. H. BLANK, "Studies in Deutero-Isaiah" (*Hebrew Union College Annual*, 15 [1940], 1 ff.) and "Israel's God is God" and "And Israel is his Prophet" (respectively chaps. IV and V in *Prophetic Faith in Isaiah* [New York, 1958], pp. 49-73 and 74-116); cf. also JULIAN MORGENSTERN, "Deutero-Isaiah's Terminology for 'Universal God'" (*Journal of Biblical Literature*, 62 [1943], 269-280), and now "The Suffering Servant—a New Solution" (*Vetus Testamentum*, 11 [1961], 292-320, 406-431; 13 [1963], 321-332). See in general the section on "Particularism and Universality . . . of the Prophets" in my *Ancient Israel* (Cornell University Press, 1954), pp. 163 ff., with the references in n. 14 to FLEMING JAMES (*Personalities of the Old Testament* [New York, 1939], p. 263) and N. H. SNAITH (*op. cit.*, p. 191) as "Of the very few scholars who have noted the essential nationalism of Second Isaiah." So that DE BOER underestimated the numerical strength of the non-universalists (more correctly: non-internationalists) by two-thirds when he wrote (p. 84), "there are of course shades in the opinions of the interpreters of Isaiah xl-lv. . .It is the more notable that we find a virtual unanimity of opinion about universalism in the conception of God and the task of Yhwh's servant. I know but one exception, N. H. SNAITH. . ."

Let us now see how this concept manifested itself in Second Isaiah. God, we are told in 40.10,

> Like a shepherd He pastures His flock:
> He gathers the lambs in His arms. . .

whereas, in v. 17:

> All nations are as nought before Him,
> Accounted by Him as less than nothing.[1])

Throughout, Second Isaiah uses terms of endearment in reference to Israel.

> Comfort, oh comfort My people,
> Says your God.
> Speak tenderly to Jerusalem. . .[2])

is how he begins his message (40.1-2). In chapter 41 (vv. 8, 12-14) he will assert:

> (8) But you, O Israel, My servant,
> Jacob, whom I have chosen,
> Seed of Abraham My beloved. . .

One cannot get very far in this basic problem from a reading of PETER ALTMANN, *Erwählungstheologie und Universalismus im Alten Testament (Beihefte zur Zeitschrift für die alttestamentliche Wissenschaft*, No. 92, 1964, 31 pp.), where the author insists that Israel's covenant with God involves—rather than excludes—the other nations of the world. There are so many non-sequiturs and the like that the study seemed based on the motto: credo quia absurdum.

[1]) Isa. 40.10, 17   (10) הִנֵּה אֲדֹנָי יהוה בְּחָזָק יָבוֹא וּזְרֹעוֹ מֹשְׁלָה לוֹ
הִנֵּה שְׂכָרוֹ אִתּוֹ וּפְעֻלָּתוֹ לְפָנָיו:

(17) כָּל־הַגּוֹיִם כְּאַיִן נֶגְדּוֹ מֵאֶפֶס וָתֹהוּ נֶחְשְׁבוּ־לוֹ:

Similarly, in 42.22 ff. (see the Hebrew text on p. 25, n. 1), when the prophet refers to Israel's involuntary presence in Babylonia, he asserts unequivocally, in the name of God:

> Who was it gave over Jacob to despoilment,
> Israel to plunderers,
> If not the Lord Himself, against whom we sinned!
> They would not follow His ways
> And would not heed His Teaching. . .

Babylonia is but God's helpless rod for punishing Israel, and possesses no independent authority whatever.

[2]) 40.1-2   (1) נַחֲמוּ נַחֲמוּ עַמִּי יֹאמַר אֱלֹהֵיכֶם:
(2) דַּבְּרוּ עַל־לֵב יְרוּשָׁלַם · · ·

(12) Less than nothing shall be
The men who battle against you.

(13) For I the Lord am your God,
I hold you by the hand,
I say to you: Have no fear;
I will be your help.

(14) Fear not, O worm Jacob...
I will help you—declares the Lord—
I your Redeemer, the Holy One of Israel.[1]

This hardly sounds like an appeal to Babylonia or any other gentile nation to recognize God and become part of His covenanted people. Or as the prophet put it in the verses (15-16) immediately following:

(15) I will make of you a threshing-sledge,
Sharp, new, with many spikes.
You shall thresh the mountains to dust,
And make the hills like chaff.

(16) You shall winnow them
And the wind shall carry them off,
The whirlwind shall scatter them.
But you [2] shall rejoice in the Lord,
And glory in the Holy One of Israel.[3]

It is unlikely that Second Isaiah is promising here his fellow exiles military conquest of Babylonia or of any other nation; the exiles, in the midst of their mighty masters, would, with justification,

---

[1] 41.8, 12-14

(8) וְאַתָּה יִשְׂרָאֵל עַבְדִּי יַעֲקֹב אֲשֶׁר בְּחַרְתִּיךָ
זֶרַע אַבְרָהָם אֹהֲבִי:

(12) תְּבַקְשֵׁם וְלֹא תִמְצָאֵם אַנְשֵׁי מַצֻּתֶךָ
יִהְיוּ כְאַיִן וּכְאֶפֶס אַנְשֵׁי מִלְחַמְתֶּךָ:

(13) כִּי אֲנִי יהוה אֱלֹהֶיךָ מַחֲזִיק יְמִינֶךָ
הָאֹמֵר לְךָ אַל־תִּירָא אֲנִי עֲזַרְתִּיךָ:

(14) אַל־תִּירְאִי תּוֹלַעַת יַעֲקֹב מְתֵי יִשְׂרָאֵל
אֲנִי עֲזַרְתִּיךְ נְאֻם־יהוה וְגֹאֲלֵךְ קְדוֹשׁ יִשְׂרָאֵל:

[2] Note the pronoun וְאַתָּה and its emphatic position.

[3] 41.15-16

(15) הִנֵּה שַׂמְתִּיךְ לְמוֹרַג חָרוּץ חָדָשׁ בַּעַל פִּיפִיּוֹת
תָּדוּשׁ הָרִים וְתָדֹק וּגְבָעוֹת כַּמֹּץ תָּשִׂים:

(16) תִּזְרֵם וְרוּחַ תִּשָּׂאֵם וּסְעָרָה תָּפִיץ אוֹתָם
וְאַתָּה תָּגִיל בַּיהוה בִּקְדוֹשׁ יִשְׂרָאֵל תִּתְהַלָּל:

regard him as mad. In good rhetorical manner he is simply assuring them that God and His covenant would prevail over all else. TORREY, his theory of Israel's mission to the gentile nations rather embarassed by the blunt statement of our passage, resorts to this kind of exposition (p. 317), "Those whom Israel is to 'thresh' and 'shatter' are not the heathen nations in general nor any of the surrounding nations in particular, but *the wicked* [italics in original], of all races and lands; the incorrigible enemies of Yahwè and the religion of righteousness..."
It is interesting how the utterly nationalistic statements of our prophet are diluted and "extended" in order to make them express internationalism and to support Israel's alleged mission to the world. Thus DE BOER (p. 90), recognizes well that "No other conclusion can be drawn from our texts than the statement: Second-Isaiah's only purpose is to proclaim deliverance for the Judean people. 'Yhwh bares his holy arm before the eyes of all the nations, and all the ends of the earth see the salvation of our God['] lii 10. Foreign nations are but mentioned as peoples to be conquered, in whose hands the cup of wrath will be put, li 23; or as the instrument of Yhwh to deliver his people; or, in rhetorical manner of speaking, to be witness of Yhwh's glory. Yhwh's glory will be shown only in his elected people, raised up from their humiliation. If the interpretation which reads a world-wide missionary task of the servant in the so-called first and second song of Yhwh's servant and in chapters li and lv is right, we must state that the expressions where upon this interpretation is based are a *corpus alienum* in the book of Second-Isaiah. Are they an alien element indeed?..." One may well ask: Would anyone, prior to the rise of post-biblical Judaism and Christianity, have thought of creating such a *corpus alienum* and then introducing it into the text and context of Second Isaiah as the basic, original element? Herein lay the crux of the matter: scholarship unfree of the tradition and interests of time and place.

Whether or not the reference to "Cyrus" in 44.28 and 45.1 is original, the fact is that the gentile nations and kings will be—not saved or converted—but mercilessly overcome, all for the sake of God's name and Israel's welfare; as put in the first part of the chapter (vv. 4-6):

...(4) For the sake of My servant Jacob,
Israel My chosen...

(6) That it may be known,

From the rising of the sun and from the west,
That there is none besides Me,
I am the Lord, there is none other. . .[1]

When we read in chap. 43 (vv. 3-6):

(3) For I the Lord am your God,
The Holy One of Israel who brings you triumph. . .
(5) Do not fear, for I am with you:
I will bring your offspring from the east,
And from the west I will gather you;
(6) I will say to the north, "Give up!"
And to the south, "Do not withhold!". . .[2]

it is hardly "good tidings" that the prophet was announcing to the
gentile peoples of the earth. And the same is true, e.g., in chap. 48,
where God calls out (vv. 12-14):

(12) Hearken to Me, O Jacob,
Israel whom I called. . .
(14) The Lord loves him.

whereas, so far as Babylonia is concerned,

He shall perform His will on Babylonia,
And His arm on the Chaldeans.[3]

---

1) 45.4-6

(4) לְמַעַן עַבְדִּי יַעֲקֹב וְיִשְׂרָאֵל בְּחִירִי
וָאֶקְרָא לְךָ בִּשְׁמֶךָ אֲכַנְּךָ וְלֹא יְדַעְתָּנִי:
(5) אֲנִי יהוה וְאֵין עוֹד זוּלָתִי אֵין אֱלֹהִים
אֲאַזֶּרְךָ וְלֹא יְדַעְתָּנִי: (6) לְמַעַן יֵדְעוּ מִמִּזְרַח־שֶׁמֶשׁ
וּמִמַּעֲרָבָה כִּי־אֶפֶס בִּלְעָדָי אֲנִי יהוה וְאֵין עוֹד:

2) 43.3-6

(3) כִּי אֲנִי יהוה אֱלֹהֶיךָ קְדוֹשׁ יִשְׂרָאֵל מוֹשִׁיעֶךָ
נָתַתִּי כָפְרְךָ מִצְרַיִם כּוּשׁ וּסְבָא תַּחְתֶּיךָ:
(4) מֵאֲשֶׁר יָקַרְתָּ בְעֵינַי נִכְבַּדְתָּ וַאֲנִי אֲהַבְתִּיךָ
וְאֶתֵּן אָדָם תַּחְתֶּיךָ וּלְאֻמִּים תַּחַת נַפְשֶׁךָ:
(5) אַל־תִּירָא כִּי אִתְּךָ־אָנִי
מִמִּזְרָח אָבִיא זַרְעֶךָ וּמִמַּעֲרָב אֲקַבְּצֶךָּ:
(6) אֹמַר לַצָּפוֹן תֵּנִי וּלְתֵימָן אַל־תִּכְלָאִי
הָבִיאִי בָנַי מֵרָחוֹק וּבְנוֹתַי מִקְצֵה הָאָרֶץ:

3) 48.12-14

(12) שְׁמַע אֵלַי־יַעֲקֹב וְיִשְׂרָאֵל מְקֹרָאִי
אֲנִי־הוּא אֲנִי רִאשׁוֹן אַף אֲנִי אַחֲרוֹן:
(13) אַף־יָדִי יָסְדָה אֶרֶץ וִימִינִי טִפְּחָה שָׁמָיִם

One may well ask at this point: Is it for this that Israel is supposed to have suffered vicariously? Of course the "problem" disappears if "Babylonia" and "Chaldeans" are deleted from the text—which is what TORREY does. But then, those who hold to the theory of Israel's mission to the gentile nations and her vicarious suffering for their welfare, must, as in all the passages cited above, and below, likewise ignore the clear import of such a passage as 48.20-22: "Depart from Babylon, Flee from the Chaldeans! With a shout of joy...Say: the Lord has redeemed His servant Jacob...There is no peace, said, the Lord, for the wicked." [1]) Why should the Judeans "flee" from exile and amidst "shouts of joy," and why should it be Israel, rather than gentile nations, whom the Lord is about to redeem—unless it is precisely because Israel is God's people whom He is redeeming among the idolatrous gentile nations in whose midst Israel was exiled in punishment for her sins.

Or take chap. 49. Verse 7 asserts clearly:

> Thus says the Lord,
> The Redeemer of Israel and his Holy One,
> To one deeply despised, abhorred by the nations,
> The servant of rulers:
> "Kings shall see and stand up;
> Princes, and they shall prostrate themselves,
> Because of the Lord, who is faithful,
> The Holy One of Israel, who has chosen you." [2])

קְרָא אֲנִי אֲלֵיהֶם יַעַמְדוּ יַחְדָּו:

(14) הִקָּבְצוּ כֻלְּכֶם וּשְׁמָעוּ מִי בָהֶם הִגִּיד אֶת־אֵלֶּה
יהוה אֲהֵבוֹ יַעֲשֶׂה חֶפְצוֹ בְּבָבֶל וּזְרֹעוֹ כַּשְׂדִּים:

[1]) 48.20-22

(20) צְאוּ מִבָּבֶל בִּרְחוּ מִכַּשְׂדִּים
בְּקוֹל רִנָּה הַגִּידוּ הַשְׁמִיעוּ זֹאת
הוֹצִיאוּהָ עַד־קְצֵה הָאָרֶץ
אִמְרוּ גָּאַל יהוה עַבְדּוֹ יַעֲקֹב:

(21) וְלֹא צָמְאוּ בָּחֳרָבוֹת הוֹלִיכָם
מַיִם מִצּוּר הִזִּיל לָמוֹ וַיִּבְקַע־צוּר וַיָּזֻבוּ מָיִם:

(22) אֵין שָׁלוֹם אָמַר יהוה לָרְשָׁעִים:

[2]) 49.7

כֹּה אָמַר־יהוה גֹּאֵל יִשְׂרָאֵל קְדוֹשׁוֹ
לִבְזֹה־נֶפֶשׁ לִמְתָעֵב גּוֹי לְעֶבֶד מֹשְׁלִים
מְלָכִים יִרְאוּ וָקָמוּ שָׂרִים וְיִשְׁתַּחֲוּוּ
לְמַעַן יהוה אֲשֶׁר נֶאֱמָן קְדֹשׁ יִשְׂרָאֵל וַיִּבְחָרֶךָּ:

Lest, however, the reader jump to the conclusion that the expression "they shall prostrate themselves" (וְיִשְׁתַּחֲווּ) points to conversion, to acceptance of Israel's God and His teachings, let him but continue to read on, to the end of the chapter (vv. 8-26). He will read, e.g., in v. 13,

> Sing for joy, O heavens, and exult, O earth!
> Break forth, O mountains, into song!
> For the Lord comforts His people,
> Will show compassion to His afflicted ones,

whereas, the Lord assures His people (v. 22a),

> Thus said the Lord God:
>
> I will lift up My hand to (or: against) the nations
> And raise My standard to (or: against) the peoples.[1]

Indeed, it is in this very context that the most vigorously nationalistic statements of the prophet are expressed:

(22b) And they [2]) shall bring your sons in their bosoms,
   And your daughters shall be carried on their shoulders.
(23) Kings shall be your foster fathers,
   And their queens your nursing mothers.
   With their faces to the ground they shall bow down to you
   And lick the dust of your feet. . .
(26) I will make your oppressors eat their own flesh,
   And they shall be drunk with their own blood as with wine.
   Then all flesh shall know
   That I the Lord am your Savior,
   The Champion of Jacob, your Redeemer! [3]

---

[1]) 49.13, 22a

(13) רָנּוּ שָׁמַיִם וְגִילִי אֶרֶץ וּפִצְחוּ הָרִים רִנָּה
כִּי־נִחַם יהוה עַמּוֹ וַעֲנִיָּו יְרַחֵם:
(22a) כֹּה־אָמַר אֲדֹנָי יהוה
הִנֵּה אֶשָּׂא אֶל־גּוֹיִם יָדִי וְאֶל־עַמִּים אָרִים נִסִּי

[2]) Viz., the gentile nations, i.e., the whole world. This is, of course, pure hyperbole—just as, e.g., "Proclaim it to the ends of the earth" in 48.20a (see n. 1 on p. 46) is not to be taken literally.

[3]) 49.22b-26

(22b) וְהֵבִיאוּ בָנַיִךְ בְּחֹצֶן וּבְנֹתַיִךְ עַל־כָּתֵף תִּנָּשֶׂאנָה:
(23) וְהָיוּ מְלָכִים אֹמְנַיִךְ וְשָׂרוֹתֵיהֶם מֵינִיקֹתַיִךְ
אַפַּיִם אֶרֶץ יִשְׁתַּחֲווּ לָךְ וַעֲפַר רַגְלַיִךְ יְלַחֵכוּ
וְיָדַעַתְּ כִּי־אֲנִי יהוה אֲשֶׁר לֹא־יֵבֹשׁוּ קֹוָי:

It is almost beyond comprehension how the plain meaning of this chapter is sometimes subverted by the "universalists" in order to attribute to the prophet the idea of ". . .the 'restoration,' the conversion of the heathen nations, and the final status of Jews and Gentiles in God's kingdom. . ." (TORREY, pp. 380 f.). Far from thinking of the alleged "conversion of the heathen nations," Second Isaiah expresses but contempt for them; cf., e.g. the scorn manifested for them precisely in passages where Israel is exhorted to prepare for liberation (52.1, 11):

עוּרִי עוּרִי לִבְשִׁי עֻזֵּךְ צִיּוֹן
לִבְשִׁי בִּגְדֵי תִפְאַרְתֵּךְ יְרוּשָׁלַם עִיר הַקֹּדֶשׁ
כִּי לֹא יוֹסִיף יָבֹא־בָךְ עוֹד עָרֵל וְטָמֵא:

and

סוּרוּ סוּרוּ צְאוּ מִשָּׁם טָמֵא אַל־תִּגָּעוּ
צְאוּ מִתּוֹכָהּ הִבָּרוּ נֹשְׂאֵי כְּלֵי יהוה:

Again, TORREY asserts (p. 387), "The phrase עֲפַר רַגְלַיִךְ יְלַחֵכוּ [49.23, "They shall lick the dust of your feet"] means no more (and no less) than the omnipresent 'he kissed the ground before him' in the stories of the *Thousand and One Nights*, wherever king or caliph is approached by one of his subjects." Of course not only is this "explanation" less than convincing in context, but the statement three verses farther on ("I will make your oppressors eat their own flesh, And they shall be drunk with their own blood as with wine") is similarly dismissed with the statement (p. 388), "But the poet would have been horrified by the thought that any one would take his words here as a literal prediction or wish"! It is clear that this is hardly a *literal* prediction or wish; but then neither is it exactly an expression of affection on the part of a conquered and humiliated people for her mighty and insolent conqueror! One may rightly wonder by which statement the poet would be horrified, by his own or by TORREY's.

Something of a climax is reached in chapter 52. It begins with the exhortation (see the Hebrew text above):

(24) הֲיֻקַּח מִגִּבּוֹר מַלְקוֹחַ וְאִם־שְׁבִי צַדִּיק יִמָּלֵט:
(25) כִּי־כֹה אָמַר יהוה
גַּם־שְׁבִי גִבּוֹר יֻקָּח וּמַלְקוֹחַ עָרִיץ יִמָּלֵט
וְאֶת־יְרִיבֵךְ אָנֹכִי אָרִיב וְאֶת־בָּנַיִךְ אָנֹכִי אוֹשִׁיעַ:
(26) וְהַאֲכַלְתִּי אֶת־מוֹנַיִךְ אֶת־בְּשָׂרָם וְכֶעָסִיס דָּמָם יִשְׁכָּרוּן
וְיָדְעוּ כָל־בָּשָׂר כִּי אֲנִי יהוה מוֹשִׁיעֵךְ וְגֹאֲלֵךְ אֲבִיר יַעֲקֹב:

> Awake, Awake,
> Clothe yourself in splendor (or: might), O Zion,
> Put on your robes of majesty
> O Jerusalem, holy city!
> For the uncircumcised and the unclean
> Shall enter you no more

because (verses 10-11)

> The Lord will bare His holy arm
> In the sight of all the nations,
> And the very ends of the earth shall see
> The victory of our God.
> Away, away,
> Depart from there!
> Unclean! Touch it not!
> Depart from her midst,
> Cleanse yourselves,
> You who bear the vessels of the Lord!

TORREY asserts (p. 406) that " 'There shall no longer enter thee the uncircumcised and the unclean'. . .means simply: Jerusalem will be pure and holy, the abode of upright and God-fearing men; not foul and wicked, as it is at present. . .The sentence has in it no hatred of Gentiles, nor does it express a wish that Jerusalem may be reserved for Jews only; see on the contrary 60: 11 and the many similar passages. . ." One may well ask what עָרֵל וְטָמֵא in 52.1 and טְמֵא אַל־תִּגָּעוּ in v. 11 signify, if not the alien and heathen peoples, which is likewise the only—and natural—frame of reference in which the term עָרֵל fits.

As to 60.11 ("Your gates shall always stay open, Day and night they shall not be shut, To let in the wealth of nations, With their kings conveying it [or, led in procession]"), not only is v. 10 immediately preceding ignored in context ("Aliens shall rebuild your walls, Their kings shall wait upon you, [For in anger I struck you down, But in favor I take you back]"), and not only is v. 12 immediately following ("For the nation or the kingdom That does not serve you shall perish; Such nations shall be laid waste") obliterated as "an addition by a later hand, an exegetical appendage to נְהוּגִים (misunderstood)" (p. 451), but the clear force of the *hiph'il* ("to bring in; be brought in; let in"; as against *qal* "to come in") is suppressed, חֵיל is rendered as "throng" (as against "wealth"), and נְהוּגִים arbitrarily interpreted as "conducted in state; personally conducted!"

As a matter of fact, not only will the uncircumcised and unclean never again enter Israel's Holy City, but even those heathens who had previously conquered and occupied the territory of Israel will now be forced to quit her land. This is how our prophet put it (54.2-3; the historical background is II Ki. 17.24 ff.):

> (2) Enlarge the site of your dwelling,
>   Let the cloths of your tent be extended;
>   Do not stint!
>   Lengthen the ropes, and drive the pegs firm.
> (3) For you shall spread out to right and left,
>   As your offspring shall disposses nations
>   And settle the desolate towns.[1]

Someone—I am unable at the moment to locate the reference—went so far as to assert that while it is true that God sent Israel into exile as punishment for her sins, once Israel was already in exile God decided to exploit the occasion and use Israel as a *vicarius* for the benefit of Babylonia and other gentile nations; God, as it were, decided as an afterthought to kill two birds with one stone. But apart from the clear fact that the gentile nations, Babylonia included, were not going to benefit from Israel's exile and God's restoration of His people, this sort of "reasoning" smacks of subterfuge (on which see CADBURY's *caveat*, Introductory Statement above).

If there is any purpose in Israel's presence in Babylonia, other than Israel's punishment for her sins, it is that the gentile nations (i.e., Babylonia and the world in general) may witness and experience, to their great chagrin and discomfiture, God's might in behalf of Israel, His boundless and exclusive love for His chosen people, exclusive because the gentile nations were never associated with God's love.

For in contrast to his attitude toward the non-Israelite world, our prophet constantly uses terms of endearment, compassion, and consolation for his fellow Israelites and for the devastated homeland.

---

[1] 54.2-3

(2) הַרְחִיבִי מְקוֹם אָהֳלֵךְ וִירִיעוֹת מִשְׁכְּנוֹתַיִךְ יַטּוּ
אַל־תַּחְשֹׂכִי הַאֲרִיכִי מֵיתָרַיִךְ וִיתֵדֹתַיִךְ חַזֵּקִי:

(3) כִּי־יָמִין וּשְׂמֹאול תִּפְרֹצִי וְזַרְעֵךְ גּוֹיִם יִירָשׁ
וְעָרִים נְשַׁמּוֹת יוֹשִׁיבוּ:

Without attempting here the compilation of a complete list of these terms, attention may be drawn, e.g., to such expressions as "Comfort, oh comfort My people. . .Speak tenderly to Jerusalem" (40.1-2; there is never any comfort or tenderness for non-Israelites); Israel alone as God's flock and lambs whom He will gather (v. 11); the Israelite exiles—never the gentile peoples—as weary and spent, but whose trust in God will bring them renewal of strength (v. 31); Israel—never any gentile nation—as "My servant," "Jacob, you whom I have chosen," and Abraham as "My beloved" (or favorite, friend; אֹהֲבִי; 41.8); Jacob as God's "worm" and God as Israel's—never anyone else's— "Redeemer" and "Holy One" (v.14); the Israelites as "the poor and the needy, seeking water. . ." (v. 17); the exiles as blind and imprisoned (42.17); Israel—never the other peoples—frequently exhorted not to fear; God as Israel's "Maker," "Creator," and "Fashioner" (43.1; 44.21, 24); and so on.

In fine, then, Israel cannot be the central personage in Isaiah 53.

C

VICARIOUS SUFFERING IN ISAIAH 53—A THEOLOGICAL AND SCHOLARLY FICTION

It is generally agreed among scholars that the original Hebrew text of our brief chapter of twelve verses is not altogether intact: there are several verses that cannot be translated as they stand, and other verses hardly belong there in the first place. However, we shall propose no emendations and deal with the passages that concern us in their preserved, traditional form.

The aspect of vicariousness has been found in our chapter by theologian and scholar alike for nigh on two thousand years. But does this aspect really obtain in our text? Is the personage in chapter 53, whoever it may be, a *vicarius*: did he really act as a substitute for the guilty who deserved punishment because of their iniquity, but who escaped it because this personage, while himself innocent of sin, bore their punishment for them?

It is remarkable how virtually every scholar dealing with the subject has merely taken it for granted that the principle of vicariousness is present in Isaiah 53; thus, e.g., NORTH has no discussion of it at all, nor TORREY, et al. No one proves it, everyone assumes it. So that when EISSFELDT, e.g., asserts ("The Ebed-Jahwe," etc., p. 265), "Finally, the last Servant Song, which by its unique content (the discovery of the significance of vicarious death) stands on a pinnacle by itself. . .," it is actually he himself, in common with the other members of the theological and scholarly guilds in post-biblical times, who has made the discovery, not the author of Isaiah 53. (See below, § D and nn. 1-2 on p. 60, for evidence that even "death" is a post-biblical discovery in Isa. 53). Not only that, the gratuitous assumption of vicariousness in this chapter has led directly and uncritically to the widespread opinion that this is "the most wonderful bit of religious poetry in all literature" (TORREY, p. 409; I wonder whether anyone has read the "religious poetry in all literature!"); or cf. NORTH's approval (p. 176) of LUDWIG KÖHLER's statement that " 'he opened not his mouth' (ver. 7). . .is 'the most beautiful and expressive *Nachklang* in the whole writing. . .'." What would the scholars have said of Jer. 11.19 and many other passages had vicariousness been discovered there?

KISSANE is typical of scholarship in assuming vicariousness in Isaiah 53. Thus he writes (*The Book of Isaiah*, vol. II, p. 178), and correctly so, "There is still less reason for identifying the suffering servant with the prophets or the teachers. Individual prophets were innocent and suffered (e.g. Jeremiah), but their suffering was not the expiation of the sins of men. . ." Yet he assumes "vicarious suffering of the servant" in vv. 3d-5 (p. 186), and asserts sweepingly (p. 177), in v. 10b-d, "Here the servant is a sacrificial victim chosen by God to make expiation for the sins of men by his suffering and death. . . Jahweh's purpose. . .is fulfilled by the servant's vicarious suffering and death."

Even more revealing in this connection is the forthright statement by LINDBLOM (p. 50), "It is true that the idea of vicarious suffering is not indicated in the parts of the text which surround the fourth Servant oracle [viz., chaps. 52-53]." Yet this most sober and reliable of all the Scandinavian scholars follows immediately with: "But this is of no import. To the compiler of the Book of Deutero-Isaiah it was quite sufficient that the whole section played variations on this leading theme, abasement and glorifying, in accordance with the sublime plan of Yahweh."

To realize the absence of vicariousness in Second Isaiah, one need but read carefully CUTHBERT LATTEY, "Vicarious Solidarity in the Old Testament" (*Vetus Testamentum*, I [1951], 267-274), where the statement is made (p. 272), "From the scapegoat I turn naturally to Isa. liii, which hardly calls for much expostion, being such a clear case of vicarious solidarity. . .”; or SAMUEL H. HOOKE on “The Theory and Practice of Substitution” (*Vetus Testamentum*, 2 [1959], 2-17). There is, actually, nothing there to connect the Mesopotamian data adduced, or the biblical scapegoat (Azazel), with our chapter 53. On the scapegoat, note THEODOR H. GASTER's statement (s. “Azazel,” *Interpreter's Dictionary of the Bible*, vol. I, p. 26), “. . .in view of the very fact that sin and impurity are unloaded upon them [viz. the scapegoats], they can be (and are) used only as vehicles of elimination, but not of propitiation.”

The crucial passages in our chapter are verses 4-6:

(4) Surely he has borne our sickness
And carried our pains;
Yet we thought him stricken,
Smitten, and afflicted by God.
(5) But he was wounded because of our transgression,
Crushed because of our iniquities;
The chastisement of our welfare (or, that made us
whole) was upon him,
And through his stripes we were healed.
(6) Like sheep we had all gone astray,
Each of us had gone his own way;
And the Lord caused to fall upon him
The guilt of us all.[1])

with which compare “and he shall bear their iniqities”/ וַעֲוֺנֹתָם הוּא יִסְבֹּל in verse 11, and “and he bore the sins of many”/וְהוּא חֵטְא־רַבִּים נָשָׂא in verse 12—though these clauses may be out of place; both verses seem to have experienced conflation.

It is evident at once that neither Babylonia nor any other gentile nation can be involved here: they had experienced no sickness and no pain, and, as is clear from the preceding section, they were guilty of no transgression or iniquity, and they were not going to be healed; quite

---

[1]) 53.4-6
(4) אָכֵן חֳלָיֵנוּ הוּא נָשָׂא וּמַכְאֹבֵינוּ סְבָלָם
וַאֲנַחְנוּ חֲשַׁבְנֻהוּ נָגוּעַ מֻכֵּה אֱלֹהִים וּמְעֻנֶּה:
(5) וְהוּא מְחֹלָל מִפְּשָׁעֵנוּ מְדֻכָּא מֵעֲוֺנֹתֵינוּ
מוּסַר שְׁלוֹמֵנוּ עָלָיו וּבַחֲבֻרָתוֹ נִרְפָּא־לָנוּ:
(6) כֻּלָּנוּ כַּצֹּאן תָּעִינוּ אִישׁ לְדַרְכּוֹ פָּנִינוּ
וַיהוה הִפְגִּיעַ בּוֹ אֵת עֲוֺן כֻּלָּנוּ:

the contrary: the prophet held out for them nothing but shame and ignoble defeat. There is only one party who had transgressed and sinned, who had, consequently, experienced sickness and pain, and who would soon be healed of its wounds—and that was the people Israel, now in exile. And if Israel is the party of the first part, then it is only an individual person, be it the prophet himself or someone else, who can be the party of the second part.

It is our contention that the concept of vicarious suffering and atonement is not to be found either here or anywhere else in the Bible; it is a concept that arose in Jewish and especially Christian circles of post-biblical times. I know of no person in the Bible, nor has any scholar pointed to any such, who took it upon himself, or who considered himself, or who was appointed or considered by others, to be a *vicarius* for wicked people deserving of punishment. This should hardly be surprising in the light of the covenant.[1]

All scholars are in agreement, and rightly so, that the covenant lay at the heart of biblical thought. God and Israel voluntarily entered into a pact according to which God promised on oath to prosper Israel if she remained faithful to him, and Israel undertook to worship Him alone in return for His exclusive protection. This altogether legal contract, then, assured both the obedient and the rebellious, both the

---

[1] The origins of the biblical concept of covenant have in recent years been considerably discussed, perhaps not always critically enough. It has sometimes been overlooked that the ancient Near Eastern concepts and formulae of covenant, while very important *per se* and for background, are yet not really crucial for the correct understanding of how the prophets—half a millennium and more subsequent to, e.g., the *floruit* of the Hittites—structured this cornerstone of their faith; the prophets must be permitted to speak for themselves rather than in terms of the extra-biblical data that derive from cultures with which they had no direct, or only the most indirect association. Out of an already large and rapidly growing literature on covenant, one may cite GEORGE E. MENDENHALL, "Covenant Forms in Israelite Tradition," *Biblical Archaeologist*, 17 (1954), 50-76; DENNIS J. Mc-CARTHY, *Treaty and Covenant: Study in Form in the Ancient Oriental Documents and in the Old Testament* (= *Analecta Biblica*, 21, 1963) and the review by ERHARD GERSTENBERGER in *Journal of Biblical Literature*, 83 (1964), 198 f.; F. CHARLES FENSHAM, for example his articles on "The Treaty between Israel and the Gibeonites," *Biblical Archaeologist*, 27 (1964), 96-100 (with references there to his discussions in 1963 in *Vetus Testamentum* and *Zeitschrift für die alttestamentliche Wissenschaft*) and "Did a Treaty between the Israelites and the Kenites Exist?" *Bulletin of the American Schools of Oriental Research*, 175 (Oct. 1964), 51-54; DELBERT R. HILLERS, *Treaty Curses and the Old Testament Prophets* (*Biblica et Orientalia*, N. 16; 1964), along with the acute review by P. WERNBERG-MØLLER in *Journal of Semitic Studies*, 10 (1965), 281-3; E. GERSTENBERGER, "Covenant and Commandment," *Journal of Biblical Literature*, 84 (1965), 38-51; and GENE M. TUCKER, "Covenant Forms and Contract Forms," *Vetus Testamentum*, 15 (1965), 486-503.

guiltless and the wicked, their proper due. Nothing could be farther from this basic concept of *quid pro quo*, or from the spirit and letter of biblical law, or from the teachings of the prophets, than that the just and faithful should suffer vicariously for the unjust and faithless; that would have been the greatest injustice of all, nothing short of blasphemy, that the lawless be spared their punishment at the expense of the law-abiding. Nowhere in the Hebrew Bible did anyone preach a doctrine—which would have superseded the covenant!—which allowed the sacrifice of the innocent in place of and as an acceptable substitution for the guilty.

Thus the prophet Ezekiel, immediately before Second Isaiah, observed (14.14, 20) that if the three models of righteousness, Noah, Daniel, and Job, were dwelling in wicked Jerusalem, they themselves would escape harm in the catastrophic destruction of the city, but the inhabitants of the city, transgressors of the Lord's commandments, would suffer the full punishment due them. It would have occurred to no one in the Bible that such blameless persons as Noah, Daniel, and Job bear vicariously the suffering and punishment due to the wicked populace of the Holy City. (Similarly, Moses and Samuel, and Jeremiah himself, in Jer. 15.)

Even in the well-known story in Genesis 18, where Abraham bargains with God in the matter of the impending destruction of Sodom and Gomorrah, there is not to be found the slightest hint of vicariousness. Abraham asks God whether He would insist on destroying these wicked cities if some innocent men (*ṣaddiqim*) were found dwelling in their midst, be they fifty, forty, thirty, twenty, or even ten in number. God replies that He would spare the guilty for the sake of the innocent; but in no case is there any question of a *ṣaddiq* being a *vicarius* for the wicked (*rashaʿ*).

Or, finally, in Exodus 32, when Moses came down from Mt. Sinai to behold Israel rejoicing in the golden calf. For this idolatrous act, God wanted to destroy His people Israel. According to vv. 9-10 God said to Moses, "I see that this is a stiffnecked people. Now let Me be, that My anger may blaze forth against them and that I may destroy them, and make of you a great nation." But Moses dissuades God from such drastic action (vv. 11-14), reminding Him of what the Egyptians would say and of the oath that He swore to the patriarchs. In another version of this same event, vv. 30 ff., Moses said to God, "Alas, this people is guilty of a great sin. . .And yet, if you would only forgive their sin! If not, erase me from the record which You have written!" But the Lord said to Moses, "He who has sinned against Me, him

only will I erase from My record. . ." Here, too, then, there is no
hint of anything vicarious being sought or offered by either party.

Turning back now to our passage in Isaiah 53, it will probably come
as an anticlimax to learn that in point of fact the text has nothing to
say in the first place about vicariousness; this was only read back into
the text many centuries after Second Isaiah's time. All that our text
says is that the individual person, whoever he was, suffered on account
of Israel's transgressions. Let us try to comprehend this statement in
historical perspective.

Throughout the Hebrew Bible, whoever came in the name of God
to the representatives of the people to rebuke them for breaking faith
with God—and for what other reason did a spokesman for God make
public appearance?—automatically suffered because of the nature of
his mission. No prophet ever appeared in order to tell Israel and her
leaders that they were just and upright in the eyes of God. On the
contrary: it was when they had to be rebuked and condemned, and be
made to repent and return to God, that a prophet appeared on the
public scene. And because of their "uncompromising vehemence, the
prophets continually risked and sometimes suffered abuse and even
death at the hands of those they attacked. . .Elijah had to flee for his
life because of his vehement denunciations of Ahab and Jezebel.
Micaiah was hit on the jaw and thrown into prison. . .Amos the Judean risked life and limb. . .at Bethel, and he minced no words in
telling the royal house and its supporters what lay in store for them as
retribution for their rebellion against the Lord. Because he bitterly
denounced the domestic and foreign policy of his government,
Jeremiah's life was threatened, he was beaten, he was put in stocks,
and he was thrown into a dungeon, so that he was constrained to cry
out (11.19), 'and I was like a docile lamb that is led to the slaughter'. . .
Ezekiel was told by God, 'And you, son of man, be not afraid of them
[namely, your fellow Judean exiles in Babylonia], neither be afraid of
their words, though briers and thorns be with you and you dwell
among scorpions'. . .Uriah the prophet was killed by King Jehoi-
akim. . .and Zechariah was stoned to death (II Chron. 24.20-21)." [1]

---

[1] This quotation derives from the section "The Fate of the Prophets and their
Teachings" (in chap. VII: "The Hebraic Spirit: The Prophetic Movement and
Social Justice") in my *Ancient Israel*, pp. 156-7. As to Zechariah, see S. H. BLANK,
"The Death of Zechariah in Rabbinic Literature" (*Hebrew Union College Annual*,
12-13 [1937-38], 327-346), where three different Zechariahs, including the prophet,
are involved.

It should be noted here that insufficient attention has been paid to the clear

Every one of these spokesmen of God suffered because of the nature of their calling; it was their occupational hazard.[1]) None of them had committed any sin for which they were suffering, for which they were experiencing punishment. It was simply that, innocent as they themselves were of any transgression against the Lord, their extremely unpopular occupation and mission as God's spokesman necessarily brought into their wake suffering, and abuse, and jail, and even death. In this respect, the personage of Isaiah 53 was no more a sufferer than so many of those who preceded or followed him as spokesman of God.

Read straightforwardly, then, all that the pertinent verses in our chapter actually assert is that the person in question bore the griefs and carried the sorrows of the people, having been wounded for their transgressions and bruised for their iniquities. Like all spokesmen and prophets of God, from first to last, this person too suffered on account of and along with the people at large, the latter directly because of their transgressions and the former, though not guilty of transgression, because of his unpopular mission. And when the people were made whole again, when their wounds were healed, it was only because the prophet had come and suffered to bring them God's message of rebuke and repentance. That, and that alone, is the meaning of such a statement as (vv. 5-6) "The chastisement of our welfare (or, that made us whole) was upon him, And through his stripes we were healed. . .And the Lord caused to fall upon him the guilt of us all."

It may be noted, further, that if the author of these verses had intended here something of vicariousness, he would probably have employed not (מֵעֲוֹנֹתֵינוּ) (מִפְּשָׁעֵינוּ מְדֻכָּא) (וְהוּא מְחֹלָל) but ב...ב (the *bet* of exchange). Similarly, in Lamentations 4.13, where nothing vicar-

---

distinction between vicariousness and atonement, or even martyrdom. Thus "vicariousness" is treated together with and subsumed under "Atonement" in *Jewish Encyclopedia* (vol. II, pp. 275-284; article by K. KÖHLER) and in *Interpreter's Dictionary of the Bible* (vol. I, pp. 309-313; article by C. L. MITTON—most inadequate for the Old Testament)— and quite confused with it. Or cf. "Suffering and Evil" (pp. 450-453; article by O. A. PIPER), where, again, it is simply assumed (§ 2a) that "the Servant of God has taken vicariously upon himself the punishment of his nation (Isa. 53: 2-12)." In general, it is most unfortunate that so many of the "theological" articles in the *Interpreter's Dictionary* involving the Old Testament were written by scholars who are specialists only in the New Testament.

[1]) This may well be one of the reasons for the virtually stereotyped manner in which one called by God to be His spokesman reacts to the summons, viz., he is hesitant to accept the calling and may even reject it. One thinks, e.g., of Moses, Elijah, Jeremiah, Ezekiel, and Jonah. But the matter requires further study.

ious is involved, it is, again, the *mem* that is employed: (מֶ(חַטֹּאת נְבִיאֶיהָ

עֲוֺנֹת כֹּהֲנֶיהָ ... , 'It was because of (the sins of her prophets, the iniqui-

ties of her prophets. . .)." And as it stands, the *mem* in (מִ(פֶּשַׁע עַמִּי נֶגַע לָמוֹ

in our verse 8, usually rendered "because of (the transgressions of my

people he was stricken)," is likewise causal. So that the significance of

the single instance of *bet* in our section, viz.,   (וּ(בַחֲבֻרָתוֹ נִרְפָּא־לָנוּ:) ,

can hardly be made to prove anything for vicariousness. But the ar-

gument goes beyond this: How could our author be talking of vicar-

iousness, that is, how could he be asserting that sinful Israel would

be spared punishment, when Israel had alrealy experienced that

punishment—in the form of destruction at home and two generations

of captivity abroad—and had thereby fully expiated her sinfulness

(40.1-2)?

ALFRED GUILLAUME's discussion of "The Servant Poems in the

Deutero-Isaiah" (*Theology*, 11 [1925], 254-263, 309-319; 12 [1926],

2-10, 63-72), is typical of the gratuitous assumptions and confusion

that characterize so much of the scholarship on our problem. He

writes (p. 5), "the difference between the sufferings of the nation and

the sufferings of the Servant is fundamental. The nation suffered be-

cause of its disobedience to Jehovah: the Servant because of his obe-

dience. All his countrymen had wandered from the path of obedience

like silly sheep, and Jehovah brought down upon the Servant the

guilt of them all. Through these verses the emphasis and antithesis of

the *we* and the *he* are everywhere marked, so that the sense is '*we*, not

he, wandered from the right way, and *he*, not *we*, bore the guilt.'

No explanation of this vicarious atonement is offered by the writer

except that it was the pleasure or will of God to save Israel and the

world in this way. . .The Servant's suffering was voluntary: he could

have escaped it by disobedience to God and refusal to deliver his

message. But he chose to suffer without protesting. Like a lamb borne

to the slaughter: and like a sheep before her shearers." Having noted

correctly that "*we*, not *he*, wandered from the right way," it is a pity

that GUILLAUME followed with the utterly incorrect assertion, "and

he, not *we*, bore the guilt": what was Israel doing in exile, its sover-

eignty destroyed, its land devastated, its Temple defiled, its population

enslaved, if not bearing the guilt? And where is the evidence that "the

world," as distinct from Israel, was to be saved? And as for the ob-

servation that "No explanation of this vicarious atonement is offered

by the (biblical) writer"—why should an explanation be expected of something that did not exist in the mind of that writer?

It is interesting how LEROY WATERMAN's article on "The Martyred Servant Motif of Is. 53" (*Journal of Biblical Literature*, 56 [1937], 27-34) has been ignored; ROWLEY's very detailed survey has overlooked it, and NORTH makes no reference to it at all, though he lists it in the bibliography. WATERMAN wrote, rather bluntly (p. 28), "The Christian tradition seized upon the factor of vicariousness and seeing only Christ in the servant figure lifted it bodily out of its context and gave to the language unwarranted implications that cling to it to this day." And after discussing verses 4-5 he concludes (p. 29) that "The element of actual vicariousness thus disappears from the verse and the context"— this despite the fact that WATERMAN himself argues in favor of an "ideal servant" and "a world service that transcends nationalism . . ." (p. 32).

The fundamental fact should not be lost sight of, that neither in this chapter nor elsewhere in the Bible do the sinful get off scot-free, at the expense, as it were, of the prophets or of anyone else. Quite the contrary: the people whom the prophet was addressing had experienced the greatest catastrophe in their history. The central element in the phenomenon of vicariousness, that the wicked go upunished, is lacking altogether here.

D

THE "SUFFERING SERVANT" IN
ISAIAH 53—A THEOLOGICAL AND SCHOLARLY FICTION

With the recognition that no inkling of vicarious suffering obtains in Isaiah 53, the concept "Suffering Servant" will readily emerge for what it really is, an equally post-biblical phenomenon.

Our chapter is full of hyperbole, not least in precisely the passages that deal with suffering. Verses 7-9 read: [1])

> (7) He was oppressed, and he was afflicted,
> But he opened not his mouth;

---

[1]) Following more or less the Revised Standard Version. But nearly each verse has its difficulties, as may be seen readily, e.g., in KÖNIG, KISSANE, NORTH, SNAITH, LINDBLOM, G. BEER ("Die Gedichte vom Knechte Jahwes in Jes 40-55. Ein textkritischer und metrischer Wiederherstellungsversuch," in WOLF BAUDISSIN Festschrift, ed. WILHELM FRANKENBERG-FRIEDRICH KÜCHLER [Giessen, 1918], 29-46); or cf. *The Fifty-Third Chapter of Isaiah according to the Jewish Interpreters*, ed. ADOLPHE NEUBAUER-S. R. DRIVER, 2 vols. (Oxford and London, 1876-77). All too many of the "text-critical" studies of this chapter are vitiated by prior theological views and superficial analysis.

Like a lamb led to the slaughter
And like a sheep that is dumb before its shearers. . .
(8) By oppression and judgment he was taken away. . .
For he was cut off from the land of the living,
Stricken for the transgression of my people.
(9) He made his grave with the wicked,
And his tomb [1]) with the rich. . .[2])

The well known expression "Like a lamb led to the slaughter" (כַּשֶׂה לַטֶּבַח יוּבָל), as everyone has recognized, reminds one at once—in all probability it actually derives from—Jeremiah's plaint (11.19), "and I was like a docile lamb led to the slaughter" (וַאֲנִי כְּכֶבֶשׂ אַלּוּף יוּבַל לִטְבוֹחַ). No one has ever accused Jeremiah of being docile as a lamb, of accepting his suffering serenely; on the contrary, he was one of the most vigorous spokesmen of God in the entire Bible, full of fire and brimstone, complaint and vengeance (cf., e.g., verse 20 immediately following). As for the (universally assumed) literalness of "Like a lamb led to the slaughter," note in Isaiah the immediately following—non-fatal—parallel, "And like a sheep that is dumb before its shearers," and the expression in verse 10, יִרְאֶה זֶרַע יַאֲרִיךְ יָמִים (dis-cussed immediately below). The poet is merely asserting, in normal poetic exaggeration, that God's spokesman to His people Israel bore unflinchingly the suffering that such spokesmen frequently experienced.

By the same token, Second Isaiah's lament, "For he was cut off

---

[1]) Taking במותי as a form of root *bmh* "tomb" or the like (// קִבְרוֹ "his grave"); so, e.g., Ibn Ezra, S. D. LUZZATTO (with reference also to LOWTH, MARTINI, LOCKENMACHER, and GESENIUS; see p. 359 of the *Texts* in vol. I, or p. 422 of the *Translations* in vol. II, in *The Fifty-Third Chapter in Isaiah*, etc.; cf. also Jacob ben Reuben the Qaraite, I, p. 60 = II, p. 62), Jewish Publication Society Translation (1917), American Translation, *La Sainte Bible* (1956); see most recently SAMUEL IWRY, *JBL*, 76 (1957), 232. The traditional interpretation, according to which our word derives from ב and root *mwt* "to die," is not easily defended.

[2]) 53.7-9

(7) נָגַשׂ וְהוּא נַעֲנֶה וְלֹא יִפְתַּח־פִּיו
כַּשֶׂה לַטֶּבַח יוּבָל וּכְרָחֵל לִפְנֵי גֹזְזֶיהָ
נֶאֱלָמָה וְלֹא יִפְתַּח פִּיו:
(8) מֵעֹצֶר וּמִמִּשְׁפָּט לֻקָּח וְאֶת־דּוֹרוֹ מִי יְשׂוֹחֵחַ
כִּי נִגְזַר מֵאֶרֶץ חַיִּים מִפֶּשַׁע עַמִּי נֶגַע לָמוֹ:
(9) וַיִּתֵּן אֶת־רְשָׁעִים קִבְרוֹ וְאֶת־עָשִׁיר בְּמֹתָיו
עַל לֹא־חָמָס עָשָׂה וְלֹא מִרְמָה בְּפִיו:

from the land of the living" (כִּי נִגְזַר מֵאֶרֶץ חַיִּים), recalls at once Jeremiah's cry (11.18-20), "(. . .I did not know that it was against me that they devised schemes, saying, 'Let us destroy the tree with its fruit), let us cut him off from the land of the living (וְנִכְרְתֶנּוּ מֵאֶרֶץ חַיִּים), (that his name be remembered no more).' " Of course Jeremiah lived long enough after this outburst to be taken down to Egypt against his will.

As a matter of fact, Isaiah 53.10 tells us very plainly that the central character of the chapter did not die in the midst of his mission; we read: ". . .he shall live to see his offspring, he shall have a long life. . ." (יִרְאֶה זֶרַע יַאֲרִיךְ יָמִים וְחֵפֶץ יהוה בְּיָדוֹ יִצְלָח).[1]) This expression can only mean that the person did not die, but, instead, would live a long life on earth. (It is scarcely necessary to observe that it could not mean that after dying and rising, he would then die again, and remain dead forever). In Job 42.16-17, Job is said to have lived after his bitter ordeal, "a hundred and forty years, and he lived to see (וַיִּרְאֶה) children and children's children, four generations; and Job died in ripe old age." Note also Gen. 50.23, "And Joseph lived to see (children of the third generation of Ephraim. . .)"/(וַיַּרְא יוֹסֵף לְאֶפְרַיִם בְּנֵי שִׁלֵּשִׁים גַּם בְּנֵי) in יַאֲרִיךְ יָמִים. . .יִרְאֶה יִשְׂבָּע; and for מָכִיר בֶּן־מְנַשֶּׁה יֻלְּדוּ עַל־בִּרְכֵּי יוֹסֵף: 53.10-11 cf. Ps. 91.16, אֹרֶךְ יָמִים אַשְׂבִּיעֵהוּ וְאַרְאֵהוּ בִּישׁוּעָתִי:. Finally, attention may be drawn to the fact that the expression הֶאֱרִיךְ יָמִים ("to live a long life"; lit. "to prolong days") is characteristic of Deuteronomy (cf. S. R. DRIVER, *Introduction to the Literature of the Old Testament*, 9th ed., 1913, p. 99), where afterlife and resurrection are unknown.

TORREY, who regards the Gentiles as speaking here about Israel, says about our v. 9 (p. 420), "It is certain that where 'death' is spoken of in these verses, it is either in hyperbole or else (as in the present case) in the description of what the onlooking Gentiles *expected* [all italics in original]. They did not *dig* his grave; they 'assigned' it, 'designated' it. . .They were all ready to bury him with the criminals, as soon as the last spark of life should be gone. He was 'as good as dead.' But of course the whole significance of the poem rests on the

---

[1]) The expression וַיהוה חָפֵץ דַּכְּאוֹ הֶחֱלִי אִם־תָּשִׂים אָשָׁם נַפְשׁוֹ in the first part of the verse is both of uncertain meaning and corrupt—and this on any interpretation of the verse as a whole; so that translators and commentators render this passage on the basis of emendation, whether implicit or explicit. None of these translations may be used for any theory.

fact that the Servant did *not* die, but lived to be brought to triumph. 52: 13-15 and especially 53: 12 are entirely conclusive on this point. . . [and on v. 10, "He will see his seed"] The Servant not only escapes the death which came so near, but sees the sure promise of long life and a blessed posterity. . ."

One could easily multiply such instances of hyperbole; the book of Job, e.g., is full of it. Outside the Bible one calls readily to mind the well known Mesopotamian composition *Ludlul bel nemeqi* ("I will praise the lord of wisdom"), where the "righteous sufferer" lives to lament:

> The grave was open still when they rifled my treasures,
> While I was not yet dead, already they stopped mourning.[1]

Accordingly, the expressions in 53.7-12, "Like a lamb led to the slaughter,/And like a sheep that is dumb before its shearers/. . .For he was cut off from the land of the living/. . .And he made his grave with the wicked,/And his tomb with the rich/. . .And he bared (the meaning of הֶעֱרָה is quite uncertain) his life (= exposed himself) to death. . ." indicate, rhetorically, nothing more than that the person in question suffered much in the course of his mission from God to Israel, but did not die in consequence of it; instead, he would live long after that chore, long enough to enjoy several generations of progeny and victory over his adversaries. And they may be right who believe that the career of ancient Job—not in the (later) dialogue but in the very much earlier background of the prologue-epilogue [2]—may well have suggested this to Second Isaiah.[3]

---

[1] THORKILD JACOBSEN, in his section on "Mesopotamia" in *The Intellectual Advanture of Ancient Man*, ed. HENRI and H. A. FRANKFORT (Chicago, 1946; appeared in 1949 as a Pelican Book, without the chapters on "The Hebrews," under the title *Before Philosophy*), pp. 212-216; or cf. ROBERT H. PFEIFFER's translation on pp. 434-437 of *Ancient Near Eastern Texts relating to the Old Testament*, ed. JAMES B. PRITCHARD (Princeton, 1950).

[2] Cf. N. SARNA, "Epic Substratum in the Prose of Job," *Jouranl of Biblical Literature*, 76 (1957), 13-25. The universal tendency to see resurrection in vv. 10-12aα following death (vv. 8-9, 12aβ), reminds one of Job 19.27-29, where the irrevocably corrupt text is made by numerous scholars to yield resurrection, in spite of all the other perfectly clear data to the contrary; cf. chap. III, § C, "Alleged Concept of Afterlife," in ORLINSKY, "Studies in the Septuagint of the Book of Job" (*Hebrew Union College Annual*, 32 [1961], 241-249; 19.25-27 is treated on pp. 248 f.).

[3] It should ordinarily not be necessary to add here the obvious *caveat* that because Second Isaiah made use of earlier writers or ideas, this does not indicate

It is clear that the concept "Suffering Servant," with capital "S," could not have derived from within our Hebrew text in biblical times. The central figure in chapter 53—regardless of whether the term "My servant" in 52.13 is really applicable to him or not (see § *A* above)— was no more a "sufferer," in some instances he was even less, than God's spokesmen elsewhere in the Bible. Certainly there is no evidence that he "suffered" more than, say, Elijah, or Jeremiah, or Uriah, or Job; and none of these ever became known, either during or after the biblical period, as a "suffering servant."

E

SOME ALLEGED ANCIENT NEAR EASTERN PARALLELS
TO ISAIAH 53

The attempts to discover elsewhere in the ancient Near East pertinent parallels to our problems in Isaiah 53 have been less than successful, partly because there are none and partly because our own biblical problems were not comprehended correctly in the first place. For having assumed that a suffering servant and vicarious suffering and atonement were involved in our chapter, and that the servant accepted the suffering in meekness, humility, and uncomplaining silence, scholarly procedure dictated a search in comparative materials for parallels.

Unfortunately, the parallels that have been discovered scarcely stand up as such under careful scrutiny. Thus the generalizing statement has been made (WILLIAM F. ALBRIGHT, *From the Stone Age to Christianity: Monotheism and the Historical Process* [Baltimore, 1940], p. 254), lacking real pertinence to the problems at hand, "Humility, silence, and meekness became increasingly characteristic of ancient oriental piety after the late second millennium B.C." [1]) But how this

---

that he had any earlier worthy specifically in mind as the central personage in chap. 53. Yet that is precisely what so many critics have proceeded to do, so that not many biblical figures have escaped identification as the "Suffering Servant"; see, e.g., the list of candidates for this dubious role in NORTH's "Contents" on p. v.

[1]) This quotation follows immediately upon, ". . .The combination of these two concepts, vicarious suffering and purification through suffering, lies behind Deutero-Isaiah's doctrine of salvation. The most obvious characteristic of the Servant of Yahweh is his humility and meekness in the presence of his tormentors" —differently, one might well ask, from Jeremiah and so many other prophets? Indeed, this is the least obvious characteristic of Second Isaiah's *'ebed*—unless one insists on disregarding altogether not only the plain meaning of so many passages

sweeping statement bears upon our specific problems is not made
clear; for what can this kind of statement prove, even if only in the
matter of chronology, for the period of Second Isaiah over half a
millennium later? As for the assertion that follows immediately,
"The inscriptions of the Neo-Babylonian kings (sixth century B.C.)
often begin with the words (following the titulary), 'the meek and
humble one,' " it is well known that such inscriptions are generally
characterized from the very beginning by formulaic humility, conventional meekness and politeness. These are but official formulas,
and have no pertinence for Isaiah 53 which has no association with
royal historical inscriptions; thus, no one would assume that the—
likewise only alleged—meekness and humility of Jeremiah ("But I
was like a docile lamb led to the slaughter . . .,"followed in the
very next verse by "But, O Lord of Hosts. . .let me see Your vengeance upon them. . .!") derives likewise from Neo-Babylonian royal
inscriptions.

Again, attention is drawn to the fact that "The words 'I am a
humble man' appear at the commencement of an inscription of a king
of Hamath about 800 B.C." But apart from the fact that the reading
and meaning of the original are not beyond dispute,[1]) how can the
alleged concept in Isaiah 53 be demonstrated by finding the word for
"humble" in the dialect of another culture, region, and period?

And, finally, the statement is made, "Humility is also a characteristic of the worshipper in late Egyptian and Assyrian prayers
to the gods"; however, this is usually the case in all prayers among
all peoples in all times, including the prayers in the Bible itself.

---

of the Hebrew text but also the characteristic and vigorous nationalism of our
prophet, in relation to both his own people and to the non-Israelite peoples.

[1]) Line 2 of the Zakir inscription is generally read (ʾish) ʿaneh (ʾanah) and
translated "(A) humble (man am I)." M. BLACK, on the other hand (Documents
from Old Testament Times, ed. D. WINTON THOMAS [1958; now a Harper Torch-
book]), pp. 242 ff. (following M. LIDZBARSKI, Ephemeris für semitische Epigraphik
[Giessen, 1909-1915], vol. III, p. 6), renders "I am a man of ʿAnah" (p. 248,
"ʿAnah seems more likely to have been a place name than an adjective"), and ob-
serves that "The name could also, however, be read as ʿakko (the middle letter is
uncertain) and identified with a place of this name in Phoenicia." Reproductions
of the Zakir inscription are given e.g., in H. POGNON, Inscriptions sémitiques de la
Syrie, etc. (Paris, 1907), plates IX and XXXV (with the discussion of our word on
p. 159); col. 198 of ALBRIGHT's article on "Hamath" in Encyclopaedia Miqraʾit,
vol. III (1958), cols. 193-200 (with recent bibliography).

It may also be noted that Isaiah 53 is not a prayer, and lacks a wor-shipper.[1])

In fine, there are no ancient Near Eastern parallels to our problem, a conclusion that is not surprising in view of the fact that our problem did not come into being in the first place until some six hundred years after the days of Second Isaiah.

Whatever Second Isaiah's style and thought may owe to the specifically Babylonian part of his environment, I cannot take seri-ously the attempts to associate chapter 53, say, with the mythology and cult of Tammuz (see the survey in ROWLEY, pp. 42 ff.). As a matter of fact, Tammuz (or the Ugaritic material adduced) would never have suggested itself in this connection had it not been for the "dying-and-rising" element which was read into our Hebrew text in the early days of Christianity. Neither am I impressed by the attempts to attach the concept of "divine kingship" to our chapter; Second Isaiah's concept of the character and role of God, amply attested by every chapter in his Book, precludes these attempts—apart from the not insignificant fact that the entire problem of "divine kingship" in relation to the Hebrew Bible is still very much *sub judice*.

Modern scholars, all too prone to read the dying-and-rising element in the ancient Near East and then into the Bible, may now study EDWIN M. YAMAUCHI, "Tammuz and the Bible" (*Journal of Biblical Literature*, 84 [1965], 283-290); cf., e.g., pp. 289 f., ". . .the resurrection of Tammuz was based, in the words of (SAMUEL N.) KRAMER, 'on nothing but inference and surmise, guess and conjecture'. . .More-over, the resurrection of Inanna-Ishtar offers a contrast and not a comparison. . .Inanna, instead of rescuing Tammuz from hell, sent him there." And A. F. RAINEY, in one of his several stimulating ar-ticles on aspects of "The Kingdom of Ugarit" (*Biblical Archaeologist*, 28 [1965], 102-125), has noted (p. 121) that "Baal is admittedly a dying and rising fertility deity, but his cycle of victories and defeats in the struggle with Mot (Death) is not a seasonal affair. The agricultural

---

[1]) The theory of a "fluctuating" servant is well put by ALBRIGHT (p. 255), ". . .When not only the leaders themselves, but also every pious Isra-elite is ready to give himself as a vicarious victim for his people, then God will restore Israel and will give it a glorious future. In this interpretation the different aspects of the Servant of Yahweh receive due consideration. The Servant is the people of Israel, which suffers poignantly in exile and affliction; he is also the pious individual who atones for the sins of the many by his uncom-plaining agony; he is finally the coming Savior of Israel. . ." But this is pa-tently — though well meant — homiletics, not scholarship.

seasons of Syria and Palestine do not recognize an alternation of fertile and infertile seasons. . ." (with reference to CYRUS H. GORDON; also to ALBRIGHT for noting the same lack of alternation in the Gezer Calendar).

J. PHILIP HYATT, "The Sources of the Suffering Servant Idea" (*Journal of Near Eastern Studies*, 3 [1944], 79-86) has taken it for granted that the "Suffering Servant Idea" obtained in Isaiah 53 and—even if only potentially—in the Bible proper. EDWARD J. YOUNG, *Studies in Isaiah* (London, 1955), chap. 5, "The Origin of the Suffering Servant Idea" (pp. 127-141), has criticized in some detail one of HYATT's four sources (the myth of the dying and rising god); but one cannot get very far in the scholarly comprehension of the problem in the face of such dogmatic assertions as (p. 129), ". . .Who is the Servant? The answer, we believe, is that He is the redeemer Messiah whom God had long ago promised to His people as their Deliverer from sin. In other words, the Servant is Jesus Christ"; and (pp. 140 f.), ". . .The righteous Servant suffering for the sins of those who are unrighteous is a conception which could never have been conceived by the unaided mind of man. . .If, therefore, we are to look for the sources of the idea of the Suffering Servant, we shall find them not in the religions of antiquity, but in a special revelation from God. . ."

And so one can but express the fullest sympathy with G. ERNEST WRIGHT's vigorous rejection of the attempts by those scholars (e.g., IVAN ENGNELL, "The Ebed Yahweh Songs and the Suffering Messiah in 'Deutero-Isaiah,' " in *Bulletin of the John Rylands Library*, 31 [1948], 54-93) to interpret Isaiah 53 in the light of Mesopotamian royal ritual; he asserts, *God Who Acts: Biblical Theology as Recital* (= *Studies in Biblical Theology*, No. 8, 1952), p. 80, n. 1, ". . .For my part, I can only say that the evidence adduced for such an interpretation of the suffering servant is so meagre, tenuous and strained that the theory is most difficult to accept. . ."

F

THE CHRISTIAN ORIGIN OF

"SUFFERING SERVANT" AND "SERVANT OF THE LORD"

AS TECHNICAL TERMS

It is, naturally, outside the scope of this study to determine precisely when and under what circumstances Jesus came to be associated with the personage in Isaiah 53; I say "naturally," because the present-day specialist in Old Testament, no matter how learned and gifted he may be, can hardly lay claim to the competence of the specialist in New Testament. Yet by the same token the former is not absolved of acquainting himself with the work of the latter—and the latter, no less, with that of the former—when a problem such as ours is involved. Unfortunately, Old Testament scholarship since the days of Duhm has gotten so deeply in the rut of taking it for granted that such concepts as "Servant of the Lord" and "Suffering Servant" were technical terms already in Second Isaiah and the Hebrew Bible that it did not think of investigating them in their New Testament setting. (Note the same attitude on the part of Old Testament scholars to the concept of vicarious suffering, chapter III, § C above.)

ROWLEY has noted (*The Servant of the Lord*, etc., p. 55, n. 1) that some scholars hold "that the ascription to Jesus of an interpretation of His mission in terms of the Servant is an unhistorical creation of the post-resurrection church." Thus F. J. FOAKES JACKSON-KIRSOPP LAKE, *The Beginnings of Christianity, Part I: The Acts of the Apostles*, vol. I (1920), in their chapter (IV) on "Christology" (§ III, Primitive Christianity), have asserted (p. 385)—and this in spite of the fact that they permitted themselves to be misled by their Old Testament colleagues into believing that "In the parts of the Old Testament which develop this relation of suffering with service considerable importance attaches to the word 'Servant of the Lord' ($\pi\alpha\tilde{\iota}\varsigma$ $\varkappa\upsilon\rho\acute{\iota}\upsilon$). . . and the consciousness of this connexion reached its highest literary expression in the Psalter and in the second part of Isaiah" (pp. 384-5)—"In none of these, however, do the writers appear to have had in mind any prophetic description of a great Sufferer and certainly had no idea of relating their descriptions of suffering to the Davidic Messiah or to the Son of Man in the Apocalypses"; or cf. p. 386, "In Mark and in Q there are no clear signs of any identification of Jesus with the sufferer of Isaiah liii. . ." It may be observed here, too, that JACKSON-LAKE did not note that it is not with the "Servant of the Lord" but with the "Suffering Servant" that Jesus first came to be associated.

B. W. BACON, "New and Old in Jesus' Relation to John" (*Journal of Biblical Literature*, 48 [1929], 40-81; part of a symposium on *Primitive Christianity and Judaism*), p. 61, put it this way, ". . .Nevertheless the earliest intimations are all opposed to Jesus' application of the figure to himself. Not the 'Servant' but 'the Son of Man' is Jesus 'self-designation. . uniformly the identification of him with the Isaian suffering Servant is represented as a post-resurrection discovery. . ." And

C. T. CRAIG begins his survey discussion of "The Identification of Jesus with the Suffering Servant" (*Journal of Religion*, 24 [1944], 240-245), as follows: "From countless pulpits, congregations are told that Jesus found the clue to his ministry in the fulfilment of the Suffering Servant prophecies of the Book of Isaiah. Indeed, many modern scholars have affirmed the same belief. . .On the other hand, it seems to me that at few points has wishful thinking dominated the judgment of scholars more than in the consideration of this issue. . ."

The concept "Servant of the Lord," no more than any of the so-called *Ebed-YHWH* sections, had no special significance for anyone until after the career of Jesus had come to an end; the attempts to find this significance in an earlier period flounder on the simple fact that mere reference to passages in Second Isaiah, even to chapters 52-53, do not yet demonstrate technical terms and significant concepts such as "Servant of the Lord" and "Suffering Servant". This fact may be determined from a careful analysis of the references compiled, e.g., in NORTH (pp. 5-27); ROWLEY, chap. I (pp. 3 ff.); ZIMMERLI-JEREMIAS, chaps. III ("Παῖς Θεοῦ [read "The term 'Servant of the Lord' "] in Late Judaism in the Period after the LXX") and IV ("Παῖς Θεοῦ in the New Testament"), respectively 43-78 and 79-104. In the last-named, it is interesting to note how the absence of either all reference or any specific reference to Isa. 53 is frequently turned into proof that it is precisely Isa. 53 that was uppermost in the mind of those who failed to cite from it or gave it no special prominence. Thus, it is conceded that "In the N.T. Jesus receives the title Παῖς Θεοῦ strikingly seldom. . ." (p. 80), and that "There are strikingly few N.T. passages where in specific quotation a word relating to the servant of Deut. Isa. is applied to Jesus. . ." (p. 88); to the question "Can Jesus have known himself to be the servant of God?" Jeremias gives immediate reply, "The gospels say so. . ." (p. 98); ". . .the silence of Jesus before his judges (Sanhedrin, Pilate, Herod). . ." (p. 99) in reference to his role as Deutero-Isaiah's *Ebed-YHWH*—this and other serious related problems are solved with one stroke by the gratuitous assumption, and in the face of reasonable analysis of the data available (or altogether absent), that ". . .Jesus only allowed himself to be known as the servant in his esoteric and not in his public preaching. Only to his disciples did he unveil the mystery that he viewed the fulfilment of Isa. 53 as his God-appointed task. . ." (p. 104). There is far more of eisegesis than exegesis to be found here; thus when JEREMIAS asserts, "The gospels say so," one has but to examine carefully each passage quoted from the gospels along with each alleged source in Isa. 53 and it will be apparent at once that JEREMIAS has simply pulled out individual and isolated words or common expressions— virtually never, incidentally, from the Septuagint text of Isa. 53!— and made these justify his dogmatic assertion, "The gospels say so." Indeed, the gospels do *not* say so; it is only JEREMIAS who says that they say so. JEREMIAS' treatment of this all-important subject is an unjustifiable retrogression from the scholarly treatment given it, e.g., by FOAKES JACKSON-LAKE three and a half decades earlier.

JEREMIAS' presentation appears particularly inadequate and misleading in the light, e.g., of HENRY CADBURY's *multum in parvo* Note on "The Titles of Jesus in Acts" in vol. V of FOAKES JACKSON-LAKE, *Beginnings of Christianity* (1933; pp. 354-375), especially § 9 on ὁ παῖς (364-370). There he noted (p. 366), *inter alia*, "The use of παῖς with Jesus is generally regarded as a definite reference to the so-called Suffering Servant of parts of Isaiah, notably Isaiah liii. It may be an act of temerity to question this origin. . .Conversely the influence of the Isaiah passages on early Christianity is fortified by references to these passages in Acts, with the further assumption that because they are liturgical their concepts are early. Such a connexion was questioned in Vol. I. p. 391, but in view of its all but general acceptance it is worth while to indicate how little basis it has to rest on.

"The use of Isaiah's interpretation is exceedingly scanty. Modern expositors, hard put to it to find predictions of Christ's death in the Old Testament, seize upon Isaiah liii as the proof text. But there is little evidence that it played so central a rôle. Paul and Luke refer frequently in a general way to the Scriptural expectation of Christ's passion, but Paul never uses Isaiah's words and Luke but once (Acts viii.32 f.).

"The abundance of the vicarious clauses in Isaiah liii. also attracts modern commentators with their preconceived notion of what primitive Christology must have been like. Luke, however, as I have pointed out elsewhere [*The Making of Luke-Acts*, p. 280, and note], not only omits 'vicarious' phrases found in Mark, but the one time that he does quote Isaiah liii almost unbelievably escapes all the vicarious phrases with which the passage abounds. . ." [1]

Following on a fine critique of ADOLF VON HARNACK's use of words

---

[1] MORNA HOOKER (p. 4) quotes this last sentence. On my view, there is nothing of vicariousness in Isaiah in the first place, and so there was no reason for Luke to make use of this non-existent concept.

and passages in the Old and New Testament in his "Die Bezeichnung Jesu als 'Knecht Gottes' und ihre Geschichte in der alten Kirche" (pp. 212-238 in the *Sitzungsberichte* of 1926 of the Berlin Akademie der Wissenschaften, Philosophisch-historische Klasse); with references also, e.g., to L. L. CARPENTER and C. C. TORREY), CADBURY concludes this Note with the statement (pp. 369-370), "In their atomistic use of Scripture the early Christians were very different from the modern theologian who, gathering together the four 'servant passages' of Isaiah, derives from them a complete concept, treating them as a whole, and then assumes that this Christological concept underlies the passages mentioned, and even such passages as have no more echo of Isaiah than the simple παῖς."

(The sort of eisegesis practiced by most scholars in this area of research is well brought out by ROBERT P. CASEY's Note on Μάρτυς, on pp. 30-37 of the same vol. V of *Beginnings of Christianity*: "In studying the history of the word μάρτυς, scholars have been principally interested in explaining how, in early Christian documents, it gradually lost its usual sense of a witness [Hebrew עֵד] at a trial and came to mean one who testified to the truth of Christianity by sacrificing his life. . .the transition from 'witness' to 'martyr'. . ." It is really only after the idea of Jesus' resurrection began to develop, when his death came to be associated with special significance, that "the passion and resurrection of the Messiah and the universal opportunity for repentance" became the subject of the testimony of the μάρτυρες. But we may not pursue here any further the fascinating and all-important subject of eisegesis at large).

It is above all in MORNA D. HOOKER's remarkable book on *Jesus and the Servant: The Influence of the Servant Concept of Deutero-Isaiah in the New Testament* (London, S.P.C.K., 1959) that the flagrant eisegesis that has so long usurped all authority and methodology in the scholarly study of our subject has been exposed. The book would appear to have been generally unread or slighted, perhaps even suppressed; reference to it is rather meager (e.g., it is unmentioned among the extremely full bibliographical data offered in the new English version by PETER R. ACKROYD of EISSFELDT's *The Old Testament: An Introduction* [HARPER & ROW, 1965]).

As in the case of FOAKES JACKSON-LAKE, CADBURY, and others (e.g., WILHELM BOUSSET and RUDOLF BULTMANN, referred to on pp. 4-5 of her book), MORNA HOOKER's argument would have been fortified many times over had she realized fully that what Old Testament scholarship had to say about Second Isaiah and Isaiah 53 and the Hebrew Bible generally about Servant of the Lord, Suffering Servant, Vicarious Suffering and Atonement, and the like, was to be taken with no fewer grains of salt than were the results of New Testament scholarship in its domain. Nervertheless, her reasoning and conclusions are of the fullest significance. The following excerpts are intended chiefly to present her viewpoint and to send the sincere student of the subject scurrying to the book itself.

Following on chapters on "General Survey of Recent Work on the Problem" (I, pp. 1-24), "The Servant Passages: their Meaning and Background" (II, 25-52), and "Jewish Interpretation of the Servant" (III, 53-61), Miss HOOKER deals in chapter IV with "The Servant in the Synoptic Gospels" (pp. 62-102; the notes are on pp. 181-191) and arrives at the conclusion that "There is. . .very little in the Synoptics to support the traditional view that Jesus identified his mission with that of the Servant of the Songs. . ." (p. 102). Her analysis of "The Servant in the Early Church" (V, 103-133) leads her to the conclusion that "In these early extra-canonical documents there is nothing to suggest that the identification of Jesus with the Servant was widely known or used in the primitive Church. Only in one passage in the Epistle of Barnabas is the fifty-third chapter of Isaiah applied to Jesus, through whose sufferings Christians receive the forgiveness of their sins. Elsewhere the passage is taken, either merely as a prophecy of the fact of his sufferings, or as the description of the one whose example of humility Christians are to exhorted to follow.

"We have now examined the literature of the early Church up to the middle of the second century A.D., a period sufficiently long to show whether or not the failure of the New Testament writers to make much use of Isa. 53 was accidental; the paucity of positive evidence in the extra-canonical material supports the conclusion to which the evidence of the New Testament has already led us, that the early Church did not attach any great significance to the Servant passages, or regard them as the key to their understanding of the Atonement" (p. 133).

The chapter (VI, 134-146) on "The Concept of Suffering" ends with this statement, "Finally, any direct equation of Son of Man and Messiah makes nonsense of the evidence of the gospels, which shows clearly that neither the disciples of Jesus, nor the Jews in general, understood the title 'Son of Man' as a Messianic term."

In her final chapter (VII, 147-163), "The Servant Concept in the

Thought of Jesus and the Early Church," Miss HOOKER concludes
inter alia: "The account of the beliefs of the early Christians which is
given in the Acts of the Apostles does not suggest that the primitive
community ever thought of Jesus as 'the Servant' of Deutero-Isaiah.
Nor is there any evidence that the author of the book himself made
such an identification. We found no reason for linking either the title
'παῖς' or the term 'δίκαιος' with Deutero-Isaiah in particular, nor for
understanding the references to the prophets as pointing only to Isa.
50 and 53. The use which is made of Isa. 49.6 and of 42.6 f. in Acts
13 and 26 shows clearly that no identification of Jesus with any
'Servant figure' is intended; the concepts have been found to be
relevant to both Jesus and Paul.

"These facts are the more significant, since in Acts 8 we find a
quotation from Isa. 53 actually applied to the sufferings and death of
Christ. While it is evident from the context, however, that Philip
interpreted the passage as a description of the Passion of his Lord,
this by no means implies that he must have in mind an equation of the
nature: Jesus = the Servant. For it must be stressed once again that
the words which are quoted speak only of the *fact* of the sufferings
and death of the Servant, and do not mention their *significance*. These
facts, however, are precisely those features which were *already present
in the primitive* kerygma, *and which need no passage from the Old Testament
to suggest them*. The significance of this quotation, therefore, must lie,
not in any interpretation of the *meaning* of Christ's death, but in the
fact that it is a foreshadowing of the events of the Passion: in other
words, Isa. 53 is used here in precisely the same way as in Luke 22.37,
and with the same motive as lies behind the introduction by both
Matthew and Luke of quotations from Deutero-Isaiah in other contexts. The passage is used, not as a theological dogma, but as a
'proof-text' from the Old Testament that these things could—and
did—happen to the Messiah.

". . .Paul apparently makes no use whatever of the 'Servant figure',
although he quotes twice from the fourth Song. In view of the complete lack of evidence for any identification of Jesus with the Servant
in the tradition underlying either the gospels or Acts, it is impossible
to accept the view that certain words which Paul uses are echoes of
such a belief in the primitive community. Certainly if Paul himself had
thought of Jesus as 'Servant' he would have made it plain. The absence
of this concept from his thought is the more significant, in view of his
continual emphasis upon the atoning value of the death of Christ.

"In St. John's gospel. . .There is no connection with the concept of vicarious atonement, as expressed in Deutero-Isaiah. . (pp. 150 ff.; cf. pp. 105 f.).

"How was it, then, that apparently neither Jesus nor his disciples made use of an idea [the Servant idea] which to us seems so obvious? Why did both Jesus, who spoke of the necessity of his death, and the early Church, which grapples with the perplexing problem of his Passion, and actually quoted the fourth Servant Song in their apologetic, fail to identify him with the Servant?

"The solution to this problem would seem to lie in the fact that modern scholarship, in over-estimating the importance of the Servant concept for Jesus and the early Church, has also inevitably exaggerated the part played by the same concept in contemporary Judaism. Consequently, too much emphasis has been placed, first upon the figure of the Servant himself, and secondly upon his experience of suffering" (p. 155).

Miss HOOKER has hit the nail on the head. But she could have gone even further and stated more sweepingly: neither the Old Testament—including especially Second Isaiah and its chapter 53—nor the Judaism of the intertestamental period knew anything of the concepts of Servant of the Lord, Suffering Servant, and Vicarious Suffering and Atonement as they came to be developed by the followers of Jesus some time after his death.

FOAKES JACKSON-LAKE, pp. 390 ff., have some pertinent remarks to make on Acts 8 (the full text may be seen below, in chapter IV § D end). Thus they wrote (p. 391) ". . .it is tempting to suggest that the interpretation of Isaiah liii. as a prophecy of Jesus was first introduced by Hellenistic Christians, for there is no positive evidence of its existence in sources which certainly represent the thought of the first disciples in Jerusalem but it was clearly part of the teaching of Philip." Previously (pp. 384 ff.) they had noted (p. 390), "There is no more trace of a Christian interpretation of the 'Servant' in Isaiah regarded as a sufferer, than there is in Mark or Q. The situation is markedly different in Luke and Acts. . ." And even "In Acts the Passion of Jesus is identified with the suffering of the Servant, but nowhere is described as giving salvation to men. . ." (p. 391).

It is not difficult to surmise that if these two learned editors of *The Beginnings of Christianity*—not to mention any of the other New Testament specialists referred to above—had been aware that none of Servant of the Lord, Suffering Servant, or Vicarious Suffering and

Atonement was known to biblical or intertestamental Judaism, they would have been far more positive in explaining these concepts and their association with Jesus as from specifically pagan sources, as the product of a non-biblical milieu in the Greco-Roman world. Thus it was also from a non-biblical Hellenistic milieu that the idea of virgin birth emanated, to be associated with Jesus and then read back into both the Hebrew word 'almah and its Septuagint rendering παρθένος in Isaiah 7.14 so that the Hebrew word was made to mean here—contrary to all pertinent data—"virgin" instead of "young woman," and the Greek word was made to mean—again incorrectly—exclusively "virgin."

Interestingly, in pre-New Testament times it is yaskil (52.13), not 'ebed, that is seized upon for purpose of identification and interpretation. Thus it has long been recognized that the maskilim in Daniel (11.33, 35; 12.3, 10) derive from our own yaskil; but nothing vicarious is involved here, nor any such concept as a Suffering Servant of the Lord.[1]) And this is true likewise of the Dead Sea Scroll material, into which some scholars have tried, beyond the call of scientific duty, to read their own notions of Isaiah 52-53 and Jesus as the fulfillment of them (cf., e.g., A. DUPONT-SOMMER, The Essene Writings from Qumran [Meridian Books, 1962], chap. VIII, § 2, "The Man of Sorrows," pp. 364-366; this whole section is a homiletical disservice to the Scroll material, with n. 1 on p. 366 being particularly revealing); nothing vicarious is involved there. Indeed, it is, again, only by wishful thinking (viz., eisegesis) that Qumran's "Righteous Teacher" is identified with Second Isaiah's servant; cf., e.g., M. BURROWS, More Light on the Dead Sea Scrolls (New York, 1958), pp. 66, 316 f., 328, 335 f.—reiterating with greater emphasis the brief statements in his earlier volume, The Dead Sea Scrolls (New York, 1955); F. M. CROSS, Jr., The Ancient Library of Qumran and Modern Biblical Studies (Anchor Books, rev. ed., 1961), p. 222, n. 52. I suppose that it would not be easy to associate the concept of vicariousness with a group that could produce a treatise dealing with the ruthless and total war of the righteous (children of light) against the wicked (children of darkness).

---

[1]) Miss HOOKER (n. 1 to p. 53 and n. 4 to p. 56, respectively on pp. 177 and 178) takes WILLIAM H. BROWNLEE severely to task for the wholly uncritical manner in which he seeks and finds evidence for the Servant concept in Daniel and in the Dead Sea Scrolls; she finds that his "sweeping statement is based upon the flimsiest of evidence" and is "unconvincing."

CHAPTER FOUR

THE IDENTITY OF THE "SERVANT" IN SECOND ISAIAH

We have seen that nothing especially significant was attached in biblical times to the so-called 'ebed sections in Second Isaiah; were it not for the theological needs of early Christianity that brought emphasis for the first time to the concept "servant" in Isaiah 52-53, it is altogether doubtful that scholars would subsequently have paid special attention and granted special status to Second Isaiah's servant passages. We shall deal here with the four generally recognized major servant sections, though not in very great detail, in the hope of clarifying the identity of the servant in them. For bibliography or more detailed analysis, see, e.g., NORTH, 117 ff.; SNAITH; LINDHAGEN, 197-228; LINDBLOM, 14 ff.; ROWLEY, *passim*; DE BOER; ZIMMERLI-JEREMIAS, 23-34.

A. 42.1 ff.

(1) הֵן עַבְדִּי אֶתְמָךְ־בּוֹ בְּחִירִי רָצְתָה נַפְשִׁי
נָתַתִּי רוּחִי עָלָיו מִשְׁפָּט לַגּוֹיִם יוֹצִיא:

(2) לֹא יִצְעַק וְלֹא יִשָּׂא וְלֹא־יַשְׁמִיעַ בַּחוּץ קוֹלוֹ:

(3) קָנֶה רָצוּץ לֹא יִשְׁבּוֹר וּפִשְׁתָּה כֵהָה לֹא יְכַבֶּנָּה
לֶאֱמֶת יוֹצִיא מִשְׁפָּט: (4) לֹא יִכְהֶה וְלֹא יָרוּץ
עַד־יָשִׂים בָּאָרֶץ מִשְׁפָּט וּלְתוֹרָתוֹ אִיִּים יְיַחֵלוּ:

(5) כֹּה־אָמַר הָאֵל יהוה בּוֹרֵא הַשָּׁמַיִם וְנוֹטֵיהֶם
רֹקַע הָאָרֶץ וְצֶאֱצָאֶיהָ נֹתֵן נְשָׁמָה לָעָם עָלֶיהָ
וְרוּחַ לַהֹלְכִים בָּהּ:

(6) אֲנִי יהוה קְרָאתִיךָ בְצֶדֶק וְאַחְזֵק בְּיָדֶךָ
וְאֶצָּרְךָ וְאֶתֶּנְךָ לִבְרִית עָם לְאוֹר גּוֹיִם:

(7) לִפְקֹחַ עֵינַיִם עִוְרוֹת לְהוֹצִיא מִמַּסְגֵּר אַסִּיר
מִבֵּית כֶּלֶא יֹשְׁבֵי חֹשֶׁךְ: (8) אֲנִי יהוה הוּא שְׁמִי
וּכְבוֹדִי לְאַחֵר לֹא־אֶתֵּן וּתְהִלָּתִי לַפְּסִילִים:

(9) הָרִאשֹׁנוֹת הִנֵּה־בָאוּ וַחֲדָשׁוֹת אֲנִי מַגִּיד
בְּטֶרֶם תִּצְמַחְנָה אַשְׁמִיעַ אֶתְכֶם:

Scholars differ on the length of the first 'ebed section, the vast majority undecided between vv. 1-4 and vv. 1-7 or 8; some regard vv. 5-9 as a separate unit, but disagree on how to associate it with vv. 1-4. Regardless of these sundry differences, (1) it can be only an individual person that vv. 1-4 and 7-9 allude to, and (2) it is Israel in exile that is the object of his efforts.

(1) *The servant an individual person rather than the people Israel*

(a) When God is said to have summoned the servant in order (v. 7)

> To open eyes that are blind,
> To rescue prisoners from the dungeon,
> From the prison those who sit in darkness,

the terms "blind" (sometimes with its parallel "deaf"), "prisoners," and "those who sit in darkness," as elsewhere in Second Isaiah (cf., e.g., vv. 18 ff. in our very chapter) can refer only to Israel in exile.[1]) Thus the servant can only be an individual person.

(b) It will be seen from the Appendix below, "A Light of Nations," etc., that neither of the two expressions in v. 6, לברית עם and לאור גוים, points to Israel in relation to the nations, but rather to an individual in relation to Israel (לברית עם) and in relation to the world at large (לאור גוים).

(c) It is not easy to identify the people Israel with anything in vv. 1-4 (on additional "Jacob. . .Israel" in the Septuagint of v. 1a, see § B 3 below). Thus God does not "put His spirit upon" (נתן רוח על-) an entire people, not even His own people Israel; so that "I have put My spirit upon him" (v. 1bα) would naturally indicate an individual person. (It need hardly be noted that *rúaḥ* in v. 5—"Who gives. . . spirit/life to those who walk in it"—parallel to *nᵉshamáh*, is something else again. R.V.S., e.g., spells it "Spirit" in v. 1, but "spirit" in v. 5.)

(d) It makes no sense to assert about Israel in exile (vv. 2-3) that "He will not cry out or raise his voice and cause it to be heard in the open. A bruised reed he will not break, a dimly burning wick he will not quench. . ." Rather, this is the sort of statement that is made about God's individual spokesmen, who submit to His will in their unpopular mission.

(e) Regardless of how one renders the three clauses with *mishpáṭ* in vv. 1, 3, and 4, "(he shall) bring forth/execute/establish/promulgate judgment/justice (to the nations/in the earth)," it is hardly captive

---

[1]) Cf. chap. III, § B above; LINDHAGEN, p. 210; LINDBLOM, p. 78 and n. 25. Thus in vv. 18 ff. in this same chapter, Israel in exile is referred to as "deaf" and "blind." Of course even those who identify the servant here with Cyrus (against this identification see immediately below) must identify the "blind" here with Israel in exile; Babylonia was hardly to be freed by Cyrus!

Israel that will achieve this; Israel will be liberated by God and restored to her homeland. It is natural, on the other hand, both in specific context and in general, to think in terms of an individual as the one who will proclaim God's will. By the same token, it is not a people, but an individual spokesman for God, who will publicize God's teachings (v. 4b).

(2) *The servant is the prophet himself rather than King Cyrus*

(a) King Cyrus, great military hero, is hardly one to be described in such terms as (vv. 2-4)

> He will not cry out or raise his voice
> Or cause it to be heard in the open.
> A bruised reed he will not break,
> A dimly burning wick he will not quench. . .

In his fine study of "The Use of Figurative Language in Deutero-Isaiah" (Chap. IV of his *The Servant Songs*, etc., pp. 75-93), LINDBLOM has noted some of the metaphors used by our prophet for—as LIND-BLOM believes—Cyrus. Interestingly, the expressions quoted here are nowhere cited by LINDBLOM in connection with the Persian monarch; how could they be?

(b) It is hardly Cyrus who will bring God's *torah* ("instruction," or the like) to the world (v. 4). This is evident, e.g., from the blunt statement of v. 8:

> I am the Lord, that is My name;
> I will not yield My glory to another,
> Nor My renown to idols

with which one may compare 51.4a, "For from Me will instruction go forth" (כִּי תוֹרָה מֵאִתִּי תֵצֵא). Cyrus is not yet God's devoted servant, nor is the God of Israel also his chosen God; he is rather, as stated clearly in 44.28 and 45.1 ff., merely God's instrument for crushing Babylon and liberating Israel.

(c) Elsewhere in Second Isaiah, it is the prophet himself, not Cyrus, who will bring light and freedom to his fellow exiles who live in darkness and in prison (v. 7).

The precise language employed for the prophet in this section need not concern us here. Many scholars recognize "kingly features in the servant of Isa. XLII. . .a prophet, but with regal features. . .," some referring to him as "servant [of God]-king" or "vassal-king" (cf. LINDBLOM, pp. 18 ff.); but that is largely because they regard the "servant" as being Cyrus. There are also those who associate messianism and/or eschatology with our passage; but while these concepts are outside the immediate cope of this study, it is very dubious indeed that they possessed any significance during the biblical period, the kind of significance that they acquired in post-biblical times, in the Judaism of the last centuries of the Second Temple and in early Christianity. Thus LINDBLOM (chap. V, "The Problem of Eschatology in Deutero-Isaiah," pp. 94-104) has commented (103 f.), "The Second Isaiah has often been labelled by scholars as an 'eschatologist', and even as the originator of the Israelite-Jewish eschatology as a whole. If eschatology means a doctrine, or a message, concerning the end of history and a new age including 'new heavens and a new earth', there is no eschatology in Deutero-Isaiah at all. Nor do the Servant Songs contain any eschatology. . .In my opinion scholars. . .have not seldom treated metaphors, symbols, figurative pictures as precise and exact descriptions of reality, quite in opposition to Hebrew modes of expression. Thus many passages in the Old Testament have been understood as eschatology, while they in fact are simply poetry. The whole question of the eschatology of the Old Testament must be taken up afresh along new lines. . ." (and cf. in this connection LINDBLOM's chap. IV, "The Use of Figurative Language in Deutero-Isaiah," pp. 75-95, and his subsequent article, "Gibt es eine Eschatologie bei den alttestamentlichen Propheten?" in *Studia Theologica*, 6 [1953], 79-114). More is the pity, therefore, that LINDBLOM permitted himself to be sidetracked, along with so many others, by the concept of Messianism, a concept that lacks justification for our problem no less than eschatology does.

In a recent discussion of "The Interpretation of Deutero-Isaiah" in *Interpretationes ad Vetus Testamentum Sigmundo Mowinckel Septuagenario Missae* (Oslo, 1955), C. R. NORTH stated (p. 139), ". . .I find myself entirely in agreement with VOLZ when he says. . .'Deutero-Isaiah is shot through and through with eschatology. . .'" One may well wonder to what extent the sweeping eschatology seen here in the Old Testament derives from the New Testament period. In a clear statement on "Realized Eschatology" (*JBL*, 56 [1937], 17-26), C. T. CRAIG observed (pp. 17 f.): "There is so much that is true in the general position advocated by Professor (C. H.) DODD that the point at issue must be clearly isolated. Four positions may be named upon which we

are in substantial agreement. 1. Our gospels are primary sources for
the church at the time when they were produced, rather than for the
life-time of Jesus. . . 2. The message of Jesus was 'eschatological.'
In proclaiming the coming of the kingdom, Jesus did not have anything in mind which was akin to our evolutionary conception of
progress. . . 3. Jesus believed that the power of the kingdom of God
was present in his own ministry; in other words, eschatology was
already realized. . ."

B. 49.1-6

(1) שִׁמְעוּ אִיִּים אֵלַי וְהַקְשִׁיבוּ לְאֻמִּים מֵרָחוֹק
יהוה מִבֶּטֶן קְרָאָנִי מִמְּעֵי אִמִּי הִזְכִּיר שְׁמִי:

(2) וַיָּשֶׂם פִּי כְּחֶרֶב חַדָּה בְּצֵל יָדוֹ הֶחְבִּיאָנִי
וַיְשִׂימֵנִי לְחֵץ בָּרוּר בְּאַשְׁפָּתוֹ הִסְתִּירָנִי:

(3) וַיֹּאמֶר לִי עַבְדִּי־אָתָּה יִשְׂרָאֵל אֲשֶׁר־בְּךָ אֶתְפָּאָר:

(4) וַאֲנִי אָמַרְתִּי לְרִיק יָגַעְתִּי לְתֹהוּ וְהֶבֶל כֹּחִי כִלֵּיתִי
אָכֵן מִשְׁפָּטִי אֶת־יהוה וּפְעֻלָּתִי אֶת־אֱלֹהָי:

(5) וְעַתָּה אָמַר יהוה יֹצְרִי מִבֶּטֶן לְעֶבֶד לוֹ
לְשׁוֹבֵב יַעֲקֹב אֵלָיו וְיִשְׂרָאֵל לוֹ [K= לֹא ; Q =] יֵאָסֵף
וְאֶכָּבֵד בְּעֵינֵי יהוה וֵאלֹהַי הָיָה עֻזִּי:

(6) וַיֹּאמֶר נָקֵל מִהְיוֹתְךָ לִי עֶבֶד לְהָקִים אֶת־שִׁבְטֵי יַעֲקֹב
וּנְצוּרֵי [Q = ;וּנְצִירֵי [K = יִשְׂרָאֵל לְהָשִׁיב וּנְתַתִּיךָ לְאוֹר גּוֹיִם
לִהְיוֹת יְשׁוּעָתִי עַד־קְצֵה הָאָרֶץ:

Allowing for the difficulties in v. 5, both *per se* and in context, and
leaving *yisra'ēl* in v. 3 untranslated, our section may be rendered as
follows:

(1) Listen to me, O coastlands,
Hearken, O distant peoples!
The Lord called me from the womb,
He singled me out from my mother's body.
(2) He made my mouth like a sharp sword,
In the shadow of His hand He sheltered me;
He made me a polished arrow,
He concealed me in His quiver.
(3) He said to me, "You are My servant,
. . .In whom I will glory (or: By whom I will be glorified)."
(4) But I thought: I have labored in vain,
I have spent my strength in utter futility.
Yet (or: Assuredly) my vindication is with the Lord,

And my recompense with my God!
(5) And now the Lord has declared—
   Who formed me from the womb to be His servant—
   That He will bring Jacob back to Him,
   That Israel shall be gathered to Him.
   Thus I shall gain honor in the sight of the Lord,
   And my God has been my support.
(6) He said, "It is too slight for you to be My servant
   To set up again the tribes of Jacob
   And to restore the survivors of Israel;
   But I will make you a light of nations,
   That My triumph may reach to the ends of the earth."

It is almost two hundred years since JOHANN D. MICHAELIS, in his *Deutsche Uebersetzung des Alten Testaments, mit Anmerkungen für Ungelehrte*[!] (Der achte Theil, Göttingen, 1779), p. 249, cast suspicion on the genuineness of the word ישראל in v.3.[1]) But scholars have not yet reached agreement on the quality of the word: Is it original or secondary? Clearly this word has been crucial for many scholars in the attempt to determine the identity of the servant mentioned in the verse: Is it Israel or is it an individual person?

By and large, those who identify the 'ebed in Second Isaiah with the people Israel tend to keep our "Israel" here, whereas those who see in the 'ebed an individual generally delete our word. Some scholars have labored hard to be impartial in their analysis of the problem, regardless of how they identify Second Isaiah's 'ebed. Thus LINDBLOM, to whom (p. 103) "the servant of the songs is thought of as an individual. . .but he symbolizes allegorically a community, namely Israel. . .," has argued (p. 30 and notes 40-42), "The second problem refers to the much discussed word 'Israel' in v. 3. From a metrical point of view nothing certain can be said about the genuineness of the word. In accordance with my interpretation. . .the word 'Israel' can be very well justified if we translate. . .'And he said to me: You, my servant, you are (i.e. symbolize) Israel, and through you I shall be glorified.' . . .If this explanation is unacceptable, the only satisfactory alternative is to delete the word as an interpretation. .." ZIMMERLI (-JEREMIAS), committed as he is to "the collective interpretation of

---

[1]) "Dis Wort steht im hebräischen, allein es ist mir verdächtig, und deswegen habe ich es in Klammers eingeschlossen: es könnte vielleicht hier eben ein solcher Zustaz sehn, als Cap. XLII, 1. in der griechischen Bibel." MICHAELIS had translated the verse (p. 96): "du bist mein Knecht, (Israel) dessen ich mich rühme."

Israel as a whole" (p. 24; and cf. his § iii on pp. 17-18), nevertheless asserts (p. 25), "In the ישראל of 49.3 we shall have to see an early, but in the text a secondary *midrash* made in a collective sense while the original text will have to be interpreted in an individual sense. . ." And finally, NORTH has wrestled mightily with the text and his scholarly conscience (pp. 118 f.; and cf. 143 ff.): " 'Israel'. . .Metrical grounds have been urged both for and against its retention. It is clearly a case where the scholar's judgement is liable to be determined by his attitude to the problem as a whole. Manuscript evidence is not sufficient to compel deletion. Yet the retention of the word, even on the collective interpretation, is difficult if the Servant is called Israel in ver. 3, and then given a mission to Israel in ver. 5 f., unless the infinitives there are to be taken as gerundives, with Yahweh as the subject, which is very doubtful. . .It would greatly simplify the whole problem if we could with a good conscience delete 'Israel'. For that very reason I hesitate to do so, since I have a suspicion that it would be on theoretical rather than on manuscript or metrical grounds. I therefore retain it, but with what I feel, in all the circumstances, is justifiable hesitation. It cannot be said that the stichos is very euphonious, and there may be deep-seated corruption. . .Finally, it may be remarked that the case for the retention of 'Israel' is not so strong that the collective interpretation may without more ado be assumed."

And so, the philologian will disregard any *a priori* identification of the *'ebed* elsewhere in Second Isaiah and apply to *yisra'él* in verse 3 the same canons of textual criticism that he would to any problem of this kind.

(1) *The term "Israel" (and "Jacob") in Second Isaiah*

A question that requires a clear-cut answer is one that involves the precise manner in which the term "Israel" (and "Jacob") was used elsewhere in Second Isaiah. This crucial point has been dealt with in the past only in passing and quite inadequately. Thus JULIUS A. BEWER ("Two Notes on Isaiah 49.1-6," in *Jewish Studies in Memory of George A. Kohut*, ed. Salo W. Baron-Alexander Marx [New York, 1935], 86-90) closes his study of manuscript Kennicott 96 (see further below) with the statement (p. 88), " 'Israel' is mentioned without the parallel 'Jacob' also in Is. 45.17.25 46.13"; and TORREY is content with a sweeping reference (p. 380) to "numerous parallel passages (*e.g.*, 41: 8; 43: 10; 44: 1, 2, 21)." The data offered immediately below will indicate how incomplete and misleading the statements by BEWER and TORREY really are.

Fortunately, the occurrences of the term "Israel" in chapters 40-55 of Isaiah are numerous enough—43 in all, not counting 4 instances where "Jacob" alone (not in parallelism with "Israel" but in the same manner as "Israel") is used—to bear statistical analysis.

(a) In no less than 17 instances "Israel" and "Jacob" are used in parallel lines, exactly as in vv. 5 and 6 in our chapter: 40.27; 41.8, 14a; 42.23; 43.1, 22, 28; 44.1, 5, 21a, 23; 45.4; 46.3; 48.1a, 12; 49.5, 6. Chosen at random, the following passages may be reproduced in part: 40.27 וְאַתָּה יִשְׂרָאֵל עַבְדִּי; 41.8 לָמָּה תֹאמַר יַעֲקֹב וּתְדַבֵּר יִשְׂרָאֵל; 43.1 יַעֲקֹב אֲשֶׁר בְּחַרְתִּיךָ (וְעַתָּה כֹּה־אָמַר יהוה) בֹּרַאֲךָ יַעֲקֹב וְיֹצֶרְךָ יִשְׂרָאֵל; 48.12 שְׁמַע אֵלַי יַעֲקֹב וְיִשְׂרָאֵל מְקֹרָאִי.

(b) In one instance (44.2) "Jeshurun" stands for "Israel" in parallelism with "Jacob": (כֹּה־אָמַר יהוה · · ·) אַל־תִּירָא עַבְדִּי יַעֲקֹב וִישֻׁרוּן בָּחַרְתִּי בוֹ.

(c) In one instance (46.13) "Zion" is essentially parallel to "Israel": וְנָתַתִּי בְצִיּוֹן תְּשׁוּעָה לְיִשְׂרָאֵל תִּפְאַרְתִּי.

(d) In 21 passages "Israel" is combined with another word to constitute an expression for God, usually in parallelism with *YHWH*. The expressions are: "The Holy One of Israel"/קְדוֹשׁ יִשְׂרָאֵל(41.14b, 16, 20; 43.3, 14; 45.11; 47.4; 48.17; 49. 7b;54.5—11 instances in all); "The God of Israel"/אֱלֹהֵי יִשְׂרָאֵל (41.17; 45.3, 15; 48.1b, 2; 52.12—for a total of 6 instances); "Creator of Israel"/בּוֹרֵא יִשְׂרָאֵל (43.15); "King of Israel"/מֶלֶךְ יִשְׂרָאֵל גֹּאֵל יִשְׂרָאֵל (46.6); and "Redeemer of Israel"/גֹּאֵל יִשְׂרָאֵל (49.7a).

(e) In only 3 passages does "Israel" stand by itself: 44.21 זְכָר־אֵלֶּה יַעֲקֹב וְיִשְׂרָאֵל כִּי עַבְדִּי־אָתָּה יְצַרְתִּיךָ עֶבֶד־לִי אַתָּה יִשְׂרָאֵל לֹא תִנָּשֵׁנִי; 45.17 יִשְׂרָאֵל נוֹשַׁע בַּיהוה תְּשׁוּעַת עוֹלָמִים לֹא־תֵבשׁוּ וְלֹא־תִכָּלְמוּ עַד־עוֹלְמֵי עַד 45.25 בַּיהוה יִצְדְּקוּ וְיִתְהַלְלוּ כָּל־זֶרַע יִשְׂרָאֵל.

(f) As for "Jacob" by itself, the 4 passages are: 41.21 קָרְבוּ רִיבְכֶם יֹאמַר יהוה הַגִּישׁוּ עַצְמוֹתֵיכֶם יֹאמַר מֶלֶךְ יַעֲקֹב, where "King of Jacob"—cf. "King of Israel" in 44.6—is parallel to *YHWH*; 45.19 לֹא אָמַרְתִּי . . . לְזֶרַע יַעֲקֹב תֹּהוּ בַקְּשׁוּנִי · · ·, where "seed of Jacob" may be compared with "seed of Israel" in verse 25; 48.20 · · ·, אִמְרוּ גָּאַל יהוה עַבְדּוֹ יַעֲקֹב with which compare the use of "Israel" on several occasions with

. . . וְיָדְעוּ כָּל־בָּשָׂר כִּי אֲנִי and 49.26 ;[1]("both "servant" and "redeem
יהוה מוֹשִׁיעֵךְ וְגֹאֲלֵךְ אֲבִיר יַעֲקֹב.

It will be readily apparent that "Israel" is not used in 49.3 in the manner that one might expect in the light of its other 42 occurrences— and the 4 of "Jacob"—in Second Isaiah.

(2) *Kenn 96*

It is well known that one Hebrew manuscript, Kenn 96, lacks our word "Israel." The closest study yet made of this phenomenon is that of BEWER; unfortunately, BEWER was so intent on identifying Second Isaiah's *'ebed* with collective Israel that his analysis is less than objective and his conclusion less than conclusive.

Every textual critic knows that it is extremely rare for a medieval Hebrew manuscript of the Bible to be closer to the original text by having preserved, or by lacking, a certain reading. So that while our word is present in all the primary and secondary versions and in all the other Hebrew manuscripts, including both the complete and incomplete scrolls of Isaiah commonly designated IQIsa[a] and IQIsa[b], the absence of *yisra'él* in Kenn 96 is *a priori* an important factor in the textual analysis of our passage.[2] In his study, BEWER was so determined to prove Kenn 96 as having no value whatever that he concentrated on singling out the errors of that manuscript elsewhere in Second Isaiah, where single words were missing and scribal errors had been made. He did not try to find out whether other variant readings in

---

[1] Thus BROWN-DRIVER-Briggs, e.g., has noted (p. 145b, *Qal* § 2*c*; which should include also Isa. 52.3, listed there under *Niph.* § 2) the use of גאל in Isaiah 40-66 for God's redemption of Israel in exile. Or cf. NORTH, *The Second Isaiah*, 99 f. (with additional reference to AUBREY R. JOHNSON's discussion of "The Primary Meaning of √גאל," *Supplements to Vetus Testament*—the Copenhagen Congress Volume, 1 [1953], 67-77), though care should be taken to distinguish between the considerable eisegesis prevalent in the book and the exegesis (see the review by PREBEN WERNBERG-MØLLER in *Journal of Semitic Studies*, 10 [1965], 283-5). Neither do I understand the usefulness of such a statement as (p. 13), ". . .But VON RAD [*Theologie des Alten Testaments*, vol. II] is right when he says that for DI [Deutero-Isaiah] 'create' (*bara'*) and 'redeem' (*gā'al*) are almost synonymous. Yahweh created and has redeemed Israel (xliii. 1, 14 f.). . ."; but this is not the place to analyze *ga'al* in relation to *bara'*.

[2] An excellent parallel to this kind of phenomenon is the unique reading in Kenn 223, שדי אלהים (for received אלהים) at Job 5.8; see my discussion of this in "Job 5.8, a Problem in Greek-Hebrew Methodology," *Jewish Quarterly Review*, 25 (1934-35), 271-278; and chap. V, "The Hebrew *Vorlage* of the Septuagint of Job: the Text and the Script," § A 3, of my *Studies in the Septuagint of the Book of Job*, *Hebrew Union College Annual*, 35 (1964), 61 ff.

Kenn 96 were noteworthy, he did not study any other Kennicott manuscripts to determine their characteristics, nor did he attempt to relate Kenn 96 to other manuscripts recensionally. In fine, our manuscript is still in need of objective and adequate evaluation, and its lack of *yisra'él* may not be dismissed as lightly as BEWER would have us do.

(3) *The Septuagint*

A word about the Septuagint (LXX). Some scholars, e.g., LUDWIG KÖHLER (*Deuterojesaja* [*Jesaja* 40-55] *Stilkritisch Untersucht* [*BZAW*, 37, 1923, p. 37) and SIGMUND MOWINCKEL,[1]) had asserted that some LXX manuscripts likewise were lacking "Israel" in our verse. This is not the case at all; a direct consultation of the data (in JOSEPH ZIEGLER's Göttingen edition of *Isaias*, 1939) reveals the fact that two manuscripts read Ιακωβ in place of Ισραηλ—which is something else again. The two manuscripts are **Q** (Codex Marchalianus, sixth century) and 534 (eleventh century cursive), which constitute part of a subgroup of the **A**-recension (ZIEGLER, pp. 21 ff., 29 f.).[2])

It has, further, been noted that the term "Israel" is a gloss elsewhere in Second Isaiah, in the case of the LXX at 42.1; but here too there has been a lamentable lack of understanding of this version. For preserved הֵן עַבְדִּי אֶתְמָךְ־בּוֹ בְּחִירִי רָצְתָה נַפְשִׁי (נָתַתִּי רוּחִי עָלָיו מִשְׁפָּט לַגּוֹיִם יוֹצִיא) the LXX reads Ιακωβ ὁ Παῖς μου, ἀντιλήμψομαι αὐτοῦ, Ισραηλ ὁ ἐλεκτός μου, προσεδέξατο αὐτὸν ἡ ψυχή μου. Since it is not "Israel" alone but "Jacob...Israel" (note the order!) that is present, I am inclined to believe that the LXX-*Vorlage* read יעקב (עבדי אתמך בו.[3]) בְּחִירִי רצתה נפשי) ישראל. This fuller version is overlong, and it is likely that יעקב···ישראל constitutes a gloss already in the Hebrew

---

[1]) in *De senere profeter* (1944; = vol. III in *Det gamle testamente*), p. 233 (ad loc.), repeated in his *Han som Kommer*, etc. (Copenhagen, 1951), 334 f. and more especially in the English version *He That Cometh* (Oxford, 1956), p. 191 and Additional Note XI on pp. 462-4 (cf. also p. 466); the "Note," incidentally, is not exactly a model of how to deal with a textual problem.

[2]) ROWLEY, *The Servant of the Lord*, etc., p. 8 and n. 4—also on p. 51 of the 1957 *Book List* of the (British) Society for Old Testament Study—has been especially critical of MOWINCKEL.

[3]) I have much respect for the Septuagint of Isaiah, as a result of my study of "The Treatment of Anthropomorphisms and Anthropopathisms in the Septuagint of Isaiah," *Hebrew Union College Annual*, 27 (1956), 193-200. JOSEPH ZIEGLER, *Untersuchungen zur Septuaginta des Buches Isaias* (= *Alttestamentliche Abhandlungen*, XII, 3, 1934), does not appear to have discussed our passage; in his commentary on *Isaias* (Würzburg, 1948), p. 145, n. 3, ZIEGLER deletes "Israel" as "wahrscheinlich Glosse nach 44.23..."

Vorlage of the LXX. But the problem merits a closer study than it has yet received.

(4) *The Meter*

The problem of meter is far less troublesome than is generally admitted (cf., e.g., MOWINCKEL, *He That Cometh*, 462-4, 466). The "collectivists," being most eager to retain "Israel," will sometimes assert bluntly, as BEWER did (p. 87), "the metre requires it"; or cf. TORREY (p. 381), "the rhythm of the verse. . .is sadly impaired by its omission." The fact is that both the verse that precedes our own and the verse that follows it end in 3: 2 meter—v. 2 וַיְשִׂמֵנִי לְחֵץ בָּרוּר בְּאַשְׁפָּתוֹ הִסְתִּירָנִי; v. 4 אָכֵן מִשְׁפָּטִי אֶת־יהוה וּפְעֻלָּתִי אֶת־אֱלֹהָי—exactly the meter that our v. 3 exhibits with the deletion of *yisra'él*. KÖHLER deletes *yisra'él* and construes the verse as 2: 2: 2.

(5) *Emendation*

The problem of meter, along with other problems, falls by the wayside entirely if one resorts to emendation or transposition. Thus RUDOLF KITTEL (*Biblia Hebraica*³), following others, ponders the deletion of *yisra'el* (> 1 MS; dl?) and notes on אֶתְפָּאָר: "trsp huc v. 5b." ARNOLD B. EHRLICH (*Randglossen zur hebräischen Bibel*, vol. IV, 1912, p. 178) believes that "ישראל ist in seiner jetzigen Stellung unerklärlich. . ."; he reconstructs the verse so that *yisra'el* appears at the end and אֶתְפָּאָר becomes אֲפָאֵר: "du bist mein Knecht, durch den ich Israel verherrlichen will."

(6) *"Israel" in v. 5*

It has been noted by many scholars that it is simply impossible for "Israel" to be original both in our verse 3 and also in verse 5: how can Israel be given a mission to Israel? And so those who retain "Israel" in v. 3 are compelled to construe the infinitives in vv. 5 (לְשׁוֹבֵב) and 6 (לְהָקִים · · · לְהָשִׁיב) such that God Himself is their subject.

The complicated character of this construction is clearly apparent from the well-intentioned manner in which NORTH, e.g., deals with it. In his *The Suffering Servant* (pp. 118 f.) he writes, "Yet the retention of the word [*yisra'el*], even on the collective interpretation, is difficult if the Servant is called Israel in ver. 3, and then given a mission to Israel in ver. 5 f., unless the infinitives there are to be taken as *gerund-*

ives [italics mine], with Yahweh as the subject, which is very doubtful," whereas in his recent commentary on *The Second Isaiah* (Oxford, 1964; p. 189) he asserts, "There is obvious difficulty in these words, if the Servant is the nation Israel. How can Israel 'bring back' Israel? Accordingly, protagonists for the collective theory have argued that the infinitives in this and the next verse are *gerundial* [italics mine] (cf. *GK* 114 *o*), with Yahweh as their subject. Two translations have been offered on the basis of this interpretation: (i) 'But now, says Yahweh ...in that he brings back Jacob to himself, and that Israel will not be swept away (*Qere* reading). . .' (so HITZIG. . .); (ii) 'And now, says Yahweh. . .in that he brought back Jacob (out of Egypt) to himself and gathered Israel to himself (in the wilderness). . .it is too little. . . that I should raise up Jacob's tribes. . .' (so K. BUDDE. . .). These translations are grammatically possible, but they are awkward and involved, and most exponents of the collective theory have now abandoned them." [1]) But there is a considerable difference between "gerund" and "gerundive," and it is sheerest desperation to drag in these terms and constructions in order to justify what is patently unjustifiable. The cure is worse than the disease.

In the second of his "Two Notes on Isaiah 49.1-6" (§ 2. Indirect Speech in Isaiah 49.5), BEWER argued (pp. 89 f.) "that the infinitive construct with ל in Is. 49.5, is another example of indirect speech. . . 'And now Yhwh, who formed me from the womb to be his servant, has said that he would bring Jacob back to himself and that Israel would be gathered to him.' The direct speech does not begin till verse 6 and there it is introduced by another יאמר). . ." But surely the very presence of (ועתה אמר יהוה) יצרי מבטן לעבד לו immediately before לשובב יעקב אליו וישראל לו יאסף is sufficient not only to indicate the עבד (rather than יהוה) as the subject of לשובב—why else should the expression "who formed me from the womb to be His servant" have been as used here?—but the identical statement is made in v. 6 immediately following:

> He said, "It is too slight for you to be My servant
> To set up again the tribes of Jacob
> And to restore the survivors of Israel. . ."

---

[1]) For the sake of completeness, I quote the last sentence of this statement, "Instead, it is quite properly argued, Israel could have a mission to Israel, very much as we say that the first mission of the Church is to the Church." Incidentally, the data in GK § 114 *o* (p. 351 top) hardly bear on our problem.

To get out of this difficulty, BEWER rendered *v.* 6 as follows: "That I should raise up the tribes of Jacob, and restore the survivors of Israel is less significant than that thou art my servant. . ."—which is plainly not what the Hebrew says.

(7) *Some Significant Expressions*

The significance of the expressions employed in our section is worthy of greater attention than it has attracted hitherto. Such expressions as "The Lord called me from the womb, He singled me out from my mother's body" (v. 1) and "And now the Lord has declared—Who formed me from the womb to be His servant" (v. 5) are how a prophet will describe the origin of his calling. One thinks at once of the prophet from whom Second Isaiah drew most, viz., Jeremiah, who begins his message (1.4-5) with "The word of the Lord came to me: Before I formed you in the belly, I selected you; Before you issued from the womb, I consecrated you." It is not natural to associate our own verses 1 and 5 with the people Israel.

Again, it is only natural that the expressions "He made my mouth like a sharp sword. . .He made me a polished arrow" (v. 2) refer to the prophet himself; they make no sense if applied to the people Israel. This is true no less for the second and fourth lines in the same verse 2: "In the shadow of His hand He sheltered me. . .He concealed me in His quiver," which would be absurd if used for suffering Israel in exile.

(8) *The "I" Construction*

An excellent picture of the utter incongruity of *yisra'el* in context can be seen from the use of the first person (the prophet himself clearly being the speaker throughout) in vv. 1-6: · · · קְרָאָ֫נִי · · · אֵלַ֫י
אִמִּי · · · שְׁמִי · · · פִּי · · · הֶחְבִּיאָ֫נִי וַיְשִׂימֵ֫נִי · · · הִסְתִּירָ֫נִי: וַיֹּ֫אמֶר לִי עַבְדִּי־אַתָּה
[יִשְׂרָאֵל!] אֲשֶׁר־בְּךָ אֶתְפָּאָר: וַאֲנִי אָמַ֫רְתִּי · · · יָגַ֫עְתִּי · · · כֹּחִי כִלֵּ֫יתִי · · · מִשְׁפָּטִי · · · וּפְעֻ֫לָּתִי אֶת־אֱלֹהָי: · · · יֹצְרִי · · · וְאֶכָּבֵד · · · וֵאלֹהַי הָיָה עֻזִּי:

In stating categorically that "The textual evidence sustains יִשְׂרָאֵל, the metre requires it, and the strict parallel in Is. 44.21 confirms it" (p. 87), BEWER has failed completely to note—*inter alia*—that the entire context of our section in chapter 49 revolves about the "I", in sharp distinction from the pertinent section in chapter 44, where the context revolves about "Israel."

(9) *The Secondary Origin of "Israel"*

The origin of *yisra'el* as a secondary intrusion in v. 3 may be readily accounted for variously. One plausible suggestion (cf., e.g., NORTH, p. 119) has it that 44.23b, (כִּי־גָאַל יהוה יַעֲקֹב וּבְיִשְׂרָאֵל יִתְפָּאָר), was the source of inspiration for the glossator. Others would prefer 44.21b as that source: (וְכָר־אֵלֶּה יַעֲקֹב וְיִשְׂרָאֵל כִּי עַבְדִּי־אָתָּה) יְצַרְתִּיךָ עֶבֶד־לִי אַתָּה לֹא תִנָּשֵׁנִי; thus, e.g., *La Sainte Bible* places "Israel" within parentheses and offers this note: "Cette précision, difficilement campatible avec les vv. 5-6, cf. **42** 1+, est sans doute une glosse, inspirée de **44** 21." On the other hand, they may be right who believe that "there may be deep-seated corruption" (NORTH, ibid.); indeed, all of v. 3 (*N.B.* the length of vv. 1-2 and 4-6) may be secondary here, with v. 4 follwing directly on v. 2 in the original. But this need not concern us here.

To sum up. The argument altogether aside as to who the *'ebed* of Second Isaiah in general and of 49.1-6 in particular is, the textual analysis presented here makes it amply clear that *yisra'el* has no place in v. 3: its presence makes for grievous syntactical and contextual difficulties; it is lacking in a Hebrew manuscript; its deletion results in the elimination of every difficulty; and its secondary origin is readily accounted for. In fine, *yisra'el* in 49.3 should be deleted.[1]

With the deletion of *yisra'el* in v. 3, the entire section, whether it be vv. 1-4 or vv. 1-6, becomes a natural unit and crystal clear: the *'ebed* can only refer to the prophet himself. Calling upon the universe as his witness (v. 1a), he declares his calling as God-inspired and determined (1b). God had sent him forth under His protection to speak forthrightly to His people (2-3). But he feels that his mission has been in vain (4). God, however, has now assured him that not only will he serve His purpose in restoring His exiled people, but he will also make this great triumph of God evident to the whole world (5-6). The reader will not fail to note that every one of these themes is to be found elsewhere in Second Isaiah.

In keeping with this, verse 7 continues immediately with the assertion:

> . . .Kings shall see and stand up,
> Princes, and they shall prostrate themselves. . .

---

[1] This section is a somewhat reworked version of my article "*Israel* in Isa. XLIX, 3: a Problem in the Methodology of Textual Criticism," written for the Sukenik Memorial Volume, *Eretz-Israel*, 7 (5725/1965).

i.e., the whole world will recognize God's unprecedented victory
in behalf of His exalted people Israel.

C. 50.4-9

(4) אֲדֹנָי יהוה נָתַן לִי לְשׁוֹן לִמּוּדִים
לָדַעַת לָעוּת אֶת־יָעֵף דָּבָר
יָעִיר בַּבֹּקֶר בַּבֹּקֶר יָעִיר לִי אֹזֶן לִשְׁמֹעַ כַּלִּמּוּדִים:

(5) אֲדֹנָי יהוה פָּתַח־לִי אֹזֶן
וְאָנֹכִי לֹא מָרִיתִי אָחוֹר לֹא נְסוּגֹתִי:

(6) גֵּוִי נָתַתִּי לְמַכִּים וּלְחָיַי לְמֹרְטִים
פָּנַי לֹא הִסְתַּרְתִּי מִכְּלִמּוֹת וָרֹק:

(7) וַאדֹנָי יהוה יַעֲזָר־לִי עַל־כֵּן לֹא נִכְלָמְתִּי
עַל־כֵּן שַׂמְתִּי פָנַי כַּחַלָּמִישׁ וָאֵדַע כִּי־לֹא אֵבוֹשׁ:

(8) קָרוֹב מַצְדִּיקִי מִי־יָרִיב אִתִּי נַעַמְדָה יָחַד
מִי־בַעַל מִשְׁפָּטִי יִגַּשׁ אֵלָי:

(9) הֵן אֲדֹנָי יהוה יַעֲזָר־לִי מִי־הוּא יַרְשִׁיעֵנִי
הֵן כֻּלָּם כַּבֶּגֶד יִבְלוּ עָשׁ יֹאכְלֵם:

Allowing for the difficulties in v. 4, this section may be rendered:

(4) The Lord God gave me the tongue of the instructed,
To know how to speak timely words to the weary.
Morning by morning, He rouses,
He rouses my ear
To give heed like the instructed ones.
(5) The Lord God opened my ears
And I did not disobey,
I did not run away.
(6) I offered my back to the floggers
And my cheeks to those who tore out the hair.
I did not hide my face
From insult and spittle.
(7) But the Lord God will help me,
Therefore I feel no disgrace;
Therefore I have set my face like flint,
And I know I shall not be shamed.
(8) My Vindicator is at hand—
Who dare contend with me?
Let us stand up together!
Who is my opponent?
Let him approach me!

(9) Lo, the Lord God will help me—
Who can put me in the wrong?
They shall all wear out like a garment,
The moth shall consume them.

The vast majority of scholars limit this section to vv. 4-9, though the term *'ebed* does not occur here; ironically, it appears just outside the section, in v. 10. It is doubtful that anyone would have designated this an *'ebed* section were it not for the fact that vv. 6 ff. deal with the suffering of the speaker; and "suffering," as we saw above, is precisely what theologians and scholars have—gratuitously—attributed especially to Second Isaiah, turning him into the "Suffering Servant" par excellence.

Actually, of course, the entire chapter, no less than chapters 49 preceding and 51 following, constitutes a statement by the prophet himself (he is the *'abdô* in v. 10 [1])) in which he rebukes his fellow Judean exiles for not having more faith than they do in God's determination and ability to deliver them from exile and to restore them to a rebuilt Jerusalem and Judah. In this connection, he laments (vv.4-9), as other spokesmen of God have lamented—e.g., Moses, Elijah, Amos, Jeremiah, Ezekiel—his trials and tribulations, brought on by his own people's stubborness and hostility, and at the same time he expresses his faith in God and his determination to persevere in his mission to his hapless brothers in exile until its successful completion. Verses 10-11; 51.1-3, 4-6, 7-8, 9-11, etc., are all exhortations by the prophet to his own people to heed his divinely inspired words.

Some scholars (e.g., LINDBLOM, p. 32; ZIMMERLI[-JEREMIAS], p. 31) refer to this section of vv. 4-9, as to similar passages in Jeremiah, as "confessions." But such post-biblical concepts and terminology, with their own theological overtones, should be avoided for the biblical period; thus the discussion of "Confession" (by WARREN A. QUAN-BECK) in *Interpreter's Dictionary of the Bible*, 1 (1962), 667a-668b, offers

---

[1]) Isa. 50.10

מִי בָכֶם יְרֵא יהוה שֹׁמֵעַ בְּקוֹל עַבְדּוֹ
אֲשֶׁר הָלַךְ חֲשֵׁכִים וְאֵין נֹגַהּ לוֹ
יִבְטַח בְּשֵׁם יהוה וְיִשָּׁעֵן בֵּאלֹהָיו:

Who among you reveres the Lord,
Heeds the voice of His servant?
Though he has walked in darkness
And had no light,
Let him trust in the name of the Lord.
And rely upon His God.

four books as "Bibliography," all four revolving about early Christianity. The Jewish view revolved about "Confession of Sin" (*Jewish Encyclopedia*, IV, 217b-219b); there is no confession of sin, or prayer, in our section. By the same token, the common term "Lieder"/ "Songs" ought to be shunned; our passages and sections are anything but "Songs," and it would have occurred to no one to designate passages such as ours as "Songs" had it not been for the Christian aura that was cast upon them.

It would not be easy for scholars in other fields of humanistic research to believe that such "methodology" is still widely prevalent in biblical research. Thus NORTH (*The Suffering Servant*, etc., 146 f.) sees our section "as it were, the Gethsemane of the Servant," so that the Hebrew text of the sixth century B.C. is explained in the light of a twentieth century A.D. interpretation of a first century A.D. event! (In his commentary on *The Second Isaiah*, our section is given the heading, p. 201, "THE GETHSEMANE OF THE SERVANT.") The same procedure was followed in a recent article on "The Anonymity of the Suffering Servant" by W. M. W. ROTH (*Journal of Biblical Literature*, 83 [1964], 171-179)—except that the unscholarly principle of *obscurum per obscurius* was also followed: Jesus intentionally left his "Beloved Disciple" anonymous, and just so did Second Isaiah treat his *'ebed*. Or cf. LINDHAGEN, "The Servant of the Lord" (*Expository Times*, 67 [1955-56], 279-283, 300-302), p. 302, ". . .We may venture to believe that in the purpose of God the Servant-Songs were primarily intended to afford guidance to Jesus"; there isn't very much that a scholar *qua* scholar can say in the face of such a statement.

It is interesting how a "collectivist" like TORREY dealt with our section. First of all, the reader of his commentary is told (p. 389) that "Verse 10 is the *résumé* of verses 4-9, and verse 11 of verses 1-3, and there is certainly no obscurity in the mutual relation of these two! It is not easy to see how this device could be improved upon." But apart from this bland assurance of "certainly no obscurity"—for what kind of a "device (not to be) improved upon" is it to have vv. 1-3 summarized by v. 11, and vv. 4-9 by v. 10?!—it is no accident that his so-called *'ebed* section is not dealt with here in its proper place, but the reader is told (at v. 5, p. 392): "On the general meaning of this and the following verses, see the introduction to 52: 13-53: 12, and the chapter on the Servant." However, in these two other sections (respectively pp. 409 ff. and 135 ff.) our own section is not analyzed as a unit at all; either a single verse or two is treated out of context—so that, e.g.,

50.5-6 (really only v. 6: "I offered my back to the floggers And my cheeks to those who tore out the hair. I did not hide my face From insult and spittle") is made by TORREY (p. 413) to "approach very nearly" (it is not easy to believe this!) the idea of "vicarious atonement"—or else sweeping allusion is made to our section as a whole. On p. 140 TORREY talks of "certainly a *collective* designation (of the *'Ebed Yahwè*) in chapters 50 and 53. . ."; on the very next page this becomes "In 50: 4-9 the Servant seems to be Israel's better self, the *repentant* nation as it should be and might be, listening to Yahwè's instruction. . ."; and on p. 147 we read, "The Messianic leader, who stands at Yahwè's right hand. . .must be the *'righteous Servant,'* endowed with God's own spirit. . .an example of gentleness and humility (42: 2, 50: 4 ff., 61: 1); ὁ δίκαιος of Acts 7: 52. . ." The interested and uncritical theologian of two thousand years ago could hardly have improved on this kind of eisegesis.

D. 53.1-12

We saw above (chap. III, § *A*) that there is insufficient reason for regarding 52.13-53.12 as a unit; it is more likely that 53.1-12 is to be treated separately from 52.13-15, the latter dealing with Israel and the former with an individual person (see chap. III, § *B*). On this division, the section that includes the term *'ebed* deals with Israel, whereas the section that lacks the term deals with an individual. The identical situation obtains also in the third of the four so-called *'ebed* sections (§ *C*. 50.4-9 immediately above); there the *'ebed* section deals with an individual and lacks the term *'ebed*, whereas v. 10 immediately following, outside the *'ebed* section, contains the term *'ebed* and deals with Israel.

Is it possible to identify the individual in chapter 53? Once it is realized that the person in 53 did not die but would live to see grandchildren (see Chap. III, § *D*), that his career was essentially the same as that of so many other prophets in the Bible (see Chap. III, § *C*)—indeed 50.4-9 supplies a good parallel to this— and that he suffered (but not vicariously!) at the hands of the very Israelites to whom he was sent by God to admonish and persuade, then it is only natural that it is our prophet himself, Second Isaiah, who is that person. For a restored exile and homeland are precisely what the prophet—facing insult and perhaps even physical violence—came to announce and what he would see achieved, he himself enjoying some of that restoration.

The career of no other such spokesman of God, say Jeremiah or

Moses, fits the picture. Nor is there sufficient reason for abandoning, and avoiding responsibility for, the problem by describing this person as one utterly unknown to us, the "Great Unknown." [1]) Why should this person be different from all other persons in Second Isaiah? Put differently: would any scholar have thought of treating chapter 53 differently from all other chapters in Second Isaiah had it not been for the very much later theological atmosphere created for it in Christanity? This is borne out particularly clearly by the well-known passage in the Book of Acts, chap. 8. We read there (reproducing the Revised Standard Version):

(1) ...And on that day a great persecution arose against the church in Jerusalem; and they were all scattered throughout the region of Judea and Samaria, except the apostles...(4) Now those who were scattered went about preaching the word. (5) Philip went down to a city of Samaria, and proclaimed to them the Christ...(26) But an angel of the Lord said to Philip, "Rise and go...to the road that goes down from Jerusalem to Gaza"...(27) And he rose and went. And behold, an Ethiopian, a eunuch, a minister of Candace the queen of the Ethiopians, in charge of all her treasure, had come to Jerusalem to worship (28) and he was returning; seated in his chariot, he was reading the prophet Isaiah. (29) And the Spirit said to Philip, "Go up and join this chariot." (30) So Philip ran to him, and heard him reading Isaiah the prophet, and asked, "Do you understand what you are reading?" (31) And he said, "How can I, unless some one guides me?" And he invited Philip to come up and sit with him. (32) Now the passage of the scripture which he was reading was this:

"As a sheep led to the slaughter
or a lamb before its shearer is dumb,
so he opens not his mouth.
(33) In his humiliation justice was denied him.
Who can describe his generation?
For his life is taken up from the earth." [Isaiah 53.7-8]

(34) And the eunuch said to Philip, "About whom, pray, does the prophet say this, about himself or about some one else?" (35) Then

---

[1]) For some recent literature along these lines see EISSFELDT, *The Old Testament: An Introduction* (1965), 330 ff. (pp. 448 ff. in the 3rd German edition of his *Einleitung*).

Philip opened his mouth, and beginning with this scripture he told him the good news of Jesus.

It is clear that the central personage of Isaiah 53 was naturally identified with the prophet himself; [1] it was only "supernaturally," through forced interpretation and alien eisegesis, that the simple, forthright exegesis of the chapter came to be perverted.

E. The Term 'Ebed in Second Isaiah

In recapitulation, this is what emerges from our analysis of 'ebed in Isaiah 40-55. The noun 'ebed in all its forms is found a total of 21 times; this does not include the two verb forms in 43.23, 24 (הֶעֱבַדְתַּנִי and הֶעֱבַדְתִּיךָ).

(1) In 10 of these 21 instances, the reference is clearly to the people Israel: 41.8, 9; 43.10; 44.1, 2, 21 (bis); 45.4; 48.20; 49.7. In 2 additional instances, both in 42.19 (I am not certain that the preserved text is original; 44.26 would suggest some reasonable emendation), the reference must be to Israel in exile (cf. verses 15, 18, 20; 43.8). In 52.13 (see Chap. III, § A) the 'ebed is likewise Israel. And, finally, in 54.17, the plural form, "(Such is the lot of) the servants/'abdé (of the Lord, Such their triumph through Me—declares the Lord)," refers to God's loyal Israelites. So that a total of 14 instances of 'ebed is to be associated with Israel.

(2) In 6 passages the 'ebed refers to the prophet himself, to Second Isaiah: 42.1; 49.3 (see § B above), 5, 6; 50.10; 53.11 (see Chap. III, § A).

(3) One passage remains. In 44.26, 'ebed refers to Second Isaiah if the preserved text is retained:

מֵקִים דְּבַר עַבְדּוֹ וַעֲצַת מַלְאָכָיו יַשְׁלִים
הָאֹמֵר לִירוּשָׁלַם תּוּשָׁב וּלְעָרֵי יְהוּדָה תִּבָּנֶינָה וְחָרְבוֹתֶיהָ אֲקוֹמֵם:

(24) Thus said the Lord. . .I am the Lord. . .
(26) Who fulfills the words of His servant

---

[1] It is scarcely necessary to note here that the Ethiopian eunuch was made to add "or about some one else" to his query to Philip, "About whom, pray, does the prophet say this, about himself?" because Philip was ready with "the good news of Jesus." On the Hellenistic, non-biblical origin of the "suffering servant" idea, see chap. III, § F. HEINZ A. FISCHEL has published a useful survey of "Die Deuterojesajanischen Gottesknechtlieder in der juedischen Auslegung" in *Hebrew Union College Annual*, 18 (1944), 53-73 (with a chart on pp. 74-76).

And carries out the message of His messengers;
Who says of Jerusalem, "She shall be inhabited,"
And of the cities of Judah, "They shall be rebuilt.
I will restore its ruins."

· Many scholars, however—and I agree with them—would read עֲבָדָ(י)ו in place of preserved עַבְדּוֹ. The change is not only plausible *per se* but accords well with παιδῶν in Codex Alexandrinus, עַבְדּוֹהִי צַדִּיקַיָּא in the Targum, and parallel מַלְאָכָיו. The "servants" would then be the earlier prophets and spokesmen of God to His people Israel. (CROSS, p. 277, n. 20, would see in "His servants," as in Job 4.18, "the heavenly attendants of Yahweh.") TORREY, on the other hand, who insists on finding the Messiah (with capital "M") here, suppresses altogether the evidence for עֲבָדָ(י)ו, emends מַלְאָכָיו to singular מַלְאָכוֹ on the basis of 42.19, and identifies עַבְדּוֹ with the Messiah.[1]

---

[1] TORREY (p. 357, at 45.1) has gone so far as to suggest—after deleting "Cyrus" in both 44.28 and 45.1—that "The Second Isaiah seems to have been the first to use the term 'Messiah' (משיח) as a designation of the ideal leader of Israel and viceregent of God (*cf.* Ps. 2: 2). Fortunately, we know from another passage whom the poet intended by the title, for in 61: 1 the Servant introduces himself with the words, 'the Lord hath *anointed* me.' " The contextual justification for these sweeping declarations is hardly apparent.

TORREY has devoted an entire chapter (VIII) to "The 'Servant' and the Messiah" (pp. 135-150). The reader will seek in vain even an attempt to prove that the Hebrew Bible knew of a superhuman Messiah. By the same token, many scholars talk freely of a "Messiah-King" with whom they identify Second Isaiah's *'ebed* (cf. n. 70 in ZIMMERLI [-JEREMIAS], p. 25); but the concept is entirely foreign to the Old Testament, and its origins are to be sought, rather, in early Christianity. The Bible knows of kings, priests, prophets, and objects that are anointed, but it does not know of a "Messiah-King" or "Messiah-Priest" or "Messiah-Prophet" or "Messiah-Object" (e.g., pillar, tabernacle, vessels).

FOAKES JACKSON-LAKE put it this way (pp. 362 f.), ". . .The point in the previous discussion most important for the investigation of early Christianity is that 'Messiah' is essentially an adjective meaning consecrated or appointed by God, and was not the prerogative title of any single person until later than the time of Christ. . .It therefore follows that though the title was undoubtedly applied by his disciples to Jesus, their meaning must be sought from the context in which the word is used rather than from its established significance. . ." And in vol. II (1922), p. 199, they wrote, ". . .the interpretation of the figure of the Servant of the Lord in Isaiah as a reference to the Messiah is markedly characteristic of Luke and is not found in Paul, although one would have supposed that, had he known it, Paul would certainly have made use of it to support his soteriological arguments." And cf. the cogent analysis by MORNA HOOKER.

ERNST JENNI has a useful, sober article on "Messiah, Jewish" in *Interpreter's Dictionary of the Bible*, III (1962), 360a-365b; on p. 363b he writes, "As in Amos,

In fine, every clear context of the 21 occurrences of *ʿebed* in Second Isaiah points either to the people Israel or to Second Isaiah himself as that *ʿebed*. (Parenthetically, not even Cyrus, whether or not the term "Cyrus" is a later gloss in 44.28 and 45.1 and whether or not he was ever intended elsewhere in Second Isaiah, is ever designated as an *ʿebed* of God).

Zephaniah, and other prophets, we find in Deutero-Isaiah (Isa. 40-55) no expectation of a Messiah. . .''; and on pp. 360b-361a he asserts, "Only in NT times is there evidence of the 'anointed one' (מָשִׁיחַ; Aram. מְשִׁיחָא; χριστός) as one of the various designations for the eschatological king. . .''

APPENDIX

"A LIGHT OF NATIONS" (אוֹר גּוֹיִם)—
"A COVENANT OF PEOPLE" (בְּרִית עָם) [1])

[This analysis is a reworked version of my article "A Light of the Nations: A Problem in Biblical Theology," written for the 75th Anniversary Volume of *Jewish Quarterly Review* (1966). It was read originally before the Middle-Atlantic States Section of the Society of Biblical Literature, New York, April 4, 1965, under the title, "I Will Make You a Light of Nations."]

A

It has long been axiomatic among biblical scholars that when Second Isaiah used the expression (49.6) וּנְתַתִּיךָ לְאוֹר גּוֹיִם "I will make you a light of nations" (or cf. 42.6, וְאֶתֶּנְךָ לִבְרִית עָם לְאוֹר גּוֹיִם , "I will make you a covenant of people, a light of nations"), he meant that he, the prophet, would serve as God's servant not only to restore the Judean captivity to its homeland but also to bring light and redemption to the heathen nations of the world.

TORREY *The Second Isaiah*, 380 ff., has put it as eloquently and clearly as anyone: "This chapter may well occupy the central place in the book. . .It thus affords an excellent starting point for the study of (the prophet's) ideas in regard to the Servant, the 'restoration,' the conversion of the heathen nations, and the final status of the Jews and Gentiles in God's kingdom. . .The 'rescue' which had been promised to Israel, and which was the Servant's first mission (verses 5, 6) is to include the Gentiles as well; even the most remote nations are to be gathered in." JAMES SMART, "A New Approach to the 'Ebed-Yahweh Problem" (*Expository Times*, 45 [1933-34], 168a-172b)—one of the all too few analyses that breathes freshness and independence in the midst of stale and rehashed discussions—and KISSANE, *The Book of Isaiah*, vol. II, pp. 37, 128, interpret similarly.

On the other hand, SNAITH—who has long stood alone in his "nationalistic" interpretation of "The Servant of the Lord in Deutero-

---

[1]) See chapter IV, § 1 b.

Isaiah" (in *Studies in Old Testament Prophecy* [the Theodore H. Robinson Volume], ed. H. H. ROWLEY, 1950, 187-200)—put it this way (p. 198): "But it is far too small a thing to bring back all the Babylonian exiles (the tribes of Jacob and the preserved of Israel). The servant's mission is to be 'a light of Gentiles,' i.e., a light throughout all the Gentile lands 'that my salvation may be to the end of the earth,' i.e., my salvation of Israel, since this is the only salvation in which the prophet is interested. The servant will be a light to guide every Israelite wanderer home. His mission is to gather in all exiles wherever they may be scattered." SNAITH received considerable support from DE BOER's independent researches on *Second-Isaiah's Message* (1956), in the chapter (V) on "The Limits of Second-Isaiah's Message" (p. 94: "SNAITH observed rightly that the servant's mission is limited to his own people"). On p. 90 he asserted, "No other conclusion can be drawn from our texts than the statement: Second-Isaiah's only purpose is to proclaim deliverance for the Judean people. . ."; and he rendered 42.6b (pp. 9, 84), "(I, Yhwh . .) put you to a consolidation of the people, a light respected by the nations" (and cf. 92, "The renewed people will be set as a light, openly seen and respected among the nations לאור גוים, xlii 6; לאור עמים, li 4"). By ברית עם DE BOER understands (p. 94) ". . .the consolidation of the people after a period of disintegration."

But LINDBLOM, *The Servant Songs*, etc. (1951)—a fine antidote to some of the studies on this subject that have emanated from his Scandinavian colleagues—took issue with SNAITH (p. 27, n. 29). He would agree with the general view that (p. 26) "In this critical moment the prophet received a new revelation from Yahweh: he was told that he had been set apart to be a light to the nations, that is to say: he was to perform a missionary task in order that the Gentiles might be saved. The future of Israel is for the moment left out of consideration, the chief stress being laid on the new task in relation to the Gentiles. . ." This conventional view may be found also, e.g., in NORTH, *The Suffering Servant*, etc., 143 ff.; or in ZIMMERLI-JEREMIAS, *The Servant of God*, 29 f., ". . .the servant will be a light for the whole earth. His activity. . .glorifies the sole honour of Yahweh and thus becomes the light and salvation of the whole world"; or BLANK, *Prophetic Faith in Isaiah* (1958), 110 f. (and n. 85 on p. 221), 143 (and n. 4 on p. 223), and 157 (and n. 26 on p. 223).

On the generally accepted view, than, the prophet's message is one of internationalism, and on an unusually high level, a level that has not been achieved—for that matter, not even attempted—by any people in history. There is good reason, however, to believe that nothing of the sort was meant by the author; indeed, it is our contention that the prophet was here, as elsewhere in his argument (cf., e.g., chap. III, § *B*), utterly nationalistic, and that the concept of internationalism was only later, over half a millennium later—after Jesus and his contemporaries had come and gone—read back into our passage and into Second Isaiah as a whole. In this, our prophet stood four-square in the biblical tradition,[1]) even if thus he disappoints modern scholars and theologians who would see in his statements the *Weltanschauung* of our own Twentieth Century supporters of the League of Nations and the United Nations.

Let us deal here with the terms אוֹר גּוֹיִם and בְּרִית עָם in context, both the literary and historical context.

B

In 49.1 ff. (for the argument in detail, see chap. IV, § *B* above) the prophet proclaims to the whole world the fact that God has designated him from the outset as His spokesman to Israel, for the purpose of leading his fellow Judean exiles back to God. Up to this point, however, the prophet had labored in vain, for the condition of his fellow exiles had not changed. But now a new era was to begin: not only had God designated the prophet as His servant to restore His people to their homeland but, in addition, He would make him "a light of nations," with God's victory becoming a world phenomenon.

If one ignores what precedes and what follows this last assertion of verse 6 (לִהְיוֹת יְשׁוּעָתִי עַד־קְצֵה הָאָרֶץ:), "That My triumph [2]) may

---

[1]) I have in mind such passages as Lev. 19.18, "You shall love your neighbor as yourself," where "your neighbor" is simply "your fellow Israelite, countryman"; or Mal. 2.10, "Have we not all one Father? Did not one God create us?. . .," where it is not at all the heathern nations that are associated with Israel—as scholars have perverted the context to indicate—but where the priests and levites on the one hand, and the Israelite commoner on the other, are involved. Also, e.g., Amos 9.7; Zech. 2.14-16; Isa. 14.1-2; 19.18-25; 56.3-8; 66.18-24; Ps. 24—all of which I have dicussed either in chap. III, § **B** above or in my article on "Who Is the Ideal Jew: The Biblical View" in *Judaism*, 13 (Winter Issue; 1964), 19-28 (from the Hebrew original מִי יַעֲלָה בהר ה',pp. 521-528 in the David Ben-Gurion Jubilee Volume, עֹז לדוד ,קובץ מחקרים בתנ'׳ך מוגש לדוד בן גוריון למלאת בו שבעים ושבע שנים ה׳תשכ׳׳ד ירושלים); and cf. the section on "Particularism and Universality in the Teachings of the Prophets" in my *Ancient Israel*, pp. 163 ff.

[2]) Hebrew יְשׁוּעָה is best rendered "triumph, victory, vindication." Traditional "salvation" has become quite misleading with its almost wholly post-biblical theological overtones and associations.

reach to the ends of the earth"), then, I suppose, it is possible to assert
that the prophet was to bring God's teachings to the heathen nations
and therby afford the entire world the rewards that derived from
acknowledging Him as their Deity; and this is—as stated above—
exactly what has been universally asserted. But this view is precluded
by the context itself. For not only does verse 5a state that God had
destined the prophet from birth to be His servant for the purpose of
restoring His people Israel (וְעַתָּה אָמַר יהוה יֹצְרִי מִבֶּטֶן לוֹ לְשׁוֹבֵב יַעֲקֹב אֵלָיו
וְיִשְׂרָאֵל לוֹ [= Q ; לֹא = K] יֵאָסֵף, "And now the Lord has declared
—Who formed me from the womb to be His servant—That He will
bring Jacob back to Him, That Israel shall be gathered to Him"),
but verse 7 no less clearly expresses what may be termed the other side
of one and the same coin, viz.:

> Thus said the Lord,
> Redeemer (and) Holy One of Israel,
> To (or: Concerning) the one [1] despised by men,
> Abhorred by nations,
> The slave of rulers:
> Kings shall see and stand up,
> Princes, and they shall prostrate themselves—
> Because of the Lord, who is faithful,
> The Holy One of Israel, who has chosen you.[2]

In other words, far from bringing "salvation" to the heathen nations,
the prophet's task in the service of the Lord is to lead exiled Israel to
redemption and thereby cause the nations and their leaders—who
until then held the exiles in contempt—to acknowledge abjectly the
omnipotence of Israel's faithful God. And the prophet continues
(vv. 8-9, 13):

> (8) Thus said the Lord:
> In a time of favor I have answered you,

---

[1] Israel in exile is clearly meant here. Note that whenever a major category
such as "nations," "peoples," "ends of the earth," "ruler," "kings," "potentates,"
"princes," and the like is employed in Second Isaiah, the counterpart is "Israel";
see chap. III, § B above, where mention is made also of the hyperbolic use of these
and other terms in relation to Israel.

[2] 49.7

כֹּה אָמַר־יהוה גֹּאֵל יִשְׂרָאֵל קְדוֹשׁוֹ
לִבְזֹה־נֶפֶשׁ לִמְתָעֵב גּוֹי לְעֶבֶד מֹשְׁלִים
מְלָכִים יִרְאוּ וָקָמוּ שָׂרִים וְיִשְׁתַּחֲוּוּ
לְמַעַן יהוה אֲשֶׁר נֶאֱמָן קְדֹשׁ יִשְׂרָאֵל וַיִּבְחָרֶךָ׃

In a day of triumph I have helped you;
I have kept you
And I have made you a covenant of people,[1]
To restore the land,
To allot the waste heritages,
(9) To say to the prisoners,[2] "Go free!"
To those in darkness, "Show yourselves!". . .

(13) Sing, O heavens,
Exult, O earth,
Break forth into song, O mountains!
For the Lord has comforted His people,
Will have compassion on His afflicted ones.[3]

One could readily go on in this vein, not only for the rest of the chapter but throughout Second Isaiah, citing chapter and verse in every instance, to show the comfort that Israel in exile would receive from the Lord, in sharp contradistinction to the treatment that the heathen nations would receive in the process. In the light of the data offered above in chapters III and IV, the following quotation from the last five verses of our chapter will suffice here (vv. 22-26):

(22) Thus said the Lord God:
I will raise My hand to nations
And lift up My standard to peoples;
And they shall bring your sons in their bosoms,
And carry your daughters on their shoulders.
(23) Kings shall be your attendants,
Their queens shall serve you as nurses.

---

[1] For the expression וְאֶתֶּנְךָ לִבְרִית עָם see § E below.

[2] Such expressions as "prisoners," "those (who dwell) in darkness," and "the blind" always refer in Second Isaiah to Israel in exile; see chap. III, § B.

[3] 49.8-9, 13

(8) כֹּה אָמַר יהוה
בְּעֵת רָצוֹן עֲנִיתִיךָ וּבְיוֹם יְשׁוּעָה עֲזַרְתִּיךָ
וְאֶצָּרְךָ וְאֶתֶּנְךָ לִבְרִית עָם
לְהָקִים אֶרֶץ לְהַנְחִיל נְחָלוֹת שֹׁמֵמוֹת:
(9) לֵאמֹר לַאֲסוּרִים צֵאוּ לַאֲשֶׁר בַּחֹשֶׁךְ הִגָּלוּ
עַל־דְּרָכִים יִרְעוּ וּבְכָל־שְׁפָיִים מַרְעִיתָם
(13) רָנּוּ שָׁמַיִם וְגִילִי אֶרֶץ וּפִצְחוּ הָרִים רִנָּה
כִּי־נִחַם יהוה עַמּוֹ וַעֲנִיָּו יְרַחֵם:

They shall bow to you, face to the ground,
And lick the dust of your feet.

(26) I will make your oppressors eat their own flesh,
They shall be drunk with their own blood as with wine.
And mankind shall know
That I the Lord am your savior,
The Mighty One of Jacob, your redeemer.[1])

In fine, it is but eisegesis—the clear perversion of the original and
plain meaning of the text—to make the prophet as "a light of nations"
mean that Israel was in exile in order to bring redemption to the world.
In point of fact, Israel was in exile only because she had transgressed
her covenant with the Lord, and she would be restored because—the
prophet maintained, as all the prophets did—God would never cast
her off.

C

Our expression "a light of nations" occurs also in 42.6. The prophet begins with the assertion (vv. 1-5) that God, creator of the world
and author of all life on it, has decided that the time has come for His
servant [2]) to execute His judgment throughout the world. In the words
of the prophet (vv. 5-6):

(5) Thus said God the Lord,
Who created the heavens and stretched them out,

---

[1]) 49.22-26

(22) כֹּה־אָמַר אֲדֹנָי יהוה
הִנֵּה אֶשָּׂא אֶל־גּוֹיִם יָדִי וְאֶל־עַמִּים אָרִים נִסִּי
וְהֵבִיאוּ בָנַיִךְ בְּחֹצֶן וּבְנֹתַיִךְ עַל־כָּתֵף תִּנָּשֶׂאנָה:
(23) וְהָיוּ מְלָכִים אֹמְנַיִךְ וְשָׂרוֹתֵיהֶם מֵינִיקֹתַיִךְ
אַפַּיִם אֶרֶץ יִשְׁתַּחֲווּ לָךְ וַעֲפַר רַגְלַיִךְ יְלַחֵכוּ
וְיָדַעַתְּ כִּי־אֲנִי יהוה אֲשֶׁר לֹא־יֵבֹשׁוּ קֹוָי:
(24) הֲיֻקַּח מִגִּבּוֹר מַלְקוֹחַ וְאִם־שְׁבִי צַדִּיק יִמָּלֵט:
(25) כִּי־כֹה אָמַר יהוה
גַּם־שְׁבִי גִבּוֹר יֻקָּח וּמַלְקוֹחַ עָרִיץ יִמָּלֵט
וְאֶת־יְרִיבֵךְ אָנֹכִי אָרִיב וְאֶת־בָּנַיִךְ אָנֹכִי אוֹשִׁיעַ:
(26) וְהַאֲכַלְתִּי אֶת־מוֹנַיִךְ אֶת־בְּשָׂרָם וְכֶעָסִיס דָּמָם יִשְׁכָּרוּן
וְיָדְעוּ כָל־בָּשָׂר כִּי אֲנִי יהוה מוֹשִׁיעֵךְ וְגֹאֲלֵךְ אֲבִיר יַעֲקֹב:

[2]) I have argued above (chap. IV, § A) that the servant in 42.1 ff. is the prophet
himself (as against, e.g., Cyrus). However, our analysis of the expression "a
light of nations" is not affected by this problem.

Who spread out the earth and what it brings forth,
Who gave breath to the people upon it
And life to those who walk on it:
(6) I the Lord have summoned you for triumph;
I have grasped you by the hand,
Have guarded you and made you
A covenant of (a) people, a light of nations

(וְאֶצָּרְךָ וְאֶתֶּנְךָ לִבְרִית עָם לְאוֹר גּוֹיִם: ···).[1]

Once again, as in 49.6 (§ **B** above), if this passage is isolated from
the context of chapters 40-55 as a whole and from the verses immediately following in particular, one may, I suppose, agree with the
virtually unanimous opinion of scholars that God had summoned His
servant in order to achieve a covenant of all nations. Unfortunately for
this—albeit universally held—view, it is flatly precluded by the verse
immediately following (v. 7), one which is connected with it most in-
timately syntactically. For our prophet proceeds at once to assert
vigorously and unequivocally that the function of God's servant is

To open the eyes of the blind,
To set free prisoners from confinement,
From the dungeon those who sit in darkness.

i.e., to liberate from captivity His people Israel. And it is scarcely
necessary to add that—again as in the case of 49.6 ff. (§ **B** above)—the
rest of the chapter, and what follows thereafter, is essentially but an
elaboration of this theme; cf., e.g., vv. 8 and 13:

(8) I am the Lord, that is My name;
I will not yield My glory to another,
My renown to idols.
(13) The Lord goes forth like a warrior,
Like a fighter He whips up His rage;
He yells, He roars aloud,
He charges upon His enemies.[1]

Or finally, contrast v. 16, which describes God's restoration of exiled

---

[1] For the entire Hebrew text of this section, see chap. IV, § A, p. 75.
[2] 42.8, 13

(8) אֲנִי יהוה הוּא שְׁמִי וּכְבוֹדִי לְאַחֵר לֹא־אֶתֵּן וּתְהִלָּתִי לַפְּסִילִים:
(13) יהוה כַּגִּבּוֹר יֵצֵא כְּאִישׁ מִלְחָמוֹת יָעִיר קִנְאָה
יָרִיעַ אַף־יַצְרִיחַ עַל־אֹיְבָיו יִתְגַּבָּר:

Israel, with v. 17, which asserts the utter discomfiture of the heathen nations:

(16) I will lead the blind by a road they did not know,
    I will make them walk by paths they never knew.
    I will turn darkness before thm to light,
    Rough places into level ground.
    These are the promises,
    I will keep them without fail.

(17) Driven back and utterly shamed
    Shall be those who trust in an image,
    Shall be those who say to idols,
    "You are our gods." [1])

D

Isa. 60.1 ff. is pertinent for any discussion of our expression "a light of nations." Thus OTTO A. PIPER, in his article on "Light" in *The Interpreter's Dictionary of the Bible*, III (1962), has observed (p. 131a), "...thus faithful Israel is to become a light for the Gentiles (Isa. 49: 6; 60: 3, 5; 62: 1)." Whether the author of 42.6 and 49.6 was also responsible directly for 60.1 ff. or only indirectly (i.e., the author of 60.1 ff. being influenced by him; cf., e.g., KISSANE, p. 255; LINDBLOM, p. 65 and n. 27) is immaterial at this point.

It should come as no surprise by now to learn that the internationalistic interpretation—read: eisegesis—of scholars to the contrary, the context of chap. 60, exactly as that of chapters 42 and 49, affords no support whatever for the view that Israel was something of a goodwill missionary to the heathen nations; the text of 60.1 ff. declares forthrightly against this:

(1) Arise, shine, for your light has dawned,
    The Presence of the Lord has shone upon you!

(2) Behold! Darkness shall cover the earth,
    And thick clouds the peoples;

---

[1]) 42.16-17

(16) וְהוֹלַכְתִּי עִוְרִים בְּדֶרֶךְ לֹא יָדָעוּ בִּנְתִיבוֹת לֹא־יָדְעוּ אַדְרִיכֵם
אָשִׂים מַחְשָׁךְ לִפְנֵיהֶם לָאוֹר וּמַעֲקַשִּׁים לְמִישׁוֹר
אֵלֶּה הַדְּבָרִים עֲשִׂיתִם וְלֹא עֲזַבְתִּים:

(17) נָסֹגוּ אָחוֹר יֵבֹשׁוּ בֹשֶׁת הַבֹּטְחִים בַּפֶּסֶל
הָאֹמְרִים לְמַסֵּכָה אַתֶּם אֱלֹהֵינוּ:

But upon you [1]) the Lord will shine,
And His Presence over you be seen.

(3) And nations shall walk by your light,
Kings, by your shining radiance.

(4) Raise your eyes and look about:
They are gathered all, they come to you;
Your sons shall come from afar,
Your daughters shall be carried on their shoulders.[2])

(5) As you behold, you will glow:
Your heart will throb and thrill—
For the sea's abundance shall pass on to you,
The wealth of nations shall flow to you.

(6) Trains of camels shall cover you,
Dromedaries of Midian and Ephah—
All of them coming from Sheba...

---

[1]) Note the sharp antithesis syntactically between (כִּי־הִנֵּה הַחֹשֶׁךְ יְכַסֶּה־אֶרֶץ) וַעֲרָפֶל לְאֻמִּים in the first part of the verse and (יִזְרַח־יהוה) וְעָלַיִךְ in this second half.

[2]) It need scarcely be noted here that it is the "nations...kings" in verse 3 immediately preceding who will do the carrying; that is why they are mentioned in the first place.

In this connection it may be noted that preserved (בָּנַיִךְ מֵרָחוֹק) יָבֹאוּ probably harbors original יָבִיאוּ, "they (viz., "the nations...kings"/מְלָכִים ... גּוֹיִם in v. 3) shall bring (your sons from afar)." Our vv. 3-4 recall at once v. 9 below ("to bring"/לְהָבִיא), and 43.5-6 (where God addresses Israel in captivity; the Hebrew text may be found in chap. III above, p. 45, n. 1):

(5) Fear not, for I am with you:
I will bring (אָבִיא) your seed from the east,

And I will gather you from the west;

(6) I will say to the north, "Give up!"
And to the south, "Hold not back!"
Bring (הָבִיאִי) My sons from afar

And My daughters from the ends of the earth.

and 49.18, 22 f.:

(19) Look up all around you and see:
They are all assembled, are come to you!...

(22) Thus said the Lord God:
I will raise My hand to nations
And lift up My ensign to peoples;
And they shall bring (וְהֵבִיאוּ) their sons in their bosoms,

And carry their daughters on their shoulders.

(23) Kings shall be your attendants,
Their queens shall serve you as nurses...

(7) All the flocks of Kedar shall be assembled for you,
    The rams of Nebaioth shall serve your needs. . .

(9) Behold the coastlands await Me,
    With Tarshish-ships in the lead,
    To bring your sons from afar
    And their silver and gold as well. . .

(10) Aliens shall rebuild your walls,
    Their kings shall wait upon you—
    For in anger I struck you down,
    But in favor I take you back.

(11) Your gates shall always stay open,
    Day and night they shall never be shut,
    To let in the wealth of nations,
    With their kings conveying it.

(12) For the nation or the kingdom
    That shall not serve you shall perish;
    Such nations shall be laid waste. . .

(14) Bowing before you shall come
    The children of those who tormented you;
    Prostrate at the soles of your feet
    Shall be all those who reviled you. . .[1]
        Etc. etc.

---

[1] 60.1-14

(1) קוּמִי אוֹרִי כִּי בָא אוֹרֵךְ וּכְבוֹד יהוה עָלַיִךְ זָרָח:

(2) כִּי־הִנֵּה הַחֹשֶׁךְ יְכַסֶּה־אֶרֶץ וַעֲרָפֶל לְאֻמִּים
    וְעָלַיִךְ יִזְרַח יהוה וּכְבוֹדוֹ עָלַיִךְ יֵרָאֶה:

(3) וְהָלְכוּ גוֹיִם לְאוֹרֵךְ וּמְלָכִים לְנֹגַהּ זַרְחֵךְ:

(4) שְׂאִי־סָבִיב עֵינַיִךְ וּרְאִי כֻּלָּם נִקְבְּצוּ בָאוּ־לָךְ
    בָּנַיִךְ מֵרָחוֹק יָבֹאוּ וּבְנֹתַיִךְ עַל־צַד תֵּאָמַנָה:

(5) אָז תִּרְאִי וְנָהַרְתְּ וּפָחַד וְרָחַב לְבָבֵךְ
    כִּי־יֵהָפֵךְ עָלַיִךְ הֲמוֹן יָם חֵיל גּוֹיִם יָבֹאוּ לָךְ:

(6) שִׁפְעַת גְּמַלִּים תְּכַסֵּךְ בִּכְרֵי מִדְיָן וְעֵיפָה
    כֻּלָּם מִשְּׁבָא יָבֹאוּ זָהָב וּלְבוֹנָה יִשָּׂאוּ
    וּתְהִלֹּת יהוה יְבַשֵּׂרוּ:

(7) כָּל־צֹאן קֵדָר יִקָּבְצוּ לָךְ אֵילֵי נְבָיוֹת יְשָׁרְתוּנֶךְ
    יַעֲלוּ עַל־רָצוֹן מִזְבְּחִי וּבֵית תִּפְאַרְתִּי אֲפָאֵר:

(8) מִי־אֵלֶּה כָּעָב תְּעוּפֶינָה וְכַיּוֹנִים אֶל־אֲרֻבֹּתֵיהֶר:

(9) כִּי־לִי אִיִּים יְקַוּוּ וָאֳנִיּוֹת תַּרְשִׁישׁ בָּרִאשֹׁנָה
    לְהָבִיא בָנַיִךְ מֵרָחוֹק כַּסְפָּם וּזְהָבָם אִתָּם
    לְשֵׁם יהוה אֱלֹהַיִךְ וְלִקְדוֹשׁ יִשְׂרָאֵל כִּי פֵאֲרָךְ:

E

So too, the expression בְּרִית עָם in 42.6 and 49.8, however it be translated, must be understood strictly within the limits of Judean nationalism; the context—the same as that of אוֹר גּוֹיִם—precludes any broader interpretation.

In 42.6 (see § **C** above, p. 103), it will be recalled, the prophet proclaims to his fellow exiles:

> I the Lord have summoned you for triumph,
> I have grasped you by the hand,
> Have guarded you and made you
> A covenant of (a) people, a light of nations
> (וְאֶצָּרְךָ וְאֶתֶּנְךָ לִבְרִית עָם לְאוֹר גּוֹיִם: ··).

Exactly as in the case of "a light of nations," so do the verses that precede and follow our own make it amply clear that Israel alone is to benefit from God's actions; the purpose of the "covenant" is the liberation of captive Israel. As put in verse 7 immediately following:

> To open the eyes of the blind,
> To set free prisoners from confinement,
> From the dungeon those who sit in darkness.

or in verse 16:

> I will lead the blind by a road they did not know,
> I will make them walk by paths they never knew.
> I will turn darkness before them to light,
> Rough places into level ground.
> These are the promises,
> I will keep them without fail.

‏(10) וּבָנוּ בְנֵי־נֵכָר חֹמֹתַיִךְ וּמַלְכֵיהֶם יְשָׁרְתוּנֶךְ
כִּי בְקִצְפִּי הִכִּיתִיךְ וּבִרְצוֹנִי רִחַמְתִּיךְ׃

‏(11) וּפִתְּחוּ שְׁעָרַיִךְ תָּמִיד יוֹמָם וָלַיְלָה לֹא יִסָּגֵרוּ
לְהָבִיא אֵלַיִךְ חֵיל גּוֹיִם וּמַלְכֵיהֶם נְהוּגִים׃

‏(12) כִּי־הַגּוֹי וְהַמַּמְלָכָה אֲשֶׁר לֹא־יַעַבְדוּךְ יֹאבֵדוּ וְהַגּוֹיִם חָרֹב יֶחֱרָבוּ׃

‏(13) כְּבוֹד הַלְּבָנוֹן אֵלַיִךְ יָבוֹא בְּרוֹשׁ תִּדְהָר וּתְאַשּׁוּר יַחְדָּו
לְפָאֵר מְקוֹם מִקְדָּשִׁי וּמְקוֹם רַגְלַי אֲכַבֵּד׃

‏(14) וְהָלְכוּ אֵלַיִךְ שְׁחוֹחַ בְּנֵי מְעַנַּיִךְ וְהִשְׁתַּחֲווּ עַל־כַּפּוֹת רַגְלַיִךְ כָּל־מְנַאֲצָיִךְ
וְקָרְאוּ לָךְ עִיר יהוה צִיּוֹן קְדוֹשׁ יִשְׂרָאֵל׃

The context in 49.8 is identical. As asserted in verse 8-9 (see § **B** above, pp. 100 f.):

 (8) Thus said the Lord:
   In a time of favor I have answered you,
   In a day of triumph I have helped you;
   I have kept you (וְאֶצָּרְךָ)
   And I have made you a covenant of people (וְאֶתֶּנְךָ לִבְרִית עָם)
   To restore the land,
   To allot the waste heritages,
 (9) To say to the prisoners, "Go free!"
   To those in darkness, "Show yourselves!". . .

How much clearer could anyone wish the author to be in explicating וְאֶצָּרְךָ וְאֶתֶּנְךָ לִבְרִית עָם (8aα) than by following immediately (8bβ) with לְהָקִים אֶרֶץ לְהַנְחִיל נְחָלוֹת שֹׁמֵמוֹת, "To restore the land [of Judah, or Israel], To allot the waste heritages"? And note, further, how enthusiastic the prophet waxes in describing the return of the captivity (vv. 9 ff.):

(9) לֵאמֹר לַאֲסוּרִים צֵאוּ לַאֲשֶׁר בַּחֹשֶׁךְ הִגָּלוּ
  עַל־דְּרָכִים יִרְעוּ וּבְכָל־שְׁפָיִים מַרְעִיתָם:
(10) לֹא יִרְעָבוּ וְלֹא יִצְמָאוּ וְלֹא־יַכֵּם שָׁרָב וָשָׁמֶשׁ
  כִּי־מְרַחֲמָם יְנַהֲגֵם וְעַל־מַבּוּעֵי מַיִם יְנַהֲלֵם:
(11) וְשַׂמְתִּי כָל־הָרַי לַדָּרֶךְ וּמְסִלֹּתַי יְרֻמוּן:
(12) הִנֵּה־אֵלֶּה מֵרָחוֹק יָבֹאוּ וְהִנֵּה־אֵלֶּה מִצָּפוֹן וּמִיָּם וְאֵלֶּה מֵאֶרֶץ סִינִים:

reaching a climax in v. 13 with an outburst of joy:

רָנּוּ שָׁמַיִם וְגִילִי אֶרֶץ וּפִצְחוּ הָרִים רִנָּה
  כִּי־נִחַם יהוה עַמּוֹ וַעֲנִיָּו יְרַחֵם:

Or we may read on a verse or two (14-15):

(14) וַתֹּאמַר צִיּוֹן עֲזָבַנִי יהוה וַאדֹנָי שְׁכֵחָנִי:
(15) הֲתִשְׁכַּח אִשָּׁה עוּלָהּ מֵרַחֵם בֶּן־בִּטְנָהּ
  גַּם־אֵלֶּה תִשְׁכַּחְנָה וְאָנֹכִי לֹא אֶשְׁכָּחֵךְ:

But there is hardly need to go on and on in this vein; Second Isaiah is full of it, from beginning (40.1-2, "Comfort, oh comfort My people, Says your God. Speak tenderly to Jerusalem. . .") to end (55.12-13, "Yea, you shall leave [the Babylonian exile] in joy And be led home secure. Before you, mount and hill shall shout aloud, And all the trees of the field shall clap their hands. . .").

The same picture of ברית is painted in chap. 55, where the "eternal covenant" (בְּרִית עוֹלָם) involves God and His people Israel (e.g., vv. 3-5): if only they will heed Him, He will make them an everlasting covenant and fulfill the promise made to David to establish a powerful dynasty of his seed.[1]) And whoever be their author and whatever the source of their influence, the statements in 59.20-21 and 61.9 can only make this theme even more crystal clear. In chap. 59 the prophet addresses himself to purified Israel:

(20) And He [viz., God] will come to Zion as a redeemer,
To those in Jacob who turn from transgression—
Said the Lord.
(21) As for Me, this is My covenant with them,
Said the Lord:
My spirit which is upon you
And My words which I put in your mouth
Shall not depart from your mouth,

---

[1]) 55.3-5

‏(3) הַטּוּ אָזְנְכֶם וּלְכוּ אֵלַי שִׁמְעוּ וּתְחִי נַפְשְׁכֶם
וְאֶכְרְתָה לָכֶם בְּרִית עוֹלָם חַסְדֵי דָוִד הַנֶּאֱמָנִים:
(4) הֵן עֵד לְאוּמִּים נְתַתִּיו נָגִיד וּמְצַוֵּה לְאֻמִּים:
(5) הֵן גּוֹי לֹא־תֵדַע תִּקְרָא וְגוֹי לֹא־יְדָעוּךָ אֵלֶיךָ יָרוּצוּ
לְמַעַן יהוה אֱלֹהֶיךָ וְלִקְדוֹשׁ יִשְׂרָאֵל כִּי פֵאֲרָךְ:

There is, clearly, some hyperbole in vv. 4-5; but scholars generally are not aware of hyperbole, a literary phenomenon that would interfere greatly with theology. I note this statement by LINDBLOM, who is one of the exceedingly few to recognize rhetoric in the Bible (cf., e.g., his chap. IV, "The Use of Figurative Language in Deutero-Isaiah," in *The Servant Songs*, etc.), p. 55, "As king David was a witness (עד) to the peoples, a leader and commander of the nations, Israel will call upon nations it does not know, people who do not know Israel will run unto it, since they have realized the power of Yahweh, the God of Israel. In this passage (LV. 1-5), which deals with the spiritual empire of Israel, we meet with another expression of the idea of ברית עם, the confederation of peoples with Israel as its centre...The idea of the conversion of the Gentiles is common to nearly all oracles of this group." I suspect that the author of our passage and his audience were more realistic, and less concerned about post-biblical theology and messianism and eschatology, than the interpreters of the post-biblical era have been. In the note (15) on his statement, LINDBLOM had asserted (p. 56), "...the expressions in vv. 1-2 seem to me to be entirely metaphorical..." In the first part of this same note (p. 55) LINDBLOM had observed that "In his Commentary BENTZEN says that this is the first occurrence of the invitation to the eschatological Messianic meal"; LINDBLOM surely went far beyond the call of scholarly politeness in limiting his comment on this weird notion to little more than "I cannot agree..." The "Two Prophecies from 520-516 B.C." by JULIAN MORGENSTERN (*Hebrew Union College Annual*, 22 [1949], 365-431) constitute studies of our 55.1-5 and 60.1-3, 5-7.

Or from the mouth of your children and children's children—
Said the Lord—
From now on and forever.[1])

And in 61.8-9—again it is Israel that is addressed:

(8) For I the Lord love justice,
　　I hate robbery and wrong;
　　I will faithfully give them their recompense,
　　And I will make an everalsting covenant (וּבְרִית עוֹלָם)
　　with them.

(9) Their descendants shall be known among the nations,
　　And their offspring among the peoples;
　　All who see them shall acknowledge them,
　　That they are a people whom the Lord has blessed.[2])

The expression (וְאֶתֶּנְךָ לְ) בְּרִית עָם has been variously translated.
The American (Chicago) Translation rendered "(I have made you)
a pledge to the people"; Revised Standard Version "(I have given you
as) a covenant to the people;" La Sainte Bible (Jerusalem Bible)
"(Je t'ai désigné comme) alliance du peuple." Perhaps "a people's
(i.e., national) covenant" was intended. The rendering "a covenant-
people," i.e., a covenanted people, would be acceptable but for the
fact that this idea would more likely have been worded לְעַם בְּרִית in
Biblical Hebrew. On EHRLICH's view there is no problem in the first
place; he emends לברית עם in both instances to לְפְדוּת עָם (Randglossen,
IV, ad locc.), whence MOFFAT's "(I have formed you) for the rescue
of my people." Finally, out of the very many comments on our term,
I should like to quote that of Rashi: קראתיך, לישעיה הוא אומר (i.e.,
God is addressing the prophet); ואצרך, זאת היתה מחשבתי שתשי'(=שתשים
שתשיב) את עמי לבריתי ולהאיר להם or (i.e., when I formed you, this

<hr>

[1]) 59.20-21

(20) וּבָא לְצִיּוֹן גּוֹאֵל וּלְשָׁבֵי פֶּשַׁע בְּיַעֲקֹב נְאֻם יהוה:

(21) וַאֲנִי זֹאת בְּרִיתִי אוֹתָם אָמַר יהוה רוּחִי אֲשֶׁר עָלֶיךָ וּדְבָרַי אֲשֶׁר־
שַׂמְתִּי בְּפִיךָ לֹא־יָמוּשׁוּ מִפִּיךָ וּמִפִּי זַרְעֲךָ וּמִפִּי זֶרַע זַרְעֲךָ אָמַר
יהוה מֵעַתָּה וְעַד־עוֹלָם:

[2]) 61.8-9

(8) כִּי אֲנִי יהוה אֹהֵב מִשְׁפָּט שֹׂנֵא גָזֵל בְּעוֹלָה
וְנָתַתִּי פְעֻלָּתָם בֶּאֱמֶת וּבְרִית עוֹלָם אֶכְרוֹת לָהֶם:

(9) וְנוֹדַע בַּגּוֹיִם זַרְעָם וְצֶאֱצָאֵיהֶם בְּתוֹךְ הָעַמִּים
כָּל־רֹאֵיהֶם יַכִּירוּם כִּי הֵם זֶרַע בֵּרַךְ יהוה:

was My purpose, that you would make My people My covenant [or: that you would bring back My people to My covenant] and bring light to them).

F

Something should be said here about another expression, one that is quite pertinent to our own וּנְתַתִּיךָ לְאוֹר גּוֹיִם of 49.6, viz., נָבִיא לַגּוֹיִם נְתַתִּיךָ in Jer. 1.5. The whole passage reads (vv. 4-5):

(4) The word of the Lord came to me:
(5) Before I formed you in the belly, I selected you;
Before you issued from the womb, I consecrated you;
I designated you a prophet to (or: for) the nations.[1]

One has but to proceed to read all of the book of Jeremiah—regardless of whether this or that passage or chapter is generally accepted by scholars as original with Jeremiah or as of secondary origin—to realize that Jeremiah was God's spokesman to Judah alone.

Thus when Jeremiah protests—as was characteristic of God's spokesmen generally (cf. chap. III above, §C, pp. 56 f.)—that he is but a youth and without skill as a speaker (v. 6), God's reply (v. 8) is, "Do not be afraid of them, for I am with you to deliver you." Whom did Jeremiah fear? From the hands of which nation would God rescue him? Clearly (cf., e.g., 1.17-19) it is his fellow Judeans of whom Jeremiah need fear, and from whom God stood ready to deliver him. Indeed, this was precisely the occupational hazard of every prophet: harm at the hands of his fellow Israelites, whom he had come to rebuke and threaten.

What follows is a series of declarations to Judah about what would happen to her if she persisted in her evil ways; but as to the heathen nations, they were nothing more than God's rod of anger and punishment, mere tools in His hands, against sinful Judah; cf., e.g., 1.14-16; 4.16-18; 5.15-17; 6.22-26; etc. Jeremiah will be ordered to proclaim "in the hearing of Jerusalem" (בְּאָזְנֵי יְרוּשָׁלַ͏ִם, 2.1-12), but never in the hearing of any heathen nation; God will tell Jeremiah to "speak"

---

[1] Jer. 1.4-5

(4) וַיְהִי דְבַר־יהוה אֵלַי לֵאמֹר:
(5) בְּטֶרֶם אֶצָּרְךָ בַבֶּטֶן יְדַעְתִּיךָ וּבְטֶרֶם תֵּצֵא מֵרֶחֶם הִקְדַּשְׁתִּיךָ
נָבִיא לַגּוֹיִם נְתַתִּיךָ:

(‏וְדִבַּרְתָּ‎ . . .) to his Judean countrymen (1.17; 7.22; 22.1 ff.; 26.2; 35.2),
but never to any non-Israelite people; only Israelites—never any of the
gentile nations—will be exhorted to "listen" (‏שִׁמְעוּ‎ . .) to God's word
(2.4; 5.20-21; 7.2, 23; 10.1; 11.2, 4, 6, 7; 13.15; 17.20; 19.3; 21.11;
29.20; 42.15; 44.24, 26). Significantly, in each of the two passages in
which ‏שִׁמְעוּ‎ is clearly associated with ‏גּוֹיִם‎, the "nations" are treated
hyperbolically, exactly as when the "heavens" and the "earth" are
called upon to be witness to God's message or action in regard to
Israel; they are 6.18-19:

> (18) Therefore, hear, O nations,[1])
>   And know, O congregation,
>   What will happen to them;
> (19) Hear, O earth:
>   I will bring harm upon this people. . .[2])

and 31.9-11

> (9) . . .For I am a father to Israel
>   And Israel is my first-born.
> (10) Hear the word of the Lord, O nations,
>   And declare it in the distant coastlands.
>   Say: He who scattered Israel will gather him,
>   And He will guard him as a shepherd his flock.
> (11) For the Lord has ransomed Jacob,
>   Has redeemd him from hands too strong for him.[3])

---

[1]) Mention should be made of the fact that the identity of the terms ‏גּוֹי (ם)‎ and
‏ממלכה‎ in Jeremiah is not always readily determined. Thus in 1.5 ‏גּוֹיִם‎ is interpreted
by RASHI as the Judeans; in 1.10 the phrase ‏עַל־הַגּוֹיִם וְעַל־הַמַּמְלָכוֹת‎ is regarded
by some scholars as secondarily derived from 18.7, where the context is wholly
Judean. Scholars generally tend to overlook the frequency with which the term
‏גּוֹי (ם)‎ is used in the Bible for the people Israel: this is probably a Jewish even more
than a Christian prejudice. But the exposition of our problem, it will be noted,
is based on the received text and the generally accepted interpretation of it.

[2]) Jer. 6.18-19   (18) ‏לָכֵן שִׁמְעוּ הַגּוֹיִם וּדְעִי עֵדָה אֶת־אֲשֶׁר־בָּם:‎
(19) ‏שִׁמְעִי הָאָרֶץ הִנֵּה אָנֹכִי מֵבִיא רָעָה אֶל־הָעָם הַזֶּה פְּרִי מַחְשְׁבוֹתָם‎
‏כִּי עַל־דְּבָרַי לֹא הִקְשִׁיבוּ וְתוֹרָתִי וַיִּמְאֲסוּ־בָהּ:‎

(9) ‏בִּבְכִי יָבֹאוּ וּבְתַחֲנוּנִים אוֹבִילֵם‎
‏אוֹלִיכֵם אֶל־נַחֲלֵי מַיִם בְּדֶרֶךְ יָשָׁר לֹא יִכָּשְׁלוּ בָּהּ‎
‏כִּי־הָיִיתִי לְיִשְׂרָאֵל לְאָב וְאֶפְרַיִם בְּכֹרִי הוּא:‎

[3]) Jer. 31.9-11   (10) ‏שִׁמְעוּ דְבַר־יהוה גּוֹיִם וְהַגִּידוּ בָאִיִּים מִמֶּרְחָק וְאִמְרוּ‎

Indeed, Jeremiah's attitude toward the nations is readily apparent from what he himself has to say, frequently. In 2.18 he declares scornfully:

> Now why are you on the road to Egypt,
> To drink the waters of the Nile?
> Why are you on the road to Assyria,
> To drink the waters of the Euphrates? [1]

And far from being a prophet (i.e., God's spokesman) to the nations, Jeremiah warns his fellow Judeans (2.36):

> How lightly you gad about,
> Changing your way!

מְזָרֵה יִשְׂרָאֵל יְקַבְּצֶנּוּ וּשְׁמָרוֹ כְּרֹעֶה עֶדְרוֹ:

(11) כִּי־פָדָה יהוה אֶת־יַעֲקֹב וּגְאָלוֹ מִיַּד חָזָק מִמֶּנּוּ:

In 49.20 and 50.45, גוים is either, again, purely rhetorical (as also, e.g., in 18.13) or else is directed to the Judeans. In such a passage as 16.19,

> O Lord, my strength and my stronghold,
> My refuge in the day of trouble,
> To You nations shall come (אֵלֶיךָ גּוֹיִם יָבֹאוּ)
> From the ends of the earth (מֵאַפְסֵי־אָרֶץ) and say:
> Mere delusion (אַךְ־שֶׁקֶר) our fathers inherited,
> Folly (הֶבֶל) that can do no good.

it is naive to take the Hebrew literally, that nations will come from all over the world to Jerusalem to admit that the worship of any god but Israel's can do no good; neither Jeremiah nor his audience was that naive. All that Jeremiah meant— and was understood to say, *rhetorically*, was: The whole world will recognize God's uniqueness and omnipotence. Would scholars dare take literally such a similar expression as (Isa. 55.12) "...mount and hill shall break into song, And all the trees of the field shall clap their hands"? (See on this LINDBLOM, p. 101, and his favorable references to ROBERT H. PFEIFFER, H. H. ROWLEY, and ALFRED GUILLAUME; cf. also DE BOER, pp. 89-90). If one wishes to take literally Jeremiah's rhetorical declaration (2.1):

> Cross over to the isles of the Kittim and see,
> Send to Kedar and observe carefully,
> (See if aught like this has happened:
> Has any nation changed its gods?
> —And they are not even gods!—...)

then he should also take literally the equally rhetorical statement in the verse following:

> Be appalled, O heavens, at this!
> Be horrified, utterly desolate!
> —declares the Lord.

[1] Jer. 2.18

וְעַתָּה מַה־לָּךְ לְדֶרֶךְ מִצְרַיִם לִשְׁתּוֹת מֵי שִׁחוֹר
וּמַה־לָּךְ לְדֶרֶךְ אַשּׁוּר לִשְׁתּוֹת מֵי נָהָר:

You shall be put to shame by Egypt
As you were put to shame by Assyria! [1]

In 9.24-25; 10.1 ff., Jeremiah expresses outright contempt for the heathen nations and their ways:

(24) Behold, the days are coming, declares the Lord, when I will punish all those who are circumcised and yet uncircumcised—(25) Egypt, Judah, Edom, the Ammonites, Moab, and all who dwell in the desert that cut the corner of their hair; for all these are uncircumcised, and all the House of Israel is uncircumcised in heart.[2]

(1) Hear the word which the Lord speaks to (or: concerning) you, O House of Israel. (2) Thus says the Lord:

Learn not the ways of the nations,
Nor be dismayed at the signs of the heavens
Because the nations are dismayed at them.
(3) For the customs of the peoples are false. . .[3]

And the chapter is climaxed by this passage (v. 25):

Pour out Your wrath upon the nations that know You not,
And upon the peoples that invoke not Your name;
For they have devoured Jacob,
Devoured him and consumed him,
And laid waste his habitation.[4]

---

[1]) Jer. 2.36   מַה־תֵּזְלִי מְאֹד לְשַׁנּוֹת אֶת־דַּרְכֵּךְ
גַּם מִמִּצְרַיִם תֵּבוֹשִׁי כַּאֲשֶׁר־בֹּשְׁתְּ מֵאַשּׁוּר:

[2]) The text (e.g., at the end of v. 24) is not in order; yet the general meaning seems clear enough.

[3]) Jer. 9.   (24) הִנֵּה יָמִים בָּאִים נְאֻם־יהוה וּפָקַדְתִּי עַל־כָּל־ מוּל בְּעָרְלָה: (25) עַל־
24-25; 10.1-3   מִצְרַיִם וְעַל־יְהוּדָה וְעַל־אֱדוֹם וְעַל־בְּנֵי עַמּוֹן וְעַל־מוֹאָב וְעַל כָּל־
קְצוּצֵי פֵאָה הַיֹּשְׁבִים בַּמִּדְבָּר כִּי כָל־הַגּוֹיִם עֲרֵלִים וְכָל־בֵּית יִשְׂרָאֵל
עַרְלֵי־לֵב:

(1) שִׁמְעוּ אֶת־הַדָּבָר אֲשֶׁר דִּבֶּר יהוה עֲלֵיכֶם בֵּית יִשְׂרָאֵל: (2) כֹּה אָמַר יהוה
אֶל־דֶּרֶךְ הַגּוֹיִם אַל־תִּלְמָדוּ וּמֵאֹתוֹת הַשָּׁמַיִם אַל־תֵּחָתּוּ
כִּי־יֵחַתּוּ הַגּוֹיִם מֵהֵמָּה:

(3) כִּי־חֻקּוֹת הָעַמִּים הֶבֶל הוּא כִּי־עֵץ מִיַּעַר כְּרָתוֹ
מַעֲשֵׂה יְדֵי־חָרָשׁ בַּמַּעֲצָד:

[4]) Jer. 10.25   שְׁפֹךְ חֲמָתְךָ עַל־הַגּוֹיִם אֲשֶׁר לֹא־יְדָעוּךָ
וְעַל מִשְׁפָּחוֹת אֲשֶׁר בְּשִׁמְךָ לֹא קָרָאוּ
כִּי־אָכְלוּ אֶת־יַעֲקֹב וַאֲכָלֻהוּ וַיְכַלֻּהוּ וְאֶת־נָוֵהוּ הֵשַׁמּוּ:

G

Among the many additional passages that might be discussed in this connection, I may mention in passing Isa. 11.10-12:

(10) In that day,
> The stock of Jesse that has remained standing
> Shall become a standard to peoples:
> Nations shall seek his counsel,
> And his abode shall be honored.

(11) In that day, the Lord will set His hand again to redeeming the remaining part of His people [viz., those outside the land of Israel-Judah] from Assyria, from Egypt, from Pathros, from Ethiopia, from Elam, from Shinar, from Hamath, and from the coastlands.

(12) He will hold up a signal to the nations
> And assemble the banished of Israel;
> He will gather the dispersed of Judah
> From the four corners of the earth.[1]

Taken out of context, as has so often been done, one might assume that the unnamed scion of the Davidic Dynasty "shall become a standard to peoples" (v. 10) and that He (viz., God Himself; or "he", viz., this same scion of David) will lift up a signal to the nations" (v. 12), in the sense that something good will come to the gentile nations through Israel's leader and through Israel's God. However, one has but to read these expressions in context to see how completely nationalistic the prophet—or whoever it was who composed these verses—is. Thus in verses 1-9 the "shoot from the stump of Jesse" will restore justice to the land of Israel, so that "it shall be filled with recognition of the Lord." And everything that follows v. 12—indeed the entire section from 10.32 through 12.6, which constitutes the Haftarah for the Eighth Day of Passover—glorifies the deliverance of

---

[1] Isa. 11.10-12   (10) וְהָיָה בַּיּוֹם הַהוּא שֹׁרֶשׁ יִשַׁי אֲשֶׁר עֹמֵד לְנֵס עַמִּים
אֵלָיו גּוֹיִם יִדְרֹשׁוּ וְהָיְתָה מְנֻחָתוֹ כָּבוֹד:
(11) וְהָיָה בַּיּוֹם הַהוּא יוֹסִיף אֲדֹנָי שֵׁנִית יָדוֹ
לִקְנוֹת אֶת־שְׁאָר עַמּוֹ אֲשֶׁר יִשָּׁאֵר מֵאַשּׁוּר וּמִמִּצְרַיִם
וּמִפַּתְרוֹס וּמִכּוּשׁ וּמֵעֵילָם וּמִשִּׁנְעָר וּמֵחֲמָת וּמֵאִיֵּי הַיָּם:
(12) וְנָשָׂא נֵס לַגּוֹיִם וְאָסַף נִדְחֵי יִשְׂרָאֵל
וּנְפֻצוֹת יְהוּדָה יְקַבֵּץ מֵאַרְבַּע כַּנְפוֹת הָאָרֶץ:

Israel's exiles, the reunion of Israel and Judah, and Israel's God who achieved it all.

To sum up. However such expressions as וּנְתַתִּיךָ לְאוֹר גּוֹיִם and וְאֶתֶּנְךָ לִבְרִית עָם לְאוֹר גּוֹיִם in Isaiah and נָבִיא לַגּוֹיִם נְתַתִּיךָ in Jeremiah are translated, all the contextual data in these Books make it amply clear that nothing international was implied in them. These prophets, God's spokesmen all, were not sent on any mission to any nation other than their own one,[1]) to God's covenanted partner, Israel. When they were not simply the means by which God punished His erring people, the pagan peoples were merely helpless witnesses—just like the heavens and the earth and the mountains—to God's exclusive love and protection of His people. This is the essential meaning of such passages as Jer. 26.6 and 4.2:

((4) Thus said the Lord:
  If you will not listen to Me. . .)
 (6) I will make this House [of Judah] like Shiloh,
  And I will make this city [Jerusalem] a curse
  For all the nations of the earth.

((1) If you return, O Israel,
  Declares the Lord. . .)
 (2) And if you swear "As the Lord lives"
  In true justice and uprightness,
  Then nations shall bless themselves in (or: through)
   him [viz., Israel],
  And in him they shall glory.[2])

---

[1]) In my article on "The Seer in Ancient Israel" (*Oriens Antiquus*, 4 [1965], 153-174; written originally in 1958, and revised in 1959, for vol. II of *The World History of the Jewish People*, ed. BENJAMIN MAZAR—the volume is now in its final stages), I wrote (pp. 159-160), ". . .it is worth noting that since divination was a universal craft, recognized in all countries and cultures of the ancient world, it is not surprising that the activities of the Israelite seer sometimes ranged beyond the Israelite population and border. Thus Elijah is said to have been ordered by God to go to Damascus and there anoint Hazael as king of Syria—after which he was to return to his own country and anoint Jehu as king of Israel. . .Elisha. . . Naaman. . .Ahaziah. . .Baal-zebub. . .But one cannot imagine a canonical prophet in Israel being consulted by a foreign power, or going to another country to address a ruler, or to interfere with his rule, directly; or of a foreign ruler coming to Israel to consult one of the canonical prophets"; and see n. 18 there on Jonah.

[2]) Jer. 26.6 and 4.2

(6) וְנָתַתִּי אֶת־הַבַּיִת הַזֶּה כְּשִׁלֹה וְאֶת־הָעִיר הַזֹּאת אֶתֵּן לִקְלָלָה לְכֹל גּוֹיֵי הָאָרֶץ:

(2) וְנִשְׁבַּעְתָּ חַי־יהוה בֶּאֱמֶת בְּמִשְׁפָּט וּבִצְדָקָה וְהִתְבָּרְכוּ בוֹ גּוֹיִם וּבוֹ יִתְהַלָּלוּ:

i.e., the heathen nations shall say: May we be as prosperous and protected as Israel—if all goes well with Israel; but: Cursed shall you be like Israel—if Israel is in degradation af the hands of God for her sins.

In a word: Israel will be "a light of nations" in the sense that Israel will dazzle the nations with her God-given triumph and restoration; the whole world will behold this single beacon that is God's sole covenanted people. Israel will serve to the world at large as the example of God's loyalty and omnipotence.

CONCLUSIONS

1. Neither *'ebed Adonai* (*YHWH*)/"servant of the Lord" nor any form of *'ebed*/"servant" was employed as a technical term in Second Isaiah or—with the apparent exception of *'ebed Adonai/Ha-Elohim* for Moses —anywhere else in the Bible. The expression *'Ebed Adonai*/"Servant of the Lord" first became a technical term in Christian circles, after the career of Jesus on earth had come to an end, only after the significance of the life and death of Jesus had come to be reinterpreted. Consequently, the term has no special meaning in the exegesis of Second Isaiah; its meaning, rather, belongs to the area of post-biblical eisegesis.

2. The concepts "Suffering Servant" and "Vicarious Suffering" are likewise post-biblical in origin (probably from a pagan, Hellenistic, not a Judaic source), and deserve no place in the analysis of the Hebrew Bible in its historical development. It was only after suffering— vicarious suffering—came to be associated with Jesus that these concepts were read back into the passage of the Hebrew Bible most favorable for such interpretation, chapter 53 of Isaiah.

3. There is insufficient reason to isolate *'ebed* sections in Second Isaiah, apart from their natural context, in the preserved Hebrew text; no one would have thought of such procedure had not the alien, post-biblical concept of "Servant of the Lord" been permitted to intrude into the biblical text. Whatever the problems that the so-called *'ebed* sections manifest for scholarship, they do not differ from those that non-*'ebed* sections offer the unbiased and inquisitive scholar.

4. In all the four so-called *'ebed* sections—though the term *'ebed* is not found in two of the four—it is the prophet himself who is the central personage.

BIBLIOGRAPHY

ALBRIGHT, W. F., *From the Stone Age to Christianity: Monotheism and the Historical Process* (Baltimore, 1940).
——, "Hamath," *Encyclopaedia Miqra'it*, III (1958), 193-200.
ALTMANN, P., *Erwählungstheologie und Universalismus in Alten Testament (Beihefte zur ZAW*, No. 92, 1964).
An American (The Chicago) Translation: The Complete Bible, rev. ed. by T. J. MEEK.
AVIGAD, N., See s. SUKENIK, E.L.

BACON, B. W., "New and Old in Jesus' Relation to John," *JBL*, 48 (1929), 40-81.
BARDTKE, H., "Die Parascheneinteilung des Jesajarolle I von Qumrān," *Festschrift Franz Dornseiff*, ed. H. KUSCH (Leipzig, 1953), 33-75.
BEER, G., "Die Gedichte vom Knechte Jahwes in Jes 40-55. Ein textkritischer und metrischer Wiederherstellungsversuch," *Wolf Baudissin Festschrift*, ed. W. FRANKENBURG-F. KÜCHLER (Giessen, 1918), 29-46.
BEWER, J. A., "Two Notes on Isaiah 49.1-6," *Jewish Studies in Memory of George A. Kohut*, ed. S. W. BARON-A. MARX (New York, 1935), 86-90.
BLACK, M., "The Zakir Stele," *Documents from Old Testament Times*, ed. D. WINTON THOMAS (London, 1958; now a Harper Torchbook), 242-250.
BLANK, S. H., "The Death of Zechariah in Rabbinic Literature," *HUCA*, 12-13 (1937-38), 327-346.
——, "Studies in Deutero-Isaiah," *HUCA*, 15 (1940), 1-46.
——, *Prophetic Faith in Isaiah* (New York, 1958).
DE BOER, P. A. H., "Second-Isaiah's Message," *Oudtestamentische Studiën*, XI, Leiden, 1956).
BUDDE, K., "The So-called 'Ebed-Jahwe Songs' and the Meaning of the Term 'Servant of Yahweh' in Isaiah Chaps. 40-55," *American Journal of Theology*, 3 (1899), 499-540.
——, *Die sogenannten Ebed-Jahwe-Lieder und die Bedeutung des Knechtes Jahwes: ein Minoritätsvotum* (Giessen, 1900).
BURROWS, M., *More Light on the Dead Sea Scrolls* (New York, 1958).

CADBURY, H. J., "The Titles of Jesus in Acts," pp. 364-370 of Vol. V of *Beginnings of Christianity*, ed. F. J. FOAKES JACKSON-K. LAKE (1933).
——, "Motives of Biblical Scholarship," *JBL*, 56 (1937), 1-16.
——, *The Making of Luke-Acts*, 2nd ed. (New York, 1958).
——, "Gospel Study and our Image of Early Christianity," *JBL*, 83 (1964), 139-145.
CASEY, R. P., "Note on Μάρτυς," pp. 30-37 of Vol. V of *Beginnings of Christianity*, ed. F. J. FOAKES JACKSON-K. LAKE (1933).
COBB, W. H., "The Servant of Jahveh," *JBL*, 14 (1895), 95-113.
COOK, S. A., "The Prophets of Israel," *Cambridge Ancient History*, III (1925), Chap. XX, pp. 458-500.
CRAIG, C. T., "Realized Eschatology," *JBL*, 56 (1937), 17-26.
——, "The Identification of Jesus with the Suffering Servant," *Journal of Religion*, 24 (1944), 240-245.
CROSS, Jr., F. M., "The Council of Yahweh in Second Isaiah," *Journal of Near Eastern Studies*, 12 (1953), 274-277.
——, *The Ancient Library of Qumran and Modern Biblical Studies*, rev. ed. (Anchor Books, 1961).

DRIVER, S. R., *An Introduction to the Literature of the Old Testament*, 9th ed. (New York, 1913).

——, See *s.* NEUBAUER, A.

DUHM, B., *Die Theologie der Propheten* (Bonn, 1875).

——, *Das Buch Jesaia* (Göttingen, 1892).

DUPONT-SOMMER, A., *The Essene Writings from Qumran* (Meridian Books, 1962).

EHRLICH, A. B., *Jesaia* (in *Randglossen zur hebräischen Bibel*; Leipzig, 1912).

EISSFELDT, O., "The Ebed-Jahwe in Isaiah xl.-lv. in the Light of the Israelite Conceptions of the Community and the Individual, the Ideal and the Real," *Expository Times*, 44 (1932-33), 261-268.

——, *Einleitung in das Alte Testament*, 2nd ed. (Tübingen, 1956).

——, *The Old Testament: An Introduction* (New York, 1965; English translation by Peter R. Ackroyd).

ELLIGER, K., *Deuterojesaja in seinem Verhältnis zu Tritojesaja* (*BWANT*, 1933).

ENGNELL. I., "The Ebed Yahweh Songs and the Suffering Messiah in 'Deutero-Isaiah,' " *Bulletin of the Johns Rylands Liberary*, 31 (1948), 54-93.

ENSLIN, M. S., "Biblical Criticism and its Effect on Modern Civilization," Chap. IV in *Five Essays on the Bible* (American Council of Learned Societies, New York, 1960), 30-44.

FENSHAM, F. C., "Did a Treaty between the Israelites and the Kenites Exist?" *BASOR*, 175 (October, 1964), 51-54.

——, "The Treaty between Israel and the Gibeonites," *Bib. Arch.*, 27 (1964), 96-100 (with references to his articles in *VT* and *ZAW*).

FISCHEL, H. A., "Die Deuterojesajanischen Gottesknechtliedes in der jüdischen Auslegung," *HUCA*, 18 (1944), 53-76.

FISCHER, J., *Isaias 40-55 und die Perikopen vom Gottesknecht. Eine kritisch-exegetische Studie* (*Alttestamentliche Abhandlungen*, VI, 4/5, 1916).

GASTER, T. H., "Azazal," *IDB*, I (1962), 26.

GERSTENBERGER, E., Review of D. J. McCarthy, *Treaty and Covenant*, in *JBL*, 83 (1964), 198 f.

——, "Covenant and Commandment," *JBL*, 84 (1965), 38-51.

GINSBURG, C. D., *Introduction to the Massoretico-Critical Edition of the Hebrew Bible* (London, 1897; reissued by KTAV Publishing House, New York, 1966).

GINZBERG, L., *Legends of the Jews*, 7 vols. (Philadelphia, 1909-1946).

GOODENOUGH, E. R., "The Bible as Product of the Ancient World," Chap. I in *Five Essays on the Bible* (American Council of Learned Societies, New York, 1960), 1-19.

GRAY, G. B., *International Critical Commentary on Isaiah* I-XXVII (1912).

GUILLAUME, A., "The Servant Poems in the Deutero-Isaiah," *Theology*, 11 (1925), 254-263, 309-319; 12 (1926), 2-10, 63-72.

HAMLIN, E. J., "The Meaning of 'Mountains and Hills' in Isa. 41.14-16," *Journal of Near Eastern Studies*, 13 (1954), 185-90.

HARAN, M., *Between Riʾshonot (Former Prophecies) and Ḥadashot (New Prophecies): A Literary-Historical Study in the Group of Prophecies Isaiah XL-XLVIII* (in Hebrew; Jerusalem, 1963-5723).

VON HARNACK, A., "Die Bezeichnung Jesu als 'Knecht Gottes' und ihre Geschichte in der alten Kirche," *Sitzungsberichte der Berliner Akademie der Wissenschaften* (*Phil.-hist. Klasse*), (1926), 212-238.

HILLERS, D. R., *Treaty Curses and the Old Testament Prophets* (*Biblica et Orientalia*, N. 16; 1964).

HOOKE, S. H., "The Theory and Practice of Substitution," *VT*, 2 (1959), 2-17.

HOOKER, Morna D., *Jesus and the Servant: The Influence of the Servant Concept of Deutero-Isaiah in the New Testament* (London, S.P.C.K., 1959).

HYATT, J. P. "The Source of the Suffering Servant Idea," *Journal of Near Eastern Studies*, 3 (1944), 79-86.

IBN EZRA, Abraham, Commentary on Isaiah (in Rabbinic Bible).

IWRI, S., "*MAṢṢĒBĀH* and *BĀMĀH* in Isaiah^A 1Q 6₁₃," *JBL*, 76 (1957), 225-232.

JACKSON, F. J. FOAKES-LAKE, K., *The Beginnings of Christianity*, 5 vols. (1920-1933).

JACOB BEN REUBEN (the Qaraite), Commentary in *The Fifty-Third Chapter in Isaiah according to the Jewish Interpreters*, ed. NEUBAUER-DRIVER.

JACOBSEN, T., Chapters on "Mesopotamia" in *The Intellectual Adventure of Ancient Man*, ed. H. and H. A. FRANKFORT (Chicago, 1946; appeared in 1961 as a Penguin Book, without the chapters on "The Hebrews," as *Before Philosophy*).

JAMES, F., *Personalities of the Old Testament* (New York, 1929).

JANOW, H., *Das hebräische Leichenlied im Rahmen der Völkerdichtung* (*Beiheft zur ZAW*, 36, 1923).

JENNI, E., "Messiah, Jewish," *IDB*, III (1962), 360a-365b.

JEREMIAS, J., See *s.* Zimmerli, W.

Jewish Publication Society Translation of *The Holy Scriptures* (1917). See also *s. The Torah.*

JOHNSON, A. R., "The Primary Meaning of √גאל," *Supplements to VT*, Vol. I (1953; the Copenhagen Congress Volume), 67-77.

KAUFMANN, Y., תולדות האמונה הישראלית, 8 vols. (Tel-Aviv, 5716/1956).

KISSANE, E. J., *The Book of Isaiah*, 2 vols. (Dublin, 1943).

KITTEL, R., ed. *Librum Jesaiae* in *Biblia Hebraica*³.

KOEHLER, K., "Atonement," *Jewish Encyclopedia*, II, 275-284.

KOEHLER, L., *Deuterojesaja [Jesaja 40-55] Stilkritisch Untersucht* (*Beiheft zur ZAW*, 37, 1923).

KÖNIG, E., "Deuterojesajanisches," *Neue Kirchliche Zeitschrift*, 9 (1898), 895-935, 937-997.

——, *Das Buch Jesaja* (Gütersloh, 1926).

LAKE, K., See *s.* Jackson, F. J. Foakes.

LATTEY, C., "Vicarious Solidarity in the Old Testament," *VT*, 1 (1951), 267-274.

LAUE, L., *Die Ebed-Jahwe-Lieder im II. Teil des Jesaja exegetisch-kritisch und biblisch-theologisch untersucht* (Wittenberg, 1898).

——, "Nochmals die Ebed-Jahwe-Lieder im Deuterojesaja," *Theologische Studien und Kritiken*, 77 (1904), 319-379.

LEMKE, W. E., "Nebuchadrezzar, My Servant," *CBQ*, 28 (1966), 45-50.

LIDZBARSKI, M., *Ephemeris für semitische Epigraphik*, 3 vols. (Giessen, 1909-15).

LIEBREICH, L. J., "The Compilation of the Book of Isaiah," *JQR*, 46 (1955-56), 259-277; 47 (1956-57), 114-138.

LINDBLOM, J., *The Servant Songs in Deutero-Isaiah* (*Lunds Universitets Årsskrift*, N.F., Avd. 1, Bd. 47, Nr. 5; Lund, 1951).

——, "Gibt es eine Eschatologie bei den alttestamentlichen Propheten?," *Studia Theologica*, 6 (1953), 79-114.

LINDHAGEN, C., *The Servant Motif in the Old Testament: A preliminary Study to the 'Ebed Yahweh Problem' in Deutero-Isaiah* (Uppsala, 1950).

——, "The Servant of the Lord," *Expository Times*, 67 (1955-56), 279-283; 300-302.

LOEWINGER, S., "The Variants of DS II," *VT*, 4 (1954), 155-163.

LUZZATTO. S.D., Commentary on Isaiah, in *The Fifty-Third Chapter in Isaiah according to the Jewish Interpreters*, ed. A. Neubauer-S. R. Driver, 2 vols. (Oxford and London, 1876-77).

MARTI, K., *Das Buch Jesaja erklärt* (Tübingen, 1900).

MCCARTHY, D. J., *Treaty and Covenant: Study in Form in the Ancient Oriental Documents and in the Old Testament* (*Analecta Biblica*, 21, 1963).

MENDELSOHN, I., *Slavery in the Ancient Near East* (New York, 1949).

——, "Slavery in the Old Testament," *IDB*, IV (1962), 383a-391a.

MENDELSOHN, S.(-KOEHLER, K.): "Confession of Sin," *Jewish Encyclopedia*, IV (1903), 217b-219b.

MENDENHALL, G. E., "Covenant Forms in Israelite Tradition," *Bib. Arch.*, 17 (1954), 50-76.

MICHAELIS, J. D., *Deutsche Übersetzung des Alten Testaments, mit Anmerkungen für Ungelehrte* (Göttingen, 1779); Isaiah in Part VIII.

MITTON, C. L., "Atonement," *IDB*, I (1962), 309-313.

MOFFAT, J., *A New Translation of the Bible*.

MONTEITH, J., "A New View of Isaiah liii," *Expository Times*, 36 (1924-25), 498-502.

MORGENSTERN, J., "Deutero-Isaiah's Terminology for 'Universal God,' " *JBL*, 62 (1943), 269-280.

——, "The Two Prophecies from 520-516 B.C.," *HUCA*, 22 (1949), 365-431.

——, "The Suffering Servant—a New Solution," *VT*, 11 (1961), 292-320, 406-431; 13 (1963), 321-332.

MOWINCKEL, S., *De senere profeter* (Vol. III in *Det gamle testamente*; 1944).

——, *Hans som Kommer*, etc. (Copenhagen, 1951) = *He That Cometh* (Oxford, 1956).

NEUBAUER, A.-DRIVER, S. R., ed.: *The Fifty-Third Chapter of Isaiah according to the Jewish Interpreters* (Oxford and London, 1876-77).

NORTH, C. R., *The Suffering Servant in Deutero-Isaiah: An Historical and Critical Study* (Oxford, 1948; 2nd ed. 1956).

——, "The Interpretation of Deutero-Isaiah," in *Interpretationes ad Vetus Testamentum Sigmundo Mowinckel Septuagenario Missae* (Oslo, 1955).

——, *The Second Isaiah* (Oxford, 1964).

ORLINSKY, H. M., "Job 5.8, a Problem in Greek-Hebrew Methodology," *JQR*, 25 (1934-35), 271-278.

——, "Studies in the St. Mark's Isaiah Scroll, III: Masoretic חֵמָה in Isaiah XLII, 25," *Journal of Jewish Studies*, 2 (1951), 151-154.

——, *Ancient Israel* (Ithaca, N.Y., 1954).

——, "The Treatment of Anthropomorphisms and Anthropopathisms in the Septuagint of Isaiah," *HUCA*, 27 (1956), 193-200.

——, "Alleged Concept of Afterlife," § C in Chap. III of "Studies in the Septuagint of the Book of Job," *HUCA*, 32 (1961), 241-249.

——, 'Who is the Ideal Jew: the Biblical View," *Judaism*, 13 (1964), 19-28 (Originally in Hebrew, מי יעלה בהר יהוה, in David Ben-Gurion Jubilee Volume, עֹז לדוד, Jerusalem, 5724-1964, 521-528).

——, *The So-Called "Suffering Servant" in Isaiah 53* (Goldenson Lecture of Hebrew Union College-Jewish Institute of Religion, Cincinnati, 1964, 49 pp.).

——, "The Hebrew *Vorlage* of the Septuagint of Job: the Text and the Script," Chap. V of "Studies in the Septuagint of the Book of Job," *HUCA*, 35 (1964), 57-78; 36 (1965), 37-47.

——, "The Seer in Ancient Israel," *Oriens Antiquus*, 4 (1965), 153-174 (to appear in much revised form under the title "The Seer-Priest in Ancient Israel" as Chap. 26 in *The World History of the Jewish People*, vol. II, ed. B. MAZAR, Massadah Publishing Co., Tel-Aviv, 1967).

——, "*Israel* in Isa. XLIX, 3: a Problem in the Methodology of Textual Criticism," *Eretz-Israel*, 8 (1967); the Sukenik Memorial Volume), 42*-45*.

——, "Old Testament Studies," in *Religion*, ed. P. RAMSEY (in series *The Princeton Studies: Humanistic Scholarship in America*; Prentice-Hall, 1966), 51-109.

——, "A Light of the Nations: a Problem in Biblical Theology," *JQR*, (the Seventy-fifth Anniversary Volume), 409-428.

——, see also *s. The Torah* (1962).

PFEIFFER, R. H., Translation of *Ludlul bel nemeqi* in *Ancient Near Eastern Texts relating to the Old Testament*, ed. J. B. PRITCHARD (Princeton, 1950), 434-437.

PIPER, O. A., "Light, Light and Darkness," *IDB*, III (1962), 130b-132b.

——, "Suffering and Evil," *IDB*, IV (1962), 450a-453b.

POGNON, H., *Inscriptions sémitiques de la Syrie*, etc. (Paris, 1907).

QUANBECK, W. A., "Confession," *IDB*, I (1962), 667a-668b.

RAINEY, A. F., "The Kingdom of Ugarit," *Bib. Arch.*, 28 (1965), 102-125.

Revised Standard Version of *The Holy Bible* (1952).

ROTH, W. M. W., "The Anonymity of the Suffering Servant," *JBL*, 83 (1964), 171-179.

ROWLEY, H. H., *The Servant of the Lord and other Essays on the Old Testament* (London, 1952).

La Sainte Bible (sous la direction de L'École Biblique de Jérusalem; Paris, 1956).

SARNA, N., "Epic Substratum in the Prose of Job," *JBL*, 76 (1957), 13-25.

SCHIAN, M., *Die Ebed-Jahwe-Lieder in Jesaias 40-66*, etc. (Halle, 1895).

SMART, J. D., "A New Approach to the 'Ebed-Yahweh Problem," *Expository Times*, 45 (1933-34), 168a-172b.

SNAITH, N. H., "The Servant of the Lord in Deutero-Isaiah," in *Studies in Old Testament Prophecy presented to Professor Theodore H. Robinson*, ed. H. H. ROWLEY (Edinburgh, 1950), 187-200.

STAERK, W., *Die Ebed Jahwe Lieder in Jesaja 40 ff. Ein Beitrag zur Deuterojesaja-Kritik (Beiträge zur Wissenschaft vom A.T.*, XIV, 1913).

SUKENIK, E. L.(-AVIGAD, N.), ed. *The Dead Sea Scrolls of the Hebrew University* (Jerusalem, 1955).

The Torah ... A New Translation of The Holy Scriptures (Jewish Publication Society, Philadelphia, 1962), editor-in-chief, H. M. Orlinsky.

TORREY, C. C., *The Second Isaiah* (New York, 1928).

TUCKER, G. M., "Covenant Forms and Contract Forms," *VT*, 15 (1965), 486-503.

DE VAUX, R., *Ancient Israel, its Life and Institutions* (New York, 1961).

WATERMAN, L., "The Martyred Servant Motif of Is. 53," *JBL*, 56 (1937), 27-34.

WEINFELD, M., "Universalism and Particularism in the Period of Exile and Restoration" (in Hebrew), *Tarbiz*, 33 (1964-5724), 228-242.

WERNBERG-MØLLER, P., Review of D. R. Hillers, *Treaty Curses*, etc., in *Journal of Semitic Studies*, 10 (1965), 281-283.

——, Review of C. R. North, *The Second Isaiah*, ibid., 283-285.

WRIGHT, G. E., "The Terminology of Old Testament Religion and its Significance," *Journal of Near Eastern Studies*, 1 (1942), 404-411.

YAMAUCHI, E. H., "Tammuz and the Bible," *JBL*, 84 (1965), 283-290.

YOUNG, E. J., *Studies in Isaiah* (London, 1955).

ZIEGLER, J., *Untersuchungen zur Septuaginta des Buches Isaias* (*Alttestamentliche Abhandlungen*, XII, 3, 1934).

——, *Isaias* (Göttingen edition of Septuagint; 1939).

——, *Isaias* (*Die Heilige Schrift in Deutscher Übersetzung*; Würtzburg, 1948).

ZIMMERLI, W.-JEREMIAS, J., *The Servant of the Lord* (*Studies in Biblical Theology*, No. 20, 1957) = "Παῖς θεοῦ" in *Theologisches Wörterbuch zum Neuen Testament*, ed. G. Kittel-G. Friedrich (1954), 653-713.

INDEX OF BIBLICAL AND OTHER REFERENCES

Genesis
18 — 55
50.23 — 61

Exodus
7.3-5 — 28
32 — 55

Leviticus
19.18 — 41n, 99n

Numbers
14.24 — 7
23.10 — 18 (and n)

Deuteronomy
32.15 — 18 (and n)
33.5, 26 — 18 (and n)

Joshua
1.1, 13, 15 — 9
8.31, 33 — 9
11.12 — 9
12.6 (*bis*) — 9
13.8 — 9
14.7 — 9
18.7 — 9
22.4, 5 — 9
24.29 — 9

Judges
2.8 — 9

II Samuel
22.1 — 9

I Kings
11.34 — 8n
14.18 — 7
15.29 — 7

II Kings
14.25 — 7
17.24 ff. — 50
18.12 — 9
19 — 35

Isaiah
1.1 — 32

Isaiah
7.14 — 3, 74
10.6 ff. — 28
10.32-12.6 — 115
11.10-12 — 115
13.1-14.23 — 12n
14.1-2 — 38 (and n), 99n
14.12-16 — 28
19.18-25 — 40, 99n
22.20 — 7
34-35 — 12n
34.5 — 9
37.23 ff. — 28
40-48 — 12n, 14
40-55 — 12n, 15, 41n
40-66 — 12n, 21
40 ff. — 10, 12n
40.1-2 — 42 (and n), 51, 88, 108
40.1, 9 — 19 f. (and n)
40.2 — 24 (and n)
40.9-11 — 28 (and n)
40.10 — 42 (and n)
40.15-31 — 29 (and n)
40.17 — 42 (and n)
40.27 — 82
40.28 — 34n
41.1 — 34n
41.2-3, 5 — 30
41.8 — 51, 81 f.
41.8, 9 — 14, 94
41.8, 12-14 — 42 f. (and n)
41.8-16 — 30 f. (and n)
41.10-12 — 20 (and n)
41.11-12 — 32 (and n)
41.14, 16, 20 — 82
41.14-16 — 34n
41.15-16 — 43 (and n)
41.17 — 51, 82
41.21 — 82
42.1 — 84, 94
42.1 ff. — 3, 12 ff., 14, 75 ff.
42.2 — 92
42.2-3 — 76
42.2-4 — 77
42.6 — 97-117
42.6 f. — 72
42.7 — 76, 77
42.8 — 77, 103 (and n)

Isaiah
42.10-12 — 33 (and n)
42.15, 18, 20 — 94
42.16-17 — 104
42.17 — 51
42.18 — 103
42.18 ff. — 76 (and n)
42.19 — 8 f. 18 (and n), 94, 95
42.19 ff. — 8-9, 14
42.22 — 20 (and n)
42.22-25 — 25 (and n), 42n
42.23 — 82
42.23-24 — 32
43.1 — 51, 82
43.3 — 34n, 82
43.3-6 — 33 f. (and n), 45
43.8 — 94
43.10 — 14, 81, 94
43.14, 15, 22, 28 — 82
43.23, 24 — 94
43.24-25 — 25 (and n)
44.1 — 82
44.1, 2 — 14, 18n, 81, 94
44.2 — 18 (and n),82
44.3 — 84n
44.5,6 — 82
44.21 — 14, 51, 81, 82, 88, 94
44.21-22 — 26 (and n)
44.23 — 82, 88
44.24 — 51
44.26 — 94
44.28 — 8n, 44, 77, 95n, 96
45.1 — 8n, 44, 77, 95n, 96
45.3 — 82
45.4 — 14, 82
45.4-6 — 44 f. (and n)
45.11 — 80
45.14-17 — 33 ff. (and n)
45.17 — 81, 82
45.19 — 82
45.25 — 81, 82
46.3, 6 — 82
46.13 — 81, 82
47.4 — 82
47.5-15 — 35 f. (and n)
48.1-8 — 26 f. (and n)
48.1, 2, 12, 17 — 82
48.12-14 — 45 f. (and n)
48.18 — 27 (and n)

INDEX OF AUTHORS AND SUBJECTS

(Also of some Key Words and Phrases)

ISAIAH 40-66
A STUDY OF THE TEACHING OF THE SECOND ISAIAH
AND ITS CONSEQUENCES

BY

NORMAN H. SNAITH

TABLE OF CONTENTS

INTRODUCTION

These studies of the last twenty-seven chapters of the Book of the Prophet Isaiah are lectures delivered as Speaker's Lecturer in Biblical Studies in the University of Oxford in the year 1961/2. They consist of an examination of the teaching of the Second Isaiah and of the results of his teaching. The Second Isaiah had what is known in these days as 'a one track mind.' He was the Prophet of the Return. He was an intense nationalist, and he looked forward to a resurrection to abounding prosperity and world dominion for the exiles in Babylonia. Central in his thought was the conception of the Servant of the LORD. This was primarily those who went into exile with the young king Jehoiachin in 597 B.C., but the concept broadens to include all the Babylonian exiles. One of the marked features of his presentation of the Servant is the sudden surprise of the Servant's triumph. The Servant is a hidden Servant.

There are two applications of this ideal of the Hidden Suffering-but-triumphant Servant of the LORD. One is that by Jesus of Nazareth. I believe that Jesus deliberately modelled His life on the Servant of the LORD. He saw Himself as the Servant: not the Suffering Servant, but the Servant who triumphed out of his undeserved sufferings. Not only is this conscious following of the pattern of the Servant concerned with His passion and death and resurrection, but with His whole ministry. This accounts for the so-called Messianic secret, the way in which He told men 'not to make him known' and the remarkable silences at the trials. In our view, it also explains the nationalistic aspect of the earlier part of the Ministry.

The second application is the exclusive, nationalistic attitude of the returned exiles, and all the unease and ultimate strife between the Israel which returned from exile and the Israel which never left Palestine. This culminates in a high priest murdering his brother in the very Temple itself and the expulsion of all who could not prove their descent from the returned exiles. Here was the establishment by Ezra of post-exilic Judaism.

I have to thank the electors for the honour they have done me in putting my name forward as Speaker's Lecturer, and also Professor

H. H. Rowley for his comments and criticisms of these studies when
in manuscript form. Needless to say, I am wholly responsible for the
conclusions reached, especially when they vary from those commonly
accepted.

Thetford,   Norman H. Snaith
February 1965.

PART ONE

THE SECOND ISAIAH

CHAPTER ONE

ISAIAH 40-55 AND 60-62

When we say 'The Second Isaiah', do we mean the author of chapters 40-55 only? Or do we include any or all of chapters 56-66?

There has actually been much greater division of opinion than is generally realised concerning the authorship of the twenty-seven chapters 40-66. CHEYNE [1]) gives long lists of examples both in syntax and in vocabulary to show that there are two sections in 'The Book of the Prophet Isaiah', one of which is chapters 1-39 and the other chapters 40-66. The inference to be drawn from these lists is that chapters 40-66 are the work of one author. There had been various other earlier suggestions of composite authorship, culminating in that of DUHM,[2]) who held that chapters 40-55 consist of the work of an unknown prophet in Babylonia, the Second Isaiah (Deutero-Isaiah). The majority of modern scholars hold to this view. Indeed this view is the modern orthodoxy.

It is also generally agreed that chapters 40-48 were written prior to the fall of Babylon in 538 B.C., but not long before. This is on the basis of such assumptions as that 46: 1 f. refer to orders given by Nabonidus for the evacuation to a place of safety of the idol-gods of Babylon, the fall of the city being virtually imminent. Further, if, as most agree, the references to Cyrus in 44: 28 and 45: 1 are genuine and not interpolations, then chapters 40-48 will be later than (say) 546 B.C., the date of Cyrus's capture of Sardis. These two datings appear to be perfectly sound.

Chapters 40-48 and 49-55 are, then, from the same source, but they have strong affinities with chapters 60-62. These three chapters stand out markedly from the remainder of chapters 56-66. Indeed, we are of the opinion that they also are from the same source; they come from the hand of the author of chapters 40-55, the Second Isaiah.

---

[1]) *Introduction to the Book of Isaiah*, 1895.
[2]) *Das Buch Jesaia*, 1892.

SKINNER [1]) says: 'The main features can be paralleled from chapters 49-55, and the strong resemblance to 49: 14 ff.; 51: 7 ff.; 54 would lead naturally to its being assigned to the same author.' He is referring to chapter 60. He continues: 'Had the chapter occupied a different position doubt on this point would hardly arise; it could be accepted without difficulty as a prophecy of return from exile, written in Babylon.' He thus assumes that chapter 60 is early post-exilic. This is partly, at least, because it follows a series of gloomy chapters such as can scarcely be from the hand of a jubilant Babylonian Isaiah who is full of hope for the future. But the argument is based on the assumption that chapters 40-55 form one editorial whole, and that chapters 56-66 form another, but distinct, editorial whole. If, on the other hand, we assume that chapters 40-66 form an editorial whole, then there is no *a priori* reason why there should not be material in chapters 56-66 which are from the hand of the author of chapters 40-55. It is the situation of chapters 56-59 that causes the difficulty. These are certainly of different origin from what precedes them and equally from what follows them. The attitude of the writer is different, and so is the content; so, indeed are the whole background and the attendant circumstances.

It is true that the return of exiles in 60: 4, 9 apparently refers to Jews who are dispersed among the Gentiles generally. It is also true that the ingathering of these dispersed Jews, the Diaspora, was an object of prophetic concern and anticipation in the years following the reestablishment of the Jewish community in Palestine in the late sixth century B.C. But these are no reasons for assuming that 60: 4, 9 are therefore of later date than chapters 40-55. Compare 43: 5 f.: 'I will bring thy seed from the east, and gather them from the west; I will say to the north, Give up; and to the south, Keep not back; bring my sons from far, and my daughters from the end of the earth'. Or again, see 41: 9: 'Thou (Israel) whom I have taken hold of from the ends of the earth, and called thee from the corners thereof.' To these we would add 49: 6, which we translate: 'I will also make thee a light of Gentiles, that my salvation may be to the end of the earth'.[2]) C. C. TORREY [3]) claimed that 'chapters 34-66. . .(with the exception of 36-39, which

---

[1]) *Isaiah*, vol. ii, Cambridge Bible (revised 1917), p. 195.

[2]) See p. 155. This translation entails no alteration of the text. It is merely more accurate. I take 'light of Gentiles' (the 'to' has been inserted by the translators) to mean 'a world-wide light' to guide every far-away Israelite home.

[3]) *The Second Isaiah*, 1928, p. 53.

have a different origin) form a homogeneous group and are the work of a single hand'. For a man who did not accept the historicity of any exile in Babylonia, it is easy to see that some such statement is inevitable. There are certainly enough similarities between chapters 40-55 and parts of chapters 56-66 to warrant the assumption of a common authorship. TORREY was, we hold, justified so far as chapters 60-62 are concerned, however wide of the mark he may have been in other respects. There are many passages in 40-55 and 60-62 which speak of the gathering of the outcasts from far way. So much is this the case, that either TORREY is right and they all belong to a later date and all refer to the Diaspora, or TORREY is wholly wrong and they all belong to the closing years of the Babylonian exile. What certainly seems to be the case is that, so far as this matter of outcasts returning is concerned, 40-55 and 60-62 go together. Something of this was realised by STADE [1]) when he said that chapters 59 and 63-66 were by a writer later than the author of chapters 40-55, and by CORNILL [2]) who regarded chapters 40-62 as the work of the Second Isaiah, adding that chapters 40-48 were written by him in Babylonia.

The claim that chapters 40-55 and 60-62 have a common authorship and origin is based on the following considerations: similarities in style, vocabulary, a common theme of deliverance, references to a return to Jerusalem.

60: 4.   Compare 49: 18a, of which it is an exact repetition: 'Lift up thine eyes round about, and see: they all gather themselves together, they come to thee.' The argument is sometimes advanced that 60: 4 must be either a gloss or the work of a copyist or a devoted pupil. The argument is far from being as forceful in the case of the Second Isaiah as it might be in the case of another author. There is no rule, either in law or in custom, against any author, modern or ancient, repeating on occasion his own phrases and illustrations. All of them can, and many of them do, both in written and even more in spoken words. But the Second Isaiah (40-55) has 'a few favourite phrases' and he 'constantly reverts to a few fixed themes.' [3]) Of these recurrent themes

---

[1]) *Geschichte des Volkes Israel*, 1887, S. 70n.
[2]) *Einleitung in das Alte Testament*, 1891, SS. 151 f.
[3]) SKINNER, *op. cit.*, p. xxii.

'children from afar' and references to 'the isles' are perhaps the most marked, whilst references to the return to Jerusalem are frequent. In the case of this particular author, therefore, repetitions tend to confirm authorship rather than suggest copyists. The remainder of 60: 4 has close affinities in referring to the return with other passages within chapters 40-55. Compare 'thy sons shall come from afar' (60: 4) with 'bring my sons from afar' (43: 6); also 'and thy daughters shall be nursed at the side' (60: 4) with 'and they shall bring their sons in their bosom, and thy daughters shall be carried upon their shoulders. And kings shall be thy nursing fathers and their queens thy nursing mothers' (49: 22 f.).

60: 9.   'for the isles shall wait for me' לי איים יקוו: compare 51: 5 'for me the isles shall wait' אלי איים יקוו.

60: 9.   The verse ends with 'and for the Holy One of Israel, because he hath glorified thee,' which is exactly the end of 55: 5. Such repetitive conclusions are taken elsewhere (e.g. the Holiness Code) as proof of a common origin. Surely the same argument applies to this author. Also the root פאר (glorify) is characteristic of the Second Isaiah; 44: 23; 49: 3; 55: 5 and 60: 7; 60: 9 (here); 60: 13; 60: 21; 61: 3, eight times altogether against five elsewhere.

60: 10.   'for in my wrath I smote thee, but in my favour have I had mercy upon thee.' Compare 54: 7: 'for a small moment have I forsaken thee, but with great mercies will I gather thee.'

60: 13.   'the fir tree, the plane tree (תדהר, RV 'pine') and the cypress (תאשור, RV 'box') together,' which is found exactly in 41: 19. These descriptions of a bountiful nature are influenced by the tree-gardens (heb. *pardes*, Zend. *pairi-daêza*) of the Persian kings. Cf. Neh. 2: 8; Cant. 4: 13; Ec. 2: 5.

60: 15.   'forsaken and hated.' See similar ideas in 49:14; 49: 21; 54: 6; 54: 11. The words for the most part are different, but the ideas are the same.

60: 16.   'suck the milk of the nations, and shall suck the breast of kings.' Cf. similar ideas in 49: 23.

60: 16.   'and that thou shalt know that I the LORD am thy saviour, and thy redeemer the Mighty One of Jacob,' which is a near repetition of 49: 26.

61: 1. 'the spirit of the LORD God is upon me.' Cf. 42: 1: I have put my spirit upon him.' See also 48: 16.

61: 1. Note the use of the *pi'el* of the root בשׂר, used of announcing the glad tidings of release and restoration: 40: 9; 52: 7.

61: 1. The release from exile is described under the figure of the release of prisoners from darkness and dungeons; cf. 42: 7 and 49: 9. Compare also Ps. 107: 10-14. We prefer the margins of RV and RSV: 'opening of eyes to them that are bound.' The root פקח in biblical Hebrew is confined to the opening of eyes and ears, and it is not the word for 'opening of prison' (AV, RV, RSV). In modern Hebrew the root means 'be wide awake, be smart.' Further, the association of blindness and darkness is found in 49: 9, and the 'blind eyes' of 42: 7 are those of prisoners in dungeons and those that sit in the darkness of prison-houses. See also Ps. 107: 10.

61: 2. 'the acceptable year.' Compare 49: 8 'an acceptable time' רצון. See also 40: 2: 'her punishment has been accepted' (the verb is the root רצה: RV has 'her iniquity is pardoned').

61: 3. 'a failing spirit' (RV 'a spirit of heaviness'). The root is כהה, 42: 3.

61: 4. building up the old wastes, etc.; cf. 49: 8; also 58: 12; 60: 10.

61: 6. 'the wealth of the nations.' The phrase itself is found in 60: 5 and 6. Note also the characteristic omission of the definite article in chapters 60-62, itself a feature of chapters 40-55. In the main, the article occurs in the Hebrew in these chapters only when it can be inserted without inserting a consonant, i.e. with the inseparable particles. We very rarely have the consonant *be*.

61: 7. 'double' משׁנה, occurring twice. Compare 40: 2, where כפלים is used. Both words mean 'twice as much,' Zech. 9: 12; Job 42: 10.

61: 8. 'an everlasting covenant' ברית עולם with the verb כרת and the preposition ל. Compare 55: 3. The phrase and the idea become increasingly common in the P-tradition.

61: 11.   The metaphor of seed sown and springing up is found in
            42: 9; 43: 19 and especially 55: 10.

62: 4.   The simile of the forsaken and deserted שְׁמָמָה (RV 'De-
            solate') is found in 54: 1. See also 49: 14 ff; 54: 4 f.
            CHEYNE regarded 61: 1 ff.; 62: 1 ff.; 62: 6 ff. as either
            soliloquies of the Servant, or that ideal as reflected in the
            mind of a later disciple.

62: 8.   'the LORD hath sworn by his right hand.' The idea of God
            swearing a binding oath, which must necessarily be 'by
            Himself,' is found in 45: 23; 54: 9. Compare the frequent
            occurrence in Deuteronomy, much of which comes from
            substantially the same time and venue as chapters 40-55,
            60-62. The idea of 'the right hand of the LORD' as the
            instrument by which He delivers Israel is found in Exod.
            15, some Psalms, Isa. 41: 10 and here. The similar phrase
            'the arm of the LORD' belongs in the main to Deuterono-
            my, Jeremiah, some Psalms, and the Second Isaiah:
            51: 9; 52: 10; 53: 1 and here. For the picture of the shep-
            herd gathering the lambs, see 40: 11.

62: 9.   'in my holy courts' קָדְשִׁי (RV, 'courts of my sanctuary').
            It is not necessary to assume that this phrase as used here
            involves the temple already having been rebuilt. There are
            many references to the gates and walls of Jerusalem which
            must belong to the period between the destruction of the
            Temple and city and the time before Nehemiah managed
            to rebuild the walls and set up the gates once more. Nor
            need the writer have necessarily been domiciled in Palestine,
            though this may possibly have been so. The reference to
            firstfruits is plain, and it is plain also that the writer has
            in mind the Deuteronomic rule that the firstfruits must be
            eaten at Jerusalem, Dt. 12: 17 f.; 14: 23 f.; 16: 9-16. But
            these verses refer to the future. The reference in v. 8 to the
            enemies of Israel and foreigners eating and drinking
            Israel's corn and wine does not of necessity refer to de-
            predations which took place after the return, those which
            Nehemiah sought to stop by rebuilding the walls. Such
            depredations could belong to any period of Judaean
            weakness and foreign domination, but especially to the
            years following 586 B.C., when there had been no return
            from Babylon of any kind.

62: 10-12. Those who think of these chapters as belonging to the
period following the Return from Babylonia, find themselves in difficulty here. They have to make these verses
refer either to Jews still in Babylon or to the complete
ingathering of the Diaspora at some distant date. Much is
made of the lack of mention of the desert; but why must
any writer mention everything every time? But the desert
is not absent to the extent to which some allege. Compare
v. 10 'prepare the way of the people' with 40: 3 where the
desert is actually mentioned. See also the common use of
the word מסלה (highway) in v. 10 and in 40: 3. If the desert
had been actually, instead of virtually mentioned in 62: 10,
the argument would then have been that it was a sure sign
of a copyist. Note also the characteristic repetition of the
opening word עברו (pass through), a well-known feature
of the style of the Second Isaiah: 40: 1; 51: 9; 51: 17;
52: 11 and 'I even I', 43: 11; 43: 25; (48: 11); 48: 15;
51: 12.

62: 10.   'cast up, cast up' סלו סלו is another characteristic repetition,
as in the previous line. This 'throwing up' and 'gathering
the stones' is an aditional detail in the picture of building a
raised highway מסלה across the desert.

62: 10.   The lifting up of an ensign to אל the peoples (note the
plural: it means the Gentiles) is found also in 49:22.
The meaning is not universalist either there or here; see
p. 159.

62: 11.   'proclaim', using the *hiph'il* of שמע; 45: 21; 43: 12; 48: 2;
44: 8; 48: 5; 48: 6; 41: 26; 52: 7; 42: 9; 42: 2; 43: 9. There
are 29 cases in all of this use of this form of the verb, and 12
of them are in chapters 40-55 and 60-62.

62: 11.   'unto the end of the earth' קצה הארץ. Compare 48: 20:
49: 6; 42: 10; 43: 6.

62: 11.   'behold, his reward is with him, and his recompense before
him', which is exactly 40: 10.

62: 12.   Once more we have the theme of the redeemed, no longer
forsaken.

We see therefore that there are many repetitions, near-repetitions
and similarites of style and ideas in chapters 40-55 and 60-62. We find
occasional reproductions of actual phrases and on occasion the repeti-

tion of a whole line. Often there is a repetition of words combined with other words and phrases. Sometimes the same theme is expressed in a closely allied but different way. We judge that all this is precisely the same mixture, here in chapters 60-62, of repetition, near-repetition and non-repetition, exact phrases and near-exact phrases, that we meet with in chapters 40-55, the kind of thing we would expect to find in anything which the writer of chapters 40-55 wrote. Our conclusion, therefore, is that we can safely include chapters 60-62 in the writings of the Second Isaiah.

Most scholars of modern times are of the opinion that chapters 40-48 as a whole are earlier than chapters 49-55, the first nine chapters belonging to the period between 546 B.C. and 539 B.C., and the rest after 539 B.C. The idea of chapters 40-55 being a series of detached, separate poems is not incompatible with this.[1] The idea of detached pieces seems to be sound, but at the same time there are three distinct sections, 40-48, 49-55 and 60-62. These three sections come from three different periods of the unknown prophet's life and activity. Chapters 40-48 belong to the period when the hope of rescue from exile appears after the first successes of Cyrus, especially with his capture of Sardis in 546 B.C. Chapters 49-55 belong to the period immediately following the fall of Babylon when the release became very much more of a probability, even approaching a certainty. Chapters 60-62 belong to the time of waiting after the fall of Babylon, and probably towards the end of that waiting time. After all, no one would suppose that Babylon fell one night and that the exiles set out for Palestine early the next morning. There must have been a measurable time between the fall of Babylon and the movement of Jews towards Palestine, whether under Sheshbazzar or another. The note of triumph appears intermittently in the first group; it is much more pronounced in the second group; it is positively rampant in the third group. The style is substantially the same throughout all the nineteen chapters, except that the ecstatic, exuberant elements are heightened in chapters 60-62. The sense of release and future triumph becomes more pronounced and imminent from section to section.

---

[1] C. R. NORTH, *The Second Isaiah* (1964), pp. 4-12. For a discussion of 40-55 as a series of separate poems, see pp. 166 f.

CHAPTER TWO

THE PROPHET OF THE RETURN

The author of chapters 40-55 and 60-62, the Second Isaiah, is generally recognised as being the Prophet of the Return, that is, of the return of the exiles from Babylonia to Jerusalem. Most scholars, however, go much farther than this and they find the climax of his message in the ideal of the Servant of the LORD, usually with expiatory and intercessory functions, and in universalism, by which is meant a supra-nationalist appeal, that salvation is not for the Jews only, but for all nations on earth. Such conclusions we believe to be wrong. The Return is not merely one of the themes of these sixteen (eighteen) chapters, to be outshone by world-wide humanitarian ideals. It is the prophet's dominant theme. It is true that the prophet invests this return with idealist splendour, and it is also true that the ideal of the Servant is involved in it, but basically the Return is this prophet's ONE theme, and all else is subservient to it.

Many writers regard the idea and theme of the Servant of the LORD as being the great and outstanding contribution of these chapters, whether the conception be thought to be that of the Second Isaiah himself or that of another, whether predecessor or successor.[1] For many, the very mention of the Second Isaiah sets them thinking forthwith of the Servant. Or if they think also of the Return, the thought-sequence is Prophet-Return-Servant. This is wrong: it should be Prophet-Servant-Return. The climax for him was the Return. The emphasis on the idea of the Servant as the climax of the prophet's thinking appears to be due mostly to Christian interpretations of Isaiah 53 as a preview of the Passion and Death of Christ. We hold that everything in these chapters is definitely subservient to the Return from Babylon and the Restoration of the nation. There is another thought-sequence, found more often among modern Jews but something of it also among modern Christians: Prophet-Monotheism-Humanitarianism ($s^e\underline{d}\bar{a}\underline{k}\hat{o}t$), as forming the basis of a world culture and religion. We hold this also to be wrong. The prophet certainly is a monotheist, and in him also monotheism becomes for the first

---

[1] Some scholars regard the so-called Servant Songs as interpolations into the 'main body' of the work.

time clear and definite and unadulterated. But, important as this contribution undoubtedly is, it is secondary. The one theme is the Return, and all else is brought in by means of emphasising and demonstrating the certainty of this.

The difference between this point of view and the usual universalist-humanitarian-expiatory point of view can be shown in the translation of Isaiah 53. Compare the translation usually offered (EVV and elsewhere) with the following translation of v. 12:

Therefore I-will-give-him-a-share among-the-great-ones,
And-with-the-strong-ones he-shall-share the-spoil;
In-return-for being-his-stripped-naked to-death,
and-he-was-numbered with-the-rebels.
For-it-was-he that-bore the-punishment-of-the-great-ones,
And-with-reference-to-the-rebels it-was-caused-to-light (on him).

Notes on Isaiah 53: 12.

רבים can mean either 'the many' or 'the great.' The verse consists of three synthetic couplets, and עצומים in the other half of this couplet certainly means 'the strong ones.' The whole point of the chapter is that the apparently weak and despised slave will in the end share the spoils of victory with the great and the strong.

הערה is the *hiph'il* of ערה (be naked, bare), and the construction is impersonal, cf. English 'one', French *on*, German *man*. Similarly for יפגיע at the end of the verse. For 'his (or 'his life': נפש with suffix) being stripped bare, poured out' as meaning 'death,' see Ps. 141: 8. But here the picture may even be that of the dead of the defeated being stripped bare as they lay on the battlefield.

פשעים definitely does not mean 'transgressors.' The word means 'rebels.' It is the word characteristically used by the prophets of sinners as rebels against God. It is part of their general attitude whereby sin is not a transgression of the law so much as a rebellion against God. Further, the noun פשע represents sin in its most serious aspect: Job 34: 37, 'he addeth rebellion פשע to his sin חטאת.'

והוא is emphatic: 'for it was he who': cf. v. 5. This emphatic use of the copula with a preposition or a noun is frequent in this chapter, because the author is concerned with the amazing contrast between the former and the latter state of the Servant, and his wholly unexpected victory. The point is that it was he who met with disaster and it was undeserved. The punishment which he suffered was that which ought to have fallen on the guilty rebels. It was caused to light on him instead: cf. v. 6 where this same *hiph'il* of פגע is used. This יפגיע is usually interpreted to mean 'interceded for,' but this is reading into the verb a different meaning from that in v. 6. We find here no thought of 'interceding for' the rebels, and no vicarious suffering in the sense that the Servant suffered in order to save the rebels. The writer is stating the plain fact that the Servant did not deserve the suffering and disaster, and because he did not deserve it, it must necessarily be the case that he will prosper and triumph. The writer is not interested in the fate of the Gentile rebels, but he is convinced that the law of rewards and retribution still holds. The Servant, so to speak, got in the way of the proper retribution which was properly falling upon the guilty rebels. It was not in accordance with the proper ordering of things, and when things are worked out fully the triumph of the Servant must come to pass.

Many writers have emphasised the prophet's insistence on the uniqueness of the God of Israel, and his strong emphasis on a true monotheism.[1]) As in the case of the Servant, this theme is certainly an important element in what the prophet has to say. Also, in both cases his words have borne a greater and a richer fruit than he could possibly have expected. It is also clear that here at last the monotheism of Israel is stated firmly and plainly. Nevertheless, this theme also is subservient to the declaration of the coming Return. To put all this another way. The prophet did not set out to state his doctrine of the Servant, nor did he set out to write a treatise on monotheism. He had neither subject on his list of primary objectives. He had but one theme on this list: the Return. His task was to convince the Judean exiles that the return was certain and that it was increasingly imminent. He had to open their blind eyes and make them see this. The prophet's insistence on the uniqueness of the God of Israel is his main confidence in the Return. This is why he emphasises God's incomparable majesty and power, and His effectiveness against the ineptitude of the idols of Babylon. But the Return is not proof of the unique power and might of God. Rather, the unique power and might of the ONE GOD is the guarantee of the Return. The prophet begins with the Return; he ends with it; he deals with it all the time in between. Everything in the nineteen chapters has to do with it, and everything is subordinate to it. This is his theme: the Return from the Babylonian exile, involving the resurrection as from the dead of the old Israel, and the resurgence as from a new birth of a new Israel.

Not only does the prophet speak of the Return, but he is full of immediate instancy. He is vigorous, he is urgent; he cannot

---

[1]) For an essay on the existence and development of monotheism in early times, see 'The Advent of Monotheism in Israel', *The Annual of the Leeds University Oriental Society*, vol. V, pp. 100-113.

wait. It is true that the prophets in general are speaking on the eve of great events. Indeed, it is usually a time of crisis [1]) that stings them into speech and action, and imbues them with a zeal and urgency that will not be denied. Their words which have come down to us have something to say in a special and divine way for men of every age and for us now, but their primary intention was to speak to the people of their own times. Perhaps this was their only intention; indeed, this is more likely than not. But they were speaking greater truths than they knew. However this may be, the prophets, without exception, were urgent in their message. If one is to write an account of the message of any prophet, the first heading should be 'The Time is at Hand.' This sense of immediacy is perhaps most apparent in the Second Isaiah. He is essentially the prophet in a hurry. With him, as with the writers of the apocalypses, it is a case of 'immediately, if not sooner.'

The literary style of the Second Isaiah is one of hurrying, of rushing tumultuously on. This atmosphere of hurry is enhanced by the frequent use of the 3:2 metre which he uses, with the pattern $a\,b\,c$: $b'c'$ and the alternative $a\,b\,c$: $c'b'$. For example:

> Bring my-sons from-afar
> and-my-daughters from-the-end-of-the-earth. 43:6.

which is $a\,b\,c$: $b'c'$; and

> Who-gave for-a-spoil Jacob,
> And-Israel to-robbers. 42:24.

which is $a\,b\,c$: $c'b'$. This metre is known as the *qinah* metre, because its use was first remarked by BUDDE as being found in laments and elegies. But it is the lyric metre: see the Song of Songs. It is true that the metre has what has been called 'a halting effect' and that it is used to produce or to express an atmosphere suitable for mourning, but in essence it is expressive of emotion, and in the writings of the Second Isaiah it has the effect of a man stumbling because he cannot go quickly enough. He appears to be in such a hurry that he had not the time to complete the full 3:3 couplet. He rushes on and in so doing manages to catch only a passing echo of the first line.

As an illustration of this, we discuss in detail the first couplet of his writings, 40:1 and 2a. Here the decisiveness, the thoroughness and

---

[1]) Nowhere is the fact that 'crisis' is the Greek word for 'judgment' is more apt than in the messages of the prophets.

the speedy effectiveness of the LORD's work in releasing His people is apparent. We consider the first two words in each line of the couplet.

The opening words of 40: 1 are 'comfort ye, comfort ye' נחמו נחמו. Apart from the characteristic repetition of an opening imperative which arises out of the prophet's sense of urgency, it is important from our point of view to realise clearly the precise meaning of this root נחם. Especially it is important to understand that this root does not mean 'comfort' in the ordinary modern use of the word—soothing words which may help in the midst of sorrow and trouble which continue, something to help the sufferer to continue to bear the pain and sorrow. It has little to do with any hope that is merely tentative, however pious and devoted. It has little to do with any betterment which may happen, or even with the preliminary stages of what is going to happen. The word involves a complete, a definite and a decisive change. As used here, especially when it is repeated, the word is part of the vocabulary of a confident, urgent, resurgent nationalist. For the nationalist element in this prophet's writings, see pp. 154 ff.; here we are concerned with the author's frame of mind—this vigorously religious, joyously triumphant Zionist of the sixth century B.C. Of all the prophets, this man is the prototype of the devoted, enthusiastic Israeli of today.

The Second Isaiah is called the Prophet of Comfort chiefly because of these opening words, 'comfort ye, comfort ye'. Further, Isa. 40: 1-26 is the Haftarah (Reading from the Prophets) in the synagogues for the Sabbath *Va-ethchanan* (Deut. 3: 23-7: 11). It is the first of the seven Haftarahs of Consolation which follow the Fast of Ab. The Sabbath itself is called *Nachamu* because of the use of this passage as the Haftarah for this particular Sabbath. But the root נחם does not mean 'comfort *in* sorrow.' It means 'comfort *out of* sorrow', make an effective end of all tears and woe. For evidence for this, see two articles in *The Expository Times*, the first by D. WINTON THOMAS, 'A Note on the Hebrew root נחם' (xlix, January 1933; p. 191) and the second by N. H. SNAITH (lvii, November 1945; pp. 477 ff.). The first article begins with the Arabic *naḥama* (breathe hard, pantingly: of a horse), and D. W. THOMAS shows that the connexion of this root with the idea of comfort is through the idea of the relief obtained by taking a deep breath. See Isa. 1: 24, 'I will ease me of my advesaries'; Ezek. 5: 13 refers to the relief which comes when anger is appeased; Job 16: 2 does not refer to 'miserable comforters,' but to 'breathers out of trouble.' The Syriac *naḥam* means 'make to breathe, resuscitate and quicken the dead,' because the word really means 'breathe again' and 'breathe deeply.' Thus *nouḥama* in Syriac means 'resurrection,' the idea being that of the dead being once more supplied with breath. In the second article, the main emphasis is that the meaning 'comfort' does not come through ideas of pity, compassion and the like, but through the idea of changing the mind. It is not as 'patently absurd' as Professor JAMES BARR thinks [1]) to suppose that the origin of a word has considerable influence on its subsequent usage. It is comparatively common for a word to retain something of its earlier meaning side by side with a developed meaning: e.g. the English words 'peculiar,' 'quick,' 'frank.' Thus Jer. 15: 6 is 'I am weary with changing my mind' (RV, repenting), i.e. weary of stepping in so as to change the normal sequence of sin and its punishment. See also Exod. 13: 17; 1 Sam. 15: 29, etc., In the Old Testament the word rarely means 'sympathise with in sorrow,' but rather 'comfort out of sorrow' and make an end of it, Gen. 24: 67. It involves effective comfort, the drying of tears once and for all because all has changed. Isa. 40: 1 says that such effective, convincing words are to be spoken as to ensure that Jerusalem's tears shall cease forthwith. All is conviction. The action is immediate.

The same conviction and urgent immediacy is to be seen in the first phrase of v. 2. This phrase is (AV, RV) 'speak ye comfortably to Jerusalem,' or RSV 'speak tenderly.' The Hebrew is דברו על לב, lit. speak to the heart. LEVY [2]) refers to 'sympathetic speech.' This is because the commentaries say that the phrase is used of courtship, Gen. 34: 3; Judg. 19: 3; Hos. 2: 16 (Eng. 14). But there is an error here. The association is not with tender words and soft sentimental speech, though these may well be involved. The reference is to effective, successful courtship. There are other cases of the use of the phrase where courtship is not involved, but what is involved is the idea of conviction. Ruth 2: 13 is near-courtship. In 2 Chr. 32: 6 Hezekiah speaks to the captains and instils courage into them against Sennacherib. In 2 Chr. 30: 22 he speaks with similar effect to the Levites. In 2 Sam. 19: 8 (Eng. 7) Joab speaks in such fashion as to shock David out of his inaction following the death of Absalom. There was nothing

---

[1]) *The Semantics of Biblical Literature*, 1961, p. 171. It is he that uses the word 'decisive'. BARR has rightly drawn attention to the danger of being influenced too much by the etymology of a word, but he frequently exaggerates the statements of those he attacks.

[2]) *Deutero-Isaiah*, 1952, p. 113.

tender or sympathetic in Joab's attitude. It was plain, brutal speech, the exact opposite of honeyed, sympathetic words. So also in Gen. 50: 21 Joseph speaks straightly and plainly to his brothers and shakes them out of their fear of him. Further, against the RSV rendering, the heart is not particularly the seat of the emotions, and certainly not exclusively so. The heart is the seat of thought and knowledge, memory, will and everything else. It is the innermost core of a man's being, the seat of conviction.[1] Thus 'speak to the heart' is a strong phrase used to describe speech which leads to immediate conviction. It is our 'change of heart.'

There are three instances where נחם (comfort) and דבר על לב (speak to the heart) are used in parallel lines: Gen. 50: 21 E; Ruth 2: 13; and here in Isa. 40: 1, 2a. The Syriac in Isa. 40: 2 expresses the idea of *complete* satisfaction, lit. 'fill the heart.' This is the Peshitta rendering also at John 11: 19 for παραμυθέομαι, which is used by Symmachus for נחם in Isa. 40: 2 and by LXX at 2 Macc. 15: 9.

---

[1] BROWN, DRIVER and BRIGGS, *Hebrew and English Lexicon* of the Old Testament, 1907, *in loc*.

CHAPTER THREE

THE NATIONALIST

It is usually stated that the Second Isaiah is the great universalist: that is, his message and his promises extend to all mankind on a fully liberal scale, and he looks forward to the spread of Israel's faith throughout all the world. LEVY [1]) writes of this hope of the prophet of 'seeing Yahweh's religion prevalent over the whole world.' He says (p. 23) that 'later, Israel chose not to emphasise' this universal spirit, but that 'once roused (it) never died, though often it had to fight for its existence:' which, all things considered, is a very generous description of the exclusive Judaism of the fifth and fourth centuries B.C., and, indeed, of the spirit of the Jerusalem 'hierarchy' which very nearly wrecked Christianity at the start, Acts 15; Gal. 1-2.

But statements like this of REUBEN LEVY's are typical of the general opinion. Scholars find in the work of the Second Isaiah the beginnings of what is called missionary enterprise. Actually, the beginnings of this world-wide religion are to be found in Ezekiel, though even there the thought is still nationalistic. It comes in the realisation that if God's people cannot come to Him in their need, He can come to them. The idea that God is to be found only in the centralised temple at Jerusalem breaks down under the need of God's people. When Isaiah of Jerusalem saw the throne of God, he saw it fixed and firm, immovable (Isa. 6), but Ezekiel did not see it that way. He saw (Ezek. 1) a chariot which had wheels within wheels, so fixed that each wheel could run east and west or south and north, the inner wheel being at right-angles to the outer wheel. Beside the wheels there were living creatures with wings, and these winged creatures could lift into the air the whole concern. The chariot was completely mobile, and could travel over land, and fly over any mountain or sea. Above the chariot there was a platform (RV, firmament), and on this there was the throne of God. Ezekiel 9:3; 10:4; 10:19; 11:23 and 10:20 with chapter 1, tell the story of God's reluctance to leave His ancient home, but indicate also the stern necessity. In Isa. 49: 20 the crowding is at Jerusalem, and in 54: 2 the lengthening of the tent cords and the

---

[1]) *op. cit.* p. 23.

strengthening of the stakes is also in Jerusalem. The Second Isaiah thinks in terms of bringing the people back to Jerusalem.

There are three exceptions to the general opinion that the Second Isaiah was a universalist. They are N. H. SNAITH,[1]) P. A. H. DE BOER,[2]) and R. MARTIN-ACHARD.[3]) To these we may in part add J. LIND-BLOM,[4]) who agrees that the Second Isaiah was nationalist at first, but was universalist after 539 B.C.·

The picture of the Second Isaiah as a universalist is considerably enhanced, and for many largely influenced by the usual translation of אור גוים in 49: 6 as 'a light to the Gentiles.'[5]) The usual translation is (RV): I will also give thee for a light to the Gentiles, that thou mayest be my salvation (margin: 'that my salvation may be') unto the end of the earth.' Largely on the basis of this, other passages are interpreted and translated as being universalist in intention and content. Without this particular translation of 49: 6, the universal element in the Second Isaiah is much more meagre than many realise. There are many passages which, if they are translated as though this particular rendering of Isa. 49: 6 never existed, are capable of a very different interpretation.

A strict translation of 49: 6 is: It is far too small a thing for you to be servant to me to restore the tribes of Jacob and to bring back the preserved of Israel. I will set you as a light of Gentiles for my salvation to be to the end of the earth.' The verse contains five sections, of which the last four form two couplets. Thus, like 43: 5 (for instance), the first section is without its parallel. 'Restore the tribes of Jacob' is parallel to 'bring back the preserved of Israel.' This is satisfactory. Both phrases refer to the Babylonian exiles. There are many cases where 'Jacob' and 'Israel' are in parallel and have this significance: 40: 27; 41: 8; 41: 14; 43: 1; etc., and especially 49: 5 'to bring back Jacob to him, and that Israel be gathered to him.' In the second couplet, the parallelism is 'a light of Gentiles' and 'for my salvation to be to the end of the earth (RVm),' that is, a light through-

---

[1]) 'The Servant of the Lord in Deutero-Isaiah' in T. H. ROBINSON Festschrift, *Studies in Old Testament Prophecy*, 1950, pp. 187-200.

[2]) *Second Isaiah's Message* (Oudtestamentische Studiën, Deel XI), 1956.

[3]) *Israël et les nations: la perspective missionaire de l'Ancien Testament*, 1959. English translation, *A Light to the Nations*, 1962.

[4]) *Prophecy in Ancient Israel*, 1963, p. 428.

[5]) What is written here in this chapter is largely a development of what was first put forward in the above-mentioned essay in the T. H. ROBINSON Festschrift

out all the gentile [1]) world, in order that God's salvation of Israel—the
the salvation with which the prophet is elsewhere concerned—may
reach the end of the world. That this world-wide salvation is God's
salvation of Israel can be seen from 43: 6: 'bring my sons from far,
and my daughters from the end of the earth.' Or again: 'whom I have
taken hold of החזקתיך from the ends of the earth, and from its corners
I have called thee,' where the previous verse makes it clear that the
reference is to Israel, God's servant, to Jacob whom God has chosen,
and to 'my lover' Abraham's seed.

The phrase 'a world-wide light' (49: 6, RV 'a light to the Gentiles')
is found also in 42: 6, but not in Codex B of LXX, nor in the original
hand of א. The first corrector of א has 'a covenant of my people to a
light of Gentiles' γένους μου εἰς φῶς ἐθνῶν, though other correctors
and other MSS do not have 'my.' There seems to be no sound reason
for regarding 'for a light of Gentiles' as an interpolation in 42: 6.
The structure of the verse demands the inclusion of the phrase in
spite of its omission by two leading LXX manuscripts. On the other
hand, the Hebrew text of 49: 6 is probably right as against LXX (all
major MSS except codex A; Q has it in the margin) in omitting
לברית עם (for a covenant of the people) as a gloss from 42: 6.

DE BOER [2]) interprets 'light of (to the) Gentiles' to mean that the
renewed people will be set as a light, openly seen and respected among
the nations. 'Everyone who sees the redemption of the Judean
people, even great nations, kings and princes, will be astonished and
will respect it as a wonderful salvation.' Similarly, MARTIN-ACHARD
says: [3]) 'the shining of the light of the Servant. . .does not necessarily
mean something like the evangelisation of the Hellenistic world in the
first century of the Christian era.' Or again (p. 30), 'the heathen will
learn of the redemption of the People of Israel; the salvation that
Yahweh will have given His people will be praised to the ends of the
earth.' MARTIN-ACHARD does not see in the Second Isaiah any
missionary message in the ordinary sense of the term, and no pro-
selytism. Israel is not called to go out to the Gentiles nor actively in
anyway to win them. Rather, and at most, Israel through the salvation
which God has wrought for them and through their loyalty to Him
will be such a dazzling light shining throughout the world, that the
Gentiles will come in humble, subservient awe. 'The heathen, now

---

[1]) There is nothing in the Hebrew equivalent of the preposition 'to.'
[2]) *op. cit.* p. 92.
[3]) *op. cit.* (Eng. tr.), p. 28.

subdued, will give Him the glory that is due to His name (p. 30).'
Both these scholars realise that the Second Isaiah is truly nationalist,
and that he is concerned with the salvation of Israel. Both realise
that he is not interested in the Gentiles as such, and that any place
they may have in the new economy will be entirely subservient,
definitely second-class citizens, if indeed anything more than slaves.
I still prefer my original idea, that the Servant is to be a world-wide
light to guide all scattered Israelites home; but the idea of the Gentiles
as ultimately second-class citizens, if at all, is right. On the other hand
in 51:4 DE BOER's explanation has much to commend it: the phrase
'to be a light of the peoples' (לאור עמים: note the plural) refers to the
promulgation of the Lord's judgment (i.e. the declaration of His will
in human experience: משפט) shining out among the nations.

The phrase ברית עם, usually translated 'a covenant of the people,'
42:6; 49:8, constitutes another problem. The fact that the definite
article is not found is of no account. The Second Isaiah does not
normally use the definite article. There are two cases where the word
עם is found in our chapters with the definite article *be*. The first is
40:7, which is a gloss (see below). The other is 62:10 where the
article is intended to belong to 'way' rather than to 'people'.

The Hebrew in 42:6 has עם in the singular. The Second Isaiah is
consistent about this. When he uses the singular, he means Israel, the
People of God, the true People of God. When he uses the plural, he
means mankind generally, the Gentiles. For the plural (five times),
see 49:22; 51:4; (56:7) and 61:9; 62:10. There are twenty-five
instances of the singular, with and without the suffix. In every case
except two, 42:5 and 40:7, the reference is to Israel. Sometimes it
means the Servant and sometimes it is distinct from the Servant.[1]
The case of 40:7 is as clear a case of a gloss as one could find. The
gloss is 'surely the people is grass,' and it means mankind as distinct
from God Himself. LXX and the Old Latin omit the verse, and it is
outside the scheme of versification. With respect to 42:5, the meaning
there is mankind as a whole, and it is difficult to see how else the prophet could have said what he wanted to say.

In 42:6 and 49:8 the Servant is called ברית עם 'a covenant of the
people.' He is to be the means by which God's people is to be in-
tegrated, bound together once more. Various suggestions have

---

[1] For an explanation of how this can be, see pp. 172 f.

been made as to the meaning here of the word ברית.[1]) The meaning
could be 'mediator of my covenant with,' [2]) though NORTH understands 'people' to mean all the Gentiles, interpreting the passage in a
fully universalist sense. We think that here the word ברית retains
something of its original meaning: the root ברה means 'bind together.'[3]) The Servant is to bind together the old Israel, and this to
make them once more the People of God, the new People of God.

There is, in our view, no possibility of 42:7 referring to the
Gentiles. 'Blind eyes' (v. 7) means the exiles in Babylonia. Blindness
and imprisonment in dungeons are frequent metaphors for this
captivity. DE BOER [4]) refers to KISSANE as saying that here we have a
figurative description of the conversion of the nations, but there is
no need to pick out KISSANE particularly. This interpretation is
common; it is the orthodox one. As MARTIN-ACHARD points out,[5])
the interpretation which makes עם mean 'mankind' here and so the
Gentiles generally 'is specifically based on the parallelism which is
found in 42:6 between ברית עם and לאור גוים.' But this latter phrase
('light of Gentiles') is disputed. Many hold it to be a gloss here, and
in 49:6, from where it is repeated, we hold that a nationalistic interpretation is to be accepted. The Servant's mission, we maintain, is to
release the captives from Babylon, to bring the scattered Israelites
back to Jerusalem and there to establish a restored community, the
New Israel. His task is limited to this. 'There is no question of a
message, starting off from one point and swarming off in the whole
world. . .(all is) relative to the experience of the exile. . .' [6]) The phrase
'covenant of the people' has nothing to do with the Gentiles, but
everything to do with the People of God. SKINNER [7]) agrees with this,
in spite of his general attitude whereby he regards the Second Isaiah
as a universalist. He says 'עם (people) can hardly be understood of
humanity at large (even if that were a possible use of the word),
because in 49:8 the phrase is applied exclusively to the Servant's

---

[1]) See especially MARTIN ACHARD, *op. cit*, p. 26. note 12, and more recently,
C. R. NORTH, *op. cit.*, p. 11. He thinks the phrase is an addition in 49:8.

[2]) NORTH, *op. cit.*, p. 112.

[3]) See VAN DER PLOEG, *Les Chants du Serviteur de Jahve*, 1936, pp. 30 ff, where he
cites VASCARI and VOLZ. Also DE BOER, *op. cit.*, pp. 92 ff. and MARTIN-ACHARD,
op. cit., pp. 26 ff.

[4]) *op. cit.*, p. 93.

[5]) *op. cit.*, p. 27, note 12.

[6]) DE BOER, *op. cit.*, p. 100. See also MARTIN-ACHARD, *op. cit.*, pp. 27 ff.

[7]) *op. cit.*, p. 32.

mission to Israel.' This is indeed plain in 49: 8, as we interpret it.
The Lord has called and chosen His Servant to raise up and restore
Jacob-Israel (v. 6) and thus God's salvation will reach to the end of
the earth. Or, if it be held that v. 8 is in a different context from v. 6,
it is stated in v. 8 that being 'a covenant of the people' means reesta-
blishing the land and causing the ruined properties [1]) to be occupied
once more. This refers to a desolated Jerusalem, and it is to the released
prisoners (i.e. the returning exiles) that the prophet is speaking.
Again, the returning inhabitants are 'from far,' from north and west
and from the land of Sinim, but these are not the Gentiles. These are
'his people' and 'his afflicted' (v. 13). Yet again, there is no justification
for assuming that the overcrowding of vv. 19 f. is due to an immigra-
tion of Gentiles. It is due to the many scattered children coming back
home again. The Gentiles do not appear until v. 22. They do indeed
come to a restored Jerusalem (vv. 22-26), but it is to carry Jerusalem's
sons and daughters as slaves carry the children of their masters. The
kings and queens of the Gentiles are to serve as attendants on the
returning Israelites. They are to be Israel's nursemaids, and they will
bow low before the Israelites as the most abject of slaves: 'bow down
with their faces to the earth, and lick the dust of thy feet' (v. 23). It is
then that Israel will know for certain that the LORD is their God. This
will be because of the subservience and humiliation of the Gentiles.
They will know from actual experience that those who trust in the
God of Israel will be triumphant at last. The captives of the warrior
shall be snatched from him and Israel's children shall be saved. The
chapter closes with v. 26, one of the most bloodthirsty and revengeful
verses in the Old Testament. If the Second Isaiah is the great universalist that many allege, meaning by this one who welcomes the Gentiles
on something at least approaching equal terms, something more than
a 'benevolent colonialism,' then either he has fallen very short of his
great ideals, or we must say that this verse belongs to a later time, say,
the times of Nehemiah and Ezra.

The nationalist, even anti-Gentile, attitude is plain in 43: 3 f. Here
the LORD is the Saviour of Israel and He will hand over Egypt,
Ethiopia and Seba for Israel. There can be no doubt but that here
כפר means 'the price of ransom for a life,' Job 33: 24; 36: 18; Exod.
21: 30; etc. The next verse clinches the matter: 'Because you are
precious in my eyes, you are of great value, and I prefer [2]) you above

---

[1]) נחלה means 'property' rather than 'inheritance'.
[2]) אהב here means 'preferential love,' Gen. 29: 30, 31; Deut. 21: 15.

all others; and I will give men in return for you and peoples in exchange for you.' That is, God is prepared to sacrifice the Gentile peoples for the sake of Israel.[1]) He will deliver them into slavery in order to release Israel from exile and bondage. There is nothing universalist here. It is as narrowly nationalistic as the narrowest and most fervent of modern nationalists could desire. There are times when the Old Testament reaches no higher than many in this modern world.

As we have already pointed out, one of the main barriers to the proper understanding of the nationalistic attitude of the Second Isaiah is that the English Versions have been produced under strong universalist influence. An example of this is 45: 19-25. According to SKINNER,[2]) who here is typical of most, here is 'a salvation as universal as it is eternal.' This statement is made in spite of the fact that the word of the prophet is addressed to those 'that are escaped of the nations' (20), and that the concluding verse (25) is 'in the LORD shall all the seed of Israel triumph [3]) and shall boast.' SKINNER and others are influenced by v. 22: 'Look unto me and be ye saved, all the ends of the earth,' which they interpret to mean all mankind, all the Gentiles, and to involve the open arms of modern missionary zeal. But 'all the ends of the earth' is far from involving the Gentiles in any liberal open-handed fashion. See above (p. 156) and the discussion of 43:6 and 41:9. 'The ends of the earth' is where the Israelites are, where 'my sons' and 'my daughters' are, where 'Israel, my servant' is, and 'Jacob whom I have chosen.' The phrase is a lyrical geographical exaggeration. Also, as we shall see (p. 161) the nationalistic attitude is plain to see in 52:13-15. The great ones were astonished, appalled at the Servant because he was so bedraggled and miserable. But he is no longer the slave of rulers. The tables have been turned. Now, great nations will leap to their feet to honour him, and kings will clasp their hands over their mouths. They will never have heard anything like this, and they will be forced to take particular notice of it. This new unheard of thing is the revival and triumph of Israel after a disaster so apparently final and complete.

---

[1]) Cf. DE BOER, *op. cit.*, p. 12. We are not discussing whether, then or now, nationalism is better than internationalism, or whether any degree of national feeling is right. We are not discussing whether the Second Isaiah was right for his own time or for any other time. We are seeking to find out what the Second Isaiah actually meant.

[2]) *op. cit.*, p. 71.

[3]) SO DE BOER. See also N. H. SNAITH, *The Distinctive Ideas of the Old Testament*, 1944, p. 87. This is much better than the 'be justified' of EVV.

We have translated יַזֶּה (v. 15; AV, RV 'sprinkle'; RVm, RSV 'startle', but RSVm says that the meaning is uncertain) as 'make leap to their feet.' Formerly there was general agreement that the root is נזה I (spurt, spatter: in the *hiph'il*, sprinkle). This root in the *hiph'il* is used in the Priestly Tradition with a ritual meaning associated with cleansing rites from ritual uncleanness.[1]) It is natural that many should read 'sprinkle' here in 52: 15, especially if they have certain views of the atoning value of the death of Christ, interpret chapter 53 in this way and make use of the temple ritual for disposing of ritual uncleanness. Thus we have the explanation offered that just as the nations formerly shunned the Servant as being unclean, so now he will sprinkle them and cleanse them. Something of this seems to be the basis of the English Versions and of some ancient versions also. It is combined also with the underlying assumption that the Servant's mission is to all mankind. The alternative was to assume another root נזה II (c.f. Arabic 'spring up, leap up'), and this gave rise to the translation 'startle' (RVm, RSV). This rendering is supported by the idea of astonishment which is plain in the context; and LXX has θαυμάσονται. But this second root does not really mean 'startle,' and some critics have pointed out that 'startle' is a long way from the Arabic 'leap up.' This is why there is doubt expressed in RSVm. 'Startle' could be justified as a legitimate extension of the original idea; there have been many stranger developments than this. There is, however, a better suggestion, namely the original 'leap up,' and this is what we are proposing to read. The argument is as follows: the first half of the verse is a parallel couplet. In the other half of the couplet we have (as it is usually translated) 'shut their mouths.' But compare Job 29: 8 f.: 'The young men saw me and hid themselves, And the aged rose and stood. The princes refrained from talking, And laid their hand on their mouth.' Here are two ways of showing the utmost and most reverential respect. One way is to rise to one's feet, the more quickly, the better. The other way is to be silent, close one's mouth and clasp it with one's hand. This is what we have in Isa. 52: 15. The word יַזֶּה means 'cause them to leap to their feet.' No change is involved in the Hebrew, neither of consonants or of vowels. Further, the root קפץ in the next half-line does not mean merely 'shut their mouths,' but 'place the hand over the mouth and clutch it, grasp it in the closed hand,' cf. Deut. 15: 7. The verse therefore describes the

---

[1]) e.g. Lev. 5: 9, etc, but not such passages as Lev. 1: 5 where 'sprinkle' is definitely wrong. The root there is זרק (toss), cf. RSV 'throw.'

amazement of the Gentiles, both nations and kings, at the triumph of
the Servant, especially since it involved the complete subservience of
these same nations and kings.

In 54: 2 we find that those returning will have exceeded all ex-
pectations so far as numbers are concerned. After having done
everything possible to secure the necessary living space, the returned
inhabitants will spread in all directions and their descendants will
dispossess the Gentiles. This root ירש (v. 3: possess, dispossess, in-
herit, disinherit) is the verb regularly used in the story of the conquest
of Canaan, where it involves the driving out of the original Canaanites
and taking possession of their land: Josh. 18: 3 and often in Deuteronomy and Joshua. DE BOER [1]) has 'expel', and this is not by any
means too strong a word. It is not universalism, nor anything like it.
It is the Joshua invasion all over again, for much of Deuteronomy
and virtually all of the Second Isaiah is a second occupation of Canaan.
Just as in Deuteronomy, Moses is speaking to the second invaders of
Palestine, so here the prophet is speaking to an Israel that once more
is to cross over into the land, possess it and conquer the Gentiles.
Ultimately the LORD will be called the God of the whole earth, and
this will be when His people have become dominant in it. In the end
Jerusalem will be supreme. No weapon formed to be used against her
will be effective, and no one will be able to stand against her with
weapon or tongue in any assault or accusation. 'This is the heritage of
the servants of the LORD and their victory (triumph, vindication)
which is from me,' 54: 17. All men will run to Israel, and David's
successor will be prince and commander of the peoples, 55: 4. God's
word will certainly triumph.

In the three extra chapters 60-62 the note of triumph at the expense
of and over the Gentiles is clearest of all. Chapter 60 is full of national
triumph. All the wealth of the nations is to come to Jerusalem. Verse
12 condemens to extinction the nations and the kingdoms which
refuse to serve Israel. Duhm and others object to this verse. This is a
natural attitude for all those who have made up their minds that the
Second Isaiah and his friends are universalists. Chapter 61 begins by
declaring that the Spirit of the LORD is upon the speaker (the
Servant), and the purpose is to release the captives and bring new
prosperity to Zion. In v. 6 the inhabitants of Zion are to 'eat the
wealth of the nations.' The rest of the three chapters breathes the same

---

[1]) *op. cit.*, p. 36.

general air of triumph and the acknowledgement of this by the Gentiles.

We turn to the assumed references to Cyrus in 41:2 f. and 46:11. It is generally maintained that 41:2 f. refers to Cyrus. The adjectives used are 'unquestionable,' 'obvious,' 'no further argument'—all of which create suspicion. In ordinary daily life and discussion, the use of the word 'obvious' is taken by the wise as a sure sign that what is being said is anything but obvious. It is not altogether different with what is written. The Targum and ancient Jewish authorities did not find it obvious. They saw here a reference to Abraham (cf. 51:1-3). What 'obvious' means is that a reference to Cyrus is obvious to a writer who has certain assumptions deeply seated in his own mind. These assumptions involve universalism and a belief that there is a general unity of all the material outside the four so-called servant songs. But if we establish from other passages the existence of a nationalist prophet who is looking forward to Israel's victory and triumph over the Gentiles, and if we can show that we have separate pieces everywhere and no 'main body' of prohecy, then the identification with Cyrus in 41:2 f. is neither obvious nor necessary. Why should Cyrus be intended here, when elsewhere we have the picture of a militant, triumphant, exultant Israel marching home to Jerusalem? It is extremely unlikely that anyone would think of Cyrus here unless he had first the notion of an Israel that is generous and kindly to all the Gentiles, and had previously read 45:1 f. A more natural explanation is that the 'one from the east' roused [1]) by the Lord to be a conqueror of kings is the new Israel: cf. 53:12; 52:15; 49:23. Compare the similar phraseology of 41:25 f., another passage which is often interpreted to refer to the victories of Cyrus. Here the difficulty is of 'one that calleth on my name' (41:25). It is true that in 45:3 f. the LORD speaks to Cyrus through the prophet and says, '(I have) called thee my name,' but this is a very different thing from saying that Cyrus has called on the name of the LORD, especially when, according to 45:4 and again in 45:5, it is said with particular emphasis that Cyrus did not know the LORD. The ancient Jewish identification with Abraham is worthy of consideration in view of 51:1-3. Abraham was but one when God called him, but God blessed him and made him many. The inference in 51:1-3 is that God will also call Israel, the new Israel, will call him as once He called Abraham, will make

---

[1]) The Hebrew is עוּר, not נשׂא, nor the *hiph'il* of קוּם.

him many, restore him to Zion and make that city a veritable Garden of God. Abraham was called from Ur of the Chaldees in ancient time; Israel is called from Babylonia in this latter time. Israel is the 'one from the east' who has been roused, and victory meets him at every step, cf. Gen. 30: 30. The LORD who roused him, enables him to subdue nations and kings, and his sword and bow make them like dust and wind-driven chaff.[1]) He pursues them and passes safely on by the path on foot.[2]) Verse 5 and 6 may well be a continuation of the fear and trembling of the Gentiles, with 'they drew near and came' as an addition (also outside the metrical scheme), and v. 7 a mistaken explanation of the help which each gave the other. It seems to us, therefore, to be a much more likely explanation of 41: 1-5 that it refers to a triumphant Israel roused by God to new endeavour and marching proudly to victory.

Who is the עיט (bird of prey) 'from the east', 46: 11? Most agree that it is Cyrus, but it could at least equally be a triumphant Israel, swooping down in victory. Similarly for the phrase in the same verse: 'the man who executes my counsel,' i.e. brings my plans to fruition. This again could be Cyrus, given the necessary assumptions, but assuming the idea of a triumphant, militant Israel, it is once again more likely to be a reference to that triumphant, victorious Israel.

Turning to 42: 1-4, it is customary to see here a special meaning for משפט (AV, RV 'judgment') analogous to the use of the Arabic dîn, which can mean 'true religion'. The Arabic usage arises from the idea of a man's fate being wholly in the hand of Allah (kismet, and so forth), and from the idea of submission to the will of God. The Hebrew usage (if it is correct) would arise from the idea that sound custom and the will of God are one. But if we assume that the Second Isaiah is an intensely nationalist prophet, then משפט means 'justice,' [3]) here meaning the verdict in the sense of a penalty of strict retribution. The Servant is a wick now burning dimly, but in the future he will not burn dimly, nor will he continue to be a bruised reed. He will establish justice in the earth. This is the true meaning of משפט. It is God's justice as shown in history and experience; cf. the Queen's justice, which is our English law, based on precedent and custom.

---

[1]) The exact reading of the Hebrew is uncertain. Read either (with LXX) 'he makes their sword as dust' or 'his sword makes them as dust.' The sense, however, is clear, whatever the precise construction is.

[2]) The phrase לא יבוא (he doth not come, hath not come, will not come) is not in LXX and is outside the metrical scheme.

[3]) See *Studies in Old Testament Prophecy*, p. 193. RSV has 'justice.'

Again,[1]) it is true that the Hebrew root יחל (end of v. 4) most often means 'wait expectantly' rather than 'wait with dread,' but the meaning 'hope' tends to be late and the *'aph'el* of the corresponding Syriac root means 'despair.'

This use of מֹשְׁפּט meaning 'judgment, justice' occurs again in 51: 4-6. The message is spoken to 'my people:' [2])

> For a law תורה shall go forth from my presence
> For my judgment מֹשְׁפּט shall be 'a light of peoples.'
> I will suddenly bring near ארגיע אקרוב my victory,
> My salvation shall go forth like the light
> And my arms shall judge the peoples.
> For me the isles shall tarry
> And for my arm they shall wait.

Then there follows a verse of terror, and the inhabitants of the earth are dying like gnats (reading כְּנִּים for כֵּן-thus). Also, 'like the light' does not refer to a steady and continuous illumination, but to the sudden blazing forth of the light of a new day (see p.176). Further, 'the isles' איים means 'the Gentiles.' [3])

---

[1]) *Studies in Old Testament Prophecy*, p. 143.

[2]) This is עמי and לאומי. See 42: 3, the other case of מֹשְׁפּט meaning 'justice': most read there לְאֻמֹּת? (peoples) instead of לֶאֱמֶת (in truth).

[3]) BROWN, DRIVER and BRIGGS, *in loc.*

CHAPTER FOUR

THE SERVANT OF THE LORD

There is no need here to give a summary of the many and varied attempts to identify the Servant of the LORD. This was done admirably a generation ago by A. S. PEAKE,[1]) and even more comprehensivley in recent years by C. R. NORTH.[2]) This latter volume is most detailed, and every view of importance is discussed. The bibliography is both accurate and extensive. We proceed, therefore, to discuss the identity of the Servant of the LORD with the discussions in Professor NORTH's book as a background. An outline of this present discussion has already appeared in 'The Servant of the LORD in Deutero-Isaiah,' *Studies in Old Testament Prophecy*, 1950, pp. 187-200, and a preliminary article appeared in *The Expository Times*, lvi (December 1944), pp. 79-81, entitled 'The So-called Servant Songs.'

In the first place, we maintain that the Servant of the so-called Servant Songs (42: 1-4; 49: 1-6; 50: 4-9; 52: 13-53: 12) is the Servant of the remainder of the nineteen chapters, 40-55 and 60-62. As was pointed out in the two above-mentioned essays, the existence of the four Servant Songs as distinct pieces involved their separation from 'the main body of the prophecy.' [3]) Very few have argued against such segregation,[4]) and few have realised any need for discussion. The position here maintained is that there is no such 'main body of the prophecy.' The modern attitude is to think of all four of the Latter Prophets (Isaiah, Jeremiah, Ezekiel, the Twelve) as 'collections of independent and usually short orcales, poems and the like.' [5]) This movement began with H. GRESSMANN [6]) who found 49 pieces in Isaiah 40-55, and these wholly independent of each other. He has been followed by KÖHLER (70 pieces), MOWINCKEL (45), VOLZ (54), OESTERLEY and ROBINSON (54), EISSFELDT (about 50), BEGRICH (70), and CASPARI (many pieces from many authors). MOWINCKEL and

[1]) *The Servant of Yahweh*, etc., 1931.
[2]) *The Suffering Servant in Deutero-Isaiah*, 1948.
[3]) SKINNER, *Isaiah*, vol. ii, pp. 238 f.
[4]) BUDDE (1922), GIESEBRECHT (1902), MARTI (1900), KISSANE (1943) and Roman Catholic scholars generally.
[5]) O. EISSFELDT, 'The Literature of Israel: Modern Criticism' in *Record and Revelation*, ed. H. WHEELER ROBINSON, 1938, p. 94.
[6]) 'Die literarische Analyse Deutero-jesajas,' ZATW 34 (1914), SS. 254-297.

Volz exclude the Servant Songs from their count.[1]) More recently, J. Muilenburg [2]) has written in favour of twenty-one separate poems.

If there is no main body of the prophecy, there can be no special group of pieces distinct from it. We are faced with approximately fifty separate pieces, in some of which reference is made to the Servant of the LORD. These references are of varying definiteness, but there are four where the association is particularly plain. These are the pieces which B. Duhm picked out and called *Die Ebed-Jahve-Leider*.[3]) These he isolated from the rest, and most scholars have followed him in this. But some scholars include other pieces also, and even Duhm himself varied. The fact is that the four pieces cannot be identified as markedly and definitely as Duhm first proposed. North, for instance,[4]) speaks of 'Secondary Servant Songs:' 42: 5-9; 49: 7-9a or 49: 7-12; and 50: 10 f. It has been said that 42: 5-9 is a continuation of 42: 1-4, and later Duhm agreed to this, but in doing so he said that these latter verses were so similar in style to the style of the Second Isaiah that he had at first ascribed them to him instead of associating them with the author of the Servant Songs, whom Duhm distinguished from the Second Isaiah. If Duhm could make such a 'mistake,' it is evident that the style of the Servant Songs does not differ from the style of what is called 'the main body of the prophecy' to anything like the degree which some have maintained. Often arguments depending upon style are far too subjective, but here we accept Duhm's second opinion: the style is for the most part indistinguishable.

We do not agree that 42: 5-9 forms one piece with 42: 1-4. Verses 5-9 undoubtedly refer to the Servant, but he is not specifically mentioned. Further, v. 5 begins with 'Thus saith the El, the LORD,' [5]) which Gressmann held to be an important criterion for the detection of a new piece. In 42: 1-4 the Servant is referred to in the third person, but in 42: 5-9 he is himself addressed in the second person. Again, in the first piece the message is for all who will listen and is in general terms. In the second piece the message is precise and specific. The word *rûaḥ* is used in different senses in the two pieces. In the first piece, the reference is to the Spirit of God which inspires the Servant

---

[1]) For further details, see C. R. North, *The Suffering Servant in Deutero-Isaiah* pp. 158 ff.

[2]) *The Interpreter's Bible*, vol. 5 (1956), pp. 389-392.

[3]) 42: 1-4; 49: 1-6; 50: 4-9; 52: 13-53: 12. See *Die Theologie der Propheten* (1875) and again his commentary *Das Buch Jesaia übersetzt und erklärt* (1892).

[4]) *op. cit.*, pp. 189 ff.

[5]) LXX reverses these titles.

and enables him to conclude his mission effectively. In the second piece, it is the breath which God gives to all men, the breath by which man lives. DUHM was right originally. 42: 1-4 and 42: 5-9 are separate pieces.

Similarly, we hold that DUHM was right originally in holding that 49: 1-6 is distinct and separate from 49: 7-12. In the first piece the Servant is speaking, but in the second piece the speaker is the LORD Himself. Notice also that v. 7 and v. 8 both begin with 'Thus saith the LORD.' Does this mean that v. 7 also is a separate piece, distinct from both 49: 1-6 and 49: 8-12? Certainly in v. 7, God is speaking about the Servant, whereas in v. 8 He is speaking directly to him. The difficulty about v. 7 is instanced by the fact that CONDAMIN (1910) makes the first piece end with v. 7 and not with v. 6. Evidently he connected v. 7 with what follows it rather than with what precedes it. Yet again, there is difference of opinion as to whether the second (? third) piece ends at v. 9a or continues to v. 11 or even to v. 12.

Turning to 50: 4-9, LEY (1893) and LAUE (1928) held that this piece is not a Servant Song, and VOLZ (1932) hesitated. The rhythm is different, and there is a higher proportion of unusual words. NORTH [1]) examines the vocabulary very carefully, and comes to the conclusion that, whilst there are differences, 'there are sufficient correspondences with Deutero-Isaiah to make it hazardous, on grounds of vocabulary alone, to deny his authorship.' This makes 50: 4-9 a Servant Song, since NORTH holds that all four Servant Songs are by the Second Isaiah. But what of v. 10, which has a definite reference to the Servant? The Servant is here referred to in the third person; in the first nine verses it is the Servant himself who is speaking. Later, DUHM added vss. 10 and 11 to the song. He was right originally. 50: 1-9 is one piece; 50: 10 f. is another piece.

The last of the four so-called Servant Songs is 52: 13-53: 12. Here again there are differences of the same type as those which scholars have discussed in these other pieces. In 52: 13-15 the LORD is speaking, but in 53: 1-11 the speaker is not the LORD, though apparently he is the speaker once more in 53: 11b and 12. But who is speaking in 53: 1? If 52: 13-53: 12 is a unit, then it is the kings of the Gentiles who are speaking in 53: 1. But this creates a difficulty in 53: 8, where עמי (my people) occurs, since 'my people' (the singular) usually means, in some sense, Israel. Some therefore read עמים (the

---

[1]) *op. cit.*, pp. 164 ff.

plural), whilst others read מפשענו (because of our rebellions) for מפשע
עמי (because of the rebellion of my people). This, it must be noticed,
changes the content of the piece, and makes the suffering of the servant
to be vicarious on behalf of the Gentiles. We take 52: 13-15 to be
spoken by the Gentile kings, and chapter 53, certainly as far as v. 11a
to be spoken by the prophet himself, which 'my people' means Israel
in some sense.

There are other pieces within chapters 40-55 and 60-62 which
scholars have sought to include among the Servant Songs. These are
61: 1-3, because of its contents, and 61: 4-6, because of its unmistake-
able connexion with 42: 1-4. There are also 41: 8 ff.; 44: 1-5; and
44: 21-23. Further, there are those pieces which NORTH [1]) refers to
as 'the Secondary Servant-Songs': 49: 7-9a (13); 42: 5-9; 50: 10 f.;
42: 19-21; 48: 14-16; 51: 4-(6) 8; 51: 9 (12)-16; 61: 1 ff. There has
also been hesitation as to whether 50: 4-9 ought to be included among
the Servant Songs. The very fact that other pieces can be described
as 'secondary Servant Songs,' especially by such a careful and accurate
scholar as C. R. NORTH, shows that the Four cannot be isolated as
decisively as is often supposed, whether on grounds of metre, or
literary style, or vocabulary or content. DUHM himself varied his
opinion in two cases, and he admitted, certainly in one case, that the
style is not distinguishable. Scholars have varied as to the number of
these songs. If we count all which have been proposed, the number is
sixteen.

Our conclusion is: It is reasonable to maintain that in Isaiah 40-55
and 60-62 we have between 50 and 60 separate pieces. If we were to
place these pieces in a long line so that those which have nothing to
do with the Servant of the LORD are on the left, and those which have
most to do with the Servant are on the right: if also we try to place
them in order according to the emphasis on the Servant, then we
shall have DUHM's original Four Servant-songs on the extreme right,
and next to them the so-called Secondary Servant Songs, one of which
is within the three chapters 60-62. To the left of these will come the
extra three songs, 41: 8 ff.; 44: 1-5; 44: 21-23; and so on. There is no
'main body' of the work. There are no Servant-songs in any exclusive sense. We have a whole series of pieces, in which, as we move
from left to right, the Servant motif becomes increasingly manifest.

If there are no distinct and separate Servant-songs, then the Servant

---

[1]) op. cit., pp. 127 ff, 189 ff.

of the so-called Songs is the Servant of the rest of the book. Who then is the Servant of the LORD? Our suggestion is that the Servant of the LORD in Isaiah 40-55, 60-62 is the first batch of exiles, those who went into captivity with the young king Jehoiachin in 597 B.C., together with a tendency to include also the 586 B.C. exiles. Ultimately, all the exiles in Babylonian are the true People of God, and it is they who are to return to Jerusalem and restore the situation, but with increased prestige and in the end with world-wide success. [1])

The prophet Jeremiah divided the people of Judah into two distinct groups. First, there were those who went into exile with the young king Jeconiah (Jehoiachin), 2 Kgs. 24: 8-17. Those who went at that time consisted of 'all the princes, and all the mighty men of valour, even to ten thousand captives, and all the craftsmen and smiths; none remained save the poorest sort of the people of the land' (v. 14). These who were taken to Babylon, said Jeremiah, were 'very good figs, like figs that are first ripe.' Those that were left behind in Jerusalem he called 'very bad figs, which could not be eaten, they were so bad,' Jer. 24: 2. He continued by saying that the good figs were taken to Babylon 'for good,' and that 'they shall be my people, and I will be their God; for they shall return to me with their whole heart,' Jer. 24: 5-7. He said of Zedekiah and of those who remained behind in Jerusalem that 'the residue (shall be) consumed off the land that I gave to them and to their fathers,' Jer. 24: 10.

It is usually held that Ezekiel began his ministry in Palestine in 592 B.C., and probably (so BERTHOLET) was taken away captive to exile with the second deportation in 586 B.C. However this may be, Ezekiel refers (11: 20) to those who went into exile in 597 B.C. and says of them that they 'shall be my people, and I will be their God.' He says this because a contention has arisen concerning this very matter. It is the first sign of that dispute which led ultimately to the rift between Jew and Samaritan. The inhabitants of Jerusalem have said to the rest, to those who have been 'removed. . .far off among the Gentiles' that they are 'far from the LORD,' and that God has given to them (that is, those who have remained in Jerusalem) this land for a possession, 11: 15. These exiles are far way from the Temple,

---

[1]) These suggestions were first put forward in the essay mentioned above, 'The Servant of the LORD in Deutero-Isaiah,' *Studies in Old Testament Prophecy*, pp. 187-200. C. R. NORTH (*op. cit.*) has examined the history of the attempts at the identification of this figure, and there is no need here to give an account of these studies.

the only place where properly, since the introduction of the Deuteronomic reforms, the LORD could be worshipped. The exiles therefore
are indeed 'far from the LORD,' but, says the prophet, the LORD has
become for them for a little while a Sanctuary in the lands whither
they have gone. Thus they will no longer be 'far from the LORD.'
This promise of the Presence of the LORD is fulfiilled in Ezek. 9: 3;
10: 4; 10: 19; 11: 23: with the consummation in chapter 1.[1]) These tell
the story of God's reluctance to leave the Temple of His choice,
the place where He chose to set his Name. The glory of the LORD
mounts up from upon the cherub where it has been and comes to the
threshhold of the house, that is, the outer door of Solomon's Temple.
Then the chariot-throne of the LORD with the cherubim (the 'living
creatures' of chapter 1) mounts aloft, but stays at the door of the east
gate (10: 19). It makes a third halt 'upon the mountain which is on
the east side of the city,' 11: 23. And finally the prophet sees the living
creatures, the chariot-throne, and the vision of the glory of the LORD
beside the river Chebar, 10: 22, 23; and chapter 1. The reluctant God
leaves Mount Zion, whose gates He loves more than all the dwellings
of Jacob (Ps. 87: 2), and flies across the deserts to the river Chebar
where His true people are. This is the way in which 'he became a
sanctuary for them for a little,' Ezek. 11: 16. As we have said, where
God's people are, there is He. If they cannot come to Him, He can
come to them. His people are in Babylon, not in Jerusalem, 'for a
little,' and that is why He must be there.[2])

And so the LORD goes to Babylonia to be a sanctuary to His
people who are there. These exiles in Babylonia will be given a new
heart and a new spirit (Ezek. 11: 19), but those left behind in Jerusalem are whole-heartedly following detestable idols and abominations,
Ezek. 11: 12 and chapter 5. They are doomed to complete destruction;
they are a 'rebellious house,' 2: 6; 5: 1-4; etc. But for the People of
God there is a resurrection. These, the exiles, are those who said,
'Our bones are dried up, and our hope is lost; we are clean cut off,'
37: 11. These bones, the dried bones that filled the valley, 'are the
whole house of Israel.' God calls them 'my people' and He will raise

[1]) see p. 154.

[2]) The most likely date for chapter 1 is soon after the fall of the city and the
destruction of the Temple. So SELLIN and BERTHOLET. When else would the LORD
leave Mount Zion? One answer is, because it has been destroyed. A better answer
is the true People of God can no longer come to Him there. See also 'The Dates
in Ezekiel,' *Expository Times*, lix, 12 (September 1948), pp. 315 ff.

them to new life, put His spirit in them and place them in their own land, 37: 12-14.

In Ezek. 17: 22-24 we have the parable of the tenderest twig on the topmost of the new growth. This tenderest twig will be cropped off and will be planted 'in the mountain of the height of Israel,' where it will grow into a goodly cedar. This tenderest twig is the young captive king Jehoiachin, unless the whole of the newly reborn People of God is intended.

Thus we see that both Jeremiah and Ezekiel believe the true People of God to be the exiles in Babylonia, and more specifically the 597 B.C. exiles. The first break in the dark clouds came with the release on parole of King Jehoiachin in 561 B.C. by Evil-Merodach king of Babylon, 2 Kings 25: 27-30.[1]) Here was the beginning of the fulfilment of the promise, and it was probably this event which gave the second editor of Kings courage and hope to deal with the appalling problem created by the untimely death of king Josiah. If ever a king should have lived long and prospered gloriously it was King Josiah, the true pattern of all that a Deuteronomic king should be.[2])

But the prophets found it impossible to confine the privilege of being the People of God to the 597 B.C. exiles only. Both in Jeremiah 30 and 31 and in Ezekiel 37, the People of God includes all the exiles in Babylon, all who are described as being scattered exiles 'from the uttermost parts of the earth,' Jer. 31: 8.

When we turn to post-exilic times and to the work of the Chronicler, we find the same attitude. Those who have been in exile in Babylonia are the People of God. Those who stayed behind in Palestine, 'the people of the land,' are not the People of God. These latter are contrasted with the 'people of Judah,' who are the returned exiles (Ezra 4: 4) and they try to weaken their hands. They are 'the adversaries of Judah and Benjamin' (Ezra 4: 1), who, as the Chronicler believed, went to all lengths to frustrate the returned exiles in their purpose of

---

[1]) For the cuneiform account of the details of this king's 'continual allowance', see W. J. MARTIN, 'The Jehoiachin Tablets' in *Documents form Old Testament Times*, ed. by D. WINTON THOMAS, 1958, pp. 84-86.

[2]) See *I and II Kings*, The Interpreter's Bible, vol. 3 (1954), pp. 10 f., where it is argued that the original edition of Kings ended with the word 'Moses' in 2 Kgs. 23: 25, and that this first edition was written not long before the death of Josiah, when he was at the flood tide of his success. It is difficult to see how any editor could have written as he did, if Josiah, by a comparatively early death, had falsified all his theories. Nothing which involved Deuteronomic ideals could easily have been written between the death of Josiah in 609 B.C. and some such event as the easing of the conditions of Jehoiachin's exile.

rebuilding the Temple. These adversaries claimed to be worshippers of God equally with the returned 'children of the captivity,' but Zerubbabel and Jeshua and the rest, for whatever reason, did not allow them to have anything to do with the rebuilding, and that, so the records say, was when the trouble started.

Thus the returned exiles sought to establish themselves, and themselves only, in Jerusalem as the People of God. It is for this purpose that we have the genealogies and lists of the Chronicler: 1 Chr. 1-8; Ezra 2 and 8; Nehemah 7; 10: 1-28; 12: 1-26, together with the list of those who put away their 'foreign wives' (EVV 'strange wives'), the women whom they had married from 'the peoples of the land,' Ezra 10: 2. Anyone who was to be recognised as a priest in the post-exilic community had to be able to point to his family name in the priestly genealogies. If the name was not there, he was put out from the priesthood, Ezra 2: 62. There were priestly families whose names were in the lists, but who had not been to Babylon, but that is another story and was the result of a compromise.[1]) The genealogies were lists of the People of God. If a man's name was not in the list, then he was one of 'the people of the land' עם הארץ; it is probable that here we have the origin of this term, used later on to mean 'the outsiders,' the people outside the law, those who did not observe the ritual rules of cleanness.

Thus when the founders of Judaism limited the People of God to 'the children of the captivity,' they were translating into fact the words and promises of Jeremiah and Ezekiel. Our claim is that the Second Isaiah fits into this pattern and is in this succession. He is the link between Jeremiah and Ezekiel on the one hand and the post-exilic returned exiles on the other hand, those who sought to establish themselves as the sole People of God, the story of whose struggle and success is to be found in the writings of the Chronicler, his history of the establishment of Judaism. From the Second Isaiah, in fact, there came an added edge of exclusiveness.

In the next chapter we seek to show the truth of this contention and the soundness of the identification of the Servant of the LORD, and this by dealing in detail with the various pieces of chapters 40-55 and 60-62.

It is on this basis that we would explain Isaiah 48: 1-11, a section with which the commentators have found very considerable difficulty.

---

[1]) See below, pp. 228.

Some scholars have ascribed all the strictures of this piece to an editor, holding that this kind of thing is not at all like the Second Isaiah. So DUHM, CHEYNE, MARTI and others. The most recent commentators accept the section as from the Second Isaiah.[1]) The assumption is that here as elsewhere the prophet is speaking to the exiles, and that therefore he is accusing them, or at least some of them, of all these abominations. The critics naturally find this difficult to accept, and so an alternative is that he is speaking to the Israel of history, the people which has been so prone to idolatry and such like waywardness all through the years. The writer is rightly compared with Ezekiel, but when Ezekiel is making these accusations, he is castigating the people who are still in Jerusalem. And so it is in Isaiah 48: 1-11. The prophet is attacking the non-exiles. They call themselves by the name of Israel. They have come forth 'from the bowels [2]) of' Judah. They make their oaths in the Name of the LORD, and they commemorate the God of Israel, 'but not in truth, nor in righteousness' (end of v. 1). They say that they belong to the Holy City and they rely upon the God of Israel. This is the content of verses 1 and 2. Some commentators (DUHM, etc.) hold that the whole of these two verses after 'Jacob' is an addition, and so also the strictures of verses 4, 8-10 and 11. If half a section is excised, it is not surprising that a different conclusion is reached from that which appears on the surface. An explanation which demands such wholesale excision is surely suspect. As the section stands, it refers to people whose claim to be the true Israel-Jacob is strongly denied. They are a people who claim that the Holy City is their's. Presumably this is a group actually resident in Jerusalem. They are the inhabitants of the city who were not deported either in 597 B.C. or in 586 B.C. They are 'the rebellious house' of Ezekiel; the 'bad figs' of Jeremiah; they are 'the people of the land' of the Chronicler. The claim of the author of 48: 1-11, which is the basis of all his strictures, is that exiled Israel is the People of God. This is the theme of the Second Isaiah. His nationalism has an exclusiveness which would deny even those who are of the same blood.

---

[1]) C. R. NORTH, *Isaiah 40-55* (TORCH Commentaries, 1952), pp. 101 f.; *The Second Isaiah*, 1964, pp. 174-179.

[2]) The Hebrew has וּמִמֵּי (and from the waters of). LXX omits. The Targum has 'seed', probably interpreting euphemistically. Most read וּמִמְּעֵי (and from the bowels of). Possibly the Hebrew is sound after all, the meaning being that they claim to have survived the waters which have engulfed and overwhelmed Judah, i.e. the Babylonian invasion.

The nation, the People of God, is composed only of the exiles in Babylon. See further, pp. 148 f.

Thus the post-exilic 'reformers,' those whose work culminated in the 'reforms' of Nehemiah and Ezra, were following a tradition, a principle already established. It began with Jeremiah, though he was one of the last persons in the world to desire that anything he said should even begin to establish the kind of exclusiveness which characterised post-exilic Jewry. It continued in Ezekiel. It becomes specific in Isaiah 48: 1-11 with its absolute denial that those who were still living in Jerusalem were to be reckoned among the People of God. This Israel of the exiles, this Servant of the LORD of the Second Isaiah develops into 'the children of the captivity,' and the obstinate ones of Isaiah 48: 4 who wrongly claim to be true worshippers of God become 'the adversaries of Judah and Benjamin' of Ezra 4: 1.

Our proposition is therefore: The Servant of the LORD is primarily the 597 exiles, but gradually it tends to widen in conception to include all the Babylonian exiles. Those remaining in Jerusalem are definitely not the People of God. This situation is found first in Jeremiah and Ezekiel. It crystallises in the Second Isaiah. It is put into ruthless execution by Nehemiah and even more so by Ezra.

In the next chapter, we comment on various pieces in Isaiah 40-55 and 60-62 to demonstrate the evidence for the above proposition. To some extent, it is a development of the examination of various passages in the article in SOTP, pp. 187-200. J. LINDBLOM criticised [1] these interpretations as 'somewhat original but sometimes hazardous exegesis.' Everything depends upon the initial assumptions. In reply to the charge that the majority of scholars assume that the prophet was a universalist and that this prior assumption influences their exegesis throughout, he says: 'It would be equally correct to say that their (i.e. DE BOER and I) own interpretation depends on their idea that the prophet was a consistent nationalist.' [2] This, of course, is quite right. Everything does indeed depend upon the categories of judgment which the exegete brings to his material. All that can be done is to put forward interpretations of the various sections of chapters 40-55, 60-62, based on the assumptions that the Servant is primarily the 597 B.C. exiles, and that the prophet is a convinced, persistent and consistent nationalist. The reader must judge which set

---

[1] *Prophecy in Ancient Israel* (1963), p. 428.
[2] *op. cit.*, p. 428.

of assumptions is the more likely to be those of the Second Isaiah. Was he an innovator, as the majority of scholars assume? Or is he in the line of his predecessors and successors, as we assume?

LINDBLOM goes so far as to agree that prior to 539 B.C. the prophet had a nationalist outlook,[1]) and that he became a universalist after 539 B.C. We agree that there was a change in the prophet's outlook. We agree also that the date of the change was roughly 539 B.C. But we think that the change was not one which welcomed all Gentiles, but from the narrower idea of the Servant as the 597 B.C. exiles (cf. Jeremiah, Ezekiel) to the wider idea of all the exiles and possibly all exiled Israelites, but definitely not those who remained in Jerusalem.

---

[1]) *op. cit.*, p. 428.

CHAPTER FIVE

EXEGESIS OF ISAIAH 40-55, 60-62

This chapter consists of detailed exegesis of sections and verses in the nineteen chapters of the Second Isaiah, on the basis that (i) the Second Isaiah was essentially a nationalist, and (ii) the Servant of the LORD is primarily the 597 B.C. exiles, and secondarily all the Babylonian exiles.

Isaiah 40: 1 *f.* Who is to be comforted? and who is to administer the comfort? The answer is that 'my people' are to administer the comfort to 'Jerusalem.' The passage with which we are concerned is 40: 1 and 2a:

> Comfort-ye, comfort-ye, my-people,
> saith your-God:

> Speak-ye to-the-heart-of Jerusalem,
> and-call-aloud to-her. . .

The frequent assumption is that we have here an exact parallelism between the two longer elements in this pair of 3: 2 couplets, even though there is no such parallel in the shorter lines. It is thus assumed that 'my people' is the object of the verb 'comfort'; 'comfort ye' being the equivalent of 'speak to the heart of,' and 'my people' the equivalent of 'Jerusalem.' This is what the Versions mostly do. Thus, LXX makes 'my people' the object of the verb 'comfort,' but then feels compelled to supply a vocative in order to indicate who it is that is bidden to act as comforter. LXX therefore inserts 'Ye priests' at the beginning of v. 2, and is followed in this by the Syro-hexaplar. The Targum assumed that the command to comfort is addressed to the prophets, and inserts this. Another suggestion is made by F. M. CROSS, Jr. and adopted by G. E. WRIGHT,[1] namely, that God is instructing his angels in the heavenly assembly. The Syriac took 'my people' to be the object of the verb, but makes no explanatory interpolation. But the Vulgate has *popule meus*, making 'my people' a vocative,[2] and then follows with *consolamini*, which the Douay Version

---

[1] *The Old Testament against its Environment*, 1950, p. 37n.

[2] WRIGHT has not considered this possibility, but thinks of the verb as active, and not passive.

renders 'be comforted.' But the Latin form is not decisively a passive.
It can indeed be the passive of *consolare* (and so 'be comforted'), but
this verb is markedly rare. It is much more likely that we are dealing
with the deponent verb *consolari* (and so 'give comfort'). The first
hand of codex א has λαός (vocative) instead of the normal LXX
accusative. It seems most likely that LXX intended the deponent verb
and that Douay misinterpreted the intention of the Latin under the
influence of the orthodox LXX text. It is not possible to decide from
the Hebrew accents whether the Masoretic tradition intended the one
or the other. The accents would be the same in either case, since both
involve the second word of the three being more closely connected
with the first word than with the third.[1]) The most that can be
established is that 'my people' is probably, though not certainly,
vocative, and thus that 'my people' is bidden to comfort Jerusalem.
It depends upon where 'my people' are. If 'my people' are the ones to
be comforted, then 'my people' are to be identified with Jerusalem.
If we were right in our intepretation of 48: 1-11 (end of the last
chapter), then quite definitely 'my people' is not to be identified with
Jerusalem. What we have is 'my people', now on the way back or
about to be on the way back, bringing comfort to the ruined city.

In 40: 9 the message is certainly to 'the cities of Judah,' but what is
the meaning of מבשרת ירושלם? It could mean, as LEVY[2]) suggests, that
Zion-Jerusalem is the messenger who is to announce the good news
to the cities of Judah. It is sometimes said that the Greek Versions
make Zion the messenger, but this is by no means certain. It is true
that in classical Greek εὐαγγελίζομαι takes the accusative of the messenger and the dative of the recipient, but in New Testament Greek both
are in the accusative. Who is to say what LXX intends when the noun
is indeclinable? The more natural interpretation is that the meaning
is 'Zion's messenger,' i.e. a messenger to Zion, especially since this
seems to be the case in 41: 27 and 52: 7. Therefore, we hold that in
40: 1, 2a Zion-Jerusalem is the recipient of the message and 'my
people' is the messenger. The good tidings are that the LORD is
coming back again to His Holy City, the city which He left in order to
be with the exiles, Ezek. 1; 11: 16. He is coming as a mighty one,
conquering and ruling, but leading His flock like a shepherd with the
utmost care and solicitude, carrying new-born lambs in the folds of
His cloak and leading on by easy stages the ewes that are heavy with

---

[1]) WICKES, *Prose Accents*, 1887, p. 69.
[2]) *op. cit.*, p. 117.

young.[1]) Thus 'the ransomed of the LORD shall return and come with singing unto Zion' (51: 11), and then it is that Zion once more will be 'my people' (51: 16).

If it is true that 'my people' (40: 1), the returning exiles, are to bring effective comfort and relief to Jerusalem, then it follows that the group which has committed iniquity is Jerusalem and not 'my people.' It is Jerusalem's 'warfare' (צבא here means 'period of hard service, hardship, toil') that is finished and her iniquity that is pardoned. The phrase נרצה עונה means that the punishment which she has received is adequate to compensate for the iniquity she committed: sin demands the full price and when this is paid in full, then 'sin' (or the nature of things, or God) is satisfied רצה. Whether Jerusalem received double punishment or not,[2]) the point here is that Jerusalem sinned and Jerusalem paid.

Isaiah 40: 7. 'the people is grass.' This is a gloss, and has nothing to do with our problems. See above, pp. 168 f.

Isaiah 41: 8. 'Israel my servant' is equal to 'Jacob whom I have chosen.' Jacob-Israel is either 'the seed of Abraham my loving one' or 'Abraham's seed, my loving one.' The same uncertainty occurs in 2 Chron. 20: 7, though Jas. 2: 23 speaks of Abraham as the friend of God. The phrase 'whom I have chosen' is equivalent to 'my servant' also in 44: 1 f. and 45: 4. The call is to the Servant, which is Israel, and 'I have chosen thee and not cast thee away' (v. 9). That is, the exile did not mean rejection. On the contrary, it meant their being chosen ones, recognised as being the descendants of Abraham. God is going to make these exiles conquerors ('uphold thee with my victorious [3]) right hand' v. 10, RSV). Jacob the worm and Israel the grub [4]) (v. 14) is going to be helped by God, his redeemer, the Holy One of Israel, and everything is going to be smashed flat before him. Compare our interpretation of 41: 2-3 as referring to Jacob-Israel and not to Cyrus (pp. 163 f).

---

[1]) AV 'with young' and RSV; RV 'give suck.' The Arabic *ġala* means 'give suck (while pregnant),' and the Syriac *ʿula*ʾ means both 'foetus' and 'suckling.'

[2]) The root כפל means 'double over.' The noun can mean 'the double of the jaw' Job 41: 5. It can mean being folded over, like the curtain (Exod. 26: 9) or the breastpiece (Exod. 28: 16). Thus it might mean 'equivalent' and not necessarily 'twice.'

[3]) The Hebrew is צדקי, my vindicating, rectifying, saving power.

[4]) Most read רָמָּת (grub), but G. R. DRIVER retains the text and translates 'louse' (cf. Accadian *mutu*), JTS 36 (1935), p. 399.

Isaiah 42: 1. According to LXX, this verse should read 'Jacob my servant' and 'Israel my chosen.' Evidently LXX identified the Servant with Jacob-Israel. But Jacob-Israel means the exiles, not the old Israel, not the Palestinians, but the 'good figs' of Jer. 24: 5. It means the new Israel, the one that is ransomed and redeemed (41: 14). SKINNER [1]) says: 'It is at least true that if the Servant of vv. 1-4 be Israel, he is Israel in a new character.' To which the answer is 'quite': he is the new Israel which arose as if from the dead (Ezek. 37; Isa. 53: 8 f.), triumphant and victorious.

Isaiah 42: 6-9. Here the Servant is apparently distinct from those who have blind eyes, who sit in the darkness of dungeons. The Servant has been called by God 'in righteousness': this means 'in victory, with salvation' or, as C. R. NORTH [2]) translates it, 'for a saving purpose' But whereas Professor NORTH sees the saving purpose as for the nations, our judgment is that it is for Israel as a whole. The difference between the Servant and the prisoners who are to be released is, we suggest, due to the two deportations. The first deportment of 597 B.C. was, as we pointed out earlier (p. 170), of all the leaders, so that 'none remained, save the poorest sort of the people of the land,' 2 Kgs. 24: 14. This statement may well be, at least in part, Judaean propaganda against the Palestinians (cf. 2 Kgs. 17: 24-41), but we do know that hopes for the future were centred primarily around King Jehoiachin, and that the seventy years of the exile (Jer. 25: 11 f.; 29: 10) are reckoned from 597 B.C. Further, it is these first exiles who are Jeremiah's 'good figs,' and it is those who are not the first exiles who are Ezekiel's 'rebellious house.' This first group is to be the instrument by which all the exiles return home. They are thus 'the covenant of the people,' [3]) the means by which God will bind into one again the scattered People of God, and thus bring them once more into relationship with Him. The People of God does not include any that remained in Palestine after 586 B.C., unless it includes some who were deported c. 581 B.C. In this way we explain as meaning 'Israel' passages which refer to others being rescued and restored apart from the Servant, and we are not led to identify these with the Gentiles.

---

[1]) *op. cit.*, p. 28.

[2]) *The Second Isaiah*, p. 38.

[3]) We regard it as most important to retain the singular here and not assume a plural, as NORTH does, and as LINDBLOM does, *Prophecy in Ancient Israel*. 1963, p. 400.

Isaiah 42: 18-25. As has been pointed out,[1]) much confusion has been caused by the assumption that the 'blind ones' of v. 16 and v. 18 are identical with the 'blind one' of v. 19. The 'blind ones' of v. 16 are the exiles, all of them. Also 'the blind ones' (and 'the deaf ones') of v. 18 seem to be the exiles. But suddenly the writer turns and says that 'my servant,' 'my messenger whom I send,' 'the one who is to be restored,' [2]) 'the Servant of the LORD' is the blindest of all. The Servant is blind and cannot see that it is all 'for his (i.e. God's) righteousness' sake'. As NORTH has pointed out, this means 'for his saving purpose' [3]); this is the only rendering which gives the phrase meaning. Then 'his law' (v. 21b) means 'his teaching' (NORTH). All this is why he (Jacob-Israel) is a people robbed, imprisoned, without anyone at all to deliver. The LORD did this, against whom we (not the Servant) sinned. *They* (again not the Servant) would not obey God's law, and it was upon him (the Servant) that the disaster fell, but he did not understand. Cf. 53: 1-12 which also says that the people sinned and the Servant suffered the death of exile.

Isaiah 43: 1. The LORD speaks to the newly created and newly form-ed Jacob-Israel, whom He has redeemed and to whom He has given this name,[4]) so that Jacob-Israel is His. The prophet means that God has given this name Jacob-Israel to the exiles, those who will be passing through flood and fire. The prophet uses these words 'create,'[5]) 'form,' 'make' again and again, so important is his message that God has remade, recreated Israel. He is referring to an action in the immed-iate past, actually taking place, or is truly imminent. He does not mean that God created, formed, made this Jacob-Israel long, long ago. He means that God has just created and has recently named this Jacob-Isreal. He created them for His glory, so that all the world should admire and be impressed.

Isaiah 43: 8-13. It is usual to translate הוציא as an imperative, either

---

[1]) *SOTP*, pp. 194 ff.
[2]) The heb. משלם is very difficult; see NORTH, *The Second Isaiah*, pp. 39, 118. We take the word to have the same meaning as שלום in 53; 5, 'the chastisement which brought us *prosperity, well-being, restored life.*' So either retain the vowels of the Hebrew text and think of the servant as the one who is to be restored, or (better) read as a *pi'el*, in the sense of 'restore' BDB p. 1022b (top).
[3]) *op. cit.*, pp. 39, 118.
[4]) The ancient Versions have the suffix 'I have named *thee*,' as if reading קראתיך.
[5]) 'create' ברא 43: 1; 43: 7; 43: 15.
　'form' יצר 43: 1; 43: 7; 43: 21; 44: 2; 44: 21; 44: 24; 45: 11; 49: 5.
　'make' עשה 43: 7; 44: 2; 51: 13; 54: 5.

assuming an irregularity or reading a *ṣērĕ* or making it a plural; and then to follow by translating the prefect נקבצו as 'let. . .be gathered together' (RV) or 'let. . .gather together' (RSV). But NORTH rightly translates this last as a perfect: 'all the nations have been convened.' [1] The opening verb is also a perfect, and from v. 9 it may be understood that the event is regarded as having taken place. These all may well be 'prophetic perfects,' the prophet meaning either that the event is absolutely certain or is imminent or (more probably) both. We would translate, inverting the construction in the first line:

> The people that is blind, yet has eyes,
>   has been brought out,
> The deaf ones, though they have ears.
> All the Gentiles are gathered together;
> The peoples assemble.
> Who among them foretold this,
> And announced the former things?
> Let them produce their witnesses and
>   show they are right (justify themselves),
> And let men hear and say, 'It is true.'

The passage goes on to say that the new Israel, the released ones, those who God has saved, are the living witnesses to the saving might of the Only God. There is nothing here about saving the Gentiles. They are on trial because they did not forsee the 'former things' (usually this means the first Exodus), nor did they foretell this second Exodus.

Isaiah 43: 14-21. God here speaks to the exiles. For their sake he has sent to Babylon and brought down all the honoured ones,[2] all of them, and (?) the Chaldaeans shall be bound in fetters.[3] This is the God who makes a path through the sea, as He did in the first Exodus, who brought out chariot and horse and destroyed them all. But do not look back (v. 18) at these former things. These things took place long ago. Look forward to the new thing (i.e. this second deliverance)

---

[1] SI, p. 41.

[2] G. R. DRIVER, JTS xxxiv (1933), p. 39; בְּרִיחִים, cf. Syriac *beraḫ* 'honoured'.

[3] The text is uncertain. This reading is based on LXX (אᶜᵃ and A) ἐν κλοιοῖς δεθήσονται. The normal LXX is 'ships' as the Hebrew, though this might easily be 'with lamentations' (cf. RSV). It is possible that Cod. A may be a correction because of 'bind,' but it is difficult to see how δεθήσονται could arise in the first place without κλοιοῖς.

I am about to do. God is going to make a way through the wilderness,
and rivers [1] in the desert. All this is to give drink to this newly chosen
people whom God has formed for Himself and whose duty is to
rehearse His praise. The whole passage then, refers to the journey
across the desert of the exiles, the newly chosen People of God.

Isaiah 43: 22-28. A new section begins here. The words are addressed
to the old Jacob-Israel, who did not call [2] upon God, nor did they
weary themselves in their service to Him. They brought whole-
offerings, but not to God. Their sacred meals (זבח) were not in honour
of Him. God did not make them worship [3] Him with tribute-offerings
(מנחה: the cereal-offering of post-exilic times), nor did He weary
them by insisting on them providing frankincense. It was not for Him
that they bought fragrant cane, and they did not satiate him with the
fat of their sacred feasts.[4] The old Jacob-Israel did indeed worship
(serve) God, but it was with their sins. They did indeed weary Him,
but it was with their iniquities. Then in v. 25 God says that He, even
He, is the One who blots out Israel's rebel actions, and forgets his
sins. Then (v. 26) let us see what can be done about it. Recall it all
to my memory, and let us judge the matter. Recount what you have to
say, you that you may be cleared of your sins (the verb is צדק, put
in the right, declared innocent). But no: the whole story is one of
unrepented sin, and this was so all down the years. Their first ancestor sinned, God's spokesmen to them were rebellious against Him,
His princes defiled His sanctuary.[5] And so God gave Jacob to the
ban, to be utterly destroyed, and He made Israel something for every
one to revile. The section tells of the utter and complete rejection of
the old Jacob-Israel.

Isaiah 44: 1-5. This section is linked to the previous section by the
word ועתה (and now). It seems to be outside the metrical system,
though such statements tend to be subjective in a line like this one,
but single words are found at the beginning of a piece. Here the word
provides the contrast between the old Jacob-Israel of the last section

---

[1] Qumran (A) has 'paths,' which may well be right. It makes a parallel, and
see v. 20b.
[2] Both the direct accusative and the preposition *lāmed* are found with this
meaning. The negative is carried over into the second clause, as LXX and V
realised.
[3] The word also means 'serve, act as a slave.' Cf. NORTH, SI, p. 42.
[4] All the fat of the sacred-meal זבח went to the altar, and none of the flesh.
[5] This follows LXX.

and the new Jacob-Israel of this section. God has chosen a new Jacob-Israel, Jacob who is the Servant, Israel whom God has chosen. He has made him as though newly born. The offspring of the returned exiles (water for the thirsty, streams on the dry ground) will increase and multiply like poplars and willows by the river side. They will claim that they are God's people. There is no basis for assuming that those mentioned in v. 5 are foreigners, except a basic assumption that the Second Isaiah is a universalist. The speakers in v.5 are the descendants mentioned in v. 3 .DILLMANN [1]) realised that those who are speaking are Israelites by birth.

Isaiah 44: 21-22. Here Jacob-Israel is the Servant whom God has formed and chosen. Israel was made for the express purpose of being God's Servant. Jacob-Israel will not be forgotten [2]) by God. V. 22 is difficult because these words for 'sin' sometimes mean the actual sin itself, and sometimes the punishment: which could well be the meaning here. In this case, the meaning is that the sufferings of the exile are over, and God has redeemed Israel.

Isaiah 44: 23. is the description of the triumphant return and restoration of Jacob-Israel, with all the natural world exulting. Cf. 49: 13; 55: 12.

Isaiah 44: 24-28. The great Creator God speaks to the people He has formed. He confirms what the Servant has said: Jerusalem shall be rebuilt and the cities of Judah inhabited. Cyrus is going to be the actual agent in this. The Hebrew apparently intends to say that Cyrus will give the rebuilding instructions, but LXX and V have the same construction as vv. 26a, 27, 28, all of which makes God the speaker. Probably the Hebrew is right, and the Versions are assimilating. Josephus says (*Ant. Iud.* XI i 1) that it was when Cyrus read this passage concerning the rebuilding of the city that he took appropriate action.

Isaiah 45: 1-7. Cyrus is God's anointed one. This means that he is appointed for a special purpose,[3]) in this case to free Jacob-Israel from captivity in Babylonia, to allow these displaced persons to return

---

[1]) *Der Prophet Jesaia*, 1890, *in loc.*

[2]) This is the pointing of the Hebrew, and it would appear to be correct. God will always remember His Servant, the new Jacob-Israel. Other suggestions are 'you must not forget me' (cf. RVm) and 'you must not play false with me.' When God remembers, He acts and saves.

[3]) *The Jews from Cyrus to Herod*, 1949, pp. 106-112.

home. Cyrus is chosen for the sake of Jacob-Israel, the chosen Servant of God. Cyrus never knew God, but God nevertheless gives him strength, so that all the wide world may know that the LORD is the only God there is. The call of Cyrus to rebuild the city is mentioned again in v. 13 and he is to free the exiles though no payment is to be made to secure their freedom.

Isaiah 45: 14-17. There is much dispute concerning this section. If the section is to be connected with the previous verses, then the workers of Egypt and the merchants of Ethiopia and the tall Sabaeans will come and pay homage to Cyrus and they will say "Nay, but God is in thee." Such an acknowledgement will be wholly contrary to expectation.[1] This identification with Cyrus is in Jerome, and amongst moderns it is advocated by SKINNER, MOWINCKEL, and others.[2] If, however, this section is regarded as distinct from the previous verses, then Egypt, Ethiopia and the Sabeans are to come to Jacob-Israel, astonished that God is to be found in them because of all the utter disasters which have overtaken them. It is all idolators who are to be thrown into confusion, but Jacob-Isarel will be saved and delivered once and for all with never any more disappointment or disillusion. God must be in (with) Israel because of Israel's triumph. Verse 15 looks like a pious comment by a scribe.

Isaiah 45: 18-25. As has been pointed out,[3] if verses 22 and 23 are taken separately and lifted out of their context, they can be interpreted as evidence of a generous universalism towards the Gentiles. This is what orthodox modern commentators actually do. But 'all the ends of the earth' does not mean the Gentiles: cf. 43: 5, 6. And verse 23 does not involve, as many suppose, humble worship in willing loyalty. It means 'worship' only to those who are accustomed to kneel in worship, but not to those who prostrate themselves. To kneel means to bow low in humble obeisance and subservience. The call is (v. 20) to those who have escaped from the Gentiles, and the climax is (v. 25) that 'by (through, by the agency of) the LORD all Israel's

---

[1] Both אף and אך can be used in discussion. אף means 'Yes, and. . .' with the speaker going on to add further corroboration. אך means 'yes, but. . .' with the speaker proceeding to produce an objection. Always a negative, unexpected element is involved: see 'The meaning of the Hebrew אך', VT. xiv, 2, (April 1964), pp. 221-225.

[2] NORTH, DI, p. 137, who is of the opinion that the 'thee' is Jacob-Israel. Also WHITEHOUSE, *Isaiah* (Cent. Bible), ii, p. 125.

[3] SOTP, p. 196.

descendants (i.e. the descendants of the exiles) shall be justified (seen to be in the right, vindicated, triumphant) and shall boast.' Here is conquering, boasting Israel. Verse 22 we take to refer to the exiled Israelites (cf. 49: 6 as well as 43: 5, 6). Verses 23 and 24 describe the humble subservience of the Gentiles. As they bow in humility before God, they will say (LXX, verse 24) 'Nay,[1]) but in the LORD are victorious acts and strength. All men shall come to him, and all who were formerly his antagonists shall lose face.' But all the descendants of Israel shall be gloriously vindicated.

Isaiah 46: 3-4. This section is wholly independent of verses 1-2, which describe the panic in Babylon and the rush to load the idols on to pack-animals to save them when the city is captured and sacked. The prophet here is talking about the birth of the new Jacob-Israel, not yet come to birth, but being delivered out of the womb of God.[2]) This babe to be born is the remnant [3]) of the old Jacob-Israel. However long the birth is delayed, even though the parent's hair be gray, the birth of the new Israel is certain. This new Israel is the exiles, preserved and reborn. Here is the birth of post-exilic Judaism.

Isaiah 46: 8-11. As NORTH pointed out,[4]) 'the rebels' (RV and RSV have 'the transgressors') are the prophet's own people, and not the Gentiles. We understand the reference to be to the exiles as a whole, slow to heed and respond to the words of the Servant. The 'bird of prey' (v. 11, as RSV. RV has 'a ravenous bird') from the east is the Servant, the new Israel, who is represented as being 'from the east' in 41: 2 also; see pp. 163f. above. Compare also 44: 26. All three passages hang together; either they all three refer to Cyrus, or, as we think, all three refer to the triumphant, rampant People of God. Verse 12 encourages all who losing heart (אבדי לב, cf. LXX) because they think they are far from vindication (צדקה, victory, salvation). But this vindication is near and this salvation will not be long delayed. It will be granted in Zion, and it will be for the new Israel, the returned exiles.

---

[1]) The Hebrew is אך. See note on p. 185.

[2]) See the strong anthropomorphisms of verse 4 also, where מלט means 'deliver, give birth' as in Isa. 66 7. See 'The Width and Length of Words,' ET lv 10 (July 1944), pp. 265-268.

[3]) Both שארית and שאר are used of the Remnant, though the latter comes to be the technical term.

[4]) SI, p. 166.

Isaiah 48: 1-11. See pp. 173f. above, where it is argued that verses 1 and 2 refer to those who still are in Jerusalem, men who falsely claimed to be true worshippers of God. They say they belong to the holy city and they profess to rely on the God of Israel. But it is all false. Commentators have found this section difficult, and some find more than one piece in these eleven verses. DUHM tought the whole piece has been substituted for a much milder passage. Many difficulties are removed if we think of the Jerusalemites as the rejected ones and the exiles as the remnant, those that have been refined and chosen in the furnace of affliction. The old Jacob-Israel had been told by the prophets of what would come to pass (v. 3), and now it has all happened. New things have come to pass, things that have been hidden and secret (i.e. in God's secret counsel). But they took no notice (v. 8), have not listened, born a rebel and still a rebel. Nevertheless God is not going to exterminate Jacob-Israel. He has refined the old Jacob-Israel, tested and chosen them in the furnace of affliction. In v. 10 the Hebrew is the root בחר, which means 'choose' (cf. RV) and not 'try, test' (as RSV). We see no need to alter the text to בחנתיך (tried, tested) as some do. The passage refers to the choosing of the new Israel (the exiles) out of the furnace in which the old Israel was involved.

Isaiah 48: 12-19. These verses are notoriously difficult, since the rhythm and the pronouns are constantly changing. To what extent these changes are due to the activity of scribes, either by accident or in seeking to 'improve' or 'correct', it is difficult to say. There is always the possibility that we have a number of separate pieces. Verse 12 is a summons to Jacob-Israel, the new Israel, the exiles whom God has called to be His people. Verse 14 is a call to all and sundry to hear the declaration of God concerning what is about to happen to Babylon and the Chaldeans. The LORD chose (אהב, special love, choice) Israel, and he shall fulfil His (God's) purpose (חפץ as in 46: 10) concerning Babylon, and exercise His power (lit. 'his arm,' unless we follow LXX and read 'and concerning the seed of' וּבְזֶרַע for זורעו the Chaldeans). God has spoken and He has summoned him, brought him along, and Israel has made his way prosperous.[1] Verse 16 says that God has never made any secret of all this: i.e. His intention to call the Servant and lead him and the people to prosperity. But now, NOW (ועתה, emphatic, as in 44: 1) the climax

---

[1] LXX, Targum and Syriac have first person here also, as throughout the verse.

has come, and God has sent the Servant forth (on his conquering way), and 'my spirit. . .' This is a noted crux, and it is very likely that a word has been lost, such as '(is) upon him.' In any case, the general sense is clear. God has called Jacob-Israel and now at long last God's plans are going to be fulfilled. There has been much discussion as to whether vv. 17-19 refer to the past or the future. It is agreed that the first stichos of v. 17 can be translated 'O that thou wouldest hearken. .' (so RVm), but if we follow with 'then. . .' ,the reference must be to the past. But there is a way in which the reference to the future can be maintained: and such a reference is much more in keeping with the Second Isaiah's attitude rather than useless repining for what might have been. It is best to read: 'O that thou wouldest hearken to my commandments and your peace be like a river. . .(19b) then their (your children, descendants) name shall never be cut off. . .'. This makes the verses promise unending prosperity for the future dependant on the new Israel keeping the commandments of God.

Isaiah 48: 20 f. Jacob is the LORD's servant whom He has released from Babylon. The journey back to Jerusalem is described in terms borrowed from the story of the Deliverance from Egypt, for this is a second exodus and it ends in a second entry into and occupation of the Promised Land. Verse 22 seems to be a pious addition: cf. 57: 21, possibly dating from a time when the whole of chapters 40-66 were for some reason divided into three sections of approximately equal length: 40-48, 49-57, 58-66. The division does not seem to have anything to do with the contents of the sections, and any reason offered for such division is wholly without evidence.

Isaiah 49: 1-6. This is the second of the so-called Servant Songs. The Servant is Israel (v. 3). All who insist upon an individualistic interpretation of the identity of the Servant find themselves constrained to omit 'Israel' in this verse. It is indeed missing in one Hebrew MS, but this is no. 96 in KENNICOTT's list, in many ways the least satisfactory of his manuscripts. He says of it *plurimas habet variationes*. The metrical evidence for omission is decidedly weak. Indeed, if this word is to be omitted on metrical grounds, then almost any word can be omitted anywhere. The rhythm, especially of 'the latter half of the lines, is most irregular in this section. Here the Servant is declaring his calling and his mission in the Gentile world. This mission is not only to restore the Jacob-Israel of the Babylonian exile, but to be a guiding light throughout the whole of the Gentile world in order that God's salvation may extend everywhere. But this is God's salvation of the Jews: see pp. 155 f. above.

Isaiah 49: 7-13. Here the LORD is speaking to a despondent Jacob-Israel, despised [1]) by men, abhorred by the Gentiles, and subject to tyrants. There is to be a complete change. When kings and princes see a triumphant Israel, they will leap to their feet in respect and bow low in submission, all because of the LORD who is to be relied upon, the Holy One of Israel who has chosen Isreel. Verse 8 says that God has answered and helped Israel in a time of favour רצון. This means a time when God acts favourably with goodwill. It is the same as 'a day of favourable visitation,' a day of salvation. The journey home will be without the normal hardships of desert travel. They will come from far (i.e. from far away Babylon) and others from the north and the west, and yet others from Sinim (? Syene): but they will all be Israelites.

Isaiah 49: 14-21. Here is consolation for Zion,—the city, not the inhabitants. The city complains that she is forsaken and forgotten. But God denies this. He has remembered her and has her walls in mind. Her sons [2]) will hurry to her, and those that destroyed her will go away. If Zion raises her eyes and looks, she will see her children returning, crowds of them, so many that there will not be enough living space for them. In v. 21 גלמוד (solitary) means husband away and therefore no chance of legitimate children. The two words גולה (exile) and סורה (removed) are not in LXX and seem genuinely to be outside the metrical construction. They look like realistic interpretations of a prosaic nature inserted into an elaborate metaphor. Further, they are the two words which make Zion an exile, which she definitely is not. Zion is the desolate and empty city, and is quite distinct from 'the People of God': cf. note on 40: 2.

Isaiah 49: 22-26. In these verses two things are plain. First, Zion's sons and daughters are being brought back to her from afar. Second, the Gentiles will be their humble slaves. Indeed, the kings and queens of the Gentiles will be in humble attendance on Zion's returning children. Humbly they will bow low with their faces in the dust and they will lick the dust off Zion's children's feet. Nothing could be so

---

[1]) See the full discussion by NORTH, SI, pp. 190 f.
[2]) The Versions have 'builders' בֹּנָיִךְ, which makes good sense, but the Hebrew is better.

abject, and no domination so complete. Normally it is impossible to snatch captives away from a warrior, but in this case God will free captive Israel, because He is the Saviour, the Redeemer, the Mighty One of Jacob. The section ends with brutal revenge on the oppressors of Israel. In this section, the exiles are the new Israel, and the prophet is entirely nationalistic. Note also that in v. 22 for עמים (peoples), LXX has νήσους (isles), but there is no need to assume that LXX was reading איים. It is more likely that LXX knew that the plural עמים means the Gentiles, and this is what 'the isles' means in the Second Isaiah.

Isaiah 50: 1-3. NORTH [1]) is of the opinion that the questions in v. 1 are rhetorical, and that the meaning is: There never was a divorce, and I was never so poor that I had any creditor. But Zion was divorced and the old Israel was sold. The meaning is: Let us have a look at that writ of divorce and see what it says, why the divorce took place: Let us get hold of that particular creditor and ask him why the sale took place. The answer is that it was all because of the people's iniquities that they were sold; and it was because of Zion's rebellious acts (RV, RSV 'transgressions', wrongly) that she was divorced. The difficulties arise through assuming that the metaphors of divorce and selling into slavery are both to be taken to include the exile. This is the problem of all exegesis and indeed of every discussion. When a metaphor or an illustration is used, to what extent is it to be applied? A feature in all arguments is that one man uses an illustration to illustrate a particular point, and the other man picks out other things in the illustration which the first man never intended. Here we would maintain, the reference is only to the disaster and not to the exile which followed it. The prophet is not talking about the exiles at all in verses 1 and 2, but only about Zion and the old Israel. Zion was divorced and her inhabitants sold away, so that when God came to Zion, there was nobody there; when he called there was nobody to answer. They had all been sold; the People of God were no longer there. But (v. 2a) God is able to redeem and deliver. He can dry up the sea (which is what He did in ancient time), and He can turn rivers into desert, so that the fish are in distress [2]) and die. It is not said that God will redeem the actual individuals whom He has sold, but that

---

[1]) SI, pp. 198 f.
[2]) Ugarit *b'š* (be bad). DE BOER, *op. cit.*, p. 53; G. R. DRIVER, JTS xxxi (1930), pp. 276 f.

He will redeem and deliver. We believe that it is the exiles that He will redeem and deliver, but not the old Israel.

Isaiah 50:4-9. This is the third of the so-called Servant Songs. Verse 4 is uncertain, but it speaks of the Servant learning his lessons, being roused regularly in the early dawn to hear what God has to say to him, and thus being able to declare what he, as a good pupil, has learned. It was a hard discipline, but the Servant did not rebel against his lot. He was submissive. He bore the humiliation of exile and captivity. Therefore God has helped him and he has not been shamed out of existence. He endured bravely with set teeth (lit. 'set my face like a flint'), and he is sure he will not be shamed for ever. His vindication is near. He is prepared to face any accuser and he will win, because God will help him.

Isaiah 50: 10-11. All are walking in the dark and have no light, but there are two types. One type is the man who fears God (worships Him devoutly), relies upon God and obeys the Servant. All will be well with him. The other type seeks to make its own fire and does not trust in God nor obey the Servant. Any such will walk in the fires they have made and burn with their own brands.

Isaiah 51: 1-3. The meanings of the metaphors 'rock' and 'waterpit' are discussed at length by DE BOER,[1]) but the main message is clear. Remember Abraham and Sarah, who went out from this very country where you are exiled. Abraham was but one man when I called him, but his posterity multiplied like the stars of heaven. What God did for Abraham, He can and will do for you. Zion will be changed from ruin and desert into fruitfulness and joy like that of Eden the Garden of God.

Isaiah 51: 4-6. Many follow the Syriac and 12 de Rossi MSS in verse 4 and read עמים (peoples) for עמי (my people), and לאומים (nations, peoples) for לאומי (my nation, people). G. R. DRIVER [2]) thinks they are abbreviations. NORTH [3]) suggests that the singular forms may be dogmatic emendations. We would suggest, on the contrary that the proposed changes from singular to plural are dogmatic emendations. God's fiat will go out as a shining light throughout the world. He will

[1]) *op. cit.*, pp. 58 ff. He thinks the Rock is God, not Abraham.
[2]) 'Abbreviations in the Massoretic Text' in *Textus I* (1960), p. 115.
[3]) SI, p. 107.

suddenly [1]) bring his vindication near and His salvation will go forth, and He will judge the Gentiles by His power. This is the judgment by the conqueror. The Gentiles (isles) will wait for Him and His might. Compare 42: 4 where קוה means 'wait,' but not necessarily with hope (in Syriac the root means 'wait with dread'). So also יחל means 'wait' but not necessarily with eagerness (cf. 60: 9), though this is the usual meaning. They are to wait for the might of His arm, and this, combined with the judgment in strenght of verse 4, shows that the section refers to the judgment of the Gentiles and not to their salvation.

Isaiah 51: 7-8. This section says that no faithful Israelite need have any fear of men, nor need he be disturbed by anything they say. God's vindication of those who are devoted to His law is firm and secure for ever.

Isaiah 51: 9-11. The exiles shall return to Zion. The prophet links up the coming deliverance with the Rahab-dragon myth, according to which God overthrew the forces of chaos and destruction before the beginning of the world; and also with the first deliverance from Egypt. See Exod. 15: 4 and 5; Jonah 2: 3-6; Jer. 51: 34.

Isaiah 51: 12-16. God is Israel's comforter (cf. 40: 1). Israel has no need to be afraid of mortal man, here today and gone tomorrow. There is no need to fear the fury of the oppressor when he makes preparations to destroy. The one who stoops will quickly be set loose.[2]) He will neither die nor starve. God inspires his speech, protects him. It is perhaps best to regard v. 16a as within brackets, and then the stilling (רגע II, not רגע I) of the sea (v. 15a) is made preliminary to the work of creation (v. 16b), the stretching out of the heavens and the founding of the earth.

Isaiah 51: 17-23. Jerusalem is in great distress, lying prostrate having drunk to the dregs the cup of the LORD's anger. None of her children are there to raise her up and guide her. This we take to fit in with the Second Isaiah's usual attitude that the People of God are no longer in Jerusalem, and so far as her true inhabitants are concerned, the

---

[1]) reading ארגיע with the next verse.
[2]) The verb צעה in v. 14 means 'stoop, bend down.' The meaning can be 'cringe under the fury of the oppressor' or 'bow low under the burden of a slave.' Also, הפתח can mean loosed from fear, loosed from the bonds of the burden, loosed from the bonds of captivity.

city is empty. But God has taken the deadly cup away, and others must drink it, those who have trodden down the people of God like mire in the street.

Isaiah 52: 1-2. Zion-Jerusalem is to get up from the dust and put on festive clothing. She is to be a holy city, and no uncircumcised, ritually unclean foreigners will enter her any more. The people (captive daughter of Zion) are to be released, and the rope which tied them all neck by neck in one long line is to be loosed. There always was violent antagonism in old Israel against those who were uncircumcised, but here uncircumcision is linked with ritual uncleanness and we have the beginnings of that exclusiveness which was the dominant feature of Judaism. The uncircumcised are the Babylonian conquerors and possibly also others who have infiltrated into the city, who may actually be intended by the 'unclean'. In any case, the returning exiles claimed that all 'the people of the land' were unclean.

Isaiah 52: 3-6. Some editors have regarded this section as 'an interpolation' or as an 'editorial insertion.' Phrases like this belong to the same vocabulary and set of ideas as 'the main body' of the prophecy. If there is no 'main body,' then how can there be an interpolation? If the work of the prophet is regarded as being composed of fifty or so pieces, then any change of metre or of matter does not necessarily involve an insertion. It indicates another piece. In any case, if our view of the identity of the Servant is sound, this section is very far indeed from being an insertion. It is wholly in line with the prophet's message. The prophet is speaking to the exiles, the People of God. They are bidden to remember their history. They went down into Egypt innocently to live there for a while, and they were made slaves. The Assyrians unjustly oppressed them: this refers to the time from Jehu onwards until the fall of Nineveh, except for the period of Assyrian weakness in the time of Uzziah. Now once more, an innocent people is oppressed. They are unjustly carried away into exile. This is in line with the attitude of the prophet elsewhere, and it is also the attitude of Jeremiah and Ezekiel. These exiles were the good figs. Those left behind in Jerusalem were the bad figs. They were Ezekiel's 'House of rebellion.' But the exiles, 'my people,' will know my Name: that is, they will experience the establishment of God's reputation. This will be when He rescues His people from captivity and restores them to Zion. Then they will know that 'here I am' as in the ancient days.

Isaiah 52: 7-12. Here is a lyric declaring new life for Zion-Jerusalem. The messenger is bringing good news of salvation and prosperity. His feet are on the mountains (cf. 40: 9) and he is calling (?) from the mountains of Judaea across the valley to Jerusalem. He declares that once more their God has triumphed and established His kingly rule. The phrase יהוה מלך (the LORD has become king) is the Coronation cry. God has just triumphed and has taken His seat upon His throne. He has comforted (נחם; 40: 1) and redeemed Jerusalem. God has returned to Jerusalem and once more 'Jerusalem' and 'my people' are one. This time there is no haste, as there was in the flight from Egypt. This is a triumphal march and all the wide world will see the great salvation which God has wrought for Israel.

Isaiah 52: 13-15. This piece is usually held to be the opening of the fourth and last so-called Servant Song, but it is more probably a separate piece, though it may well stand as a title and summary of chapter 53. The Servant will prosper, be exalted and extolled, and be very high. There was a time when many (? the great ones) were appalled at his plight, battered and bruised, afflicted with sickness out of all human recognition. But the time will come when great nations will leap [1]) to their feet at his approach and clasp their hands to their mouths in respect and honour. They will see such things as never were told them before, and perceive things the like of which they have never heard.

Isaiah 53. The first three verses tell of the utter astonishment of the heathen world at the unexpected triumph of the Servant. Who, say they, could possibly have believed what we have heard? Who would have thought that in him of all people the victorious might of the LORD would be revealed? He grew up [2]) like a sucker, like a weak sapling, from a root in a dry and waterless soil. He had no shape and no beauty; there was nothing at all about him to admire. Men despised, neglected him. He was a man of much suffering, brought low [3]) by sickness. Men hide their faces from such as he, and that is what the speakers did. With verse 4 we get the beginning of the explanation first

---

[1]) See p. 161 above.

[2]) There is no need to read לפנינו (before us) for לפניו (before him). The suffix is a reference back to the subject of the verb: G. R. DRIVER, JTS 38 (1937), p. 48.

[3]) The root is ידע II, Arabic *waduʻa* (be quiet, humiliated), D. W. THOMAS in *Record and Revelation* (1938), pp. 393 f.

of the suffering and then of the triumph. Why did the Servant suffer?
And why so suddenly and unexpectedly did he triumph? The acknowl-
edged theory was that it is the guilty who suffer and it is the righteous
who triumph. Surely, to have suffered so much, he must have been
the worst of sinners. Surely, to have triumphed so completely, he must
have been the most upright and righteous of all. The Second Isaiah
supplies the answers in the rest of the chapter, and he speaks on behalf
of sinful, guilty Israel. He explains why it is that the sufferings must be
temporary, and why the triumph must be complete and lasting.
Verse 4 opens with אכן, which is a stronger form of אך, itself ex-
pressing a contrast. It means: as a matter of fact, and quite contrary to
what has been supposed.

In point of fact, says the prophet, it was our sickness, but he
suffered. They were our pains, but he bore the heavy load of them.
It was he that was pierced because of our rebellious actions; he was
crushed because of our inqiuities. The chastisment which brought us
health/prosperity fell on him, and through his wound there was
healing for us. All of which is saying that the Servant was wholly
innocent, that the suffering which he bore was not his at all, he bore
it instead of the guilty ones and they went free. The prophet continues:
we all of us strayed like sheep, we turned each one of us his own way,
and the LORD caused him to encounter the penalty for all of us.
This is not saying that the Servant suffered in order than the rest might
go free. There is nothing vicarious about his suffering in this sense. It
is just a plain fact that he suffered when he ought not to have suffered,
and we did not suffer when we ought to have suffered. He was treated
brutally,[1] and he humbly submitted to such harsh treatment and
made no complaint. He was dumb and never opened his mouth, like
a sheep led to the slaughter or an ewe before her shearers. There is no
reference here whatever to any temple sacrifice; the point is the
helplessness and dumbness of the animal. He was taken away after [2]
an oppressive unjust sentence, and nobody was concerned about his
fate, for he was cut off from the land of the living, because of the
rebellion of my people the mortal blow was his. They made his grave
with the wicked (guilty) and with the rich [3] at his death, although
he had done nothing violent and had spoken no falsehood. Thus far

---

[1] נגש is used of the Egyption task-masters, Exod. 3: 7, etc.
[2] The meaning is wholly uncertain: It could mean 'without arrest and trial,'
or 'after arrest and trial.' The preposition מן is often difficult to translate.
[3] See p. 215.

(end of v. 9) the prophet has been declaring that the Servant is wholly innocent and entirely undeserving of any evil fate. But there is a divine law of retribution in this world and therefore it is entirely right and indeed inevitable that the disasters of the Servant must be temporary. If there is any justice at all in the world, then he must triumph. There was no period at which this belief was more widely held than the period from which Deuteronomy comes, and especially the period of the later sections of Deuteronomy. The prophet has referred to the exile under the figure of death, as Ezekiel did in chapter 37. The Servant must come to life again, as did the dried and apparently wholly lifeless bones in Ezekiel's vision.

It was all part of the divine purpose that the Servant was crushed. It was God who brought the sickness on him. But when [1]) the Servant provides (has provided) the compensatory payment for the wrong that has been done, then he will see his descendants living long, the greatest of earthly blessings, and the LORD's purpose will prosper in his hands. Here אשם means compensation, substitution. The so-called 'guilt-offering' was actually a compensation offering, and was presented in the Second Temple where damage had been done and the loss could usually be assessed. It could be for either inadvertent errors or deliberate offences. The essence of the offering was always that it was a compensation, a substitution.[2]) There is no record of this particular sacrifice before the post-exilic period, and we therefore see no reference here to any ritual sacrifice. The Servant was an innocent substitute for the guilty. The prophet is not concerned about what happens to the sinners, nor does he say that the Servant suffered and died for the sinners in order to save them. There was nothing vicarious in this sense about the suffering and death of the Servant, nor is there anything to do with atonement. The prophet is concerned about the Servant and he is demonstrating that the Servant was entirely innocent, and must of necessity prosper abundantly. The 597 B.C. exiles were the good figs, and those that remained behind in Jerusalem were Jeremiah's bad figs and Ezekiel's 'house of rebellion.' After (lit. away from) his suffering (trouble) the Servant will see light [3]); this means the light of life. His humiliation will give full

---

[1]) As NORTH points out (SI, p. 243) אם can be translated this way, Num. 36 4.

[2]) See 'The sin-offering and the guilt-offering,' VT XV, pp. 73-80. Also, DE VAUX, *Ancient Israel* (Eng. tr. 1961) pp. 420 f. makes a distinction between the sacrifice for sin and what he calls 'the sacrifice of reparation.'

[3]) So LXX and the Dead Sea Scrolls.

satisfaction and the righteous one, my Servant, will be vindicated to the great ones, for it was the penalty for their iniquities that he bore. (Lit. one will be satisfied with his humiliation—same verb as in v. 3—and one will vindicate the righteous one). Then in v. 12 we have the climax: God will grant him to share the spoils of victory with the great and strong ones. After all, he poured out his life in death and he was reckoned with the rebels; but it was the punishment for the sin of the many (great) that he bore and he took the place of the rebels (he intercepted). It is unfortunate that the English Versions, including RSV, have 'made intercession for' in 53: 12, because this phrase involves conscious and deliberate self-sacrifice for others and a pleading with God on their behalf. No one would dream that the same verb (and also the *hiph'il* form) is used in v. 6 and there translated 'laid on him.' We hold that the verb should be translated in the same way in both cases.

But who is 'my people' in v. 8? We deprecate reading the plural here or translating as though the word is in the plural. We maintain that the meaning is my people Israel, the sinful Israel of the days before 597 B.C., the bad figs. The Servant is the innocent victim of their rebellious apostasy, the 597 B.C. exiles, but tending, perhaps here, to include all the exiles.

Isaiah 54: 1-10. This section tells of the repopulation of a deserted Zion-Jerusalem. Not only will the city itself be full but it will be overcrowded. Her posterity will take possession of (יִרַשׁ, used in Joshua of the occupation of Palestine) of the lands of the Gentiles. God's desertion of Jerusalem was temporary. He will nevermore leave her, nor will He ever cease from His steadfast love and care for her. The picture is continued in vv. 11-17 with a glorious picture of prosperity and freedom from oppression. Once more the nationalistic element is supreme. At the very least it must be allowed that here the prophet's concern is for the resurgent Israel alone.

Isaiah 55: 1-5. God's free gift is offered to the new Israel, a prefiguration of the New Testament doctrine of grace. The ancient promises, the covenant with David will be renewed and made firm for ever. This new Israel is to be a witness to the Gentiles, and he will be a leader and a commander of the peoples. Israel will summon to his presence unknown nations, and nations who now do not know Israel will hurry to answer his summons. All this will be because Israel's God, YHVH, has glorified him.

Isaiah 55: 6-13. This last section of the sixteen chapters, 40-55 is a
call to repentance. Come now and come quickly whilst the opportunity
is here. Let the wicked leave his wicked way: let the evil man leave his
evil devices—let him turn in repentance to God who is full of mercy
and pardons to the uttermost. God's ways are not our ways, and His
thoughts are not our thoughts. He has a different way of doing things,
but be sure that His purposes will surely be accomplished. And so
(vv. 12 f.) the return home to Zion will be a glorious march through
a transformed world. All nature rejoices in this new day. Instead of the
thorns and briers of the desert there will be a veritable tree garden
like the paradises of the Persian kings.

There remain the three additional chapters, 60-62, which we hold
to be the work of the Second Isaiah.

Chapter 60. Here the glory and splendour of the restored, repopulated
city is joyously extolled in language which almost amounts to idealistic
extravagance. Everywhere else on earth and covering all the Gentiles
there will be darkness, thick obscuring cloud, but for the new Israel
there will be a new dawn and the glory of the LORD will shine out
upon them like the rising sun (זרח is used regularly of the speedy
brightening of the sunrise). This 'glory' of God is His splendour כבוד,
the haze of dazzling light which surrounds Him. It is the magnificence
and splendour of the eastern prince magnified a thousandfold. Nations
and kings will come to the bright light of this sunrise. Here (v. 4)
they all come, the Gentiles come from every direction, carrying Israel's
own children. All the wealth and plenty of land and sea will come to
Israel; camels laden with gold and frankincense, flocks and rams from
the desert tribes, all for the service of the altar in the glorious Temple
that shall rise. Here they come (v. 8) like clouds of doves. The Gentiles
(lit. isles) wait (קוה; cf. 51: 5) to bring Zion's children home with
quantities of gold and silver. In verses 10-14 we get the complete
subservience of the Gentiles. The foreigners are to build the walls,
their kings are to be attendants. The gates of the city will be open
night as well as day because of the continual inflow of wealth from
the Gentiles and the Gentile kings among the train of captives. Zion
will have absolute control over all, and all former oppressors will
bow at Zion's feet in abject humility. The prophet continues this
glorious description of Zion ruling all the Gentiles (to v. 18). The
chapter concludes with the promise of a speedy exaltation and prosperity beyond the dreams of normal men.

Isaiah 61: 1-9. This has been called a secondary Servant Song. The speaker has been anointed to proclaim a day of freedom and joy. The word 'anointed' does not of necessity involve an actual anointing: the anointed one is one chosen by God for a particular purpose (cf. 45: 1). Verse 1 speaks of release from captivity. . .and the end of the exile (p. 143). The ruined cities are to be rebuilt. Israel will all be priests and ministers of God, whilst the Gentiles will do all the menial work. The people of God will receive a doubled recompence (61: 7; cf. 40: 2) and all the world will acknowledge their superiority.

Isaiah 61: 10-11. The speaker is either the Zion of the future (Targum, etc.) or the Servant (Delitzsch, etc.), but this represents no difference of opinion, since both become one. The Servant grows into the New Israel, and it is this New Israel which is to rebuild and restore Zion. Once more we have a strongly nationalist attitude. All the Gentiles will see the vindication and triumph of Isarel.

Isaiah 62: 1-4. The restoration of Zion-Jerusalem has yet to come. The prophet refuses to be silent till the promises are fulfilled, until Zion's prosperity shines out with the brightness of a flaring torch in the darkness. Then the Gentiles and their kings will see Zion's success and splendour. There is nothing about the Gentiles having any share in all this. Zion is to have a new name: Hephzibah: 'all my delight is in her' or perhaps 'all my purpose is fulfilled in her.' The land is to have a new name: Beulah; married, happy and fruitful. There will be a complete change and a new beginning.

Isaiah 62: 6-9. Once more the triumph of Jerusalem, and its glorious future is yet to come. The 'watchmen on the walls' are the prophets who will never cease proclaiming their message. They will constantly bring the LORD's promises to His remembrance. They will give Him no rest until the promises are fulfilled. The day is bound to come when Israel eats her firstfruits once again in the Temple Courts. This is according to the rules of Deut. 12: 17 f., before the time when the firstfruits became the perquisite of the priests, as they did in the post-exilic period.

Isaiah 62: 10-12. The conclusion of the prophet's messages is the actual entrance through the city gates. The exiles are pictured returning to Jerusalem and they are 'The holy people,' the redeemed of the LORD. This message has been proclaimed to the end of the earth (cf. the phrase 'light of Gentiles'), and the message is not a worldwide salvation of all peoples, but the world-wide salvation of the people of God, the 'daughter of Zion.' The stage is now plainly and clearly set for the development of the exclusive nationalism of post-exilic Judaism.

CHAPTER SIX

JESUS THE SERVANT OF THE LORD

One aspect of the career of the Servant sometimes neglected is the suddenness of his triumph and the astonishment which this triumph occasions. This is because the Servant is hidden and obscure till the moment of triumph comes.

The great ones of earth were appalled at the dreadful plight of the Servant (52: 14). He was battered and bruised, and scarcely looked like a human being at all. They are equally amazed at his complete triumph and success: see p. 194. They spring quickly to their feet at the sudden appearance of the triumphant one, and they clasp their hands over their mouths to keep silence before him; cf. 41: 1. They never thought to see what they have seen; they have realised something the like of which they had never heard. The Servant of rulers has astonishingly become the ruler of kings.

The first of the so-called Servant songs (42: 1-4) speaks first of the choice of the Servant and his destiny, which is to bring judgment to the Gentiles. It explains that it is the quiet, the silent, the unpublicised one who is to establish the LORD's justice. The Servant makes no commotion. He does not shout. He does not raise his voice (Targum, 'roar'), nor does he make his voice to be heard in the street. He is a crushed, though not broken, reed. He is a wick faintly burning, but not extinguished. Now there comes a change. He will not burn faintly, nor will he be crushed יָרוּץ, but will be strong and will burn brightly till he has established justice in the earth, and for his law (for him to declare his law) the isles (Gentiles) shall wait. Here we have the initial silence and weakness of the Servant, and then the unexpected but complete success. The same original silence and the subsequent contrast are seen in 42: 14: 'I have for a long time held my peace; I have been still and have restrained myself. (Now) I will cry out like a woman in travail; I will gasp and pant at the same time.'

In 46: 3 f. we find the picture of the long delayed birth and at long last the delivery of the new-born child, the new Israel (p. 164). But the surprise at the sudden appearance of the Servant and the unexpected transformation of the one who is despised and abhorred is seen not only in 52: 13-15, but clearly in chapter 53 (pp. 194-197). In 53: 1-3 the whole emphasis is on the surprise and unexpectedness of the exaltation of the Servant. The silence of the Servant is emphasised in verse 7. He was harshly treated, brutally like a slave, and humiliated, but he never opened his mouth. He was silent like a sheep led to the slaughter and the ewe before her shearers, and all this in spite of being taken away because of an unjust verdict. But the silent one emerges triumphant.

In chapter 49, the silence and then the unexpected and sudden triumph of the Servant are plain to see. God made the Servant as a sharp sword, but He hid him in the shadow of His hand (verse 2). He made him as a polished arrow, but He hid him in His quiver. Here we have the picture of the Servant, chosen, called, prepared, thoroughly equipped, but hidden and kept secret. Verse 5 begins with ועתה 'and NOW saith the LORD. . .' It is true that often ועתה (and now) is used in that loose, almost meaningless way in which the word 'now' is used at the beginning of an opening sentence in modern English, or as the inevitable 'well' with which almost everyone begins to answer a question in a radio interview. But this is not so in these chapters of the Second Isaiah, especially when there is a contrast inherent in the context and where that contrast is being emphasised. The 'now' is to be shouted loudly and clearly. It is NOW that the Servant is to shine out like a light throughout the darkling world.

Some scholars have seen in 45: 14-17 a reference to Cyrus, mostly because of 43: 3, but we agree with WHITEHOUSE and NORTH that the reference is to Israel, and that the submission of Egypt, Ethiopia and the Sabeans is to Israel; see p. 159. In this case God hides Himself in Israel, the reviled, the despised Servant, of whom nobody expected anything. Another passage which speaks of submissive humiliation and insult is 50: 4-9; see p. 191.

These passages have been mentioned because of their references to the silence of the Servant and his sudden, unexpected exaltation and triumph. But there are other indications of a sudden bursting forth, an unexpected breaking through. These are to be found in the prophet's use of the metaphor of light. The usual Western use of the metaphor of light is brightness illumination, with an easy transition to its use as a metaphor for Knowledge: e.g. *Dominus illuminatio mea*. But the general biblical conception of light is a blazing forth, not a shining light, but a light that shines out. The picture is mostly drawn from the uprush of the dawn. It is not for nothing that Usha is a favourite name for a girl in India. The root אור does not mean 'be light' so much as 'become light,' 'lighten up.' The verb is used five times in all in the *qal*: four, of the shining of the sun at dawn, Gen. 44: 3; 1 Sam. 29: 10: Prov. 4: 18; Isa. 60: 1; and once of Jonathan's eyes brightening up after food, 1 Sam. 14: 27 and 29 (Qere). The same usage is found in the *niph'al*, 2 Sam. 2: 32 of daybreak; Job 33: 30 of the revival of life; Ps. 76: 5 (Eng. 4) of the shining forth of the majestic splendour of the LORD. All instances of the use of the *hiph'il* are necessarily of shining forth, of sending out light. In the case of the noun, we have the frequent phrase אור הבקר 'the shining forth of the light of the dawn,' Jg. 16: 2; 1 Sam. 14: 36; 25: 34, 36; 2 Sam. 17: 22; 2 Kgs. 7: 9; Mic. 2: 1. Also of the dawn, 2 Sam. 23: 4; Jg. 19: 26 (cf. 25); Job 24: 14; Neh. 8: 3 and so forth, often metaphorically of the shining out of light. This shining forth of light is a figure for the joyful experience of a sudden salvation, so that Ps. 27: 1 does not refer to the illumination of the mind, but to the salvation of the soul. The common word for 'morning' is בֹּקֶר; the root means 'to cleave.' It is properly the first light of the morning, that which cleaves the darkness of night. The words which accompany אור are זרח (shine forth), Ps. 97: 11 probably; 112: 4; Isa. 58: 8; 58: 10; and נגה (shine, beam: in the Targum *nôgeʰā*ʾ is the planet Venus), Isa. 9: 1 (Eng. 2); Hab. 3: 4; Job 22: 28; Prov. 4: 18. A third root is יפע (shine out, send out beams), Job 37: 15.

Other verses which relate to the sudden shining out of light are Isa. 58: 8, 'then shall thy light be cleft יבקע like the dawn': Isa. 60: 1, 'rise, shine out אורי for thy light אור has come; and the glory of the LORD has shone forth זרח upon thee'; Isa. 60: 3, 'and nations shall come to thy light אור, and kings to the bright beams נגה of thy shining forth זרח (sunrise)'.

The frequent use of the metaphor of the sudden breaking of the dawn and the uprush of light is seen in the LXX rendering of צֶמַח. This word is the 'shoot out of the stock of David,' Jer. 23: 5; 33: 15; Zech. 3: 8; 6: 12. It is a figure taken from the culture of the vine. Israel is the vine, Isa. 5; Ps. 80: 9, 15; Ezek. 17; etc., and the Messianic king is the new shoot out of the old vine stock. Nothing looks so dead as last years' vine stock, cut back to the point where it has been cut back year after year, and all gnarled and wrinkled and old. But the new shoot is virgin green and few shoots grow at a faster rate. In LXX this figure is wholly unrecognised, and the Syriac meaning of the root צמח is followed, so that the meaning is not the springing up of the new shoot of the vine as in the Hebrew, but the springing up of the dawn. Thus the noun צמח of the Hebrew become the ἀνατολή (dawn) of the LXX. The Messiah becomes 'the dayspring from on high,' Lk. 1: 78.

We turn to Jesus of Nazareth and the concept of the Servant of the LORD. In *Jesus and the Servant* (1959), Miss M. D. HOOKER discusses the 'influence of the servant concept of Deutero-Isaiah in the New Testament.' As we view the matter, she is much more in the right than those with whom she disagrees, but not wholly right. Her conclusion is summed up in the blurb: 'although the primitive (Christian) community found the prophecies of Deutero-Isaiah relevant to the *kerygma*. . .there is no evidence that the (servant) concept ever occupied any prominent position in their thought.' We would say that the whole discussion starts off in confusion. 'Servant' is taken to mean 'suffering servant.' We agree with Miss HOOKER that the concept of the Suffering Servant had little place in the thought of the primitive Church, that is, the concept of the Servant with the chief emphasis on the suffering. It had even less place in the mind of Jesus Himself, certainly with all the inferences and overtones which the phrase normally carries. The very phrase 'suffering servant' is a mistake in that it conveys a false impression of the theme and purpose of the Second Isaiah. We have sought to show that the Servant is the Triumphant Servant. The purpose of Isaiah 53 is not to provide a prophecy of or an apology for the sufferings of Christ. The purpose was to explain away the sufferings of the Servant, to show that they ought not to have been his at all. The prophet would say, if we are going to form a true estimate of the future of the Servant and what on all counts his fate should be, then we must cut the sufferings altogether out of our thinking. His sufferings were illogical. The logical outcome of his life and deeds is triumph. The suffering ought to have fallen on the 'bad figs' of Jerusalem, and none at all on the 'good figs' of the 597 B.C. deportation. It is misleading to say that the suffering of the Servant was vicarious, because so often this word carries atonement ideas, 'on behalf of' or 'deliberately instead of.' We do not find in Isaiah 53 anything to do with ideas of atonement. The suffering was an interlude in the life of the Servant. It was an illogical interruption of the proper course of events. He suffered as a result of the sinful rebellion of the old Israel. It is because he was innocent that he must necessarily triumph. His sufferings were indeed an אשם, but not in any sense in which the so-called guilt-offering is usually understood. They were a substitute; he paid the penalty of their sins. This was not *in order that* the guilty might go free. It is just a fact that he did suffer the consequences of sins that were not his.

We hold that the concept of the Servant occupied a dominant place in the mind of Jesus and of the primitive Christian community. The concept of the Servant of the LORD is: He was hidden, despised, nowhere to lay his head, suffering, but necessarily triumphant at last. It is the triumph that is the really important element: the resurrection from the death of the exile. Jesus, we hold, deliberately modelled His whole ministry on this concept of the Servant. This is why He wrought His miracles of healing, preached to the poor, opened the eyes of the blind, urged silence about His Messiahship, suddenly appeared in Jerusalem and looked confidently forward to triumph even though it was beyond and after condemnation and death.

According to Lk. 4: 16 f. the official opening of the ministry was in the synagogue at Nazareth, where Jesus read Isa. 61: 1, 2 as far as 'the acceptable year of the LORD.' Either He chose the passage Himself, or, if the passage was already a fixed Haftarah (Reading from the Prophets), then the Sabbath was the first in the month Sivan in the second year of the three-year cycle of the lectionary.[1] Either way the choice of the passage was deliberate. Having concluded the reading, which was the normal length for the first official Haftarahs, He said, 'Today hath this scripture been fulfilled in your ears.' The opening of His ministry, then, is said by Luke to be the fulfilment of the prophecy. This is the advent of the Servant of the LORD. It is true that the word 'Servant' is not actually mentioned in Isaiah 61, but the characteristic phraseology is unmistakable, so much so that some who cling to the idea of four Servant Songs find themselves thinking of these verses as a secondary Servant song (pp. 169 f.). According to Mt. 11: 2-6 (Lk. 7: 18-23) John the Baptist sent two of his disciples—two because they were to be witnesses: Dt. 17: 6; 19: 15; 1 Kg. 21: 10; Mt. 18: 16; etc.—to ask Jesus whether or not He was 'He that cometh.' Apparently Jesus made no immediate verbal reply, but took them with Him that day. They saw that He 'cured many of diseases and plagues and evil spirits: and on many that were blind He bestowed sight,' Lk. 7: 21, and as both evangelists say, He told them to tell John what they had seen and heard: 'the blind receive their sight (LXX in Isa. 61: 1 f.) and the lame walk, the lepers are cleansed, and the deaf hear, and the dead are raised up,

---

[1] See further, 'The Triennial Cycle and the Psalter,' ZAW x 3/4 (1933), pp. 302-307.

and the poor have good tidings preached to them,' Mt. 11: 5. These healings are evidently proof that Jesus was the Servant of the LORD but this means the Messianic Servant, because Jesus proceeds forthwith to identify John the Baptist with the messenger of Mal. 3: 1, the forerunner of the Messiah.

There is no attempt in the Gospels to minimise the healing ministry of Jesus, embarrassing as many moderns find it. It is mentioned again and again side by side with the preaching and the teaching. For instance, Mt. 9: 35 not only states that He taught and preached, but also that He healed 'all manner of diseases and all manner of sickness.' Again, after having called the two pairs of brothers, Simon and Andrew, and James and John, Jesus taught and preached throughout Galilee, and healed every kind of sickness and disease. The evangelist then says (Mt. 4: 24) that 'the report of him went forth into all Syria.' This report was not so much because of His preaching and teaching as because of the healings, since the rest of the verse reads: 'they brought to him all that were sick, holden with divers diseases and torments, possessed with devils, epileptic and palsied; and he healed them.' See also Mk. 1: 28: 'and the report of him (the new teaching and the fact that with authority he commanded even the unclean spirits and they obeyed him) went out straightway into all the region of Galilee round about.' In Mt. 8: 17 the account of the healing of Peter's wife's mother is followed by the healing of the large crowd at sunset (cf. Mk. 1: 32-34), but Matthew goes on to quote Isa. 53: 4 in the form 'himself took our infirmities and bare our diseases,' the association being not with the Cross and the Atonement, as perhaps theologians might expect, but with 'casting out the spirits with a word and healing all that were sick.'

Indeed, it is the healing ministry of Jesus which is usually cited as proof of the coming of the kingdom. See Lk. 11: 20: 'if I by the finger of God cast out devils, then is the kingdom of God come unto you'. Also see Lk. 10: 17-20: where the seventy return full of joy especially that the devils were subject to them and Jesus replies 'I behold Satan fallen as lightning from heaven', i.e. we have got the devil on the run; he is beaten. In Lk. 9: 43 the healing of the epileptic boy (unclean spirit) is evidence of the majesty of God. It is mostly Luke who presents the aspect that the casting out of devils is fighting against Satan and his counter-kingdom of evil, but Matthew 15: 29-31 (Mark 7: 31-37) includes the most extensive healings of every type and at the end he adds 'and they glorified the God of Israel.' So also in the case of the sick of the palsy (Lk. 5: 25) and all the crowd who were there (Mk. 2: 12; Mt. 9: 8; Lk. 5: 26). Another case is that of the widow's son at Nain (Lk. 7: 16): 'and fear took hold on all: and they glorified God saying, A great prophet is arisen among us: and God has visited his people.' Throughout the Gospels the healings are emphasised at least as much as the teaching and preaching.

Mt. 12: 22 f. is important. Here Jesus heals a man who was blind and dumb. All the crowds are amazed and they say 'Is not this the son of David?' This is an extraordinary conclusion to draw. Why should the healing of a blind and dumb man prove that Jesus is the son of David? It is because Jesus is fulfilling Isa. 61: 1 f. healing the sick, preaching good tidings to the poor, and because the Servant triumphs and rules, He is the Messiah also.

The conception of Messiah according to Jesus was not that of a suffering Messiah as against a Triumphant Messiah, but a suffering-triumphant Messiah as against a triumphant Messiah. The difference is in His interpolation, so to speak, of the suffering. This is a result of His identifying Himself in such detail with the Servant of the LORD, but it is important so far as Jesus and the primitive Church is concerned, never to mention the suffering without referring also to the Triumph.

It is essential to include and emphasise the triumph, equally in the words of Jesus as in the words of the Second Isaiah. When, according to the Gospel traditions, Jesus referred specifically to His approaching death, he also referred to His resurrection. See Mt. 17: 22 f., where it is said that while Jesus yet abode in Galilee, he told them that the Son of Man would be 'delivered up into the hands of man, and they shall kill him, and the third day he shall be raised up.' These may not be the exact words of Jesus Himself, but they certainly form part of the earliest Christian tradition, according to which the climax was not the Crucifixion but the Resurrection. See also Mt. 20: 17-19: 'the Son of Man shall be delivered unto the chief priests and scribes; and they shall condemn him to death and shall deliver him to the Gentiles to mock and to scourge and to crucify; and the third day he shall be raised up.' Note the inclusion of the mocking and scourging, both of which are part of the picture of the humiliated, maltreated Servant. See also the parallel Mk. 10: 32-34; Lk. 18: 32 f.; and the post-Transfiguration passages, Mt. 16: 21 and Lk. 9: 22. Here (Mk. 9: 9-12) we find a reference to the time 'when the Son of Man should have risen again from the dead' and also that it is 'written of the Son of

Man that he should suffer many things and be set at nought' which could possibly be Ps. 22: 6 f., though it is more likely to be Isa. 53: 2 f., but why the title 'Son of Man?'

A very great deal has been written about this title 'the Son of Man' ьnd its connexion with Jesus of Nazareth, and for details of these long discussions reference must be made to the work of students of the New Testament. It has often been pointed out that in the Gospel according to Saint Mark, the use of the title is associated with suffering and that the title appears when Jesus first refers to His approaching sufferings and death—except, that is, for 2: 10 (sick of the palsy) and 2: 28 (Lord of the Sabbath). But it is also true that with the suffering, the triumph also is mentioned. It is therefore just as true to say that when Jesus begins to refer to His ultimate triumph, He begins to use the phrase Son of Man, as it is to say that it is when He begins to talk about His suffering. It is as unexpected that the Son of Man shall suffer as it is that Messiah shall suffer. There is no direct link between the Son of Man and suffering any more than there is between Messiah and suffering. Both titles belong to the world of triumph. It was not because of His suffering that Jesus claimed to be the Messiah; it was in spite of it. It was not because of suffering that Jesus took upon Himself [1]) the title Son of Man, but in spite of it. The Servant suffers and dies, but he rises again. Jesus must suffer, must die, but He must rise again. Both the Servant and the Son of Man are to triumph and judge many nations. To triumph and to rule is the destiny of the Son of Man both in Daniel 7 and in the Book of Enoch. Both the Servant of the Second Isaiah and the 'one like unto a son of man' of Dn. 7: 13, 22 are figures of speech for a new Israel, the conquering saints of the Most High, triumphant over all peoples and nations. This is why Jesus is the Servant and this is why Jesus is the Son of Man. But first in both cases come humiliation and suffering and death. This is what Jesus added to the pattern both of Messiah and of Son of Man. See Lk. 24: 26 f.: 'Behoved it not the Christ to suffer these things and to enter into his glory? And beginning from Moses and all the prophets, he interpreted to them in all the scriptures the things concerning himself.' This we take to mean, not that He had to prove to them that He was Messiah, but that Mes-

---

[1]) Did Jesus actually use this title of Himself? Or did it become used of Him in the early post-resurrection traditions and so used at an early date as an alternative title to denote His triumph? just as the title 'Lord' (*kurios*) came to be used of Him.

siah had to suffer and die first before He could achieve the triumph which is essentially His.

We hold that Jesus deliberately modelled His ministry on the concept of the Servant of the LORD of the Second Isaiah. This is why the healing, the preaching to the poor takes so large and prominent a place in the Gospel traditions. Indeed John goes so far as to treat the miracles as signs: 'this beginning of his signs σημεῖα did Jesus in Cana of Galilee, and manifested his glory,' Jn. 2: 11. He certainly deliberately fulfilled Scripture on the first Palm Sunday. He rode on the ass, which is Zc. 9: 9. He appeared suddenly in the Temple: the journey begins in Mk. 9: 30, and according to Mk. 11: 11 He went straight into the Temple, looked round on all things, and then went straight out; this is Mal. 3: 1: 'and the LORD whom ye seek, shall suddenly come to his temple.' Again, the day was the first day of the Passover Week. If the Psalter was already recited one psalm each Sabbath to correspond to a triennial system of reading the Law, then Psalm 2 was the proper psalm for the second Sabbath of Nisan in the first year. Jesus entered Jerusalem riding the ass on the day following this Sabbath. All men knew that the Messiah would appear at Passover: see the LXX of Jer. 31: 8 (in' the feast of Passover' for 'with them the blind and the lame').

This reference to Jer. 31: 8 brings to mind the curious statement of Mt. 21: 14, where it is stated that on the occasion of the cleansing of the Temple (according to the Synoptists, the next day after the Entry) 'the blind and the lame came to him in the temple, and he healed them.' The Hebrew of Jer. 31: 8 is 'Behold I will bring them. . . with them the blind and the lame,' which, as we saw immediately above, becomes in LXX 'in the festival of Passover' (במועד פסח for בם עור ופסח). Apparently the evangelist knew the double reading, just as in Mt. 27: 3-10, the story of what happened to the thirty pieces of silver which Judas Iscariot received. There was a discussion on the part of the chief priests as to whether this money should go into the temple treasury or not, and they decided in the end to use it to buy 'the potter's field.' Zc. 11: 13 is quoted, though the reference given is Jeremiah. The Zechariah passage actually is: 'Cast it unto the potter (יוצר, but the Syriac has 'treasury' as if reading אוצר. LXX has *chōneutērion* 'smelting furnace'). . .' and 'and cast them unto the potter (Syriac again 'treasury') in the house of the LORD.' The two interpretations are actually in the Hebrew text, for how could there be a potter in the temple? There could be a treasury, and there was. It is hard to explain all this, but it is plain that the evangelist knew of the double exegesis of Zc. 11: 13. Perhaps LOISY was right when long ago he suggested that the first evangelist was the 'scribe who hath been made a disciple to the kingdom of heaven. . .which bringeth forth out of his treasure things new and old,' Mt. 13: 52.

One of the strange features of the Gospel story, common to all three synoptists, is the double tradition concerning the miracles: did Jesus seek publicity, or did he seek to avoid it? It has been the fashion to say that Jesus did not want to be known as a miracle worker, but rather as teacher and preacher. This is said with particular reference to the healing miracles, concerning some of which He enjoined silence. This is not the overall picture we get from the Gospels. There are indeed times when Jesus expressly bids the healed one not to broadcast the story of the healing, but the general picture is one of healings everywhere, with the people rejoicing in them as visible signs of the coming of the kingdom, of the manifested power and glory of God. This is what we would expect after the announcement in the synagogue in Nazareth, Lk. 4: 16-19. There was one occasion when Jesus told the cured man to tell all his friends and relations what the LORD had done for him. This was the man who had been possessed by the legion of devils (Mk. 5: 19; Lk. 8: 39, but not Mt. 8: 28-32, where two sufferers are mentioned and no legion). The incident took place on the south-east shore of the Lake, in Decapolis, which at that time was an area mostly, if not entirely, east of the Jordan. The fact that this incident took place east of the Jordan is not the explanation for the command, because the healing of the deaf man who also had an impediment in his speech also took place in Decapolis (Mk. 7: 31-37), and 'he charged them that they should tell no man.' Certainly Herod Antipas knew Him as a miracle worker (Lk. 23: 8), whilst the Greek has σημεῖον (sign), the word used regularly of healing miracles in the fourth gospel.

It is on record that Jesus many times urged silence. Why did He do this, when at the same time it is clear that healing the sick was part of the proof of His claim to be the anointed one (Is. 61: 1)? When He sent out the twelve (Mk. 6: 7; Mt. 10: 1; Lk. 9: 1) and the seventy (Lk. 10: 1 f.), He gave them power over unclean spirits and to cure diseases, and even (Lk. 10: 9) to 'heal the sick. . .and say to them, The Kingdom of God is come nigh to you.'

Our explanation is that both as the healer of sicknesses and in the silence He sometimes commanded, Jesus is following the pattern of the Servant of the LORD of the Second Isaiah. He is the hidden Servant, the silent Servant, suddenly to be made manifest and ultimately, after suffering and death, to triumph. This is the explanation of the so-called Messianic secret. It is actually stated in Mt. 12: 16 ff.: 'and many followed him; and he healed them all, and charged them that they should not make him known: that it might be fulfilled. . .' and then Is. 42: 1-3 is quoted: '(my servant) shall not strive, cry aloud, neither shall anyone hear his voice in the streets.' The two necessities tended to cut across each other. On the one hand He had to proclaim His identity with the anointed (messianic) servant by His miracles of healing and by bringing good tidings to the poor; on the other hand, He sought to conform to the pattern of the Servant, who before His unexpected triumph was to be obscure, silent and dumb.

The commands for silence are frequent. In Mk. 1: 34: 'He suffered not the devils to speak because they knew him' (BW f 1 f 28 add 'to be Christ'; f 13 f 700 etc. 'to be the Christ'; cf. Lk. 4: 41). The order to tell no one that He is the Messiah (Christ) is plain elsewhere. In Mt. 16: 20 He gives this order to the disciples. This is immediately after the declaration by Simon Peter at Caesarea Philippi. The parallel in Lk. 9: 22 agrees with this, but the Marcan account introduces a qualification (Mk. 9: 9) by saying that they are to keep silent until after the Resurrection. Both Matthew and Luke represent Jesus as saying to the disciples that the Son of Man must go up to Jerusalem, suffer many things, be killed and rise again. Luke adds 'be rejected.' Both Matthew 16: 28 and Luke 9: 22 conclude with the statement that some of them standing there shall in no wise taste of death 'till they see the Son of Man coming in his kingdom' (Luke, 'see the kingdom of God'), which means, not the final judgment with the Son of Man coming on the clouds of heaven, but the triumph of the silent, hidden, suffering, dying Servant of the LORD.

In Mt. 17: 9 on the way down from the Mount of Transfiguration, Jesus commands the disciples to tell no man the vision (Mk. 9: 9, 'what they had seen') till the Son of Man be risen from the dead. This vision was of Moses and Elijah, the two traditional witnesses to the Messiah. Lk. 9: 36 simply says 'and they held their peace, and told no man in those days any of the things which they had seen.'

Similar to this is Mk. 3: 12, where the unclean spirits 'fell down before Him, and cried, saying, Thou art the Son of God.' Whereupon Jesus charged them not to make him manifest (Mt. 12: 16). Compare the two stories in Mt. 9: 27-31 and 20: 29-34 respectively. The two stories both concern two blind men who received their sight, and the other common factor is that both pairs cry out after Jesus, 'Have mercy upon us, thou son of David.' In the earlier story Jesus commands them to see to it that nobody knows of the cure (9: 30). In the second story Jesus makes no such demand. The Marcan parallel to the second story is that of blind Bartimaeus (Mk. 10: 32-34. Did the one become two because of the name? son of a twin), and here also there is no command to silence. This last incident took place towards the end of the last journey when Jesus had already left Jericho. Perhaps the reason for the difference is that the climax is near when the secret is to be made known. Other cases of silence enjoined after healing are Mk. 8: 22-26 (the blind man at Bethsaida: 'do not even enter into the village'), and Mk. 5: 43. This latter case is that of the raising of Jairus's daughter. Nowhere are the two contradictions more evident, for Luke confirms the charge for silence (8: 56), whilst Matthew says 'and the fame thereof went forth into all the land' (9: 26).

The command to the lepers for silence is probably part of the same pattern of silence on the part of the hidden messianic Servant, though here there may possibly be a taboo reason. The men will not be ceremonially nor civically clean until the priest has examined them and satisfied himself that the leprosy is dead, Mk. 1: 44; Mt. 8: 4; Lk. 5: 14. The other passage which tells of a leprosy cure is that of the ten lepers, one of whom was a Samaritan. Here the questions of silence and of broadcasting do not arise. The story is concerned with something else: the fact that it was the Samaritan alone who came back to say 'Thank you.' But why in so many instances was it expected that the son of David should heal the sick and make the blind to see, unless it was because of Isa. 61: 1 f. and Jesus following the pattern of the Servant?

But what is most remarkable of all is the silence of Jesus at the trials. Before Caiaphas Jesus uttered not a word (Mt. 26: 63; Mk. 14: 61) until He was put on oath. When He was thus forced to speak, He said 'Thou sayest' (an admission, Mt. 26: 64) or 'I am' (Mk. 14: 62). According to Lk. 22: 67 f. he answered with what appears to be a popular saying:

'If I tell you, you will not believe:
If I ask you, you will not answer.'

But later, under pressure (v. 70), He says, 'You say I am.' But all three evangelists agree that Jesus added 'From now on (Mt. ἀπ' ἄρτι :

Lk. ἀπὸ τὸ νῦν; not Mark) you will see the Son of Man sitting on the right hand of power (Luke does not have 'you shall see') and (Matthew and Mark) 'coming on the clouds of heaven.' We suggest that Luke is right in omitting 'coming on the clouds of heaven.' This is a later idea. At first the triumph of Jesus was associated with the rising from the dead. Later His triumph was linked with the idea of the Heavenly Man, the Son of Man (cf. the Book of Enoch), the judge who is to come at the End of Days. But what is important here is that Jesus was silent until Caiaphas forced Him to speak.

Again, in the trial before the governor Jesus adopted the same attitude. Pilate asked Him if He was the King of the Jews, and Jesus answered 'Thou sayest' (Mt. 27: 11; Mk. 15: 2; Lk. 23: 3), but when He was accused by the chief priests and scribes, He kept silence, nor did He make any further reply to Pilate's questions. Before Herod Jesus did not utter a single word from first to last, in spite of Herod's questioning Him in many words (Lk. 23: 9). The chief priests and the scribes vehemently accused Him. Herod was wanting Him to work a miracle. But He maintained silence, and they ended by 'setting him at nought, mocking him and arraying him in gorgeous apparel.'

Why did Jesus keep such silence at the trials, except only to admit before priests that He was 'the Messiah, the Son of the Blessed One' (Mk. 14: 61)—Matthew has 'the Messiah, the Son of God' (26: 63), which is the same thing; Luke has the admission that He is the Son of God (22: 70) which is understandable since Luke was a Gentile, writing for Gentiles; and before Pilate that He was King of the Jews? Our answer is that He was following the pattern of the Servant of the LORD, even as He had followed it all through His ministry. He had enjoined silence concerning the healings and yet demonstrated by these and by preaching to the poor that He was the Servant, and all the time Himself had followed the pattern of the silent, hidden Servant. The demand for silence at the trials is insisted upon in Isa. 53: 7 f.

'He was brutally treated and humiliated
Yet he did not open his mouth.
Like a sheep that is led to the slaughter
And like an ewe before her shearers,
He was silent and did not open his mouth.
After an oppressive, unjust sentence
He was taken waay, and who was concerned about his fate?
For he was cut off from the land of the living. . .[1])

---

[1]) see p. 195.

Another element in the trials is concerned with the two times Jesus broke silence. In each case the accusation He admitted as being true was the one thing which would get Him into trouble in that particular court. Further, the penalty in each case was death. The only thing that would get Him into trouble before the High Priest was the claim that He was Messiah, the Son of God. Whatever this last phrase meant, it was justified by Ps. 2: 7, blasphemy or no blasphemy. The only thing that would get Him into trouble in Pilate's court was the admission that He claimed to be King of the Jews. Before Herod, He made no admission at all. There was nothing that would bring Him there under sentence of death. All this leads to the conclusion that Jesus knew He had to die, just as He knew He must rise again: this is the pattern of the Servant of the LORD which He was following. 'Behoved it not the Christ to suffer these things, and to enter into His glory? And beginning from Moses and from all the prophets, he interpreted to them in all the scriptures the things concerning himself' (Lk. 24: 26 f.).

Lk. 22: 35-38 is a curious passage. It contains a quotation from Isa. 53: 12 'and he was numbered with the rebels' (see p. 197). Jesus tells the disciples to change their ways entirely: the man who has no purse or wallet is to take one, and the man who has no sword is to sell his cloak and buy one. This is because He must be numbered with the rebels, and because the time has come for this saying to be fulfilled. And yet, strangely enough two swords are enough and in the sequel one of the disciples was rebuked for using the sword he had (Lk. 22: 49; Mk. 14: 47; Mt. 26: 51). If we follow the usual translation of 'transgressors' then we may suppose the evangelist assumes that the prophecy was fulfilled at the trial, counted with the transgressors. But if we realise that the root פשע means 'rebel,' then the prophecy 'he was reckoned with the rebels' is fulfilled by His being arrested in the company of armed men, albeit it was but a token armament. It was done 'that the scriptures might be fulfilled,' Mk. 14: 49: they 'came out as against a robber.'

There are elements in the Gospel narratives concerning which it is difficult to decide how much comes from Jesus Himself and how much belongs to the early post-resurrection traditions, the time when men began to tell the story of His life, His death and His resurrection, all of it with their knowledge of the Servant equation in their minds. There was the spitting: according to Mk. 14: 65; Mt. 26: 67 the chief priests and the whole council spat in His face, and Mk. 15: 19; Mt. 27: 30 say that the soldiers spat on him. See Isa. 50: 6. Then there was the scourging, Mk. 15: 15; Mt. 27: 26; Lk. 23: 22. See Isa. 50: 6 f. and 53: 3 f. Also, in Isa. 53: 9 it is stated that the Servant was given a grave 'with the wicked and with the rich את־עשיר in his death.' [1]) It has been suggested [2]) that in עשיר we should see a second root עשר 'his grave with the wicked and his burial-mound with the corrupt.' But Joseph of Arimathea was a rich man, and this rich man's grave was the only grave Jesus ever had. Perhaps 'with the rich' or even 'with a rich man' is right after all.

Christian exegetes have found considerable difficulty over the apparent reluctance at one stage of Jesus to have dealings with non-Jews. It is stated in Mt. 10: 5 that, having chosen twelve disciples, 'he sent them forth, and charged them, saying, Go not into any way of the Gentiles, and enter not into any city of the Samaritans, but go rather to the lost sheep of the house of Israel.' Then there follows the list of the signs of the Messianic Servant (Isa. 61: 1 f.). These they also are to make manifest and to show that 'the kingdom of heaven is at hand.' The prohibition of any dealings with Gentiles in general and Samaritans in particular gives the number twelve special and exclusive significance. When Jesus bade them not to go to the Gentiles, but definitely to go to the Jews, did He mean just that? Or are we dealing with some early pro-Jewish and non-Pauline tradition, such as is evident in the attitude of the Jerusalem leaders, Acts 11: 1-3; 15: 1-29; Gal. 2? This is not a Matthaean anti-Gentile bias, as we may see from the story of Zacchaeus, which we owe entirely to Luke (19: 1-10). Verse 9 is 'And Jesus said unto him, Today is salvation come to this house, forasmuch as he also is a son of Abraham.' So that when it says in the next verse that the Son of Man came to seek and to save that which was lost, the presumption is that here it means every lost son of Abraham. This is a Lucan tradition, and it was the Gentile Luke who realised as soon as most, that the Gospel was for the Greek as well as for the Jew. Paul had realised this long before he met Luke, but there can be little doubt but that Luke strengthened Paul's convictions on this matter. Yet it is Luke, and Luke alone, who faithfully records what appears to be a statement limiting salvation to the Jews. How could he do that unless

---

[1]) Or 'his funeral mound'; see BDB 119b with its reference to Ezek. 43: 7 and possibly here also; apparently confirmed by the Dead Sea Scroll, Isaiah A.

[2]) Reider, VT ii p. 118. This certainly makes a good parallel couplet.

in some way it was firmly embedded in the tradition he received?

The clearest example of this attitude of Jesus is the story of the Canaanitish (Syro-Phoenician) woman, Mk. 7: 24-30; Mt. 15: 21-28. According to Mt. 15: 24, the answer which Jesus gave to the woman was: 'I was not sent but unto the lost sheep of the house of Israel' (? those that had gone astray like sheep, Isa. 53: 6). This is not in the Marcan parallel, but both evangelists give evidence of marked reluctance on the part of Jesus to do anything for the woman and her daughter. Mark says (verse 27) that the children must come first, but both give the woman's reply (Mk. 7: 27; Mt. 15; 26) to the effect that even the dogs eat the crumbs that fall from their master's (the children's) table. Whereupon Jesus healed the child forthwith. The mother's faith was great, and it was this which turned the scale. Either Jesus was testing the woman (which does not seem to be altogether a 'Christian' thing to do considering the great stress of mind of the mother: most of us would not dream of causing the already distracted woman such unnecessary anxiety), or He meant what He said. The natural explanation is that He did mean what He said, and that there was up to this stage in His ministry a pronounced reluctance to have dealings with non-Jews. He welcomed publicans and sinners; they were Jews, and He was out against the exclusive legalism of the scribes, who laid down other conditions than repentance and faith. He did not avoid Samaritans, but an exclusive attitude is shown in Jn. 4:22 f.: 'for salvation is of the Jews'. But there came to be a change, so the Johanine tradition says, because 'the hour cometh, and now is, when the true worshippers shall worship the Father in spirit and in truth: for the Father seeketh such to worship him.' The Marcan saying 'Let the children first be filled' is a less exclusive attitude. It has doubtless prompted the unwarranted introduction of 'also' in the margin of RV in Jn. 4: 23, but it is reflected in the way in which Paul and Barnabas went first to the Jews during their journey in Asia Minor (Acts 13: 5; 13: 46, etc.), and then to the Gentiles when the Jews rejected them. Later Jesus rebuked James and John who wanted fire to be called down from heaven upon the inhospitable Samaritan village (Lk. 9: 52-56), but these were 'sons of Abraham' even though post-exilic Judaism had interposed barriers against them because they did not conform to their rules and regulations.

It would appear, therefore, that at first Jesus was nationalist in that He conceived Himself as bringing salvation to the Jews only. This is, we have sought to show,[1]) the attitude of the Second Isaiah, and we explain this nationalism on the part of Jesus as part of His deliberate following the pattern of the Servant of the LORD. But there came a time when He realised that there could be no such 'middle wall of partition,' nor any such limits set to the Gospel. It was the incident of the Syro-Phoenician mother which taught Him this. Nevertheless, it is plain that the leaders of the Church in Jerusalem after the Resurrection and even after Pentecost were strong in their belief that the Gospel was for Jews only, and they were very slow indeed to make any compromise on this issue. Indeed, it is likely that only the destruction of the Temple and with it the virtual elimination of these exclusive and nationalist Christian Jews prevented Christianity from remaining a sect within Judaism. But this 'Jews only,' this nationalistic attitude can be explained, in our view, only on the basis that Jesus modelled His whole life and ministry on the Servant of the Second Isaiah, and that this extended at first even to a nationalistic attitude that it was only for the Jews that salvation was come.

We find in this also the explanation of the fact that the Resurrection took so prominent a place in the first preaching. This is shown, for example, in the statement in Acts 17:18 that the Athenians thought Paul was 'a setter forth of strange gods: because he preached Jesus and Anastasis (Resurrection).' See also Acts 17: 32. The absence of emphasis in the early preaching of any vicarious, atoning element in the Cross has puzzled many. We believe with BULTMANN that any such elements 'were put in his mouth subsequently by the church,' [2]) but we think BULTMANN is mistaken when he says 'The tradition of Jesus's sayings reveals no trace of a consciousness on his part of being the Servant of God of Is. 53.' [3]) BULTMANN says this because when he thinks of 'the Servant' he thinks in terms of 'the Suffering Servant.' Here we believe he is wrong, though this is the general attitude. This is why H. J. CADBURY finds it 'almost unbelievably' [4]) so, that the one time when Luke quotes Is 53, he 'escapes all the vicarious phrases with which that passage abounds.' We do not find this omission surprising at all, because in the sense in which the word 'vicarious' is generally used (deliberate atoning self-sacrifice) we do not find anything vicarious there at all. In any case, the Gospel and Acts tradition

---

[1]) see pp. 154-165.
[2]) *Jesus and the Word* (Eng. tr. 1935), p. 214.
[3]) *Theology of the New Testament* (Eng. tr. 1952), vol. i, p. 31.
[4]) 'The Titles of Jesus in Acts' in *Beginnings*, vol. v, p. 366.

is that the suffering-and-death is mentioned with the resurrection also, and the whole point is that the Suffering Servant triumphs. We suspect that the vicarious, atoning emphasis on the sufferings and death of Jesus developed from the time when men ceased to see the triumph in the Resurrection and looked forward more and more to a Second Advent, the time when the Son of Man would come on the clouds of heaven.

PART TWO

THE THIRD ISAIAH

CHAPTER SEVEN

EXEGESIS OF CHAPTERS 56-66

Virtually all modern scholars apart from 'conservative evangelicals'[1]) agree in the separation of chapters 40-66 from chapters 1-39,[2]) but there is a much wider division of opinion concerning chapters 40-66 than is sometimes realised. Some still regard 40-66 as a unit, notably W. F. ALBRIGHT[3]) and FLEMING JAMES[4]). They place the whole section as a unity in the years 540-522 B. C. There is also C. C. TORREY[5]) who regards all references to Cyrus and to Babylon as interpolations. He holds that 34-35 and 40-66 'form a homogeneous group and are the work of a single hand' (p. 53). He holds that these chapters consist of twenty-seven successive poems, written in Palestine, probably in Jerusalem, close to the end of the fifth century B.C. They have nothing to do with any return from a Babylonian captivity which is wholly fictional, but have to do with the hope of the gathering in of the Dispersion. This position is in the main supported by G. DAHL (1929) and much of it by G. A. BARTON (1938). Others who maintain the unity of 40-66 are KÖNIG (1926, all from the exile) and GLAHN (1934: 40-55 is before and 56-66 after the Return).

The majority of scholars follow DUHM (1892) and K. MARTI (1892) who held that the Second Isaiah wrote in Babylonia and that another prophet, the Third Isaiah, wrote chapters 56-66 in Palestine as late as 457-445 B. C., dates which place him after Ezra's arrival (accepting, as they did, the earlier date for Ezra) and before Nehemiah arrived. So also LITTMANN (1899), ZILLESSEN (1906), BOX (1908), ELLIGER (1928), ODEBERG (1931) and SELLIN (1930). HÖLSCHER (1914) believed that 56-66 like 40-55 were written in Egypt. Some think in terms of one person as the author of 56-66, but find a closer association

---

[1]) HERZOG (1915), LIAS (1915 and 1918), KAMINKA (1925), ALLIS (1950).

[2]) There is a great deal to be said for adding chapter 35 to chapters 40-55 and 60-62.

[3]) *The Archaeology of Palestine and the Bible* (1932), p. 218.

[4]) *Personalities of the Old Testament* (1939), p. 363.

[5]) *The Second Isaiah* (1928).

than others with chapters 40-55 by saying that the Third Isaiah was a disciple of the Second Isaiah. ELLIGER (1928 and 1933), for instance, held that not only was the Third Isaiah a disciple of the Second Isaiah, but that, besides being responsible for 56-66, he was also responsible for the revision and publication of 40-55. This view is supported by MEINHOLD and SELLIN. Both ELLIGER and SELLIN envisage the Third Isaiah as expanding the work of his master and perhaps incorporating within 40-55 something of his own, notably 52: 13-53: 12. All of this, as WEISER rightly points out, makes the Third Isaiah a contemporary of Haggai and Zechariah 1-8. The period 457-445 B.C. is rather too late for the activity of such a man: that is, supposing him to have been an actual face-to-face pupil of the Second Isaiah. The period 457-445 B.C. involves a man of the next or third generation whose mission was to interpret the Second Isaiah to his own generation who certainly needed whatever comfort and consolation could be brought to them.

There are many variations among scholars in their opinions as to the date and authorship of these chapters 56-66. BLEEK (1859) thought that in chapters 58 onwards, but certainly in 63-66, we have prophecies written by the author of 40-55, but at a later date. On the other hand, STADE (1888) held that 56: 9-57: 13a; 58: 13-59: 21 and 62-66 could scarcely be from the hand of the Second Isaiah in their present form. BUDDE (1891) thought that 56-59 and perhaps 61 and 63-64 were later than other elements in 40-66, whilst KUENEN (1889) made 50-51 and 54-66 later than the rest. And so we come to the positions held by many scholars that 56-66 are not all by the same author, and indeed may be by many authors: CHEYNE (1901), KOSTERS (1896), CRAMER (1905), BUDDE (1909), BUTTENWIESER (1919), J. MARTY (1924), LEVY (1925), ABRAMOWSKI (1925), VOLZ (1932), LODS (1935), EISSFELDT (1934, etc.), KITTEL (1898), WEISER (1961), GRESSMANN (1898), CORNELL (1900), ZILLESSEN (1904), MOWINCKEL (1925), OESTERLEY and ROBINSON (1934), ROWLEY (1950) and others. PFEIFFER (1941) finds innumerable affinities between 40-55 and 56-66, and thinks in terms of 'one or more authors' dominated in thought and diction by the author of 40-55. He says that it is the less attractive features of the Second Isaiah's style that are copied and intensified. Possibly here he means the nationalistic elements rather than literary style.

Attempts have been made to date particular sections of these 56-66 chapters. EISSFELDT allocates 56-66 as a whole to the years 520-516 B.C., but places 57: 1-13 before 587 B.C.; 63: 7-64: 12 (Heb. 11) soon after 587 B.C.; 66: 1-4 before 538 B.C.; and 65 to the period 400-200 B.C. With this compare VOLZ, who places 56: 1-8; 57:14-21 ; 58: 1-14; 59: 9 f.; 61 in the period 500-400 B.C.; 56: 9-57: 13 as pre-exilic; 63: 7-64: 12 in c. 585 B.C.; 66: 1 f. as c. 520 B.C.; 63: 1-6 as 500-400 B.C.; and 65 and 66: 3-42 as after 331 B.C. G. W. ANDERSON (1959) writes of the whole of 56-66 as a collection possibly spanning the whole period 586-400 B.C. with now and then, as in 58, an echo of the authentic voice of pre-exilic prophecy. One of the criteria of judgment running through most of these attempts at dating the eleven chapters is to be seen in the remark of SKINNER who says [1] that 63: 7-64: 11 must have been written before the building of Zerubbabel's temple in 520-516 B.C. If we are to hold that 56-66 is a unity, then it must all have been written earlier than 520 B.C. If the rest of 56-66 cannot be conceived as being earlier than 520 B.C. then 56-66 is not a unity.

The problem is: Where are these eleven chapters to be fitted in to an accepted historical framework?

597 B.C.	Beginning of the Exile: first deportation.
568 B.C.	Destruction of the Temple: second deportation.
581 B.C.	Third deportation.
538 B.C.	Cyrus captures Babylon.
522-520 B.C.	Accession of Darius Hystaspis and consolidation of the Empire.
520-516 B.C.	Rebuilding of the Temple under the leadership of Zerubbabel and Jeshua encouraged by Haggai and Zechariah.
445/4 B.C.	Nehemiah's arrival in Jerusalem.
432 B.C.	Nehemiah's return to Jerusalem.
397 B.C.	Ezra's arrival in Jerusalem followed by the complete triumph of the Habdalah (Separation) policy. Some say the date is 457 B.C., others 433 (?) B.C.; see pp. 244-261.
331 B.C.	Alexander the Great passes by. The Samaritan schism is at some date between Ezra's arrival and this date.

We proceed to an examination, section by section, of chapters 56-66.

Isaiah 56: 1-2. A most noteworthy feature of these two verses is

---

[1] Isaiah (Camb. Bible, 1917), vol. ii, p. xliv.

the mixed nature of verse 1. The first half of the verse is a command to 'observe the ordinance' שמר משפט and to 'do right' עשה צדקה. This parallelism of משפט and צדקה is not true to the Second Isaiah. But the second half of the verse is definitely true to him: 'for my salvation has nearly arrived קרובה ישועתי לבוא and my victory is to be revealed (made manifest) צדקתי להגלות.' This parallelism of ישועה and צדקה in the sense of 'salvation, victory, the triumph of what is right' is characteristic of the Second Isaiah and the sentiment of the second half of the verse is essentially his. But the meaning of צדקה in the first half is not its meaning in the second half. That 56: 1b is in the tradition of the Second Isaiah admits of no doubt, but what of 56: 1a?

56: 1a and 56: 2 have associations with Ezek. 20: 19 f. and 11 f. See also Ezek. 22: 8 and 26. In Ezekiel 20 we find the same association of observing שמר and doing עשה God's משפטים (verses 11 and 19: cf. Dt. 12: 1 etc.) and also the immediate association of this with keeping the Sabbath holy and not profaning it. In Isa. 56: 2 the test of the true Israel is to hold fast to the ordinance משפט. This shows itself in (a) keeping the Sabbath by not profaning it שמר שבת מהללו, and (b) guarding the hand from doing any evil שמר ידו מעשות כל־רע. We are here in the beginnings of that Sabbath strictness by which this taboo Sabbath became one of the fixed elements and signs of the covenant. The first references to this are apparently in Ezekiel 20 and 22 and thus they belong to the early years of the exile (seventh year: 590 B.C.). The Sabbath is to be a sign אות between God and Israel 'to know that I the LORD sanctify them ' 20: 12. Again and again in Ezek. 20 (verses 13, 16, 21, 24) the refusal to observe the ordinances משפטים and in this way walk in God's statutes involves desecrating the Sabbath.

It was during the exile that the Sabbath became a taboo-day. Before the exile the Sabbath in old Israel was a day when it was permissible to go on a considerable journey, probably because on that day the ass and his driver were free from ordinary farm duties, 2 Kg. 4: 23. Both the new-month-day חדש and the Sabbath were days when ordinary marketing did not take place (Am. 8: 5). They were days of mirth (Hos. 2: 11) and special assemblies (Isa. 1: 12), and were condemned by eighth century prophets for their licentious-ness and debauchery. Evidently, apart from such abuses, the Sabbath was a day of joy, and herein is that tradition of joy which is still part of the Jewish Sabbath in spite of all its restrictions: the Bridal Song and the fact that no Sabbath can be a fast-day. In *The Jewish New Year*

Festival (1947) we sought to show (pp. 103-124) that the origins of the post-exilic seventh-day Sabbath with its strict taboos is to be found in the taboo days of tenth century Assyria (1, 7, 9, 14, 19, 21, 28, 29, 30), all days of strict prohibitions. Asshur-bani-pal (662-626 B.C.) reduced these to the 7, 14, 21, 28 of each month. Thus having first come into contact during the ninth/eight centuries with new-moon days (1, 29, 30) and seven-days (7, 14, 21, 28, 19—49 from the previous new-month-day—9 which was Gula's day) with all their taboos, they came into renewed contact with Mesopotamia in the sixth century when the only taboo days were the seven-days. It was thus that the word *shabbath*, which originally marked the end of a period,[1]) came to receive the meaning 'rest' in the sense of taboo, restraint from doing things (even healing the sick, as in Mesopotamia) restraint from moving about (as in Mesopotamia). This change in the Sabbath belongs to the first days of Babylonian domination, and is thus c. 590 B.C.

In Isaiah 56: 1 and 2 we are in the days following the time when the taboo-Sabbath was being established as the sign of the Covenant. This theme, as we have seen, is common to Isa. 56: 1-2 and Ezek. 20. The other crime in Ezek. 20 is following after and looking to idols (verse 16, 18, 24). This is the monotheistic theme of the Second Isaiah. He was, as we have seen, primarily concerned with the coming Return of the People of God to Jerusalem. He was not concerned particularly, even in a contributory sense, with such things as keeping the Sabbath, or with maintaining the distinctions between clean and unclean, except in a general way, 52: 11. Ezekiel 22: 8, 26 regards these things as being of great importance, and thus represents a way of thinking different from that of the Second Isaiah. Both inveigh against idols, but Ezekiel is more concerned than is the Second Isaiah with those distinctions and emphases which later became the essence of Judaism. In Isa. 56: 1 and 2 we get a combination of the two emphases, the legalistic emphasis which is beginning to find prominence in Ezekiel and the emphasis on salvation which is so strong in the Second Isaiah.

In 56: 2 we have 'man' אֱנוֹשׁ and 'son of man' בֶּן־אָדָם used in parellel. SKINNER sees [2]) here reference to mankind in general, mostly because the root of the first word basically means 'be weak' (and so the frailty of human kind) or it may be akin to the Akkadian *tenišêtu* (humanity,

---

[1]) The root originally meant 'come to an end, come to a rest'; the Sabbath originally marked the end of the month: see *op. cit.*, p. 112.

[2]) *op. cit.*, p. 164.

human race), and also because the second word strictly means 'human being,' cf. the Latin *homo* and the Greek ἄνθρωπος. But the two words can also mean 'any man' (i.e. any individual). Whether this means any man out of all mankind or any man of the Jews depends upon the context, and the criteria by which the exegete is judging. For example, 'neighbour' can mean 'neighbour Jew' (as in Lev. 19) or it can mean 'neighbour human being' (Samaritan to Jew, Lk. 10: 25-37). In 56: 2, we think it means any Israelite.

Isaiah 56: 3-8. Here we get a point of view far more liberal than the returning exiles favoured. These returning exiles claimed that they and they alone were the People of God and they would cut out entirely the foreigner. This is verse 3, where the 'stranger' of EVV is wrong, and the 'foreigner' of RSV is right. The Hebrew of 'surely separate' (RV, RSV) is הבדל יבדיל. This root belongs mostly to P and the Chronicler. It is the root of the word Habdalah הבדלה, the technical word for that principle of utter separation (cf. AV) which is the core of Judaism and has made the Jew separate and apart throughout all the centuries. It was the work of Nehemiah and Ezra finally and securely to establish this principle of Habdalah [1]) and so create Judaism. Indeed, the third [2]) and last history in the Old Testament, that contained in Chronicles-Ezra-Nehemiah, is really the story of the rise and triumph of the Jewish principle of Habdalah. The first chapter of Genesis (the Priestly tradition) is an account of Creation by Habdalah. The theory of Judaism is part of the fabric of the world. God created it that way in the beginning. Any degree of similarity in development which the first chapter of Genesis may have to any other theory of creation is wholly accidental. Here God creates by making distinctions, by dividing, and the word for 'divide' is always הבדיל, strictly 'to cause a separation.' See verses 4, 6, 7, 14, 18: always God divided this from that. He made the light to be separated from the darkness; the waters above the firmament to be separated from the waters below the firmament, and so on. And the Flood was when this separation broke down (Gen. 7: 11 ,P). God made every herb with its own separate seed, and every fruit tree separate and distinct from every other. Every creature on land and in the sea and the air was made strictly according to its own species. Everything was

---

[1]) The modern equivalent of a pure race policy, often with religious support, is *apartheid*.

[2]) The first is Deuteronomy-2 Kings. The second is Genesis-Numbers, the P-history, which embodies traditions known as J and E.

created according to the principle of Habdalah; all things were made separated. At the other end of the Old Testament (Hebrew) is Chronicles-Ezra-Nehemiah, which originally concluded with the last verse of Nehemiah: 'Thus I cleansed them from everything foreign נכר ... Remember me, O my God, for good.' This exclusiveness is what CHEYNE called 'the severe spirit of the restored exiles (cf. Neh. 13) which doubtless began to show itself during the Captivity.' [1]) It did indeed show itself during the captivity. It is the nationalism of the Second Isaiah bearing a fruit which let us hope he did not forsee. But it was not only he; the separation is found also in Ezek. 22: 26 (clean and unclean) and in Ezek. 42: 20 (holy and common). Evidently it was the temper of the exiles as a whole.

But this writer (Isaiah 56: 3-8) does not exclude every foreigner נכרי ('stranger' is wrong). He maintains that every man who keeps the Sabbath, who chooses what is well-pleasing to God and in this way holds fast to the covenant, is welcome in God's house of prayer and is not to be separated from the People of God. The word is כרת, cut off, excommunicated (see the P-tradition), thrown out. But the writer says that even if the man is a foreigner (v. 3) or a eunuch (v. 4), he is nevertheless welcome. Race does not count (which probably here means Babylonian or Palestinian Jew); circumcision does not count. Nothing counts except that a man shall sincerely desire to join himself to the LORD, to minister to Him and to love His Name. God will not separate off (the root is הבדיל) the foreigner, nor will be excommunicate כרת the eunuch.

The LORD will give the eunuch a memorial יד and a name better than sons and daughters. It shall be an everlasting name and shall never be cut off. All this has to do with posterity. It is uncertain what exactly is the nature of this memorial (lit. 'hand'), but Absalom (2 Sam. 18: 18) is said to have set up a stone pillar in the King's Vale because he had no son to keep his name in remembrance. Presumably the three sons of 2 Sam. 14:27 died in infancy. But this pillar was called 'Absalom's hand' and was apparently still there when 2 Samuel was written down. The word יד (hand), then, has to do with maintaining a man's memory when he has no issue. This certainly is what is intended in Is. 56: 5, and indeed more than this: the name will be continued for ever on the roll of the People of God. He will be more firmly one

---

[1]) *The Prophecies of Isaiah*, II, p. 64.

of God's people than those whose physical descendants are numbered
amongst them.

God will bring the foreigner (v. 6 f.) to His holy mountain, presumably Mount Zion, and will give him great joy in the House of
Prayer that is there. The foreigner's whole-offerings and his shared-
offerings[1]) זבח will be acceptable, for 'mine house shall be called a house
of prayer for all peoples (v. 7).' We understand v. 8 to mean that in
addition to God's gathered ones (the returning exiles who claim that
they alone are of true descent and truly the People of God), the LORD
will gather others to Himself, these foreigners and eunuchs. We are
here in the world of 1 Kg. 8: 41-43, a very different world from the
Judaism which was established by Nehemiah and Ezra. The writer of
56: 3-8 is thoroughly out of sympathy with the nationalism of the
Second Isaiah and its bitter fruit. He is in sympathy with Ezekiel's
insistence on keeping the Sabbath, but out of sympathy with his
nationalism. This man welcomes all who will keep the Sabbath and
seek to do what is well-pleasing to God. He does not work by genealogies, as did the Chronicler; he does not even insist upon circumcision.
The LORD will gather others besides the dispersed of Israel (cf.
Jer. 40: 12; 43: 5), those who were carried off to Babylonia. The writer
is probably one of those who never left Palestine, many of whom were
as sincere and devout in their worship of God as any Babylonian
Jew (Ezra 4: 2). Even if it cannot be proved that the writer was a
Palestinian Jew, he certainly was in full sympathy with those Pales-
tinians who are called 'the people of the land' [2]) in Ezra 10: 11.
The most likely date, therefore, for this section is the early days fol-
lowing the Return, but after the completion of the rebuilding of the
Temple in 516 B.C.—say, 510-500 B.C.

The other side of the picture is to be seen in Ezek. 44: 6-9, where a
charge is made against 'the rebellious ones,[3]) the house of Israel'
'that they have brought in foreigners, uncircumcised in heart and
flesh to be in my sanctuary to profane my house.' The charge is

---

[1]) See 'Sacrifices in the Old Testament,' VT vii 3 (Oct. 1957), pp. 308-317;
also R. DE VAUX, *Studies in Old Testament Sacrifice* (1964), p. 42. But see R. SCHMID,
Das Bundesopfer in Israel (1964), who maintains that they were covenant-offerings.

[2]) This phrase later came to mean 'the common herd,' those who did not keep
the full measure of the Law.

[3]) Lit. 'rebellion' מרי. LXX and the Targum assume an original בית מרי
(house of rebellion), and so also in 2: 7, where some Hebrew MSS and printed
books also have בית מרי. Most exegetes of modern times alter the text and read
'house of rebellion,' but we are of the opinion that this is wrong and confuses
the whole passage.

against 'the house of Israel' whom we understand to be the People of God, the returned exiles, and they are called 'rebellion' because they are disobeying what the writer believes to be the clear will of God. He does not call them 'house of rebellion,' because that means those who did not go into exile in 597 B.C., (Ezek. 2: 3, etc.), and he is not speaking to them. These are 'the people of the land' of Ezra 10: 11 and they were in favour of what Isaiah 56: 3-8 advocates and Ezek. 44: 6-9 condemns. The charge is that the house of Israel have allowed these foreigners to offer God's food on the altar, that is the fat and the blood of slaughtered animals, these being the parts of the animal which went to the altar, whatever the type of sacrifice, though probably the reference is to the shared-offering זבח. Thus the house of Israel has broken the covenant (this is why they are called מרי). All this is so exactly what is advocated in Isa. 56: 3-8 that if the writer of Ezek. 44 had seen Isa. 56: 3-8 he could scarcely have been more precise in his charges.

Thus Isa. 56: 3-8 is universal in the usually accepted meaning of the word in connexion with the Second Isaiah, but Ezek. 40-48 is nationalistic, as we believe the Second Isaiah to be. What, then, is to be said of the author of Ezek. 40-48? Most scholars are inclined to hold that these nine chapters are either wholly or in part from the hand of Ezekiel himself, the author of (possibly, substantially) chapters 1-39. Whether this is so or not, the author of 40-48 was certainly pro-Zadokite, and it is more than likely that he was a Zadokite and therefore one of, or descended from the pre-exilic Jerusalem priesthood, those who were carried off to Babylonia at the destruction of the Temple in 586 B.C. Whether the author of chapters 1-39 was a priest is not so clear from the contents of these chapters, since Ezek. 1: 1-3 may be wholly editorial, as certainly some of it is. It may well be that Ezekiel is called a priest [1]) because of the contents of chapters 40-48. We agree with BERTHOLET (*Hezekiel*, 1963) that the writer of 1-39 (at least) went to Babylonia in 586 B.C. and not 597 B.C., and the same is true of the author of 40-48, who may or may not be the same Ezekiel, or of his father.

We take Isa. 56: 3-8 and Ezek. 44: 4-8 to belong to roughly the period of the struggle for power which took place immediately upon the Return. The strict party was composed of the returning exiles, headed by the Zadokite priesthood, who had to fight for their position

---

[1]) It makes no difference whether 'the priest' in 1: 3 refers to Ezekiel or his father, since the priesthood was a matter of descent in any case.

as priests: see Zech. 3: 7 where Joshua is stripped of his filthy garments (he had been in an unclean land) and given 'right of access' (מהלכים, RSV) to the altar. He was restored to the High Priesthood which his father Jehozadak had held (1 Chr. 6: 15; heb. 5: 41). Isaiah 56: 3-8 represents the other point of view, that of the Palestinians. Our guess is that this group may have been the Aaronites, who were not priests at Jerusalem before the exile, moved in probably during the exile from (?) Bethel,[1]) and formed the minority of the priests when the final settlement was made.[2])

Isaiah 56: 9-12. There is general agreement that this section has nothing to do with the previous section. It has been held to be an excerpt from a pre-exilic prophecy. Some have equated the wild beasts with the heathen peoples generally, others with the Samaritans. It is impossible to fix the date. It may belong to any century from the eighth to the fifth, and may even be earlier or later. Blind leaders, leaders that pursue policies that lead to disaster and leaders that cannot give warning of trouble and disaster, greedy dogs that never have enough—no age and no people have a monopoly of these. The situation is similar to that of the prophet Malachi. The section is not concerned with the question as to who is and who is not the People of God.

Isaiah 57: 1-2. It is not possible to assign any date to these verses. They form two distinct couplets, and the verse division is not in accordance with the poetic sructure. We judge them to be two independent couplets placed together because of the common words אסף (gather) and צדיק (righteous). The first couplet is

> The-righteous-man צדיק perishes,
> and-no-man is-taking-it to-heart;
> And-men-loyal (to the covenant) are-taken-off אסף,
> with-no-one taking-notice.

and the second couplet is:

> For-from-the-presence-of evil

---

[1]) KENNETT, 'The Origin of the Aaronite Priesthood,' JTS vi (1905), pp. 161-186.

[2]) The priests of the P-tradition were 'the priests, the sons of Aaron,' but two thirds of them were Zadokite, reckoned as the elder branch and descended through Eleazar and Phinehas, and one third were Aaronite, reckoned as the younger branch and descended through Ithamar, 1 Chr. 24 3 f.

the-righteous-man צדיק is-taken-off אסף.
(he enters peace/prosperity)
They-rest on-their-beds,
(everyone) who-walks straight-forwardly.

The first couplet bemoans the fate of the loyal, righteous man who keeps the covenant. The second couplet says either that the righteous man is saved from evil by the peace of the grave (cf. Job 3: 13 ff.), or that he is snatched away from misfortune and prospers. Once more, the section is not concerned with the struggle of the early post exilic days between the two factions.

Isaiah 57: 3-14. If, as seems most probable, this is all one piece, then it is a tirade against people in Palestine who are charged with syncretistic worship. It has been pointed out [1]) that the scenery is Palestinian with its terebinths (RV, RSV oaks), its conifers (RV, RSV 'green-trees,' lit. luxuriant, fresh, which means evergreen, non-deciduous), the wadies (RV, RSV valleys) and the clefts of the crags. These Palestinians have charged the speaker and his friends with being 'children of rebellion' (ילדי פשע: not מרי) and of false descent זרע שקר, insults which the speaker is hurling back at them. The prophet is speaking on behalf of God's people (v. 14) who are returning from Babylonia—compare v. 14 with 40: 4; 'build up' is the same root as 'highway,' and 'prepare the way' is פנו דרך, which is translated 'prepare the way' in 40: 4. The prophet says that he will tell of (broadcast) their 'righteousness and doings,' but they will be of no avail. SKINNER says that the reference to righteousness 'must be spoken ironically,' [2]) and he rightly refers to the Samaritans (Ezra 4: 2). The charge is that they have a mixed worship. They may indeed claim to be true worshippers of YHVH, but this is combined with all kinds of heathen practices and religious rites.

In order to understand the situation in these troublous times of the latter quarter of the sixth century (say, 538-500 B.C., and the following years also), we must turn to 2 Kgs. 17: 23b-41.[3]) This section is the official basis of the later claim that the Samaritans were not true Jews, that these northerners were not the People of God. The chapter comes from the Deuteronomic editors of the Books of Kings, and is most

[1]) e.g. SKINNER, *op. cit.*, p. 171.
[2]) *op. cit.*, p. 176.
[3]) Cf. H. H. ROWLEY, 'The Samaritan Schism in Legend and History' in *Israel's Prophetic Heritage* (1962), pp. 208-222.

probably an addition by the second and final editors ca. 550 B.C., those who found new courage and hope when they saw the easing in the rigours of imprisonment which came to the deposed Jehoiachin at the accession of Evil-Merodach in 561 B.C. (2 Kgs. 25: 27-30). The basis of the argument in 2 Kgs. 17 is the statement that the whole of Israel, the northern kingdom, was deported by the Assyrian king, and that he settled in their place a miscellaneous population from Babylon, Cuthah, Ava and so forth. These settlers set up their own gods, but neglected 'the god of the land,' that is, the God of Israel. This entailed ravages by lions, which doubtless had multiplied in numbers and in boldness because of the depopulation caused by war and by the deportation. An exiled priest was therefore sent back and he settled in Bethel, with the result that a mixed cult was developed there. 'They feared the LORD, and served (worshipped) their own gods' (v. 33), and they made priests for themselves from non-priestly families. This last, in the mind of a southerner, meant from non-Levites. The reason for the long condemnation is to be found in the last verse (41): 'So these nations feared the LORD and served their graven images; their children likewise, and their children's children, as did their fathers, so do they unto this day.' This is a charge against the sixth century ancestors of the Samaritans. Duhm thought of it all as a polemic against the Samaritans, and Skinner suggested that the prophet was thinking of a paganised Judaean population closely akin to the Samaritans of the North and cultivating friendly relations with them. These suggestions involve dating the section in 2 Kgs and the section in Isa. 57 much later than is necessary. Both passages are against the Palestinian Judaeans who never left the country. They are charges by returning exiles against 'the people of the land.' The sections belong to the same religious point of view as that indicated by Ezekiel's 'rebellious house,' Jeremiah's 'bad figs' and the Second Isaiah. In these three writers the breach was not as wide as in 2 Kgs. 17 and Isa. 57: 3-14, and the controversy had not grown bitter. Time is not always a healer; somtimes he makes wounds fester.

Thus Isaiah 57: 3-14 belongs to the early days of 'the cold war' between the returning exiles who claimed to be the People of God, and those Israelites who had never been in Babylonia, who claimed that they also sought the same God (Ezra 4: 2). The charges are of licentious rites beneath the ever-green trees, child sacrifice in the valleys, sacred prostitution on the hills, household gods behind the door, spices for the cult of Molech. These are all the malpractices

which Deuteronomy condemns. They are not so much what the
Israelites found in Canaan at their first entry into the land, as what they
found when they entered the second time to occupy [1] it. Indeed, it is
as though the second Moses of Deut. 18: 15 is the Moses who is
speaking in Deuteronomy, and speaking to the new Israel about to
enter Canaan, just as the old Israel entered Canaan centuries before.
There is no need to assume with SKINNER that the highway of 57: 14
is 'an emblem of the preparation for that larger deliverance to which
the hopes of the post-exilic community were eagerly directed.' [2]) The
passage is not 5th century. It is late sixth century, the beginning of the
cold war.

Isaiah 57: 15-20. Ultimately the dating and placing of this section
depends upon the initial assumptions. This is true of many passages
in the Old Testament, but perhaps more in this case than in most.
Verse 15 in LXX differs considerably from the Hebrew text, though
the general background is the same. This particular verse is firmly
in the tradition of the Second Isaiah, especially if 61: 1 f. is included as
being his: the highly exalted One who dwells on high and at the same
time is with the crushed and humble of spirit. There is no contrast
implied (SKINNER, *in loc.*, is right here), since transcendence and
imminence are compatible. It is transcendence and immanence that
are incompatible.[3])

'The humble and contrite (lit. 'crushed') ones who are to be made to
live again (*hiph'il* of חיה, revive) are the exiles. God strove against
them (better 'took up a case as in the courts' ריב) and was angry
with them, but this was not for ever, since in that case 'their spirit
(*mem* lost through haplography) would fail from my presence, and
the breathing-beings (lit. 'breaths') which I have made.' This refers
to the punishment of the exile, as also does v. 17: 'I was angry at his
iniquity for a moment (cf. LXX) and I smote him, hiding my face in
anger. He went stubbornly in the path of his own choice. Then I gave
consideration to his ways (v. 18), and I healed him (read strong-*waw*)
and led him, and recompensed him with full relief (נחמים: see note on
40: 1), creating for his mourners the fruit of lips: [4] peace, peace,

---

[1]) This root ירש (57: 13) is usually translated 'possess, dispossess.' It means
take possession of the land by occupying it having driven out the previous oc-
cupants, and it is used regularly in the story of the conquest of Canaan.
[2]) *op. cit.*, p. 177. Presumably he means the coming of the Messiah.
[3]) 'God, Transcendent and Imminent,' ET lxviii 3 (Dec. 1956), pp. 68-71.
[4]) A most difficult phrase. It is not in LXX. Perhaps it refers to the effective
words of comfort which God speaks through the prophet—peace, peace.

saith the LORD, to both far and near.' Verse 19 is thought by SKINNER to refer to Jews still in exile and Jews who have already returned. Thus it is better to retain 'and led him' ואנחהו in v. 18 and not follow LXX with ואנחמהו (and comforted him). Many scholars understand the verse to refer to the Dispersion. Our judgment is that SKINNER is right, and we assume a date between 538 and 520 B.C. for the section.

Isaiah 58: 1-14. This chapter belongs to a period when the restoration of ruined buildings, homes and foundations and walls, was an immediate necessity (v. 12). The ancient ruins apparently had not been restored, and neither walls nor roads remade. The chapter is addressed to 'my people', 'the house of Jacob' (v. 1). The matter is of some urgency since the prophet is bidden 'cry aloud with the throat' and 'lift his voice high like the sound of an alarm' (v. 1). The people are regular in their worship and sincere. They delight to know God's ways; they do what is right and they do not desert the proper way of doing things (משפט, proper custom in life and cultus). But things are going wrong, in spite of the fact that they are rigorously abstinent (lit. 'afflict their souls,' the regular phrase in the P-tradition for 'fast,' Lev. 16: 29, etc.). The prophet says that their fasts are not true fasts. They fast for their own purposes (חפץ: cf. 53: 10) and they 'oppress (נגש, the root used for the 'taskmasters' in Exolus 3 and 8) their pains.' This phrase means that they deliberately intensify their fasts. They are using them as a weapon in their quarrels: 'behold, you fast to quarrel and to fight, and to smite with the fist of wickedness (v. 4).' There are further charges: oppression, refusing to feed the poor and care for the homeless, hiding themselves from their own flesh. The people against whom the prophet is speaking are being very religious and ultra-strict in their religious observances, and all the stricter because they are using these religious exercises to set up strife and to widen the separation between themselves and others. These others are men of their own flesh—at least, the writer maintains that they are such. What these very religious offenders must do is to put away these restrictive practices, stop pointing a scornful finger and stop speaking calumny. They must obey the Deuteronomic injunctions (Deut. 22: 1-4) concerning their treatment of their own people. They must observe the Sabbath in true fashion, make it a day of delight and honour, and not observe it for their own purposes. These charges all give support for a date not far removed from Zech. 7: 1-7, namely c.

516 B.C. The writer is pro-Palestinian. He has close affinities with the Second Isaiah (vv. 8 and 9, 10, 12), but he believes that the way in which the glorious visions of future prosperity are to be realised is by including and not excluding the Palestinian Jews.

Isaiah 59: 1-4. The question is asked: Why is it that things are going so badly? The answer is that it is not the LORD's fault. His hand is not shortened (cf. 50: 2), and He is still strong to save. It is your iniquities that are causing a separation מבדילים between you and your God. It is not He that has hidden His face from you; it is your own sins. There is no straight-forward dealing in the courts; all is trickery and sharp practice. The passage might belong to any period when things were going badly politically and economically, except for the use of the separation-root בדל, which inclines the balance in favour of the period of the early development of Judaism, c. 500 B.C.

Isaiah 59: 5-8. These verses describe the misdemeanours and mal-practices of the time in more poetical language than is employed in the previous verses. They may well belong to some collection of psalms or proverbs. Compare v. 7a with Prov. 1: 16 and Ps. 14: 3 (LXX). The section might belong to almost any period.

Isaiah 59: 9-15*a*. Here the people themselves, or the prophet on their behalf, take up the tale of woe. Verses 12 and 13 read like a General Confession and may be liturgical in origin. The speakers are concerned that salvation from their present and continuing woes is as far away as ever. This is in v. 9, where משפט (judgement, here a divine verdict which will bring them good fortune) and צדקה ('righteousness,' but rather 'being put in the right') both mean 'salvation': see the second half of the verse. Also in v. 11 משפט (judgment) is equivalent to ישועה (salvation) and in v. 14 to צדקה (righteousness: once more in the sense of being put in the right). The passage may belong to any period, though there is influence from the Second Isaiah.

Isaiah 59: 15*b*-21. This section is definitely in the style of the Second Isaiah, indeed there is a great deal to be said for including it with chapters 60-62 as actually from his hand, and placed where it is be-cause of the verbal links of verses 14-15a and 15b. There was no justice and no one among mankind to intervene.[1]) He therefore Himself took action to bring salvation and vindication to the sufferers. Thus God

---

[1]) As we pointed out in commenting on Isa. 53: 12, the regular translation of the verb פגע in the sense of interceding has been most unfortunate.

armed Himself for the fight like a warrior; armed Himself with צדקה
(actively putting things right), with salvation, with vengeance נקם
and with zeal קנאה. All this is directed agaunst his enemies, his adversaries, who are the isles איים, a word used regularly by the Second
Isaiah to mean the Gentiles. In the end all the world (19) will fear the
LORD, from east to west, so fierce will be the torrent of His onset.
Thus (20) the redeemed will come to Zion and the covenant will be
established for ever and ever.

Chapters 60-62 have been dealt with (pp. 198-200) as being definitely
the word of the Second Isaiah himself.

Isaiah 63: 1-6. This section speaks of a ruthless and bloody vengeance
on Edom. LAGARDE, DUHM and MARTI have suggested such emendations (slight as they are) as would remove Edom from the context,
and substitute 'Syria' (ארם for אדם), but the puns on Edom and its
literal meaning 'red', and on Bozrah and its literal meaning 'first-ripe
grape' make the passage too aptly macabre to warrant any such
changes. If it is allowed that there is a strong nationalistic element in
the Second Isaiah, then this section is not as alien to him and to his
sphere of influence as some suppose. The Second Isaiah is no generous-
hearted lover of all the world with kind thoughts about the Gentiles,
who have ruthlessly smashed his people and all they held dear and
still deny them nationhood and liberty and a future of their own.
The word נקם (vengeance) is found in 47: 3 and in 61: 2, a context
which all are happy to associate closely with the Second Isaiah even
if some hesitate actually to ascribe it to him. No one objects to the end
of verse 1 as being in tune with the Second Isaiah ('I that speak in
righteousness, mighty to save') and in vv. 3 and 5 we have the familiar
(50: 2; 59: 16) statement that He looked and there was none to help.
He had to act alone. The section begins with vengeance on Edom,
who rushed in to take full advantage of the downfall of Judah. It
ends with vengeance and fury on the Gentiles. All this fits in with the
rampant nationalism of the end of the sixth century B.C. The Century
Bible commentary says that 'the conception of redemption has hardened in the interval since the days of Deutero-Isaiah.' The writer of that
commentary has minimised 49: 26; 41: 26; 42: 13: 43: 3; 49: 23.
There is nothing in the section which absolutely demands a Palestinian
locale, just as equally there is nothing which demands a Babylonian
locale, but we are certainly in the world of a resurgent Jewish nationalism.

Isaiah 63: 7-64: 12. We come now to what, from our point of view, is the most important section of these eleven chapters. This piece is from a member of a group who claim (64: 7, Eng. 8) that the LORD *is* their father, no matter what anybody may say. They are the clay; He is the potter and 'we are all the work of thy hand.' The claim is emphatically made and the way in which it is phrased suggests irresistibly that they are rebutting a charge, a denial that the LORD is their father, and that they are His handy-work. See also 63: 16:

> For thou art our Father,
> Though Abraham does not know us,
> And Israel does not recognise us.
> *Thou*, O LORD, art our Father:
> Our Redeemer from of old is thy Name.'

Here is a group of people whom Abraham-Israel rejects and denies that they are the LORD's. They answer that they are indeed His, as much His as anybody else is: He has been their Redeemer from ancient time, which from the context must mean the rescue from Egypt, the passage through the Red Sea, and the journey through the Wilderness with the Entry into Canaan. L. E. BROWNE [1]) rightly saw here pro-Samaritan and indeed pre-Samaritan literature. The piece begins (63: 7):

> I-will-call-to-mind the-LORD's deeds-of-steadfast-love,
>   The-LORD's deeds-that-call-for-praise,
> According-to-all the-LORD hath-done-for-us,
>   And-the-abundant-good-fortune to-the-house-of-Israel,
> Which He-dealt-us (LXX and Lat.) according-to-his-compassion,
>   According-to-the multitude-of His-deeds-of-steadfast-love.

The next verse is:

> And-he-said: Nay-my-people are they,
>   Children that-will-not-deal-falsely.
> And-he-was to-them a-saviour
>   In-all their-distresses.

Here we have a spokesman who is looking back and calling to mind the great deeds of salvation in the past, wrought by the LORD on behalf of His covenant-people. He is speaking on behalf of a group who are being denied a place among the People of God. We are

---

[1]) *Early Judaism* (1920), pp. 70 ff.

justified in introducing the word 'covenant' here, because the word
חסד has by this time, and especially in such a context as this come
to refer to God's steadfast, sure love for Israel and His faithfulness to
the covenant between Him and them. Further as L. E. BROWNE has
made clear,[1]) the use of the root שׁקר (deal falsely) involves the idea
of the covenant, cf. Ps. 44: 18 (Eng. 17); 89: 34. The speaker uses the
word אך (63: 8), which is usually, but erroneously, translated 'surely.'
This particle involves assertion in the face of denial,[2]) and whilst it is
possible so to pronounce the word 'surely' in order to ensure this
meaning, it is better to translate it' Nay, but.' The speaker means that
in spite of all his opponents can say, he still maintains that he and his
companions are God's people. We are God's people, he says, and we
will not deal falsely in the covenant. That is why and how we can
say that God has been our Saviour in all our distresses from time
immemorial.

He says further (63: 9) that it was not a messenger nor an angel
(ציר ומלאך LXX, Latin) who saved them, but 'God's Presence and
His very Self.' Compare Exod. 33: 13 J, where the LORD says: 'My
Presence shall go with thee פני ילכו and I will give thee rest,' cf. Isa.
63: 14. The piece continues:

> In-his-love and-in-his-forbearance
>> He redeemed-them,
> And-he-lifted-them and-carried-them
>> All-the-days-of old.
> But-they-rebelled and-vexed
>> His-holy spirit,
> So-he-changed-himself to-them to-be-an-enemy
>> He-himself fought-against-them.

Here we have the story of God's continued mercy, and the cause of the
Disaster of 597 and 586 B.C. The people of God rebelled against
Him and He brought disaster upon them. But there has come a change;
they remembered the days of old (63: 11) and they pray concerning
the present situation (63: 15):

> Then-he (Israel)-remembered the-days-of old
>> Moses his-servant: [3])

---

[1]) *op. cit.*, p. 80.
[2]) 'The meaning of the Hebrew אך,' VT xiv 2 (April 1964), pp. 221-225.
[3]) These two words are not in LXX; some Heb. MSS and Syriac have 'Moses

Where-is he-that-brought-them-up from the-sea?
    Where-is (Targum) the-Shepherd-of [1]) his-flock?
Where-is he-that-set in-the-midst-of-him
    His-holy spirit?
Who-caused-to-go at-the-right-hand-of Moses
    His-glorious arm?
Who-clave the-waters before-them
    To-make-for-himself a-name (? for ever) [2])?
Who-brought-them through-the-Deeps,
    Like-a-horse in the wilderness [3])
They did-not-stumble.
Like-cattle that-go-down into-the-valley,
    The-spirit-of-the-LORD gave-him-rest.[4])
So thou-didst-lead thy-people [5])
To-make-thyself a-glorious-name.

Here we have a recounting of the details of the ancient saga, particularly of the Joseph tribes who came into Canaan under Joshua
across the Jordan near by Gilgal. These mighty deeds of old, these
mighty deeds of salvation, are claimed by the writer and his friends
as having been wrought for them and their forbears, the People of
God, and they insist on this in spite of denials by others. They admit
their rebellion against God (10) and acknowledge the justice of the
subsequent punishment, but they remember also those other days [6])
when God extended His covenant-mercy to their fathers. And so in
verse 15 there comes a prayer concerning the present situation:

Look-out from-the-heavens and-see
    from-thy-high-abode, holy and-glorious.

---

his servant' (עבדו for עמו). A two-accent line is necessary here because of the
metre, and the Syriac reading makes good sense.
  [1]) Heb. has the plural, but it is sing. in many Heb. MSS, LXX, Latin, Targum.
  [2]) Some omit for the sake of the metre.
  [3]) Having come in triumph through the depths of the Sea, they rampaged
through the Wilderness like a war-horse in battle, never stumbling, and came
gladly into the Promised land like cattle down into the valley.
  [4]) The Versions have תַּנְהֵנוּ (thou didst lead them), but the Hebrew is better,
certainly if the meaning is the rest of the Promised Land.
  [5]) After all, the experiences of the Exodus and the Wilderness belonged to the
Joseph tribes rather than to Judah, which was mostly the creation of David, and
only a comparatively small element knew of the Exodus. The South 'stole' the
North's God! This makes the plea of the North more poignant than ever.
  [6]) Compare the southern Ps. 78, especially vv. 67 f.

Where-is thy-zeal and-thy-might
   The-yearning-of thy-bowels?
And-do-not-restrain [1]) thy-great-compassion.
   For-thou-art our-Father
Though Abraham does-not-know us
   And-Israel does-not-recognise-us;
Thou, O-LORD, art-our-Father,
   Our-Redeemer from-of-old is-thy-name.

This is a plea for compassion as in the ancient days. The author and his friends claim that they are the true descendants of those whom God called out of Egypt and brought into Canaan through water and desert. Jeremiah condemned them; Ezekiel rejected them; the Second Isaiah spoke against them in Isa. 48; Zerubbabel is said to have rejected them (Ezra 4: 2). The returned exiles stated the claim of their adversaries as a statement that they had worshipped the LORD ever since Esar-haddon's time, they having all been brought there by the Assyrian king (2 Kgs. 17: 24-34), but that was Southern propaganda. Their claim was that they had been there from the beginning of the Israelite occupation.

Verse 17 begins: 'Why dost thou make us to go astray O LORD from thy ways, and hardenest our heart from fearing thee?' These phrases do not mean that God has made them err or has hardened their hearts, but that they have erred and their hearts were hardened— they were stubborn in their wickedness: cf. Isa. 6: 9-12. The Hebrews were sure concerning two things about God: one that He is the One only God, and the other that He is essentially active in this world which He has made. Their zeal for the first led them not to distinguish between *post hoc* and *propter hoc*; their zeal for the second led them to think of Him as the personal link between every cause and every effect, both small and great. The verse continues, 'Turn, for the sake of thy servants, the tribes of thy possession.' This is a plea for a return to the original relationship, that covenant which God made with all the tribes of Israel in the day when He brought them out of Egypt. The verse says 'tribes' and it means 'tribes.'

Verse 18 is 'For a little while thy holy people had possession, our adversaries have trampled thy sanctuary.' LXX and Latin have: 'for a little while we possessed thy holy mountain' (Cod. A adds 'our enemies trampled thy sanctuary'). The root בוס means 'trample,

---

[1]) So LXX and 64: 11, אל תתאפק.

tread down' and is used always of destruction or desecration, so the first thought is that the 'adversaries' are the Babylonians and that the temple is still in ruins: which places the section in the period between 538-520 B.C., though L. E. BROWNE ¹) thought of it as having been written before 538 B.C. but in Palestine by those whom we have called the Palestinian Jews. On the other had, whilst the root בוס is indeed elsewhere used of destruction and desecration, it does not follow that the reference here is to the destructive trampling of the Babylonians in 586 B.C. Compare the root רמס, which also is used of destructive trampling down, but in Isa. 1:12 is used of what Isaiah of Jerusalem held to be the irreligious, though fulsome worship of his contemporaries. Thus here in 63: 18 the writer may be referring to the fact that people are worshipping there, of whose attitude he does not approve, and whose religion he does not think is sound and right. Also, who are 'our adversaries'? It may well be that the Babylonians are intended. On the other hand, 'adversaries' is a word used in the strife between the two parties in the fifth century, Neh. 4: 5 (Eng. 11); Ezra 4: 1 especially. In this case, the reference may be to the returned exiles who have taken possession of the Temple mount and are driving out and denying access to those who had not been in exile. It is curious also that the true LXX text refers to 'holy mount' and not to 'sanctuary.' But in any case, whether the verse refers to the Babylonians having destroyed the temple or to the returning exiles having taken exclusive possession of the site, the section comes from the Palestinian Jews and belongs to the period before 520 B.C.

Verse 19 provides us with what the returning exiles said about the Palestinians. See L. E. BROWNE, *op. cit.* p. 83. He proposes that we read 'We are become "From of old thou didst not rule over them" and "Thy name was not called over them".' He takes the two sentences within the inner quotation marks to be statements made by the returning exiles about the Palestinians. See also J. ADAMS,²) who shows that the accents do actually demand this interpretation. When this verse is considered in association with 64: 7 (Eng. 8) and 64: 8 (Eng. 9), we find this section to be pro-Palestinian and anti-Babylonian, belonging to the years 538-520 B.C.

Isaiah 65: 1-7. In verse 1 RV 'I am enquired' (margin, 'I was enquired of') can scarcely be right, because of the final rejection of

¹) *op. cit.*, p. 78.
²) *Sermons in Accents* (1906), pp. 86-88.

v. 7. It is better, therefore, to follow RSV, where the verbs of v. 1a
are treated each as a *niph'al tolerativum*, and then to translate 'I was
ready to be enquired of by "they have not asked me": [1]) I was
ready to be found by "they did not seek me." ' This is the same type
of syntax as in 63: 19. The verse continues, as do succeeding verses,
with the statement of what actually happened: 'I said, Here am I,
here am I, to a nation גוי which is not called by my name.[2])' God
appealed continually to these apostate ones (the root is סור, turn aside,
not מרי, rebellion), but they persisted in following their own in-
clinations. They provoked God to His face continually. This root
הכעיס (provoke) is used 'about fifty times of Israelites provoking
the LORD to anger by deserting Him and serving foreign gods,' [3])
and once of the Samaritans hindering Nehemiah (Neh. 3: 37, Eng.
4: 5) but never of the heathen. Further the idolatries mentioned in
65: 7 are Palestinian, where we would follow LXX and Syriac and
read 'their' instead of 'your' (thus following RSV). This is a statement
parallel to 2 Kgs. 17: 41. We find the section to be strongly anti-
Palestinian and to belong to the same period as the preceding section.

Isaiah 65: 8-12. Here we have another anti-Palestinian piece. 'There
is new wine to be obtained from the cluster. They say, 'Do not destroy
it, there is a blessing in it.' The writer makes use of a vintage song
(cf. the title of Pss. 57, 58, 59, 75) to proclaim the doctrine of a remnant. The whole of Israel will not be destroyed. The remnant will be
saved and this group will take possession of 'my mountains' (the
Judaean hills). This group is the LORD's chosen, His servants. All
will be well, and there will be prosperity in Sharon and in the Valley
of Achor. There will be flocks and herds there, and all this 'for my
people that have sought me.' The rest will be slaughtered—those who
have forgotten Zion, who have turned aside to the gods of Fortune
(Gad) and of (?) Fate. They did not answer the LORD's call, nor listen
to what He said. They did what was evil, that in which He did not
delight. All these are charges made by the returning exiles against the
Palestinians. DUHM believed that this section was directed against the
Jews of the land as distinct from the returning exiles. We find this

---

[1]) LXX, Latin, Syriac and 2 Heb. MSS. have the suffix. For this use of the
niph'al, see SKINNER, *op. cit.* p. 231.

[2]) The Versions have 'who did not call on my name,' but the vowels of the
Hebrew Text are the more difficult, and the Masoretic interpretation fits the use
of גוי, which means 'a heathen nation.'

[3]) L. E. BROWNE, *op. cit.*, p. 97.

confirmed by the reference to the Valley of Achor. This was the valley through which the Israelites under Joshua first entered Canaan, Josh. 7: 24; 15: 7. It is the valley along which Hosea hoped for a second and happier entry, Hos. 2: 17 (Eng. 15). It is difficult to be precise as to the date of this piece, but it belongs to the early days of the controversy, though perhaps later than some of the pieces, since the spirit of it is much more fierce.

Isaiah 65: 13-25. This piece begins by contrasting the happy lot of the LORD's servants with the sorrowful and disastrous fate of their opponents. These wicked ones will leave a name of evil omen behind them, but the chosen ones, the LORD's servants, will have another name. Every man in the land, when he invokes a blessing on himself will use the name of the God of Amen,[1]) that is, the God who says 'Amen' to the words His people utter and confirms those words in action and result. Oaths will be made in His name. The prophet then speaks in glowing and visionary terms of the amazing prosperity which will come to God's people in Jerusalem. There shall be no more weeping and crying. Men will live to a fabulous old age, and every needs of their's will be met and satisfied before it is even expressed. The section is pro-Babylonian.

Isaiah 66: 1-2. GRESSMANN placed the first four verses in the period before Haggai and Zechariah had persuaded the people to build the second temple, 520-516 B.C. There is every reason to suppose that he was right so far as the first two verses are concerned. There is no contrast involved in v.1 between heaven and earth, nor is there any suggestion that it is wrong to build a temple on earth. The Hebrew is אי־זה, i.e. 'where, then' is the house. . . : not 'what.' Thus, the opposite is the case. Rather we have an urgent enquiry for the temple, as to why it has not been built. God may have His throne in the heavens, but He needs a resting-place on earth. The Hebrew is 'a footstool' (lit. a *pied-à-terre*!). He is looking to the man who is afflicted and broken of spirit, who trembles at His word. This last makes the piece pro-Babylonian.

Isaiah 66: 3-4. These verses return to the matter of the mixed worship, though the meaning is obscured by the insertion in EVV of 'as he that offereth' and 'as he.' The verses describe a confusion of rites,

---

[1]) v. 16. RV and RSV have 'God of truth,' but see RVm, following DELITZSCH and CHEYNE: cf. Rev. 3 14.

legitimate and illegitimate, pro-YHVH and anti-YHVH: slaughtering an ox, slaying a man sacrificing a lamb, breaking a dog's neck, offering a gift-offering מנחה, offering swine's blood, making a memorial-offering with incense, blessing an idol. Verse 3 continues: 'Yes; *they* (emphatic) have chosen their ways and *they* (again emphatic, נפשם, lit. 'their soul,' a fullsome way of saying 'they') have taken delight in abominable idols, so *I* (again emphatic) will choose. . ' Then once more we have the sentiments of 65: 12: these are the people who did not answer the LORD's call, and did not listen when He spoke. Thus, once more we have a pro-Babylonian piece accusing the Palestinians of illegimate and idolatrous religious practices.

Isaiah 66: 5-6. These verses are distinct from the previous verses, and it is difficult to see any connexion between them and verse 7. Verse 5 is a jeering challenge to men whose brethren hate them and have cast them out in the name of God. The jeer is: if, as you say, you are faithful worshippers of God, then let God prosper you and glorify His name. But, says the prophet, *they* (once more emphatic) shall be ashamed, that is, the ones who have been jeering at the outcasts will be ashamed, because there will be a roar from the city. It will be the voice of the LORD (cf. Am. 1: 2) coming from His temple, rendering recompense to His enemies. The two verses are pro-Palestinian.

Isaiah 66: 7-9. These verses are closely comparable to 49: 17-21 and 54: 1, and refer to the speedy repopulation of Jerusalem when the exiles return. This theme is carried over into the succeeding verses. This piece is pro-Babylonian.

Isaiah 66: 10-24. There are associations in phrases with the Second Isaiah. 'Suck the breasts' and 'milk': v. 11 and 60: 16. 'Peace like a river': v. 12 and 48: 18. The general attitude is that of chapters 49 and 60. 'Borne on the side': v. 12 and 49: 22 and 60: 4. Jerusalem-Zion will suck the wealth of the Gentiles. The power of the LORD will be exercised against his enemies: v. 14 ff. and 49: 26. Further, those who indulge in illegitimate worship in sacred gardens (cf. 65: 3) will be destroyed. This means the Palestinians, because this is part of the charge which the Babylonian Jews made against them. All the Gentiles will come and behold God's glory and they will bring back the scattered Jews in horses, in chariots, on mules and dromedaries. Then (v. 21) out of these who have been thus brought back, God will choose Levitical priests.[1]) This we take to be a reference to the 'the Levites the priests, the sons of Zadok' who were exiled priests and will be chosen once more and given access to the sanctuary (Zech. 3: 1-7). The new conditions shall endure for ever (v. 22), and so shall the prosperity of the faithful, until ultimately all mankind will come and worship. Lest however it be thought that v. 23 is an open-handed warm-hearted universalism the piece closes with a gory picture of the fate of all who have rebelled against God. The piece is pro-Babylonian, with the door opened to such Gentiles as are properly obedient.

We thus see that Isaiah 56-66 belong to the period following 538 B.C., when at least some of the exiles had returned to Jeruslaem, and there were sharp contentions between the Babylonian Jews who had returned and the Palestinian Jews who had remained in Palestine all the time. The argument is as to who are the true People of God. The Babylonians are in the succession of Jeremiah, Ezekiel, the Second Isaiah and Zerubabel, Nehemiah and Ezra. The Palestinians are fighting all the time against 'the establishment,' until ultimately they withdraw and form what is known as 'the Samaritan schism.' Both parties are represented in these chapters (eight: since 60-62 are held to be true Second Isaiah). The teaching of the Second Isaiah has led to strife and contention which lasted for more than one generation.

---

[1]) The Versions have 'for priests and for Levites,' as also some Hebrews MSS. We follow the Hebrew consonants, but without the *pathach* of the definite article. To make the clear distinction between priests and Levites is to anticipate a later state of affairs. Cf. Deuteronomy which has 'the priests, the Levites' (Deut. 17: 9, etc; Ezek. 44: 15 has 'the priests the Levites, the sons of Zadok.' 'The priests the sons of Aaron' and 'the Levites' as distinct from them, belong to the developed P-tradition.

CHAPTER EIGHT

JERUSALEM FROM 538 B.C. TO 397 B.C.

How did it come about that both parties and both points of view, Palestinian and Babylonian, are found in Isaiah 56-66?

There is every indication that the triumph of Judaism with its rigid policy of exclusiveness—the triumph, that is, of the returned exiles, the Babylonian Jews—did not take place until 397 B.C., which we take to be the date of Ezra's arrival in Jerusalem. This victory is described either in Nehemiah 13 or in Ezra 9-10, whichever is the later (but see below pp. 251 f.). There is less evidence than is generally supposed of any serious strife before the arrival of Nehemiah in 445/4 B.C. That there was contention and struggle for religious status there can be no shadow of doubt, but there does not appear to have been any political crisis. Most of us have given too much weight to Ezra 4: 1-6. We have not realised that there is much more opposition expressed in the English translation than there is in the Hebrew of Ezra 4: 3. Further, the theory that the breach opened wide in the time of Zerubbabel depends also on the unity of Ezra 4: 1-6.

We deal first with the problem of Ezra 4: 1-6. Chapter 4, as it stands, makes little sense. The times are all confused. The chapter opens with Zerubbabel and Jeshua taking steps to build the temple. It says that the 'people of the land' (the non-exiles, the Palestinian Jews) did everything they could to hinder and weaken the efforts of the 'people of Judah' (the returned exiles, the Babylonian Jews), and that this opposition continued all the time of Cyrus and on to the reign of Darius. In the time of Xerxes (verse 6) the Palestinians wrote an accusation against the builders, and another complaint (verses 7 ff) in the time of Artaxerxes, a copy of which is given, and after it the kings' reply. Then (verse 24) it is stated that the work on the temple ceased until the second year of Darius.

There are many strange elements in this chapter. It is composed of bits and pieces. Verse 24 (second year of Darius) brings us back to verses 1-3, since it was in this second year of Darius that Jeshua and Zerubbabel became active in building the temple, urged on by Haggai and Zechariah (Hag. 1; Zech. 4: 9). Verse 6 is dated in the reign of Artaxerxes. Whether verse 7 has anything to do with verse

6 is uncertain, but it has nothing to do with verses 8 ff. Presumably this
Artaxerxes is Artaxerxes I (Longimanus), so that here we are in the
time of Nehemiah, the period 464-424 B.C. But this section is not concerned at all with the building of the temple. It is about the rebuilding
of the walls. Whether there was contention between the two parties,
Babylonian Jews and Palestinian Jews, concerning the building of
the temple, it is difficult to say; it is certain that there was considerable
trouble whilst the walls were being built.

Ezra 4: 3 is difficult. The Revised Version has: 'Ye have nothing
to do with us to build an house unto our God; but we ourselves together will build. . .' The Hebrew reads: 'Not to you and to us לא
לכם ולנו. . ., for we together כי אנחנו יחד will build. . .' But the LXX
equivalents are different. Esdras B 4: 3 has 'Not to us and to you
οὐχ ἡμῖν καὶ ὑμῖν 'and 'for we together ὅτι ἡμεῖς ἐπὶ τὸ αὐτὸ'; Esdras
A 5: 67 f. (71) has 'Not to you οὐχ ὑμῖν' and 'for we alone ἡμεῖς γὰρ
μόνοι.' Usually the phrase לא לכם ולנו is compared to the idiom מה־
לי ולך, lit. 'what to me and to you', i.e. 'we have nothing to do with
each other' or 'this is no business of yours'. But are the two phrases
equivalent? There was nothing whatever to stop the writer saying
'What to us and. to you?' The Chronicler knew the idiom (2 Chr.
35: 21), and it was well-known at all periods: Jg. 11: 12; 2 Sam.
16: 10—ten times altogether, including two without the *wāw* (Jer.
2: 18; Hos. 14: 9). The idiom persisted into New Testament times:
Matt. 8: 29; Mk. 5: 7; Jn. 2: 4. Compare also the Arabic *mā li walahu*.
But we do not have this idiom in Ezra 4: 3. Esdras A says clearly that
the building of the temple was definitely nothing to do with the
Palestinians, but both Esdras B and the Hebrew Ezra could mean that
the building was not the sole concern of either party, but the common
concern of both. It is true that the Arabic *waḥad* in the accusative
with suffix can mean 'his solitariness,' but the usual meaning of the
word in Hebrew is 'together' and not its opposite. It is true also that
Neh. 2: 20 says that the Palestinians (Sanballat and his allies) 'have no
portion, nor right, nor memorial in Jerusalem,' but the context is the
rebuilding of the walls, and the date is eighty years later. Ezra 4: 24
is confirmed by Haggai and Zech. 4: 9 in that the building of the house
was delayed until the second year of Darius, but neither prophet
mentions anything about opposition on the part of the Palestinians.

Consider Zech. 6: 9-15. When verse 13 says that 'the counsel
of peace shall be between them both,' who are 'the both'? The
prophet is bidden to take representatives of the returning exiles and

meet with them in the house of a certain Josiah son of Zephaniah. The whole section is difficult and has evidently been interpreted later differently from what was originally intended; cf. verses 11 and 14. LXX does not recognise any of the names in verse 10 apart from that of Josiah son of Zephaniah, but has 'rulers and capable and discerning men.' They are apparently the representatives of the exiles. It difficult to identify this Josiah son of Zephaniah. The tendency is to identify this Zephaniah with the second priest who was executed by Nebuchadrezzar at Riblah (2 Kgs. 25: 18). In this case Josiah must have been getting on in years, because the Riblah incident had taken place 66 years earlier. Presumably this Josiah would have been carried off to Babylonia with the rest of the Zadokite priests of Jerusalem,[1]) but his name is not in the lists, and these lists were regarded as final and authoritative (Ezra 2: 62; Neh. 7: 64). Also, verse 10 conveys the impression that Josiah was domiciled in Jerusalem. The section tells of an agreement that 'they that are afar off shall come and build in the temple of the LORD,' and the crown is to be a token, a reminder of this arrangement. The original text mentions one **crown** only,[2]) made of silver and gold, and this crown is to be set on the **head** of the high-priest Joshua son of Jehozadak. The prophet is now to say to Joshua, 'Behold a man whose name is Branch, and from his place he shall branch out, and he shall build the temple of the LORD.' The last part of the verse looks like an addition, because the next verse continues: 'and *he* (emphatic) shall build the temple of the LORD and *he* shall bear the glory and sit (enthroned) and rule upon his throne, and shall be priest on his throne, and there shall be counsel of peace between the two of them.' LXX has two crowns and two thrones with the priest sitting on the throne 'on his right,' but the natural meaning of the Hebrew is that Joshua is the Branch and the crown is set on his head.[3]) The Branch is the צמח, the new shoot out of the old vine stock Israel, LXX's 'dayspring' ἀνατολή of the new era (cf. also Lk. 1: 78) the 'my servant' of Zech. 3: 8. Joshua the high-priest is the new ruler, the successor of David for it is of him that the messianic term 'Branch' is used. But who is the Branch in Zech. 3: 8? Once

---

[1]) LXX thought so, since it has τοῦ ἥκοντος for the Hebrew אשר באו at the end of the verse.

[2]) The Masoretic text has the plural 'crowns' in vv. 11 and 14, but it is plain in each case that the singular was intended originally and that the two plurals are a later interpretation.

[3]) The 'them' has been inserted by the English translators. There is no objective pronoun in the Hebrew text.

again we are of the opinion that it is Joshua the high-priest.[1]) Zerub-babel is not mentioned in chapter 3 just as he is not mentioned in chapter 6 and Joshua is not mentioned in chapter 4. This is very strange. The two are never mentioned together in Zechariah 1-8 but always (except in the last three verses) mentioned together in Haggai. Zech. 3 is the story of the establishment of Joshua as the indubitable high-priest in spite of his having been in an unclean land (the filthy garments). The verdict in the heavenly trial is that he is to keep God's 'charge' (משמרת, technical term in the P-tradition for service within the temple), and to have right of access (מהלכים, verse 7) among those that officiate at the altar. Verse 8 says that the others who are present are 'men of portent' מופת, that is, they are men involved in an event which is a sign of things to come, cf. 2 Chr. 32: 24 31. The portent has to do with the arrival (verse 7b: I will cause to come) of the Branch, and apparently Joshua is the Branch. The significance of the stone in verse 9 has been the subject of considerable discussion (see the commentaries), but the most satisfactory suggestion is that it is an ornament for the costume of the high-priest. The result of all this is that the iniquity of that land (Babylonia) will be removed forthwith, and the chapter ends with a picture of idyllic peace. With this promise of peace, compare 6: 13 with its promise of peace 'between them both' (see p. 245 above), and also the agreement that 'they that are far off shall come and build in the temple of the LORD,' i.e. they are to take part in the building.

Again, consider Zech. 6: 1-8, which concludes: 'they that go to the north country have quieted my spirit in the north country.' The usual interpretation is that 'the north country' means Babylon, but in this case what does 'the south country' mean (verse 6)? Commentators from WELLHAUSEN onwards seek to emend the text in verses 6 and 7, and they send the chariots east and west as well as north and south, whereas the Hebrew text sends two to the north, one to the south and the fourth on a general roving commission. It is true that often 'north country' means Babylon (Zech. 3: 6), but any explanation of 'north country' in 6: 8 should also be in line with some parallel explanation of 'south country.' Our explanation is that 'north' means Israel, the Palestinian Jews, those who had not been out of the country, and that 'south' means the Judaeans, the 'Babylonians', the returned

---

[1]) It appears to be the case that these chapters in Zech. 1-8 have been subjected to slight changes in order to make Joshua and Zerubbabel throughout to be the 'two sons of oil' (two anointed ones?) of Zech. 4: 14.

exiles, and that this section is talking about an understanding between
the two parties. Compare Ps. 89: 13 (Eng. 12) and see *Studies in the
Psalter* (1934), p. 43. See also Zech. 8: 13 where the prophet thinks of
both the house of Judah and the house of Israel as being a blessing,
and none must imagine evil against his neighbour.

Our solution, therefore is: there was at first a sharp contention
between the returning exiles and those who had not been deported,
but this was (for the time being) settled amicably. Joshua the son of
the exiled Zadokite Jehozadak received the high-priesthood which his
fathers had held, and the Zadokites obtained right of access to the
altar among the other (Aaronite) priests who were there. Perhaps
Haggai's appeal to both Joshua the high-priest and Zerubbabel the
governor marks this *rapprochement*, whereas the fact that neither are
mentioned together in Zechariah 1-8 reflects the prior state of affairs.
We would explain Ezra 4: 3 and its variations in LXX on the basis
that the Chronicler (or the editor of Ezra-Nehemiah) thought that
the enmity between the two parties began with the building of the
temple, and he was reading back the enmity which broke out with
the building of the wall. He brings the two together in Ezra 5: 3:
'. . .to build this house, and to finish this wall.' Whether anything was
accomplished in the building of the temple under Sheshbazzar is open
to doubt, but it is certain that the project was actively taken in hand in
520 B.C., the second year of Darius I (Hystaspis). We know that the
Chronicler thought in terms of four Persian kings, possibly because his
sources metioned only the names, Darius, Cyrus, Artaxerxes, Xerxes,
and this involved him in much confusion of dates and the sequence of
events. It is probable also that in his sources concerned with the
building of the temple he found 'the second year' without any specifi-
cation as to whose second year it was. He therefore confused the second
year of Darius (when the activity on the temple site took place) with
the second year of Cyrus. Thus we have two beginnings in building
the temple. Similarly 'building' appeared in his sources without spec-
ifying whether it was the building of the temple or the building of the
wall, and that brought about another muddle. Thus he writes of
'the days of Zerubbabel' and 'the days of Nehemiah' as though they
were identical, Neh. 12: 47. We shall see later how his identification
of 'Artaxerxes' in his sources always as Artaxerxes I gave rise to
another muddle.

After all, the Chronicler was writing the story of the rise and
triumph of Judaism with its exclusive Habdalah policy. He is not

interested in the northern tribes, but only in the tribe of Judah (with Benjamin). He regards the northerners of his day as apostates, semi-heathen and wholly heathen, not in any way whatsoever the People of the LORD. They are the 'people of the land,' outside the promises, by no means partakers in the covenant. Nothing is more natural than for him to read back the story of the quarrel into the immediate post-exilic period and to make it a religious and political quarrel of the first degree from the beginning. There was indeed initial disagreement and sharp contention together with a certain amount of violence in words, but there was a temporary truce. It was not 'war to the death' until Nehemiah arrived in Jerusalem and began to rebuild the city walls. It was then that the clash came. For nearly a hundred years there had been a 'cold war' with an occasional thaw. It was this period which accounts for the presence of elements in chapters 56-66 representing both parties. If the quarrel was as severe in Zerubbabel's time as many suppose it is unlikely that both parties would be represented in these eleven chapters. It is our opinion that the same mixture of contrary opinions is to be found in the Elohist Psalter.[1])

There certainly was a clash when Nehemiah arrived. He made his plans with the utmost secrecy (Neh. 2: 12-16), so that Sanballat did not know the wall was going to be rebuilt until the building of it was actually commenced (Neh. 4: 1). Sanballat and his friends were worried when they heard about Nehemiah's appointment as governor of Jerusalem (Neh. 5: 14), because he was come 'to seek the welfare of the children of Israel' (Neh. 2: 10)—so at least the Memoirs say—but they did not know at first about the wall. When they did hear about the wall, they forthwith construed it as rebellion against Persia. We are now in the realm of 'politics pure and simple,' though by no means pure and certainly far from simple. It is difficult to decide whether Sanballat really believed what he said to the Persian king or whether he was seeking to cause Nehemiah the utmost inconvenience. Perhaps Nehemiah expected trouble from the beginning and took no pains to avoid it. The whole problem of the relations between Sanballat and Nehemiah, especially the political aspect of them is reviewed by H. H. ROWLEY in an article 'Sanballat and the Samaritan Temple' in the *Bulletin of the John Rylands Library*, vol. 38, no. 1 (Sept. 1955), pp. 166-198. See also A. E. COWLEY, *Aramaic Papyri of the Fifth Century B.C.* (1923), p. 110, where he says 'no religious schism had

---

[1]) *Studies in the Psalter*, pp. 9-46.

as yet (408 B.C.) taken place.' Whether or not this great clash of 445
B.C. was the first clash depends on our view of the history of 538 B.C.
to (say) c. 390 B.C. The decisive clash came either in the events of
Nehemiah 13 or in the events of Ezra 9-10, which ever is later.

Which is later? Nehemiah 13 or Ezra 9-10? Who was it that was the
effective founder of Judaism? Was it Ezra or was it Nehemiah? If
the final success is that given in Ezra 9-10, then Ezra was the founder
of Judaism, and Nehemiah's success in Nehemiah 13 was temporary.
If the final success is that given in Nehemiah 13, then Nehemiah was
the founder of Judaism, and Ezra's success in Ezra 9-10 was temporary. One or the other is right—unless JOHN BRIGHT's solution (see
p. 255 below) can be accepted, in which case both are right 'and *all*
must have prizes.'

There are two ways in which the biblical material concerning
Nehemiah and Ezra has been arranged. One is that with which most
people are familiar, the order in the Hebrew Bible, according to
which Ezra arrived first and the final triumph is that of Nehemiah,
related in Neh. 13. But there is a second order, that of the LXX in
Esdras A (1 Esdras). Here the order is (using the Hebrew Bible
references): 2 Chronicles 35, 36; Ezra 1; 4: 7-24; the story of the
three children; Ezra 2: 1-4: 5; Ezra 5-10; Nehemiah 7: 73-8: 12. This
story ends with the triumph of Ezra. We would say that the original
order of the Chronicler is that of Esdras A with the rest of the present
book of Nehemiah following Ezra 6.[1]) This order gives a complete
and intelligible account of the establishment of Judaism and its
exclusive Habdalah policy. We have Ezra 1 (return under Sheshbazzar); Ezra 4: 7-24 (early attempts at rebuilding); Ezra 2: 1-4: 5
(return under Zerubbabel and the building of the temple); Ezra 5-10
(building of the temple); Neh. 1: 1-7: 72 and 9-13 (Nehemiah's activities); Ezra 7: 1-10 and 8-10; Neh. 7: 73-8: 13 (Ezra's activities),
plus Ezra 8: 14-18. This is the Chronicler's original account of the
attempts to establish post-exilic Judaism and of the final success.
Sheshbazzar tried and failed. Zerubbabel and Jeshua, urged on by
Haggai and Zechariah, managed to get the temple built. Nehemiah
got the city walls rebuilt in spite of considerable opposition from
within and without the city. During his second term of office as
governor he established with considerable violence a policy against
mixed marriages, here also with considerable opposition from within.

---

[1]) For a full discussion see 'The Date of Ezra's arrival in Jerusalem,' ZAW 63
(NF 22), 1951, pp. 53-66.

But this also failed; he never received support from the priesthood. Finally Ezra came and, with strong support from the high-priest of the time, succeeded in establishing once and for all the Habdalah policy based on a combined religious and political basis. The story of the Chronicler was written in the full flush of enthusiasm soon after the success of Ezra's policy in 397 B.C., just as, we would hold, the first edition of the Book of Kings (ending at the word 'Moses' in 2 Kgs. 23: 25) was written at the height of King Josiah's success. Each writer had his hero, the first had Josiah, the second had Ezra. The Greek Esdras A represents the tradition that Ezra was the founder and establisher of Judaism.

But there was another tradition, and this tradition was that Nehemiah, not Ezra, was the founder and establisher of Judaism. This tradition is represented by the editor who changed the order of the narrative into that which is now found in the Hebrew Bible. This change of order was done very neatly, and the discrepancies are not immediately obvious. Ben Sira followed this tradition. See Ecclus. 49: 11-13, where he lists among his famous men, Zerubbabel, Jeshua son of Josedek, and Nehemiah. There is no mention of Ezra. Another writer in this tradition is the author of Enoch 89:72 ('three of those sheep. . .began to build up all that was fallen down of that house'), and yet another was the author of 2 Maccabees 1 and 2. S. GRANHILD [1]) has maintained that the Chronicler himself used no Nehemiah material at all. This involves following the Greek Esdras A entirely, which contains no reference to Nehemiah as governor. The story of Nehemiah's activities is in Neh. 1: 1-7: 72 and 9-13. But the strength of the Nehemiah tradition makes it almost as certain that Nehemiah existed as the strength of the Ezra tradition makes it likely that Ezra existed. We have to say 'almost' because of the Samaritan tradition of 'the wicked Ezra.' GRANHILD supposes a 'post-Chronist' editor who inserted the Nehemiah material and also inserted all the Aramaic. This editor evidently believed that it was Nehemiah who was ultimately successful since he put Neh. 13 last. But if he also inserted the Aramaic portions, then he was responsible for Ezra 7: 11-26, the passage which contains the account of the astonishing powers which were granted to Ezra. This does not make sense. It is much more likely that Nehemiah existed equally with Ezra, and that

---

[1]) *Ezrabogens Literaere Genesis*, 1949. See also BENTZEN, *Introduction to the Old Testament*, vol. 2, p. 210.

Nehemiah's activities were in the Chronicler's original story and followed Ezra 6.

Thus we take the position that Nehemiah came to Jerusalem in the twentieth year of Artaxerxes I (Longimanus) 445/4 B.C., that he returned later, and that Ezra arrived in the seventh year of Artaxerxes II (Mnemon) 398/7 B.C. This gives a period of nearly 100 years for the two strands of Isaiah 56-66 to find a place in the composite collection, with a possibility of the period extending up to 140 years.

The traditional view (Ezra 457 B.C. and Nehemiah 445/4 B.C.) held the field until the time of A. VAN HOONACKER in 1890. It was he who introduced the idea of Artaxerxes II into the discussion.[1]) He supposed that Ezra made a visit to Jerusalem during Nehemiah's second term as governor. This part of VAN HOONACKER's theory is now generally rejected, following L. W. BATTEN, *Ezra and Nehemiah* (ICC, 1913), but see JOHN BRIGHT (p. 255 below). Many scholars follow the rest of VAN HOONACKER's hypothesis and give the date of Ezra's arrival as 398/7 B.C. This means that Nehemiah and Ezra never met, and that there was a whole genration between the times of their activities in Jerusalem. French and British scholars generally have followed VAN HOONACKER with BATTEN's modification, though there has been in recent years a revival of the traditional date for Ezra among 'conservative evangelicals' such as W. M. E. SCOTT and J. STAFFORD WRIGHT. German scholars in general have rejected the idea of an early date (485/7) for Ezra, but equally are not enamoured of the late date (398/7). They have sought to find another date for Ezra's arrival, some time when Nehemiah was not in the city, say 432 B.C. or some such date. Such theories involve a change of text as well as a dislocation of the text.

One of the most important aspects of the problem resolves itself into answering the question: Was Ezra active in Jerusalem whilst Nehemiah was there in the city? The great difficulty of the traditional dating is that Ezra appears never to have heard of Nehemiah. If they both had the authority they are said to have had and if they were both working to the same end, then why in the world did they not collaborate? There were times when each one of them was in such dire difficul-

---

[1]) 'Néhémie et Esdras, une nouvelle hypothèse sur la chronologie de l'époque de la restauration', in *Le Muséon* (1890), pp. 151-184, 317-351, etc. See also his other writings listed by H. H. ROWLEY, 'The Chronological Order of Ezra and Nehemiah' in the *Ignace Goldziher Memorial Volume* (1948), Part I, pp. 117-148. which contains in the notes a comprehensive bibliography.

ty that he would surely have clutched even at a straw, let alone any one who had virtually complete authority. If they were indeed together in the city, then we have a case of departmental government *par excellence*!, a state of affairs where one department acts in complete ignorance of anything the other may do.

There are three places where the two men are mentioned together in the same context: Neh. 8: 9; 12: 26; 12: 36.

Let us first consider Neh. 8: 9. The parallel is the Greek Esdras A 9: 49, where the name 'Nehemiah' does not occur. The Greek tells that Attharates (which is an attempted transcription of the Hebrew התרשתא—the governor, a word which evidently Greek did not understand) spoke to Esdras, the Levites and all the people. Neh. 8: 9 identifies Nehemiah as the governor and says that he and Ezra and the Levites spoke to the people. Did Esdras A leave the name out? Or did the editor of Neh 8: 9 put it in? The answer is complicated by Esdras A 5: 40 which has 'Nehemias and Attharias,' whilst the corresponding Ezra 2: 63 has 'the Tirshatha.' But that cannot possibly be Nehemiah, because Ezra 2 belongs to the time of Zerubbabel. Esdras A has certainly wrongly inserted Nehemiah here. The governor of Ezra 2: 63 was Zerubbabel: cf. Hag. 1: 1. It would appear that in both Ezra-Nehemiah and in Esdras A there has been a tendency at work always to identify the governor as Nehemiah and equally to identify 'Attharias' as the governor, and that this even brought the name 'Nehemiah' into Esdras A in one place where plainly it is wrong. The problem of Neh. 8: 9 must remain unresolved; there are too many editorial cross-currents.

Next consider Neh. 12: 36. This is the end of the list of those who took part in the procession at the dedication of the wall. One company went one way 'and after them went Hoshaiah and half the princes of Judah' (12: 31 f.), and the other company went the other way 'and I (Nehemiah) after them,' 12: 38. This looks like an adequate and complete arrangement, but the end of verse 36 says 'and Ezra the scribe was before them,' that is, at the head of the first company. This is not the way to treat such a great man as Ezra. He was either the most important member of the community or he was next in importance after the governor. At the very least his name ought to have come in with that of Hoshaiah in verse 32, but not at the tail of the whole list with the strange statement that 'he was before them'. This is too much of an addendum altogether. The mention of Ezra is an interpolation.

Lastly, Neh. 12: 26. This is as clear case of editorial interpolation as can be found. The Hebrew syntax just will not do. Some editor has added 'and of Ezra the scribe' because he thought the two men were contemporaries. Possibly this is the reason for anomalies elsewhere.

It has been pointed out [1]) that the powers which were granted to Ezra as detailed in Ezra 7: 17-27 are so wide and all-inclusive that they clash with the powers given to the governor Nehemiah. In any case Ezra did not use these powers. In our view it is precarious to rest any weight on the Memoirs either of Ezra or of Nehemiah. If Ezra 7: 17-27 is accurate and historical, then it is impossible for both Ezra and Nehemiah to have been in Jerusalem at the same time and both active; nor is it possible to imagine either of them being there and not being active. Neither was that sort of man. Whether Ezra ever had these powers may be doubted, but if he did have them and used them, then Nehemiah was not there at the time. But this is all beside the point, because we are of the opinion that MOWINCKEL was right when he said [2]) that these memoirs are actually memorials, written after the oriental (Persian) pattern to preserve the memory of great ones, especially in contrast to the wickedness of their enemies. The Memoirs of Ezra in particular are not an autobiography, but a memorial, a devotional legend (MOWINCKEL). The Ezra legend had already and early begun to grow. By the time of 2 Macc. 1: 18-36 the Nehemiah legend had developed also. Our judgment is that the arguments which have been put forward, both in favour and against Nehemiah and Ezra being contemporaries, tend to be indecisive. All fall short of definite proof. But the clearest thing that emerges is that it is unlikely that Nehemiah and Ezra were in Jerusalem together or had anything at all to do with each other.

If therefore Nehemiah and Ezra were not in Jerusalem at the same time, another date has to be found for the arrival of one or other of them. If Nehemiah 13 is to be regarded as the final act in the drama and Nehemiah as the founder of Judaism, then scholars like W. A. L. ELMSLIE[3]) may be right in making Nehemiah arrive during the reign of Artaxerxes II (ca. 380 B.C.), but this solution raises new complications because Eliashib was high-priest in Nehemiah's time. If Ezra is to

---

[1]) Most recently by H. H. ROWLEY in the *Ignace Goldziher Memorial*. p. 142
[2]) *Statholderen Nehemie*, 1916; *Ezra den Skriftlarde*, 1916. Also BENTZEN, *Introduction to the Old Testament*, I, 1948, p. 247; II, pp. 209 f.
[3]) *How Came Our Faith* (1949), p. 340.

be regarded as the founder of Judaism, then it is best, as most agree, to regard Nehemiah's arrival as a fixed point, 445/4 B.C. in the reign of Artaxerxes I. It will still be possible to regard Nehemiah 13 as the final act in the drama, if we can find a date for Ezra's arrival before (say) 426 B.C. The date of Nehemiah's return for his second term as governor must be at the very latest a little while before the death of Artaxerxes I, which was in 424 B.C. If this return was in 426 B.C., this gives us six years whilst Nehemiah was absent from Jerusalem, 432-426 B.C., and Ezra must be fitted in here. Thus KOSTERS proposed to read 'thirty-second' instead of 'seventh' in Ezra 7: 7 f. There is no justification for this change except that, if Ezra is to be fitted into this period, a change has to be made. This makes Ezra arrive in 432 B.C. as soon as Nehemiah is out of the way, but it also means that Ezra 9-10 is not nearly as final and complete a victory as the chapters themselves would lead us to believe. BERTHOLET, KENNETT, ALBRIGHT (in 1932), RUDOLPH and WEISER all hold that Ezra was active in Jerusalem between 433/2 and (say) 426 B.C. A variant of this solution has been proposed by BEWER, ALBRIGHT (in 1946) and BRIGHT, namely, to read 'thirty-seventh' instead of 'seventh'. This proposed emendation involves less disturbance in the text than the other, and if a solution has to be made involving an emendation, then this is the one to make. It makes Ezra arrive during Nehemiah's second term in 428 B.C., and 'allows us to resolve the perennial problem of the relationship of Ezra's reforms to Nehemiah's in a manner which is, I believe, both plausible and faithful to the evidence. . .Nehemiah tells his own side of it and claims the credit; the Chronicler, as one would expect, gives the credit to Ezra.' [1]

Our judgement is that the 397 B.C. date is the most likely date for the arrival of Ezra, though the case as put forward by JOHN BRIGHT (*op. cit.*, pp. 375-386) is powerful. The 397 B.C. date involves following the order of the Greek Esdras A. It involves taking Ezra 9-10 to be later than Nehemiah 13—BRIGHT makes them more or less contemporaneous by thinking of Nehemiah writing his own Memoirs and taking all the credit to himself. This view certainly is plausible, but the whole story, in our view, makes even more sense if Ezra's activity is regarded as following that of Nehemiah, and particularly if a few years passed between the two periods of activity. Nehemiah certainly ejected all those who had married foreign (i.e. Palestinian, non-exiles) wives and

---

[1]) BRIGHT, *A History of Israel* (1960), p. 386.

all foreigners, but evidently they were all there when Ezra arrived. When Ezra had completed his first four days in Jerusalem there came to him certain princes who told him that there were Israelites, both priests and Levites, who were allied in marriage with 'the people of the land.' That is, certain of the temple personnel had intermarried with families who had not been in exile in Babylonia. There were indeed four members of the high-priestly family among these (Ezra 10:18), who voluntarily put away their wives (10: 19). The complainants also alleged that certain princes and deputies were leaders in this intermarriage policy, Ezra 9: 1-2. Ezra was distressed beyond measure. He rent his garments, plucked out his hair, sat amazed until the time of the evening offering, and then prayed in deep penitence and anguish. Meanwhile Shecaniah son of Jehiel of the Elam family took action. Whilst Shecaniah and his associates were taking action, Ezra retired to fast and pray in the chamber of Jehohanan son of Elisahib. It is difficult to recognise in Neh. 13 as alternative account of all this, even allowing for Nehemiah's zeal in taking the credit to himself.

This Jehohanan was actually the grandson of Eliashib. It is not stated in Ezra 10 that Jehohanan was high-priest at the time, but he certainly was high-priest ca. 401 B.C. We know this from Josephus (*Ant. Iud.* XI, vii, 1), for it was at that time that Jehohanan the high-priest murdered his brother Jesus (Jeshua) in the temple during a quarrel about the high-priesthood. Thus, if Ezra arrived in Jerusalem in 397 B.C., then Jehohanan was high-priest at the time and Ezra had his full support. Here Ezra was more fortunate than Nehemiah had been, since Nehemiah did not have the support of Eliashib over this matter of mixed marriages (Neh. 13: 4). Josephus also says that Bagohi had promised Jeshua the high-priesthood, and that Bagohi was so incensed at the murder of his nominee that he forced his way into the temple and inflicted a heavy fine on the Jews. This Bagohi is apparently the governor of Samaria mentioned in the Sachau (Elephantine) papyrus i, 13, 14. Josephus identified him with the famous general of Artaxerxes III (Ochus), but this cannot possibly be right, because Artaxerxes III reigned from 358-338 B.C. and it was it was he who deported many Jews to Hyrcania and the country round the Caspian Sea.

In *Studies in the Psalter*, p. 13 f., I sought to identify this murdered brother of Jehohanan whose name was Jeshua. If Jeshua was a brother of Jehohanan and had any semblance of a claim on the high-priesthood, then he must have been a son of Joiada. Jeshua was a family name, since it was a Jeshua who was restored to the high-priesthood in the first days of the return, Zech. 3: 1-10. It is likely, therefore, that this Jeshua was the elder of the two brothers. This would account for him pressing his claim so strongly. It also means that he was not in Jerusalem when Jehohanan succeeded to the high-priesthood. Was he actually that son of Jehoiada who had married a daughter of Sanballat? Was he therefore the man whom Nehemiah drove out in 432 B.C. (Neh. 13: 28)? There is every likelihood that this identification is sound, and it is the situation thus involved, combined with MOWINCKEL's explanation of the two sets of memoirs (p. 254 above), which seems to us to turn the scale in favour of a 397 B.C. date for Ezra's return against the 428 B.C. date so powerfully argued by JOHN BRIGHT.

We know that there was extreme political rivalry when Ezra arrived in Jerusalem. Ezra had scarcely had time to turn round before a group of princes and deputies were seeking his support against their opponents. Jehohanan was against the mixed-marriage party. Of course he was against mixed marriages if his elder brother was involved in one. How could Jehohanan retain the high-priesthood if the mixed-marriage party got control? The anti-mixed marriage party, as we view the situation, were appealing for Ezra's help in driving out the last remnants of Jeshua's supporters. They appealed to Ezra on religious grounds but with political motives. Whether Ezra's motives for supporting them were in any way political, we cannot say. He certainly supported them from religious motives. He may have been a priestly diplomat of the medieval type. He may have been a deeply religious man who was 'used' by the politicians. Both situations have arisen more than once in human history. and doubtless they will arise again. Probably Ezra was 'used.' He did not use any special authoritative powers, and he retired into seclusion to pray whilst the politicians acted. But whichever way it was, Ezra and his supporters settled the matter once and for all. This is true on both the 397 B.C. theory and the 428 B.C. theory. Nehemiah brought the rivalry to a head because that was the only way he could get the city walls rebuilt and lay any sort of foundation for the future prosperity of the city. After his departure from Jerusalem at the end of his first term of office, one of Eliashib's grandsons married Sanballat's daughter, and Eliashib allowed his ally Tobiah to live in appartments within the temple precincts. Apparently this was the Tobiah who was Sanballat's ally during Nehemiah's first governorship (Neh. 2: 10; 4: 7; etc.). Nehemiah threw them out bag and baggage when he returned in (?) 426 B.C. But some years later this Jeshua was back again seeking to obtain the high-priesthood, to which as an elder son of Joiada he believed he had some right. The letter from Elephantine ensures that Jehohanan was high-priest in 407 B.C. Jeshua was murdered somewhat later than this time, which most likely was not long after the death of his father Joiada.

Ezra succeeded where Nehemiah failed because he (Ezra) had the full support of the regnant high-priest. Nehemiah never had proper support from Eliashib. Eliashib was far too much involved with Nehemiah's opponents, and had far too many family ties with them. Certainly when Nehemiah returned to Jerusalem we find a grandson married to the daughter of his chief enemy, and that enemy's second-in-command installed by Eliashib in the very temple itself. Nehemiah was powerful enough to put a stop to this, but there is every likelihood that as soon as Nehemiah's strong hand was removed, the whole situation changed, and the mixed-marriage party gained more influence until at the death of the high-priest Joiada they were in a position to take active steps to replace Jehohanan with Jeshua. With the death of Jeshua there could be no doubt but that the anti-mixed marriage party was the winning side. This explains why it was that such a large number of deputies and princes were willing to submit to the demands of Ezra and his supporters (Ezra 10: 18-44) even though some of them had children by these 'foreign' wives.[1] Only four held out against Ezra and Jehohanan. Their names were Jonathan, Jahzeiah, Meshullam and Shabbathai the Levite (Ezra 10: 15). 'Let their names be remembered for good'— to misquote and misapply Neh. 13: 31.

It ought not to occasion any surprise that members of the high-priestly family and especially the Jerusalem priests generally should be luke-warm for the reforms of Nehemiah and Ezra considering the basic exclusive emphasis involved. We must remember that one-third of the post-exilic priesthood was Aaronite claiming descent from Ithamar the younger son of Aaron, whilst two-thirds were Zadokite claiming descent from Eleazar the older surviving son of Aaron (1 Chron. 24: 3-4). In spite of the fact that the P-tradition refers to the priests as 'the sons of Aaron' (Lev. 1: 5, etc.), the 'covenant of everlasting priesthood' is with Phinehas son of Eleazar

---

[1] Perhaps there is a reference to this in Mal. 2: 10-4: 13, especially 2: 13-14.

(Num. 25: 13), and it was Eleazar who was 'the priest' (Num. 26: 63; cf. 20: 22-29), and not Ithamar. Thus the high-priestly family was Zadokite and had been in exile in Babylon (Zech. 3, etc.), and with them were two-thirds of the priesthood. But there was one-third of the priesthood who were not Zadokites. Their pre-exilic ancestors had not been priests at Jerusalem, and none of their families had been exiles in Babylon. They were Palestinian Jews and naturally had married 'foreign' women. A compromise was reached and both groups were admitted as Aaronic priests, but the pure-race policy was not enforced until Jehohanan's murder of his brother. Ezra's prayers and Shecaniah and his associates all combined to clear the last survivors of the mixed-marriage party out of the city once and for all. The Palestinian Aaronites had to submit or go. The great majority submitted. It is a strange commentary on the exclusive nature of post-exilic Judaism with its separation from the heathen and its 'holy', separated priesthood that the very priests themselves were one-third 'foreign.'

At first Nehemiah received good support from Eliashib the high-priest. Eliashib the high-priest and his fellow priests took their full share in the building of the wall. They built the Sheep-gate, laid its beams קרוהו, set up its doors, and built part of the wall as far as the Tower of the Hundred and the Tower of Hananel and sanctified it, Neh. 3: 1. What trouble Nehemiah had at this stage was with Sanballat, Neh. 4. Nehemiah soon found himself involved in trouble of another sort, but again this was no trouble which involved any dispute between Nehemiah and Eliashib. This time it was economic trouble (Neh. 5), and the trouble was with Jewish nobles and deputies. The complainants were 'the people and their wives' who were many and could not get food. Some said they had to borrow money in order to pay taxes. Some said they were having to mortgage their fields and vineyards to get food. It had all involved slavery for their sons and daughters, and in the end the loss of their property. It is difficult to decide who were the people who were being maltreated, whether they were descendants of the returned exiles or whether they were 'the people of the land,' descendants of those who had not been deported to Babylon. But there are two verses which suggest that perhaps Nehemiah was seeking to help 'the people of the land.' In Neh. 5: 5 the unfortunates say: 'Our flesh is as the flesh of our brethren, our children as their children'—which seems a strange thing to say unless somebody had been denying it, and who would deny it except Babylonian Jews? The other verse is Neh. 5: 17 where Nehemiah describes those who ate at his table: a hundred and fifty of the Jews and rulers, 'besides those that came to us from among the heathen that are about us'. This last group were distinct from 'the Jews.' The assumption is that they were from 'the people of the land,' descendants of the Palestinian Israelites who had never been deported.

The conclusion to be drawn from all this is that at first Nehemiah did not favour the Habdalah policy of strict separtaion to the extent that has generally been supposed. Certainly on his first visit he does not seem to have taken any steps to turn any Palestinians out of city and nation, provided they were loyal to him and willing to help in making Jerusalem secure. Indeed he was ready to welcome them if they came with good intent. He fed some of them at his own table. He regarded it as his business to get the wall rebuilt in order to ensure some sort of security. He knew that the city could never prosper until the walls were rebuilt. Sanballat's opposition was political. A walled Jerusalem was a menace, since it was very difficult to capture a fortified and well-defended Jerusalem. It took even the Romans under Titus five months in spite of dissensions among the defenders. The city seems to have held out for a long time under Hezekiah against the Assyrians. Nehemiah had enough enemies without making any more. His hatred was directed against Sanballat and his supporters.

But when Nehemiah returned to Jerusalem in (say) 426 B.C. he found that Eliashib was in alliance with Tobiah and had lodged him in the temple buildings, the very room where the perquisites of the priests and Levites were stored. Further, Eliashib's grandson had married Sanballat's daughter. He found that the levites who served in the temple had not been getting their proper supplies and had been driven out of the city. He restored that situation; he threw out Tobiah and his goods and chattels after him; he drove out Eliashib's grandson, and forbade all marriage with 'foreigners.' This was the full Habdalah policy with a vengeance, but it belongs to Nehemiah's second term as governor and not to his first term. Further, he was driven to it because he could not maintain his political independence against Sanballat if the high-priest's family were so closely allied with him. That marriage must have taken place whilst Nehemiah was away. It could scarcely have taken place during the time when the walls were being rebuilt when all the plots and counter-plots were taking place.

It could scarcely have taken place without Nehemiah's knowledge if he was in the city, and it could not have taken place with his consent. It is dangerous to be certain of these things. The ways of politicians are strange and sometimes tortuous, and when the princes of the church are also politicians still stranger things can take place. There is no need to assume that anything else took place in order to make Nehemiah take this action. To find one's chief enemy allied in marriage to the chief-priest and one's second enemy installed in comfortable quarters in the temple buildings—these two things are enough to account for the most violent action. But apparently, as soon as Nehemiah was out of the way, the mixed marriages again became allowable. When the final crisis came with the arrival of Ezra, there were four members of the high-priestly family involved in mixed marriages: Massaiah, Eliezer, Jarib and Gedaliah, and there were thirteen other priests involved, two from the house of Immer, five from the house of Harim, and six from the house of Pashur (Ezra 10: 20-22). These 'houses' were the 16th, the 3rd and the 5th course [1]) (1 Chr. 24: 7-18). All these four courses are in the lists of Ezra 2: 1 and 2: 36-39. The hard core of opposition consisted, then, of only seventeen priests plus the four men mentioned in Ezra 10: 15, out of a total number of 4289 priests (Ezra 2: 37-39). There was also a number of levites, singers and laity, Ezra 10: 23-44. The mixed-marriage party would naturally be small by this time, since Jeshua was dead. If the number had reached any serious dimensions, their suppression would not have been as easy as evidently it was.

As we have said, the two groups lived together more or less harmoniously for a hundred years, from a little after 538 B.C. when the initial compromise was reached to 426 B.C., and possibly, after a short time (if we accept the 397 B.C. date for Ezra's arrival), for another twenty years. This is how it came about that the different points of view could both be embodied in Isaiah 56-66. It was a hundred years of argument, but not open conflict until Nehemiah came back again for his second term.

This means that the nationalist elements in the Second Isaiah triumphed and became the official policy of Judaism. The contrary 'universalist' point of view never wholly died, though sometimes the 'stream ran thinly.' This is the stream which R. LEVY calls 'the

---

[1]) Pashur is another name for the 5th course, that of Malchiah: compare 1 Chr 24: 8-14 with 1 Chr. 9: 12 and Neh. 11: 12.

Deutero-Isaianic stream,' [1]) by which he means the universalist
stream, since he holds with other scholars that the Second Isaiah
was a universalist. He gives instances of this from the Talmud and
the earlier Midrashim (pp. 53-77), and also in mediaeval and modern
Jewish Literature. But the official position has always been and still
is nationalist and exclusive. Even Christianity had its early struggles
against this attitude. It was thanks to St. Paul that the universalism
which Jesus of Nazareth realised was inherent in the work of the
Servant of the Lord triumphed over the Judaising leaders of the early
Church. The battle is always having to be refought.

---

[1]) *Deutero-Isaiah* (1925), p. 54.

INDEX OF BIBLICAL REFERENCES

(excluding Isa. 40-66)